Vegetation and Biogeography of the Sand Seas of

Saudi Arabia

The sand seas of Saudi Arabia, although well-known in literature, remain poorly explored scientifically. This is the first book to analyse, both quantitatively and qualitatively, the patterns, nature, and communities of the vegetation of the sand seas, using new techniques which the authors hope will prove adaptable for similar studies in other areas. The book covers such topics as the natural environment of the sand seas, vegetative paleohistory, and the importance of the sand seas as a recreational area.

David Watts was Professor of Geography at the University of Hull. **Abdulatif H. Al-Nafie** is Professor of Geography at the Islamic University of Imam Muhammad Ibn Saud, in Riyadh.

VEGETATION AND BIOGEOGRAPHY OF THE SAND SEAS OF
SAUDI ARABIA

David Watts and Abdulatif H. Al-Nafie

Routledge
Taylor & Francis Group

LONDON AND NEW YORK

First published 2003 by
Kegan Paul Limited

Published 2013 by Routledge

2 Park Square, Milton Park, Abingdon, Oxfordshire OX14 4RN

711 Third Avenue, New York, NY 10017

First issued in paperback 2014

Routledge is an imprint of the Taylor & Francis Group, an informa business

ISBN 978-0-710-30619-7 (hbk)

ISBN 978-1-138-87000-0 (pbk)

British Library Cataloguing in Publication Data
A catalogue record for this book is available from the British Library

Library of Congress Cataloging-in-Publication Data
Applied for.

Foreword and Acknowledgements

The sand seas of Saudi Arabia are well known in literature, but still poorly explored in the scientif field. Consisting of vast areas of now largely stable sand, and often standing a few hundred metre above the surrounding land, sand seas cover about one third of the interior of the Arabian peninsul and the largest (Ar Rub'Al Khali, or The Empty Quarter) extends over 640,000 km^2, being 2.6 times the size of the United Kingdom, and slightly larger than France. Difficult to access t outsiders, they are even now best known to Bedouin groups, who are needed as guides to scientif explorers. Even so, it is unwise to attempt to penetrate them in the extremely hot, dry summers, ar research workers are advised to wait until the cooler and wetter (especially in the north) winter when profuse displays of annuals mix in with the many perennials to create a desert bloom of varie vegetation. To the south, Ar Rub'Al Khali is daunting merely in view of its scale, and is dry all ye except for 'summer' showers.

Although most of the wealth of Saudi Arabia's flora lies in the wetter and hilly south-we of the country, the sand seas are covered by a relatively diverse range of plant species, with sever distinctive plant communities. This is the first book to consider and analyse as a whole, bo quantitatively and qualitatively, the patterns, nature and communities of the vegetation of the sar seas, using new techniques which the authors hope will prove adaptable for similar studies in oth arid areas. Using mainly new data, but also harking back to some of the descriptions of old, tl book covers such topics as the natural environment of the sand seas, their development over tim their vegetative palaeohistory, the plants which grow on them and their biogeographic affinities, tl flora of the sand seas and its adaptation to a difficult environment, an analysis of the main pla communities therein, the uses of the vegetation by man (for animal grazing, food, medicin purposes, industry), and the importance of the sand seas as a recreational area. The result, we trus is a sound, complete and readable analysis of the vegetation of the sand seas, and one which will l of especial use to biogeographers, ecologists, and environmental scientists, planner conservationists, and all those interested in the preservation of Saudi Arabia's magnificent natur heritage.

In a work of this nature, the authors are clearly indebted to many people for their suppor their time and their interchange of ideas. Financial support is acknowledged from the Governme of Saudi Arabia, their Cultural Mission in London and the Islamic University of Imam Mohamme Ibn Saud, Ar Riyadh. In Saudi Arabia, sincere appreciation is expressed to Dr. S. Chaundhary fi his knowledge of many areas, and his help in the identification of plant species; Abdullah A Shanqity for his advice in the selection of soil samples; and to all Riyadh, for help in analysing oi soil samples. In the United Kingdom, Dr. T.A. Cope at the Royal Botanic Gardens, Kew; and I A.G. Miller, of the Royal Botanic Gardens, Edinburgh, both provided valuable taxonomic advic Mr Keith Scurr of the department of Geography, University of Hull, compiled most of the drawings.

Within the sand seas, special thanks go to Abdulrahman Al-Udhayb, Abdullah Al-Nafe Sulayman Al-Nafea, Khalid Al-Nussar, Sulayman Al-Utaywe, Saleh al-Ribdy, Ibraheem Al-Ridb Rafat Al-Zinaty, Ahmad Al-Shaba'an, Khalid Al-Jawfy, Mutlaq Al-Subaya'y, Abdullah A Warthan, Fahad Al-Dawsari, Hajaj Al-Subaya'y, and Ubayan Al Subaya'y for much loc information on the sand seas in their respective areas, and for their hospitality and assistance durir the reconnaissance survey, and the main field-work period; also, to the brothers of the Saudi authc Abdulmohsin, Ahmed, Badir, Nasir, muhamed, Ayman and Sami, along with other family member for their back-up support during the field seasons.

Last but not least, thanks are due to Ms Kathryn Spry, who read the original manuscript; and to Mr Mark Carmichael who word processed the final document.

*To our wives, Nancy and Amsha, without whose support
and understanding this book would not have been completed*

CONTENTS   PAGE

CHAPTER 1

PRELUDE

Saudi Arabia extends over an area of 2,200,518 km^2, or about 68.5% of the Arabian peninsula. This huge mass of land makes it the tenth largest country of the world in terms of area, covering about 1.47% of the earth's land surface, and about 5% of the Asian continent. It is nearly half the size of Europe. Saudi Arabia extends over 16 degrees of latitude, from 32 15 at the Jordanian frontier in the north to 16 30 at the border of Yemen; and between 34 E and 56 E longitude (Fig. 1.1).

Within this area, sand seas, which may be defined as extensive areas of now largely-stable sand, cover about one third of the interior, constituting one of its most prominent physical features. From north to south, they are named 1) The Great Nafud; 2) Ad Dahna; 3) a group of sand dune bodies that extend along the western side of the Tuwayq escarpment; and 4) Ar Rub' Al Khali (the Empty Quarter), including Nafud Al Jafurah. Of these Ar Rub'Al Khali is by far the largest, extending over 640,000 km^2, or an area 2.62 times the size of the United Kingdom, and just a little larger than France. The Great Nafud, or An Nafud, is the second largest body of sand, covering about 62,884 km^2. These two sand bodies are connected by the Ad Dahna sand belts, which extend approximately 1,425 kms from southeast of An Nafud to the northern areas of Ar Rub'Al Khali. These sand seas, and others that are interspersed within the interior part of the Arabian peninsula, have within them a complex variety of dune forms, including traverse, longitudinal, star and red sand mountains, some of which reach heights of 300m above the general land surface.

The Arabian peninsula, and the sand seas within it, have been largely overlooked and neglected by both biogeographers and plant geographers, though it is a very significant region for both. Its importance is the consequence of its location at the meeting point of three continents and two major plant geographic regions. Yet Saudi Arabia in particular has all too frequently been regarded by both non-professionals and many scientists as a 'lifeless' environment, even though Miller & Nyberg (1991) have recently reported 2030 plant species as being present in the country.

This inherent contradiction appears to have been derived in part at least from the great classic desert travel narratives of the nineteenth century and the first half of the twentieth century, some of which described the sand seas as being inhospitable to all forms of life and completely vegetationless. A clear example may be taken from Palgrave's (1871) description of An Nafud, which he passed through during his travels in central and eastern Asia in the summer of 1862:

'Much had we heard of (this) from Bedouins and countrymen, so that we had made up our minds to something very terrible and impracticable. But the reality, especially in these dog-days, proved worse than aught heard or imagined. We were now traversing an immense ocean of loose reddish sand, unlimited to the eye, and heaped up in enormous ridges running parallel to each other from north to south, undulation after undulation, each swell two or three hundred feet in average height, with slant sides and rounded crests furrowed in every direction by the capricious gales of the desert. In the depths between, the traveller finds himself as it were imprisoned in a suffocating sand pit, hemmed in by burning walls on every side; whilst at other times, while labouring up the slope, he overlooks what seems a vast sea of fire, swelling under a heavy monsoon wind, and ruffled by a cross-blast into little red-hot waves. Neither shelter nor rest for eye or limb amid torrents of light and heat poured from above on an answering glare reflected below.'

Such descriptions, taken during the extremely hot summer months, helped to establish a stereotypical view of the sand seas, and discouraged individuals from making even short visits to their margins, let alone penetrating deep into them to conduct more detailed investigations. But at other times of the year, it is clear that visitors to the sand seas did not experience such extreme conditions. Thus Lady Anne Blunt (1968), who also visited An Nafud, but during the winter season (January, 1879), provided a much more favourable view, and a visual image which is very similar to the impression of this particular sand sea as it appears today, for the person who has never seen sand seas of such magnitude:

'At half past three o'clock, we saw a red streak on the horizon before us, which rose and gathered as we approached it, stretching out east and west in an unbroken line. It might at first have been taken for an effect of mirage, but on coming nearer we found it broken into billows, and but for its red colour not unlike a stormy sea seen from the shore, for it rose up, as the sea seems to rise, when the waves are high, above the level of the land. Somebody called out 'the Nafud', and though for a while we were incredulous, we were soon convinced. What surprised us was its colour, that of rhubarb and magnesia, nothing at all like the sand we had hitherto seen, and nothing at all like what we had expected. Yet the Nafud it was, the great red desert of central Arabia. In a few minutes we had cantered up to it, and our mares were standing with their feet in its first waves.

January 13 - We have been all day in the Nafud, which is interesting beyond our hopes, and charming into the bargain. It is, moreover, quite unlike the description I remember to have read of it by Mr Palgrave, which affects one as a nightmare of impossible horror. It is true he passed it in summer, and we are now in mid-winter, but the physical features can not much be changed by the change of seasons, and I cannot understand how he overlooked its main characteristics. The thing that strikes one first about the Nafud is its colour. It is not white like the sand-dunes we passed yesterday, nor yellow as the sand in parts of the Egyptian desert, but a really bright red, almost crimson in the morning when it is wet with the dew. The sand is rather coarse, but absolutely pure, without admixture of any foreign substance,

pebble, grit or earth, and exactly the same in tint and texture everywhere. It is, however, a great mistake to suppose it barren. The Nafud, on the contrary, is better wooded and richer in pasture than any part of the desert we have passed since leaving Damascus. It is tufted all over with Ghada (*Haloxylon persicum*) bushes, and bushes of another kind called Yarta (Arta - *Calligonum comosum*), which at this time of the year when there are no leaves, is exactly like a thick, matted vine ... Wilfred says that the Nafud has solved for him at last the mystery of horse breeding in Central Arabia. In the hard desert there is nothing a horse can eat, but here there is plenty. The Nafud accounts for everything. Instead of being the terrible place it has been described by the few travellers who have seen it, it is in reality the home of the Bedouins during the greater part of the year.'

The relative richness of the flora of the sand-seas for grazing, especially in northern Saudi Arabia, has also been commented on by several other travellers. Y. Al-Hamawe (1178-1228 A.D.) described Ad Dahna in his geographical dictionary, Mu'agam al Buldan, as being 'one of the best and richest pasture grounds in the world, sufficient in good years for all Arab nomads' (Al-Hamawe, 1955). G.A. Wallin (Professor of Arabic in the University of Helsingfors, Finland) visited in 1845, and described the vegetation of An Nafud as being 'one of the richest pasture-grounds in Arabia, but for want of wells and sources, it can only be visited by the nomads during the spring, when the rain gathers in ponds and pools' (Wallin, 1848). Somewhat later, J.A. Philips (1882) summarised the descriptions of his contemporary travellers of the vegetation of An Nafud as follows: 'Although the Nafud has been described as a totally barren waste, recent travellers state that it is everywhere, excepting on the highest summits of the sand hills, thickly sprinkled with brushwood, garda trees, and tufts of grass, the 'fulijes' being especially well clothed with vegetation.'

During the first decade of the twentieth century, J. Lorimer rated the desert vegetation of the Nafud very positively: 'There is abundant desert vegetation and, but for the absence of watering places, the Nafud would be permanently inhabited. The grazing is excellent, and when the winter rains have made a sojourn possible the surrounding Bedouins repair to the Nafud with their flocks and herds. North of 'Alam-an-Nafud' (the middle of the Nafud) the principal plant is the Ghada (*Haloxylon persicum*) which yields good firewood and charcoal; south of that point it is the Arta (*Calligonum comosum*) which when leafless resembles a thickly matted vine. The commonest plant however is Ader (*Artemesia monosperma*) with stiff green leaves and brownish-yellow flowers: there are also Nasi (*Stipagrostis plumosa*), a good kind of camel grass, and Hamrah (Sakhbar -*Cymbopogon commutatus*), a blue, prickly plant that is excellent forage for horses' (Lorimer, 1970).

In the winter of 1909, A. Musil (Professor of Oriental Studies at Charles University, Prague) travelled through the northern parts of the Arabian peninsula. Although the motive of his journey was historical, he collected some plant species from the northern part of the Arabian peninsula which he visited, and gave some accounts of the vegetation: 'the elliptical hollows surrounded by the dunes are called ka'ar. Each of these hollows is deepest at the western end of the ellipse, where it forms a huge funnel-like pit, that is called farse. Between the hollows, or ka'ar, are larger or smaller low sandy flats called nawazi. In these, as in the hollows, raza (Ghada - *Haloxylon persicum*), arta (*Calligonum comosum*), sobot (Sabat - *Stipagrostis drarii*), kasba (Qasba - *Centropodia forsskalii* or *fragilis*), ader (Ather - *Artemisia monosperma*), tubejz (Khubbayz-*Malva parviflora*) and tarba (Turbah - *Silene villosa*) grow, and in spots even arfeg (A'rfaj - *Rhanterium epapposum*), alka (A'lqa - *Scrophularia hypericifolia*) and hamat (*Molthiopsis ciliata*), of which camels are especially fond' (Musil, 1927). From this trip, he also noted the striking coloration of many of the plants, which give An Nafud much of its distinctiveness: 'the dry plants of the Nafud are of various colours: dry hamat is like silver, nasi (*Stipagrostis plumosa*) and sobot yellow like straw, arta is ashy, ader dark green and almost black, raza brightly white, with its new young sprouts yellow with a greenish tinge'. In winter 1915, Musil carried out a further expedition to north Nadj and the southern fringes of An Nafud. He noted that 'tree-like raza plants cover the whole of the An Nafud desert', and that 'fresh grasses were springing up all around us, and the perennials arta, hamat and ader were fresh. Old withered ader is called slejg. The Nafud is all overgrown with perennials and annuals, very few tracts being completely bare' (Musil, 1928).

Between Musil's two trips, Captain G. E. Leachman of the Royal Sussex Regiment made a journey in spring 1911 to north and east Arabia. He described An Nafud as having 'a great attraction for the Bedouins, especially in the spring months, when it provides grazing far superior to any other district, and even in summer it provides dry grass for the camels. This year, owing to exceptional rains, the Nafud was covered with grass and weeds growing to a height of at least a foot, while many forms of flowers, such as dandelions and daisies, gave it a bright appearance. A bush known as arfui (A'rafja- *Rhanterium epapposum*), much appreciated by camels, is very common, and also a tree called 'sider', a species of Acacia, growing to a height of six feet or more and considered the best wood for fuel in Arabia' (Leachman, 1911).

D. Carruthers, a naturalist, in his quest for the orxy explained why the Nafud was a suitable habitat for this species: 'Once on the dunes, I realised the secret of the oryx's chosen haunt. Here was food in plenty, besides a safe retreat. There was a tall, yellow grass like hay (*Stipagrostis drarii*) (in fact the Bedouin cut and store it) and a heavy growth of tamarisk. There was the ghada, which grew into great spreading bushes above the sand, and extended its roots an incredible distance below it in search of moisture. Where the sand had been blown away, and the roots were left exposed, they straggled for fifteen yards or more over the surface. The Nafud was evidently neither rainless nor without vegetation, and therefore was not a moving sand mass, except in a minor degree. That the great dunes and their corresponding hollows were stationary was proved by the vegetation upon them, and also by the fact that recognised camping grounds and ancient wells have existed in certain localities for ages. The Nafud is considered by the nomads to be a veritable paradise during the spring months, when the pastures are full of nourishment' (Carruthers, 1935).

Although very useful in terms of their description of the appearance of the Arabian sand seas and of some of the species which occur on them, it must be admitted that there are some deficiencies in these accounts in respect of their usefulness for an analysis of their vegetation. Indeed, a review of the vegetation was not the prime reason for any of these journeys. Further, the information provided by these travellers about the vegetation is scattered throughout their narratives, and requires a great effort to be traced and compiled. Also, those species which are listed are identified by their Arabian names, which is not particularly useful for non-Arabic speakers. However, Musil (1927, 1928) provided many Latin equivalents, as well as giving very brief characterisations of the Arabian botanical terms that appear in these works.

In summary, one may say that most of the information which these reports provide is inadequate for scientific analysis except in limited areas, such as those especially close to sand dune fringes along the desert tracks: interior parts of the and seas were not accessible, and so were not described. With the exception of Musil's descriptions, most travellers also limited their observations to the large perennial species that are useful for firewood, or species which are useful for forage. Some reports are conflicting: this is no doubt due to the season of the visit, summer or winter, or to the different tracks that people followed. There is also the problem that since most visitors to the sand seas during the 19th century had of necessity to travel in disguise due to local hostilities (see Mrs Blunt, 1968); circumstances were unfavourable for detailed geographical observation. Those who travelled during summer time, such as Palgrave, further must have journeyed most of the time at night, and so did not have the opportunity to see much of the desert vegetation and its features.

The modern, scientific literature of the sand seas of Saudi Arabia is also quite scarce, and is summarised below.

In his capacity as locust officer, D. Vesey-Fitzgerald produced several papers of an introductory nature on the vegetation of Saudi Arabia. One (1957) is especially concerned with the vegetation of the central and eastern parts of the Arabian peninsula, mostly north of the tropics, which covers a large part of the northern sand seas. Broadly speaking, he suggested that the vegetation of the sand seas was characterised by a few perennial species and a wealth of annuals, this being based on observations from five different locations in the Great Nafud (An Nafud) and Ad Dahna. The dominant perennial vegetation species of the deep sand which he described were *Calligonum comosum*, *Artemesia monosperma*, *Monsonia nivea* and *Scrophularia hypericifolia*. *Haloxylon* as a common genus is not mentioned. Additionally, a variety of patchy annual mesophytic herbs and grasses grew on the sand during the winter season, especially in sheltered hollows and depressions, as well as along the sand dune footings and margins, where some moisture is available.

In a further report on locust habitats in the Arabian Peninsula, G. Popov and W. Zeller (1963) categorised the central and eastern parts of the peninsula as being sub-desert vegetation, as follows: 'Sub-desert vegetation develops in the areas receiving less than about 100 mm of rainfall, over most of the Arabian peninsula, notably on the plains and the sands of the Nejd (Najd) and the Hassa (Al Hassa) and the drier hills of Hijaz (Al Hijaz). In central and eastern Arabia, much of the sub-desert vegetation is halophytic, especially on the plains, where such genera as *Haloxylon*, *Seidlitzia*, *Salsola* and *Sevada* predominate, while extensive areas of north eastern Arabia are overgrown by aromatic bushes such as *Artemesia* and *Rhanterium epapposum*'. They suggested that the topography of the sand dunes produces a multitude of meso- and micro-ecological units, but these units were beyond the scope of their report.

A. Mighaid and A. El-Sheikh (1977) and A. Mighaid (1980), in their studies of desert habitats, classified all the sand seas of Saudi Arabia as being within the sand-dune and quick-sand habitat. This is described as being poor overall in vegetation, and treeless. Migahid (1980) indicated that the most common plant species in this habitat are *Calligonum comosum*, *Artemesia abyssinica*, *Cyperus conglomeratus*, *Neurada procumbens* and *Plantago boisseri*. All plants displayed great adaptation to the harsh desert environment.

In 1983, S.A. Chaudhary presented a very brief paper and a list of the vegetation species of the Great Nafud (An Nafud). He broadly distinguished three major communities that dominated the area. The distribution and nature of these communities were, he argued, determined by the topography and physical characteristics of the sand, as well as by seasonal factors. The communities were:

1. A *Haloxylon persicum - Artemisia monosperma-Stipagrostis* community.

2. A *Calligonum comosum–Artemesia monosperma-Scrophularia hypericifolia* community.

3. Ecotone communities, which included:

   a. A *Hamada - Calligonum - Pituranthos triradiatus* community
   b. A *Rhanterium - Calligonum - Pituranthos-Scrophularia* community.

Annual species were also observed following winter and spring precipitation.

In their report on the propagation of endangered species in Saudi Arabia, the team of AOAD (Arab League, Organisation for Agricultural Development, 1985) has indicated that the dominant plant species in the entire sand-seas habitat were *Panicum turgidum, Calligonum comosum, Ephedra alata* and *Hammada elegans*. Lists of plant species which are dominant in some selected sand seas (Al Quwayiyah, Hima Al Ghadha in Unayzah, northern Hail, Al Khasirah and southern Al Jawf in central and northern Saudi Arabia) are also given.

In 1986, E. S. Schulz and J.W. Whitney gave a very brief consolidated description of the vegetation of north-central Saudi Arabia. They described this area as being part of the large belt of semi-desert which represents a transitional zone between the Mediterranean flora and the Saharo-Sindian flora, which dominates the peneplains in the southern part of Saudi Arabia. The whole area was divided into six vegetation units, correlated to the six general landscape units in this area. These six units consist of inselbergs and escarpments, pediments, peneplains, playas, large and small wadis, and sand seas. An Nafud, Nafud As Sirr and Nafud Al Urayq were the sand seas surveyed and visited by the authors, who described their study as 'the first description of modern vegetation types and their distribution in north-central Saudi Arabia'. For the sand seas they visited, they indicated that they supported 'a diffuse plant cover of shrubs and tufted grasses. Both the number of species and plant density are greater on dunes than on the bedrock plains. *Artemisia monosperma*, *Calligonum comosum*, *Stipagrostis drarii* and *Cyperus conglomeratus* are the most common plants. Achab floras are common at the foot of dunes following rainstorms, and *Plantago*, *Monsonia*, *Stipagrostis plumosa*, *Moltkiopsis* and *Filago* are among the common herbs. A sparse cover of *Helianthemum* and *Fagonia* is found on lake beds and duricrusts that are sometimes present in the internal depressions' (Schulz & Whitney, 1986). The authors also indicated that it was too early to distinguish phytosociological units because of the limited knowledge and information relating to the floristic composition.

Baierle & Frey (1986), in their paper on 'A vegetation transect through central Saudi Arabia', described the vegetation of Nafud As Sirr and Nafud Qunayfithah. They indicated that the vegetation cover on these sand seas is irregular, and that the individual plants are scattered. The abundance and distribution of the vegetation cover on the dunes depends on the degree of sand consolidation, topography and moisture conditions. The perennial shrub *Calligonum comosum* is dominant. Other species are *Cyperus conglomeratus, Moltkiopsis ciliata, Danthonia forsskali, Dipcadi erythraeum, Panicum turgidum, Stipagrostis plumosa, Polycarpaea repens* and *Rhanterium epapposum*. *Artemisia monospermum*, which is co-dominant with *Calligonum comosum* in other areas (Ad Dahna, An Nafud and Ar Rub 'Al Khali) was not observed in Nafud As Sirr and Nafud Qunayfithah. Annual vegetation such as *Eremobium lineare, Astralagus schimperi, A. gyzensis, Plantago cylindrica* and *Neurada procumbens* were found at the bases of dunes in depressions and hollows between them.

The most recent study of Ar Rub' Al Khali by Mandaville (1986) notes that, unusually, only just over 30 species are recorded, as opposed to the 390-plus found in eastern Saudi Arabia as a whole. The vegetation here is marked by the virtual absence of the Saharo-Arabian and Mediterranean-derived annuals which are so common farther north. In the hyper-arid north-west of this area one may find large areas completely devoid of vegetation but, these apart, the main co-dominants are *Calligonum criticum* and *Cornulaca arabicum*. Mandaville (1990) later produced a further book on the Flora of eastern Saudi Arabia, in which some of the northern sand seas are covered. He divides Ad Dahna into two topographic subregions, separated by the old Riyadh-Damman road: the northern subregion is dominated by *Artemisia monosperma*, as well as *Calligonum comosum* in its eastern fringes, while the southern subregion has a similar vegetation, though with fewer emphemials and more Sudanian elements such as *Rhazya stricta*.

From the general scarcity of books, papers and reports, it is still the case that information on the ecology and flora of the sand seas is very scanty. For the flora, this is likely to remain so for some time: the forthcoming Flora of the Arabian Peninsula and Socotra, being prepared by the Royal Botanic Gardens in Edinburgh and Kew, is not likely to be finished for several years (Miller & Nyberg, 1991). For the ecology, it is also clear that the available studies are not comprehensive: they do not include all the sand seas of Saudi Arabia, and most of them were undertaken during the winter season. The studies are not based on any systematic analysis, and there are no quantitative descriptions of the vegetation of the area; nor are the environmental factors that affect the vegetation cover in the region well known. Biogeographical affinities are rarely discussed.

It was with the aim of remedying these deficiencies, while at the same time providing a quantitative and more complete presentation of vegetational communities and forms, along with environment, in the sand-seas of Saudi Arabia, that this book was originally conceived. Bearing in mind the efforts of the national conservation movement, particularly associated with the founding of the Saudi National Commission for Wildlife Conservation and Development in 1986, the effects of human activities on these vulnerable environments and plant communities, are further evaluated, along with the possible consequences of future climatic change.

CHAPTER 2

THE ENVIRONMENT

The existence, development and the vegetation of the sand seas of Saudi Arabia are controlled by environmental factors that limit or encourage them. These factors are those of geology and geomorphology, the thermal, hydrological and chemical properties of sand, and climate.

2.1. Geology, and the structure of sand seas

Saudi Arabia is divided geologically (Figs. 2.1, 2.2) into two structural provinces: 1) The Arabian Shield; and 2) The Arabian Shelf.

The Arabian Shield is an ancient land mass consisting of igneous and metamorphic rocks of Pre-Cambrian age. It covers nearly 29.4% of the Arabian peninsula, occupying an area of about 946,000 km^2, or 34%, of the total area of Saudi Arabia. Its surface was, in the post-pre-Cambrian, covered in some parts by Lower Palaeozoic basal sands. Basaltic or other volcanic rocks resulting from volcanic activities and floods of basic lava since the mid-Tertiary also are found in the form of lava fields (harrat) spread over its western parts. Since the Palaeozoic era, the Shield has been relatively stable, and only the immediate surface sediments have been affected by erosional forces. At the beginning of the Tertiary period, the Arabian Shield was separated from its neighbour, the African Shield, by rifting which led to the formation of the Red Sea. Generally, the Shield slopes very gently towards the north, northeast and east. (Powers et.al., 1966: Chapman, 1978).

The Arabian Shelf extends to the east of the Arabian Shield, forming about 70.6% of the total area of the peninsula. The Shelf is comprised of a sequence of continental and shallow water marine sedimentary rocks that range in age from Cambrian to Pliocene. These sedimentary sequences were deposited in a shallow sea (the Tethys) over the crystalline basement that forms the eastern and northern flanks of the Shield. Sand accumulations, representing the most recent and distinct geomorphological feature of the peninsula, cover about half of the Arabian Shelf, and about one third of the entire land surface of the Arabian peninsula. Only Nafud Al Urayq and a few smaller sand fields are scattered over the Arabian Shield.

Despite its reputation as a sandy desert, Saudi Arabia in fact comprises several distinctive physiographic regions (Fig. 2.3). Eastward from the narrow coastal plains that extend along the Red Sea, the western mountain ranges rise steeply, to an average 2130m in height northwest of Al Madinah Al Munawarah. Their highest peak, standing at 3050m, is at Jabal Saudah, near Abha in the southwest of the country (Farsi, 1991). To the east of these mountains are very gentle slopes extending towards the interior central plateau region of the country, which includes the pediplain Najd, the Al Hisma plateau, and the Hijaz-Asir plateau. Together, these form still a highland terrain that includes local mesas, buttes and lava fields. All these plateaux are transected by large wadis and their tributaries, such as Wadi As Sirhan, Wadi Ar Rumah, Wadi Ranyah, Wadi Bishah, Wadi Tathlith, and Wadi Ad Dawasir. The directional trend of these wadis is from the mountains in the west, eastward to the plains of Najd, responding to the general slope of the land. They are, however, not continuous, being at times covered and buried by the central sand dunes: and some of them, after passing underneath the sand dunes, emerge under a new name. For example, Wadi Ar Rumah emerges as Wadi Al Batin. The presence of these now largely dry wadis reflects the wetter climate that formerly existed in the region in the past.

The cuesta region, which dominates the topography of central Saudi Arabia, is made up of a nearly parallel sequence of prominent crescent-shaped escarpments, thinning predominately north-south. These west-facing escarpments extend along the eastern margins of the Shield between the Ad Dahna sand dunes in the east and the central plateau region in the west. The Tuwayq escarpment (or, as it is called locally, Tuwayq Mountain), which is mainly hard marine limestone capped with upper Jurassic limestone, extends for about 800 km.: its average elevation is 840m above sealevel, and 240m above the western plains. The Al Aramah Escarpment, which is capped with Upper Cretaceous limestone, extends 250km north of Riyadh, with a maximum elevation of 540m above sea-level, and 120 m above the western plains (Chapman, 1978). The wadis that cut through the central plateau region also intersect these cuestas, at which points oases, villages and cities are located.

The hard-rock plains of the As Summan plateau lie between the Ad Dahna sand dunes and the eastern Arabian coast region. This coastal strip is an irregular land surface covered with marshes, salt flats and narrow sandy plains.

2.2. Origin and geomorphology of the sand seas of the Arabian Peninsula

Sand seas represent the most recent and distinctive gemorphological features found on the peninsula. Despite the wide range of geological studies that cover the Arabian peninsula and especially Saudi Arabia, unfortunately very little information is available as to the origin of the sand area's, their age, and their development and evolution.

In general, there are four basic requirements for the formation of large sand seas and ergs, namely:

1. an abundance of unconsolidated deposits and debris;
2. aeolian forces to carry and deflate the sand.
3. a suitable topographic location for sand deposition; and
4. appropriate climatic conditions to maintain the accumulation and development of the sand fields.

The growth and evolution of the sand seas of Saudi Arabia appears to have taken place gradually but discontinuously from late Miocene to late Pleistocene times, and generally

can be attributed to the decreasing temperatures and increasing continental ice volumes of the northern hemisphere in these periods, which resulted in turn in increasing aeolian activity on a hemispheric scale (Whitney *et al.*, 1983). Brown (1960) and Holm (1960) also suggested that these aeolian sands accumulated particularly at the onset of arid phases, along with renewed weathering and denudation, following the more humid periods of the Tertiary and Quaternary. In 1984, Anton reached a similar conclusion, suggesting six main pluvial and interpluvial phases that occurred in the Arabian peninsula during the Pliocene and Quaternary periods, all of which affected sand presence.

These phases appear to have been associated with the repetitive spread and retreat of the glaciers that extended over large parts of the northern hemisphere during the Pleistocene period. The last glacial maximum was about 18000 yrs B.P. (Pye and Tsoar, 1990). During this and other similar phases, the Arabian peninsula enjoyed a cooler and wetter climate than that which exists today. Shallow lakes were formed in the great deserts, as well as in the sand seas. The large dry wadis that cross the peninsula must have been active during that time, so that material from distant areas may have been eroded, and transported by water flow (including heavy floods) to low relief areas and depressions to the east. When the region became arid again, during the interpluvial phases, aeolian processes then took over and resulted in the formation of the present sand seas. The most recent arid phase started some 6,000 years ago; during this, the major sand seas of the peninsula and neighbouring regions were activated, to arrive at their present forms. Most of the large sand areas and ergs of the world are confined to low structural basins (Wilson, 1973), and this area is no exception, except for the Nafud (An Nafud), which occupies a nearly flat plain that slopes gently downward to the northeast. Strong westerly winds sweep over the areas of abundant sediment and alluvial deposits to the west of An Nafud, and seem to be the primary reason for its existence and its evolution in this particular location (Holm, 1960).

The original and immediate sources of the sand, which comprises the sand seas of the Arabian peninsula, are the igneous and metamorphic (crystalline) rocks exposed in the uplands of the peninsulas. Following early weathering and aeolian processes, unconsolidated alluvial deposits and debris were transported by wind, as well as by water in the large wadis and their tributaries, and deposited in the low relief areas in which have accumulated the present sand seas. Deposits which are derived from ancient dry lakes and sea shores are other potential primary sources of the sand. Most of the sand deposits, however, are believed to have come from the outcrops and inselbergs of the Palaeozoic and Mesozoic sandstones, as well as the surrounding gravel plains and all the older rock formations (Holm, 1960; Brown, 1960). In addition to these sand sources, sand seas might also supply one another once established, and depending on the prevailing wind. Thus small nafuds and ergs that lie west of it are supplied directly by a large amount of sand from the Great Nafud. The major sand seas in Saudi Arabia are:

1. An Nafud (The Great Nafud)
2. Ad Dahna.
3. Smaller sand bodies:
   a. Nafud Al Madhur
   b. Nafud Ath Thuwayrat
   c. Nafud Al Ghamees
   d. Nafud Ash Shuqayyiqah
   e. Nafud As Sirr
   f. Nafud Qunayfithah
   g. Nafud Ad Dahi
   h. Nafud Al Urayq
4. Ar Rub' Al Khali (The Empty Quarter).

Their locations are indicated in Fig. 2.4, and a brief description of each follows.

2.2.1. AN NAFUD (THE GREAT NAFUD)

An Nafud is the largest sand sea in northern Saudi Arabia and the second largest sand body in the Arabian peninsula. It covers a vast area in northern Saudi Arabia between Hail and Al Jawf, occupying about 62,884 km^2 between 27 20 N and 29 45 N latitude, and 38 20 E and 32 42 E longitude, with an approximate length of 413km and a width of 272km. It forms the shape of a giant hand, with long fingers extending to the west. An Nafud lies on a flat plain that is confined between Al Hajarah and the Syrian plateau to the east and north, and the Al Hisma plateau and Jabal Shammar to the west and south.

An Nafud has a variety of sand dune shapes. It is dominated by longitudinal, transverse and star dunes (Fig. 2.5). Other sand-dune types can be found there, but on a small scale. Chapman (1978) summaries four classes of aeolian sand dunes which geologists recognise in the Arabian peninsula, these being:

1. Transverse. Predominantly simple and compound barchan dunes in areas of more mobile sands, and/or simple rounded ridges, oriented transversely to the prevailing wind direction.

2. Longitudinal. Primarily dikakah (bush, or grass-covered sand) and various types of undulating sand sheets, in general characterised by elongation of the individual forms parallel to the prevailing wind direction, often partly stabilised by the sparse vegetation.

3. Uruq (ergs). Various forms of long, nearly parallel, sharp-crested narrow sand ridges and dune chains separated by broad sand valleys usually including elements of prime sand terrain.

These forms are the result of a system of two dominant wind directions, and are equivalent to the sayf (seif) dunes of north Africa.

4. Sand mountains. Large sand massifs commonly cresting 50 to 300m above the substratum, often with super-imposed dune patterns. Common forms are giant barchans spanning several kilometres from horn to horn, giant sigmoidal and pyramidical sand peaks, as well as other less common peak forms, and other giant oval to elongated sand mounds.

Longitudinal (Linear) dunes in An Nafud are found in the north, central and north-eastern parts. Unlike the linear and seif dunes of the Sahara and Ar Rub' Al Khali, these dunes are low, broad ridges with a chain of separated crescent slip faces on the northern side of each ridge. The formation of these dunes is probably due to the prevailing south-westerly and north-westerly winds in the Holocene (Whitney *et al.*, 1983). Large star dunes (pyramidical), which rise up to 200m and have radiating sinuous arms or ridges, between two to six in number, of active sand are found in the south-eastern part of An Nafud: the formation of these dunes is influenced by the complex multimode wind regimes of this region (Holm, 1960). Simple transverse and barchanoid ridges extend over the area of south-western An Nafud, and these can be attributed to the variability of the wind direction there. Although An Nafud landscapes are dominated by sand dunes, vast parts of the region are characterised by low relief and hollows between the dunes, containing a relatively thin sand cover. The remnants of lake beds can be seen in some areas of An Nafud, exposed in some of the interdunal depressions.

Schulz & Whitney (1986) reported that these lake beds were deposited during at least the late Quaternary, within the humid phases. But, contrary to what is reported by several authors (e.g. Wilson, 1973; Pye & Tsoar, 1990), wadis and internal drainage systems are almost absent from the An Nafud landscape. Most sand dunes of An Nafud are stabilised, and are considered to be fixed and inactive dunes: active sand movement is limited to the crests of the inactive dunes, so that any contemporary large-scale sand movement must be very slow, if indeed it takes place at all.

2.2.2. AD DAHNA

This is a narrow, arc-shaped sand sea which extends approximately 1425 km from the southeast of An Nafud to northern Ar Rub'Al Khali, between 20 30 and 28 30 N latitude, covering approximately 49,200 km². It lies along the western margins of the As Summan plateau to the east, and the slopes of the cuesta region in the west, with a maximum width of 50 km.

Ad Dahna has a variety of sand-dune shapes, but parallel longitudinal dunes dominate its landscape. These longitudinal ridges are called locally uruq, and the low, relatively flat areas in between are termed *shagegah*, *khab*, and *jaw*. The main longitudinal dunes from east to west are Erg Ath Thimam, Erg Al Hamrany, Erg Imr, Erg Ruwaykib, Erg Jaham, Urayq Al Uqayhat, Erg Huwaymil and Erg Harury. Ad Dhana's longitudinal dunes are broader than those of An Nafud. They are more widely spaced, and lack sharp crescent-shaped slip faces. Their elevation ranges from between 400 and 560m above sea-level. Holm (1960) surveyed other dune systems including sigmoidal (s-shaped) dunes, tuning-fork dunes, linear dunes and pyramidical dunes. He indicated that the pyramidical dunes in north-central Ad Dahna reach 150-170m above general ground level.

Ad Dahna sand seas have been known throughout history as being a favourite grazing ground, especially during the winter and spring seasons, in which scarce water and vegetation can be found in the low-lying districts. This attracts both nomads and villagers.

2.2.3. SMALL SAND SEAS

In addition to the two major sand seas in the region, central and northern Saudi Arabia are dotted here and there by scattered and isolated dune fields. The most important and distinctive small sand seas are those elongated ones which lie along the parallel, arc-shaped north-south escarpments that extend along the eastern margin of the Arabian Shield and follow its curved structure. These sand fields resemble Ad Dahna in extension, though they do not reach the vast sand sea of Ar Rub' Al Khali; they also appear to have similar characteristics to Ad Dahna. In general, they show arid geomorphic dynamics with little or no runoff, strong aeolian activity and sparse vegetation cover. Small, flat plains are confined between these sand fields and the parallel escarpments, and in the plains some urban centres are located. Several oases as well as farms and villages also exist inside these sand fields, and these are named locally 'augual' or 'khobob'. Anton (1984) suggested that such small sand fields have been a product mainly of local conditions: their distribution and formation appear to be influenced largely by the parallel escarpments, when the sand has acted as a barrier to the flow of the prevailing wind. In such cases, sand dunes have accumulated mainly on the upwind side of the escarpments, where these sand fields are located now. From north to south, these small sand seas are: Nafud Al Madhur, Nafud Ath Thuwayrat, Nafud Al Ghamees, Nafud As Sirr, Nafud Ash Shuqayyiqah, Nafud Qunayfithat, Nafud Ad Dahi, and Nafud Al Urayq.

Nafud Al Madhur. This is a southern extension of An Nafud. It lies to the west of the Al Taysiyah plateau, which detaches it from Ad Dahna. Nafud Al Madhur extends about 281km². It consists of two or three elongated sand dunes ('uruq), dissected by rocky plains. The width of all these 'uruq from west to east is about 50km, and they reach about 600m above sea level.

Nafud Ath Thuwayrat. Covering roughly 6176 km², this extends in its northern part about 310km from north to south between the end of Nafud Al Madhur and 26 30 N latitude, to the east of Sufra Al Asyah. To the south, it changes its direction to the southeast, forming a narrow sand-dune field between Sufra Al Mustory in the east, and the Tuwayq escarpment in the west. Although its width in the north can exceed 60km, it does not exceed 25km in the south. Dome-shaped dunes are common, reaching to 1.5km in diameter, and 100 to 150m in elevation (Holm, 1953). Some dome-shaped dunes also have crescentic dune ridges in their upper surfaces, so they may be classed as complex dunes (Breed *et al.*, 1979). Some oases and small villages exist inside this sand field, which are locally called 'auqal'. This small sand sea buries the giant Wadi Ar Rumah old-river system.

Nafud Al Ghamees. Unlike the two previous small sand seas, Nafud Al Ghamees extends about 87 km south of Buraydah in the Al Qaseem region. It lies along the lower valley of the Wadi Ar Rumah, running from northeast to southwest between Al Bukayriyah and Nafud Ath Thuwayrat, covering approximately 1458km²: the field is also connected to other sand-dune fields, including Nafud as Sirr in the east and Nafud Ash Shuqayyiqah in the west. Deposits from the Wadi Ar Rumah could have been the major contributor to the formation and accumulation of this sand field.

Nafud Ash Shuqayyiqah. Extending about 83km southwest and west of Unayzah, to the south of Wadi Ar Raumah, this system covers approximately 1490km². It lies parallel to Nafud As Sirr, and to the west of the Khuf cuesta. This system is separated from Nafud Al Ghamees by the Wadi Ar Rumah. Its width ranges between 20 to 35km, and its elevation averages about 400m above sea level.

Nafud As Sirr. This lies to the west of the Al Julah cuesta, covering roughly 3890km². It runs 287km from southeast to northwest parallel to the southern part of Nafud Ath Thuwayrat, between the Al Hawtah area and Nafud Al Ghamees. Nafud As Sirr averages about 30km in width, and ranges from 600 to 750m in elevation above sea level. Like most of the small sand seas, it is dominated by dome-shaped dunes, which reach 100m in height.

Nafud At Turafiyah is a small extension to Nafud As Sirr to the north of Nafud Al Ghamees, extending for about 71km and covering about 860km².

Nafud Qunayfithah. This covers approximately 2529km², averaging 40km in width and extending about 150km between the southern ends of Nafud As Sirr and Nafud Ath Thuwayrat (Urayq Al Buldan). This sand sea is separated from the latter by Safra Butayn Al Barrah. Its elevation ranges between 730 and 790m above sea level.

Nafud Ad Dahi. This extends about 282km from Wadi Birk in Hawatat Bani Tameem to the vicinity of Wadi Ad Dazwasir, to the west of Jabal Tuwayq. Unlike Nafuds Ath Thuwayrat and As Sirr, Nafud Ad Dahi runs from northeast to southwest following the curved geological structure of the eastern edge of the Arabian Shield. It covers approximately

2684km², averages about 500m above sea level, and is dominated by longitudinal dunes.

Nafud Al Urayq. This is the only relatively large sand field in central and northern Saudi Arabia that lies completely on the Arabian Shield. It extends about 238km between 24 and 24 45N, covering roughly 2863km². It is bounded by high inselbergs to the east, Wadi Al Jaris to the west, and the tributaries of Wadi Ar Rumah to the north.

Other small sand seas are scattered here and there all over central and northern Saudi Arabia, but are much more restricted in scale to those described above.

2.2.4.

Covering some 500,000 km², with an extremely arid environment, this it the largest area of continuous sand cover in the world (Mandaville, 1990). It is structurally a basin, with the long axis running from southeast to northwest: its sands are underlain by gravels associated with the ancient river system of Wadi Ad Dawasir. The basin declines from about 800m in the southwest to close to sea level in the northeast over a distance of about 1000km. Towards the lower end, the underlying gravels grade into evaporites, with marls and sabkhahs also exposed at times. These latter customarily lie below 120m above sea level, and some may extend for hundreds of kilometres: they are complex in their extent and form, and can adjoin or even encircle individual sand dunes.

The western part of Ar Rub' Al Khali (Fig. 2.7) consists mainly of fine, soft sand, and smooth rolling sand sheets which support little vegetation. In contrast, the eastern districts have sand structures which attain immense proportions by world standards. These range from parallel strings of dunes hundreds of kilometres long to complex chains of crescentic, barchan dunes, and sand dome mountains 300m in height. Sand avalanches often occur on the larger structures. In general, the dune strings are moulded by the prevailing northerly to southerly wind patterns, though dune mountain systems are indicative of changing wind systems, which, as elsewhere in

Saudi Arabia, produce frequent pyramidical dune forms.

2.3.   Properties of sand as a vegetation base

The existence and development of vegetation cover on the sand seas are affected by several limiting factors which clearly result form the physical and chemical characteristics of the sand itself, as well as from its thermal and hydrological properties.

It should be noted at this point that characteristics of sand dune bodies and what may be termed 'sand soil' are effectively indistinguishable AR RUB AL KHALI THE EMPTY similarities and a good deal of uniformity in sand properties at different depths in the sand profile.

2.4.   Physical Properties of sand.

2.4.1. SAND TEXTURE

Sand texture is the main factor that affects vegetation presence, persistence and health in the sand seas. Resulting from its generally coarse texture, the sand has a very low water-holding capacity and a very high percolation rate, arising from the large pore space between individual particles, which tend not to stick together even when wet. The occasional spell of heavy rainfall also results in a 'washing' of the profile through the leaching process, so that elements of nutrition often appear to be less than the amount required for satisfactory vegetation growth. On the other hand, the coarse texture provides some potentially positive effects for vegetation, such as good drainage as well as aeration.

Clay and silt, which hold many elements of nutrition are largely absent or rare in the sand seas. Most of the constituents consist of medium-grain sand. From our own samples, a clay content was absent from 44.2% of the total, and in 51.7%, the clay content did not exceed 2 to 4%. The highest recorded clay content was 20%, from one sample alone taken from a flat plain (khab) between dunes in Ad Dahna. Further, in 25% of the samples, no silt was present, while in 55.8% the silt content was only 2% or less. It should however be noted that where sand is more stabilised, the percentage of silt and clay, though still small, is increased through wind accumulation. In order to analyse any possible changes in sand profile with depth, samples were collected at three depths, viz from a freshly-exposed surface to 25cm, from 25cm to 50cm and from 50 to 75cm, or to the hard pan in the case of very shallow material. It should be mentioned that in the very dry parts of individual sand dunes, it was very hard to dig a pit for the soil sample collection due to the collapse of the pit walls: however, accuracy in collecting samples at different depths was achieved to the best extent possible. At all three levels, the percentage for medium sand appeared similar. Results from our survey are recorded in Al-Nafie (1995): in general, they agree well with Ahlbrandt's (1979) findings, taken from a world survey of sand-sea materials , which indicate that in inland dune and inter-dune environments, medium and fine-sands are predominant.

2.4.2 THERMAL PROPERTIES

Sand temperature is one of the vital factors that affects both chemical and biological processes within it, and vegetation growth. The intensity of heating and cooling of the sand depends on the overall climatic condition of the area, and especially on the characteristics of solar radiation income and insulation. In the warm deserts of the world, there are two major periods of radiation income, one giving rise to heating , and the other to cooling of the sand; in Saudi Arabia, the cooling period extends from September to February, and the heating period from March to August. Inevitably, the diurnal temperature of the dry sand surface fluctuates considerably, especially in summer. Then, the shade air temperatures can reach up to 48°C at midday, while that of the sand surface can reach up to 80°C. These high temperatures are however concentrated in the topmost sand layers, to depths of perhaps no more than a millimetre (Van Wijk & de Vries, 1963); below

this, heat is then transferred to the cooler underlying sand layers by the relatively slow process of conduction. As a result, below the topmost sand layer, the temperature drops sharply in the daytime to the 30°-39°C level, and then continues to fall slowly with an increase in depth. The prime reasons for this are that quartz, the main component of sand, has a low thermal conductivity; also between 35-40% of the sand volume is occupied by air-filled pore space, and air also has a low thermal conductivity.

Observations of the temperature of the sand sub-surface between February and June were taken by means of inserting a soil thermometer in the sand after removing the top most sand layer: the process was repeated many times for each site, and the average of all readings taken. The results (Table 2.1) show a variation between the average air temperatures and the average sub-surface sand temperatures which reaches up to 12°C. The lowest variation is recorded when the sand is moist, at which time it has a better thermal conductivity. In winter, although temperatures in the topmost sand layer might fall to close to freezing point, the sub-surface strata are often considerably higher. Dincer *et al.* (1974) have observed temperature profiles in Ad Dahna from July 1972 to May 1973, as well as the diurnal temperature variation in the surface sand layer (Figs. 2.8 and 2.9), and their conclusions are very similar to our own. As far as individual dunes are concerned, surface temperatures might differ substantially from one part of the dune to another as a result of minor changes in height, slope and aspect, and degree of exposure to solar radiation of the underlying sand layers.

In his study of world deserts, Petrov (1976) has summarised a number of thermal features common to all such areas. Those that apply particularly to the sand seas of Saudi Arabia are as follows. First, the heat regimes display considerable amplitude as between the periods of summer heating and winter cooling. Secondly, in winter the sands become unusually cold due to the absence of a snow cover. In summer, in contrast, when the sands are desiccated to a maximum degree, they are overheated, and the temperatures of the main root zone then reach the maximum permissible value for the development of vegetation. Third, the increased conductivity arising from the moistening of sands after rain is extremely important for plant development, as it speeds up the establishment of a favourable water-heat regime in the sands. Fourth, in the annual march of sand temperatures and in different years, there are no substantial deviations from the mean annual indices. The largest fluctuations are associated with the sand surface, and the layers close to it. At a greater depth, the amplitude of fluctuations decreases. Fifth, the lag of the maxima with increasing depth in the sand is very marked. Sixth, a broken relief can significantly affect the degree of heating of the surface layers of sands. And seventh, dense herbaceous and shrubby vegetation can influence the temperature regime of sands considerably by reducing the amplitude of temperature fluctuations in the surface horizons.

2.4.3 HYDROLOGICAL PROPERTIES

Arising from the qualities of sand texture, sand 'soils' are characterised by a high rate of infiltration and permeability, so that moisture in the sand profile is retained, and less likely to be lost through evaporation than elsewhere. However, water might be lost by drainage (deep percolation) beyond the root zone (Noy-Meir, 1973). In active dunes that contain < 1% fines and < 1% organic matter, the field capacity varies from about 4% to 10%. Stabilised dunes that contain more fines and more organic matter can retain up to 35% moisture at field capacity (Pye & Tsoar, 1990).

Sand dune surfaces normally have no runoff: however, even very low precipitation can penetrate some distance down into the sand, a feature which has considerable significance for vegetation growth in Saudi Arabia. Dincer *et al.* (1974) and Pye & Tsoar (1990) suggest that 1mm of precipitation on medium-grained sand can penetrate to a depth of 7mm, and to 20mm on coarse sand. With this in mind, and during the period from February to May 1993, sand samples were collected at three subsurface depths for moisture analysis (Table. 2.2). In

samples that were collected one day after rain, the moisture content ranged between 2.41 and 6.12% at the three depths, with the exception of the top few millimetres. On the other hand, samples that were collected one week after rain showed, as expected, much lower moisture contents, all of which increased with depth. Samples that were collected one month after rain recorded even lower moisture percentages, ranging between 0.17 to 3.82% at all levels. The highest moisture contents were found at depths of between 30 and 50cm in the inter-dune vegetated surface, for here moisture can percolate rapidly through the top layers, and then to some extent is sealed against excessive evaporation.

From this, several general conclusions may be reached:

1. Excepting immediately after rain, the first few upper millimetres of sand 'soil' appear to be completely dry, and the depth of this dry layer increases with time after rain, reaching up to 65cm at the end of the long dry season. This is in agreement with the more comprehensive experiments conducted by Al-Tubrak & Al-Hasson in the Ad Dahna sand sea during October 1990 (1992). Dincer *et al.* (1992) also reported similar results from Ad Dahna and other sand seas in the Ar Riyadh region.

2. In all samples collected, moisture appears to increase overall with depth.

3. The crest, and high parts of individual sand dunes have lower moisture contents as a result of the velocity of the wind, and depending on the orientation of the dune, and the angle of exposure to the sun's rays. The movement and replacement of the top layer of sand by erosion and wind expose the moist layers beneath it, allowing more evaporation to occur than might be expected from the admittedly strong solar radiation.

4. There seems to be uniformity in the moisture content of all sand dunes generally in this region. However, some difference can be noticed between different parts of individual dunes,

which can be attributed to sand topography, texture, the degree of stabilisation, and orientation.

It has been suggested by Noy-Meir (1973) that in regions with arid climates, the upper 5 to 10cm are mostly dry within 5 to 25 days after precipitation. Evaporation however has no direct effect on moisture that infiltrates beyond 30cm (Bagnold, 1954; Noy-Meir, 1973). The role of vegetation in the water regime of sand seas accordingly is an interesting one. Dincer *et al.* (1974) suggested that even dense vegetation in Ad Dahna had no effect on the overall water balance of this sand area. But other authors, who have conducted similar studies in other parts of the world (Gupta, 1979; Mann *et al.*, 1976; Prill, 1968; Petrov, 1976), disagree: they conclude that vegetation cover, especially of perennial plants, rapidly depletes the moisture content of sand below 30cm. Unstabilised dunes always appear to have more moisture than stabilised, vegetated dunes, and this seems to be linked to the loss of moisture through transpiration by vegetation on the latter (Mann *et al.*, 1976). Moreover, when unstabilised dunes are vegetated, they develop moisture levels similar to those of the stabilised dunes. But probably the moisture differences between vegetated and unvegetated dunes result from a complex range of physical conditions: we consider that the lack of moisture comparatively in stabilised dunes can also be attributed to their granulometric composition and their degree of compaction, as well as the consequences of vegetation roots in making the sand more compact. This in turn limits soil permeability, and can increase loss of water through evaporation from the sand surface.

Due to their generally high levels of permeability, however, both stabilised and unstabilised sand dunes provide a major reservoir of fresh water, especially where there is regular precipitation (Petrov, 1976). Scattered oases, villages and towns in and around the sand areas of Ath Thuwayrat, As Sirr and Qunayfithah obtain some of their fresh water from such reservoirs.

Additional moisture reaches the sand seas from the temporary water courses or wadis that pass into them. In central and northern Saudi Arabia, numerous wadis and water courses, the headwaters of which lie in the mountains and higher plateaux of the west, as well as in the central escarpments, are blocked by these sand fields, and their water infiltrates into the underlying sands. Thus Wadi Ar Rumah, which extends from Al Hijaz mountain, is one of the major wadi systems of Saudi Arabia, but the obstructing high dunes of Nafud Ath Thuwayrat to the east are too massive for its flowing water to cross even after very heavy rain. Wadi Ar Rumah extends again to the east of Nafud Ath Thuwayrat, to be buried once more by the Ad Dahna sand sea. It then emerges again to the east of the latter under a new name (Wadi Al Batin). Of the wadi's total length of 1225km, about 160km is covered by the sand dunes of Ad Dahna and Ath Thuwayrat.

2.4.4. CHEMICAL PROPERTIES

Sand masses are known for their very limited biological and chemical components, a low nutrition content, and a neutral to alkaline reaction.

Organic matter

Organic matter in arid-region 'soils' is very low, and normally does not exceed 4%, averaging between 0.5 to 2% (Dregne, 1976; Halwagy *et al.*, 1982). In Saudi Arabia, organic matter does not exceed 1%, even in some arid soils under cultivation (Bashour *et al.*, 1983). Our own results (Table 2.3) indicate that organic matter within the sand seas is indeed very low, ranging from between 0.03% and 0.31%.

The highest percentages of organic matter usually are found near to cultivated areas, where organic detritus originates, and from which it may be driven by wind. The main sources of humus in the sand seas themselves are the dead roots, stems, seeds, and leaves of the sparse vegetation cover. A subsidiary source is the excreta of the large number of animals that graze and roam these vast areas, mainly during the winter and spring seasons. Wind plays an important role in distributing the organic detritus from source, or from one area to another. The highest percentages of organic matter are found in the surface layers of sand taken from underneath shrubs that intercept detritus from the wind, and also absorb litter from the falling stems, leaves and seeds, as well as animal excreta.

Organic matter levels in the Saudi Arabian sand seas are clearly much lower than those found in other relatively adjacent sand fields, such as the sand dunes of the northern Sharon plains, Israel, where it ranges between 0.81 and 0.74% , or the southern Namib dunes, where it is between 0.6 to 2% (Robinson & Seely, 1980). The more arid climate, and the more restricted vegetation cover, probably accounts for the lower values in Saudi Arabia. In general, advective influences ensure that the crests and leeward sides of individual dunes have lower organic matter values (0.03 to 0.05%) than the low areas between dunes. Consequently, fixed and more stabilised as well as sheltered areas have more organic matter in the sand seas than elsewhere.

pH

pH values in the sand seas of Saudi Arabia range from 7.5 to 9.2. However, the majority of pH values are neutral to slightly alkaline in reaction ranging from 8.10 to 8.90. No changes in pH values were observed as between the surface layers, and the sub-surface sand. Very high pH values in the soil indicate that its physical and chemical characteristics are unfavourable for plant growth. These values fall with an increase in organic matter and leaching, which might explain the relative abundance of vegetation in these areas. The lowest pH values were found in samples taken from Ad Dahna (7.5 to 7.9), where the 'soil' is stable, and the sand percentage in the subsoil is as low as 60%. The highest pH values (9.0 to 10.0) were in samples collected from unstable dunes, especially along their crests, or along dune slopes.

Conductivity

Electrical conductivity is a good indicator of the degree of salinity present in the soil, which in turn also affects plant growth and welfare. According to the US Salinity Laboratory staff (Richards, 1956), sand seas in Saudi Arabia are comprised largely of 'non-saline soil', in which the conductivity of the saturated extract is less than 4 mmhos/cm at 25°C, and the pH ranges between 8.5 and 10.0. Electrical conductivity analyses of our own sand samples indicate that they have a very low quantity of soluble salts, ranging between 0.01 and 0.89 mmhos/cm: the majority, however, lie between 0.02 and 0.11. In addition to the nature of the primary minerals found in the sand, the low values of salts present in the sand seas can be attributed to the high rates of leaching along with the high levels of permeability of the sand, especially after rainfall. The soluble salts in samples taken from sand-dune crests were relatively lower than elsewhere. No noticeable differences were recognised in the percentages of soluble salts as between layers at different depths.

Calcium carbonate

The sand seas in Saudi Arabia are calcareous, with $CaCO_3$ contents ranging from 1.94 to 64.02%; however, most of the values lie between 1.94 and 5.82%. The presence of the carbonate in the sand is attributed mainly to the parent material, as well as to the settling of airborne calcium; further, the limited rainfall means that carbonate removal is negligible. The highest amounts of carbonate were found in samples taken from a flat area (*khab*) between the Ad Dahna ergs (70 to 64.02%). These samples also had a low sand percentage (to 60%), and a high amount of silt (10 26%), resulting in the soil in this district being classified as a limestone soil/sandy loam. The high percentage of silt suggests that much of the carbonate here was derived from airborne calcium.

2.4.5. NUTRIENT LEVELS

Potassium (K)

Sand in Saudi Arabia has a low potassium content, ranging from 1.84 to 274 ppm: most of the potentially-available potassium is lost by leaching after rain. With the exception of four samples, the available soluble potassium present in the sand was below the level for adequate vegetation growth (175 ppm), as suggested by Doll & Lucas (Bashour *et al.*, 1983).

Phosphorous (P)

Phosphorous content in the samples analysed ranged from 1.02 to 21.05 ppm, although most lay between 1.02 and 5.26 ppm: this is less than the desirable level for plant growth. Phosphorous is easily washed from the sand, because of the low capacity of this medium to retain water, as well as the low buffering capacity for phosphate. Due to the sand texture, phosphorus removed from the top sand layer may not be available for vegetation with relatively short roots, in that it is washed to too great a depth.

Other macro-nutrients

Other macro-nutrients and soluble salts such as Cl, SO_4, Ca, Mg and Na are very deficient in the sand seas of Saudi Arabia; most have been removed by leaching after the occasional rains.

In summary, the physical and chemical properties of sand in the sand-sea areas of Saudi Arabia have both advantages and disadvantages for vegetation growth and welfare. The advantages are that:

1. Sand dunes are relatively mesic environments: since water percolation and movement in sand is very high, that available from even meagre rain is stored in the deeper layers of sand, and is therefore protected from evaporation.

2. Water retained below the surface of the sand dunes brings sand moisture to values above the wilting point, allowing perennials and shrubs with deep, penetrating roots to survive, and to be supplied rapidly by enough moisture to make up the losses from transpiration.

3. Arising from its texture, sand has good aeration.

The disadvantages are:

1. In all, the sand seas and dunes therein have a very low water-holding capacity, which can result in moisture deficiencies in the topmost sand layers; therefore, the growth of plants with relatively short root systems is negatively affected.

2. With the exception of calcium carbonate, sand in Saudi Arabia has a very low nutrient quotient for all other elements, due largely to the effects of leaching.

3. Wind moves and erodes sand continuously, impeding vegetation establishment, and damaging established plants.

2.5 Climate

No meteorological stations are found in the interior of the sand seas of Saudi Arabia (Fig. 2.10): Moreover, records taken from nearby stations are frequently incomplete. However, available data from these stations do serve to assist interpretation of the major climatic elements found in this region.

Due to their location, the sand seas of Saudi Arabia have an arid subtropical, desert climate. Heated air rising from the equatorial regions moves at high altitudes both southwards and northwards, eventually to descend in the vicinity of the 30th parallels north and south, at a latitude which effectively is the poleward limit of the tradewind belt. Being located where it is, Saudi Arabia accordingly receives stable air, which is adiabatically warmed and dried as it loses altitude. These processes create an at times almost complete dispersal of cloud cover under anti-cyclonic conditions, and a long-term diminution in the chances for rain, except when occasional large-scale weather disturbances move into the area from the outside. Although on a world scale, trade winds are normally north-easterly, here they are more frequently north-westerly or northerly (Fig. 2.11), resulting from locally-dominant pressure patterns over the Gulf, and the Asian land mass to the east: and these winds provide the basis for most air movement within the region.

Although this general pattern holds true throughout the year, there are some important seasonal variations, and it is from these that most rainfall reaches the sand seas. In summer (May to August), the northward shift of the Inter Tropical Convergence Zone, coupled with the monsoon circulation of the Indian Ocean, give rise to south-easterly winds which can bring regular rains to a narrow coastal fringe in Dhufar, and more spasmodic rains inland to as far as the southern Ar Rub' Al Khali. To the north there is a much clearer division of the year into hot and cool seasons, with rainfall confined normally to the cool months from October to April. These winter rains are derived from eastward-moving depressions which originate in the Mediterranean region and from which, particularly in the spring, squall lines and thunderstorms are derived, with at times torrential rains and gale-force winds. In mid-winter, there is likely to be a more prolonged period of cloud cover, with longer rains. The efficiency of these weather systems diminishes as the storms move east across the Arabian peninsula, and only rarely do they carry rain as far south as Ar Rub' Al Khali, though there are exceptions, as in February 1982, in which heavy rainfall was experienced in most of this region (Mandaville, 1990). Elsewhere, storms which result in 60-80mm of rain in one day are not unusual in the winter months, though they occur infrequently.

These changing seasonal precipitation patterns ensure that two rather undefined tropical dry climates exist in Saudi Arabia: one in the north which has winter rainfall, and the other to the south which has smaller amounts of largely summer rainfall. Under Thornthwaite's (1948) classification, the climate of the sand seas north of Latitude 24°N is classed as 'arid', in terms of the formulae which elucidate potential evapo-transpiration and temperature on a month-by-month basis: south of this line, including the Ar Rub' Al Khali, it is termed 'extremely arid', this category being reserved for those areas which may have no precipitation over an entire 12-month period.

2.5.1.

The sand seas of Saudi Arabia are noteworthy for having a clear atmosphere, and a large number of cloudless days throughout the year. The average solar radiation intensity per diem, on a monthly basis (Table 2.5), ranges between 465 langleys (one langley = 1 gram calorie/cm^2) to 541 in the north, and 314 to 542 langleys in the south. This produces shade temperatures measured by standard means which range from a maximum of 52°C (Abqaig in July) to -3C inland in January. Frosts have been reported inland on the sand seas as far south as Ar Rub' Al Khali. Average mean monthly maximum and minimum temperatures are indicated in Table 2.6. The characteristically large diurnal ranges of temperatures tend to be larger in summer: they are also quite large during the transition seasons of spring (March, April and May) and autumn (September, October, November), due to the instability of the weather at these times. Thus, the mean variation between maximum and minimum daily temperature ranges between 14° and 24°C in the autumn, and between 14° to 26°C in the spring (Al-Nafie, 1989).

Details of temperatures at the sand surface, and within the sand itself, have been given earlier, in pages 12-13.

2.5.2.

Though occasional snow has been recorded in the Najd uplands (e.g. at Riyadh, 3 January 1973), precipitation in the sand seas falls almost entirely as rain. Annual totals range from 154mm in the north and northeast, to much less than 100mm in Ar Rub' al Khali, in which in many years none is reported. Dews occur fairly frequently, though they have never been measured. The average mean monthly precipitation at selected stations is given in Table 2.7. This displays clearly its seasonality: for most stations in the northern and central sand seas, as noted previously, rainfall is derived from passing Mediterranean depressions that cross the area between September and May. Occasional and very light falls might also occur in the beginning of May and at the end of September, while in the Ar Rub' Al Khali, in some years there is a tendency for rain to fall during the summer months, from monsoonal origins.

But the most dominant characteristic of the rainfall is its variability in time, amount and location. Indeed, temporal variability is one of the main features of rainfall in the warm deserts and arid lands generally. In Ar Riyadh, for example, the average annual rainfall over a 34-year period was 94.5mm; however, some years had only a little rain (no more than 13.5mm in 1966), while on the other hand totals exceeded 216.2mm in 1967, and 257.7mm in 1976. Another example is from Hail, where the average annual rainfall over a 27-year period (1966-1993) was 119.9mm, but it reached 324.9mm in 1976, in contrast to only 50.6mm in 1977, and 33.4 mm in 1978. The number of rainy days during the rainy season is also very irregular from year to year. Rainy days in the northern and central sand seas average from 19 to 27 days a year depending on location, but some years may witness considerably more or less than this. Thus in 1988, most stations in this region recorded more than 80 days of rain (Ar Riyadh 81 days; Al Qaseem 87 days; Al Jawf 81 days). On the other hand, there were only 14 days with rain in 1978. Central and northern Saudi Arabia can lie outside the path of Mediterranean depressions and cyclones in some years, and this in itself can explain much of the irregularity in rainfall and rain days from one year to another. Also, some rainfall develops under conditions of local instability (convectional rain), so that it may come in the form of violent rain storms of short duration, and over a very localised area. Thus in 1992, the old meteorological station in Ar Riyadh recorded 96.3mm, whereas the meteorological station at King Khalid Airport, also in Ar Riyadh, recorded 192mm. Such differences in the amount of annual rainfall between two nearby stations, emphasise the irregularity, and high variation in precipitation income, which can occur from time to time over a small distance.

2.5.3. RELATIVE HUMIDITY

Relative humidity values in themselves, though useful for comparative purposes, bear little relation to transpiration and plant water use as compared to other parameters such as vapour pressure deficit. They do however provide indicators of relative aridity in the sand-sea areas of Saudi Arabia.

The interior parts of the Arabian peninsula are remote from large bodies of water, so that relative humidity does not exceed 66% (Table 2.8). However, the degree of relative humidity is most closely associated with the season. Thus higher relative humidities are recorded in the coldest and wettest months (October to April). The average relative humidity for Al Jawf ranges during this period from between 29% and 66%, but in the hottest months it falls to between 15 and 20%. In Ar Riyadh, the average monthly relative humidity ranges between 23% and 49% for the period from October to April, and between 13% and 23% for the rest of the year. In As Sulayyil, to the south, relative humidity is exceptionally low, especially during the summer months (10% to 13%), but in the rainy season it increases slightly, averaging between 19% and 44%. In general, it appears to be the case that relative humidities display a marked decrease in the northern and southern extremities in this region; and that the central stations record the highest humidities.

2.5.4. EVAPORATION

Evaporation rates, which are so important to vegetation because of their contribution to evapotranspiration, give some indication of the likelihood or otherwise of available surface moisture for plant growth. Within the sand seas, evaporation is very high in summer, as a result of the very intense incoming radiation, high temperatures and low humidities. During this season, the range of monthly and annual evaporation from 'Class A' pans (Table 2.9) shows rates ranging from 35 to

100 times the local mean incoming rainfall. Mandaville (1990) has pointed out that direct measures are not available for probably the most extreme conditions, in Ar Rub' Al Khali, though the very high rates noted from Khurais and As Sulyyil give some clues as to the expected values.

Fortunately for plant growth and survival, rainfall income in the sand seas is concentrated in the cool season, when there is much less potential evaporation than at other times. The average annual total pan evaporation ranges between 2496mm in the north, and over 4900mm in the south, the latter value exceeding by far the categorised level of evaporation for hot deserts (2000 to 4000mm)m as determined by Evenari (1985). Again, fortunately for plant growth and survival, when rain falls, much of it soaks and infiltrates immediately into the sand, and this reduces the amount of water that can be lost through evaporation, and increases that available to plant roots.

2.5.5. WIND SYSTEMS

Mean wind speeds in the sand seas are not very high by world standards, averaging between 7.6 and 21km per hour (Heathcote, 1983: see Table 2.10). This average appears to be lower than that required to transport sand, and might explain the very low percentage (10%) of active dunes within the sand seas (Whitney *et al.*, 1983). However, the winds are persistent, and can negatively affect vegetation growth and survival, increasing the already high desiccating power of the hot, dry atmosphere, quickly remoulding topography and possibly making plant root systems vulnerable in the process and, with sand particles, producing an abrasive effect on dune plants, the effectiveness of which is likely to be extreme. This effectiveness is difficult to calculate in practice, since data on extreme wind speeds are not available, and neither is information about the duration of wind storms, which involve sand movement. It may be that some sand storms last longer around midday, for there is a clear tendency for wind velocities then to increase as a result of differential atmospheric and surface warming: the hottest land areas heat the

overlying air, creating thermals that temporarily reverse the general patterns of air subsidence in the subtropics, and suck in air at speed from adjacent districts (Wallen & Stockholm, 1966).

There are also seasonal differences in wind-speed patterns, and to some extent wind direction, which are likely to be important for plant growth. Although most winds blow from the northwest in the north of the region, turning to the north and even north-east farther south (Fig. 2.11), a local, dry hot wind, As Samoon, can interrupt this pattern in late spring (May to mid-June) and early autumn (September to mid-October), causing great destruction to vegetation, especially annual vegetation. Also, strong seasonal pressure gradients and patterns over the Gulf, beginning in early summer as the seasonal low of the Asian landmass extends into this region, produce strong and persistent *shamal* winds, which may produce gusts of up to 70km per hr, usually from the northwest along the isobars. These winds raise the moisture stress for plant life, particularly during June and July , for they are inevitably dry as well as strong: by August, in contrast, they fall away in speed substantially, so that a greater number of calm days prevail, with increasing relative humidity. However, it is unlikely that mean *shamal* wind speeds per month exceed those of the winter months generally within the sand seas. To the south, strong multi-directional winds frequently occur, and these are reflected in the sand-dune patterns (p.).

As in all the world's hot deserts, sand storms can occur suddenly, causing sand movement and the remoulding of various types of sand dunes. But it is normally the case that severe sand storms, in which sand and dust is raised a metre or more above ground level, and which require exceptional wind velocities, are rare: most sand movement occurs within 0.5m of the surface, and to facilitate this, much lower wind speeds suffice. Sand drift potential generally in the Arabian peninsular is indicated in Fig. 2.12.

2.6   Summary

The data available from the weather observation stations that are located in towns and cities located along the margins of the Saudi Arabian sand seas indicate that the region is characterised by an arid climate with a hot and almost rainless summer.

On the other hand, winter is mainly cold. Limited and scattered precipitation falls, especially in the northern and central sand seas, between September and May, while in contrast there is very little in Ar Rub' Al Khali, and what there is in that location may fall just as easily in the summer, under the influence of the Indian Ocean on-shore monsoon. Precipitation occurrence and quantity is by far the most important factor affecting the presence and type of vegetation in the sand seas. That in Ar Rub' Al Khali is sparse: but the concentration of rainfall mainly in the cool season farther north means that evaporation then is potentially much less than if it were to fall at other times of the year. The result is that ephemeral plant cover will appear in the late winter and early spring in these districts, sometimes luxuriously so, as in our field season of spring 1992. Herbaceous perennials, dwarf shrubs and shrubs, on the other hand, are supported by the longer-germ moisture reserve stored in the 'subsoil', following rapid percolation after whatever rains may occur.

CHAPTER 3

PALAEOENVIRONMENTS, VEGETATION HISTORY, THE DEVELOPMENT OF THE SAND SEAS, AND BIOGEOGRAPHIC AFFINITIES

Information on the overall vegetational and environmental history of the Arabian peninsula still is fragmentary. Since faunal and floral plant remains are very difficult to obtain in such arid environments, with their high potential rates of erosion of fossil-bearing material, only a few fossil collections have been discovered, mainly relating to the Ordovician, Permo-Carboniferous, Miocene, and post-Miocene periods.

3.1 Fossil and micro-fossil evidence

3.1.1 The Palaeozoic and Mezozoic periods

The Arabian peninsula's first indications thus far of vascular plant life have been recorded from bore-hole evidence dating back to the middle of the Ordovician period, at about 465 million years ago. Although this is not sufficient to detail communities *per se*, similar evidence of a related terrestrial flora of vascular plants also has been discovered in North Africa from the same period (Gray, Massa & Bout, 1982; Mandaville, 1990.)

The first clear evidence of an assemblage of plants in the peninsula comes later in the Palaeozoic, in the central parts of the country, close to Unayzah (El-Khayal *et al.*, 1980; Al-Laboun, 1987). The most abundant and securely-determined genera within this assemblage (Table 3.1) are representatives of the fern-like genus *Pecopteris*, the early seed plant *Cordaites* and the theophyte *Annularia*. This group of plants is likely to be of the late Carboniferous to early Permian age (c. 300 million years ago), and its affinities lie with the large northern Laurasian continent of that time, rather than with the Southern continent of Gondwanaland, the northern limits of the latter then presumably lying well to the south of 'Arabia'.

During the Mesozoic, fossil spores from the Triassic in eastern Arabia are not particularly noteworthy, being similar to those found in many other parts of the world at that time: and the Jurassic was predominantly marine. But during the Cretaceous period (from c. 144 million years ago), petrified trunks and leaves recorded from many parts of the Arabian peninsula testify to the presence there of subtropical and temperate forests. In the Al Quseem area and in Unayzah city, fossil tree trunks of up to 6m in length, and more than 75cm in circumference have been reported from this period, and are believed to represent the remains of an early coniferous forest which covered an area of about 1,000 km^2, extending from the southern margins of Ar Rub' al Khali near Muqayran to the Quaybah in northern Al Qaseem, in what is now central Saudi Arabia. These forests are considered to have dominated this region at this time; and indeed they appear then to have been located over a large part of what is now the Middle East (Al-Laboun, 1990); they appear to have been closest in form and genetic structure to equivalents in Australia, and thus, in contrast to the Permo-Carboniferous assemblage, they may have been representative of part of the former southern continent of Gondwanaland which, after splitting, had drifted north by that time. The first flowering plants were added to these forests during the Upper Cretaceous, about 65-70 million years ago.

3.1.2 The Cenozoic period (Tertiary and Holocene): early origins of the sand seas.

Records of the early Tertiary (commencing c. 65 million years ago) flora and fauna in the Arabian peninsula are poor, and inferred knowledge is accordingly limited. After the decline of the Tethys Sea, which periodically covered much of the area in the Eocene, Eastern Arabia then generally lay above sea-level, although there were smaller subsequent incursions of marine waters during the Miocene and Pliocene periods. Since the African and Arabian Shields remained undivided until the Miocene, it is often assumed that a palaeo-African type of vegetation extended into the western part of the present peninsula during the Eocene and Oligocene, persisting in the present western highlands as a precursor to that region's 'Sudanian' vegetation of today (see pp 26-27). Only in the Miocene (commencing c. 25 million years ago) and the Pliocene (commencing c. 10 million years ago) are there records of life forms in the eastern part of the peninsula, which give some clues as to the nature of Tertiary environments there.

During the Miocene, the main palaeogeographic event was the splitting of the African and Arabian Shields, concomitant with the formation of the Red Sea. Major mountain ranges also were formed on a world scale. Associated climatic changes point further to the Miocene as being a transitional climatic period between the humid early Tertiary, and the extremely arid phases of the later Tertiary, leading to the more severe oscillations of the Quaternary (Anton, 1984). These several major processes no doubt encouraged the development of the environment, flora and fauna to move in different directions than formerly.

However, Miocene palaeoenvironmental information for most of the Arabian peninsula still is scanty, being confined to fossils and other remains which occur mainly in the east and south, and these are found only in a few sites. Thus fossil pollen samples have been located some 150 to 200m below the eastern Ar Rub' al Khali, close to Az-Zumul, and have been determined to be Middle Miocene at the earliest (Mandaville, 1990). These are dominated by fern and moss spores (73% of the total), among which *Ceratopteris* (which now grows in fresh water springs) is particularly significant; grass pollen (13%), and other pollen from non-forest taxa (14%), including especially Myrtaceae and Palmae, comprise the remainder of the spectrum. The environment in which these taxa were deposited would seem to be a

fresh-water swamp in a humid tropical to sub-tropical habitat.

Further to the east, rich fossil faunal remains from the early-Middle Miocene have been recovered from two sites, Ad Dabityah in the northern Summan, and Jabal Mira ash-Shamali, within the Dam formation (Hamilton *et al.*, 1978; Table 3.2). In these, remnants of mastodon, rhinoceros, pig and crocodile are particularly prevalent; also present in abundance are the remains of turtle, rodents, hyrax, giraffe and bovid, all suggesting a prevailing open savanna grassland as the dominant environment.

Mangrove root fossils found and studied by Whybrow and Melure (1980/81) at two Early-to-Middle-Miocene locations in the Dam and Houfuf formations, close to the eastern Gulf coast, also suggest a dry tropical to subtropical climate in coastal and tidal-flat habitats. The relative abundance of grass pollen and spores (Myrtaceae, Chenopodiaceae, ?*Celtis*, tubulifora Compositae, *Corlyus*, Euphorbiaceae (Alchornea), Cyperaceae and Combretaceae) in the collected samples, and the existence of Proboscidean and bovid faunal remains also are indicative of open savanna grasslands, with shallow, vegetation-fringed rivers, and streams which flowed at least seasonally, feeding areas of fresh-water and some saline swamps. Thomas *et al.* (1981 Table 3.3) further recovered pollen remains from Al-Sarrar in the eastern province of Saudi Arabia, dating from the Miocene, in which Chenopodiaceae, tubulifloral Composite and Plantagaceae are abundant (88% of the total), which again strongly suggest the presence of open savanna grasslands. In this record, the presence of pollen from *Juniperus*, *Pinus* and *Corylus*, all temperate-land plants, in the same sample, is also noted, but is explained through probable long-distance dispersal from highlands with a more temperate climate, such as Oman mountain.

Abundant invertebrate and vertebrate remains from the lower Miocene were also recovered by these authors from the same site (Table 3.4 and 3.5). At least 66 species of vertebrate remains were identified: 27 were from mammals, including two gomphotheres, one deinothere, two rhinoceroses, one tragulid, one giraffoid, one bovid, several carnivores, one bunodont hyracoid, and two suids. A few dipodis, gerbillids, pedtids and phiomorphs also were found. All these suggest the continuing presence of a tropical to subtropical savanna environment here, albeit that the existence of some of the rodents may suggest the presence of a very open environment, perhaps more so than the vegetation evidence *per se* would suggest.

Van Couvering (1976) has proposed that 'proto-savanna' environments were widespread in Africa during the Middle Miocene. The presence of a savanna-type formation in both north Africa and the Arabian peninsula during the Miocene is important for confirming the general affinities in this period between the two regions, and these habitats are believed to have covered a large part of what is now the Middle East by the late Miocene. Further to the north, it is likely that, following on from the world orogenies of the mid-Miocene, pockets of more arid vegetation, and even some semi-desert and desert environments had begun to form (Axelrod. 1952). Especially during the late Miocene, the sand areas of this region then began to emerge (Whitney *et al.*, 1983). Consequent upon this, a large number of the plant families that predominate in many of the more northerly areas today, including Gramineae, Cyperaceae, Compositeae and Caryophyllaceae, became more common towards the end of the period, while the savanna-like forms then began to retreat from the most easterly areas back into the west.

Commencing about 10 million years ago, the Pliocene period marks a stage worldwide in which gradual cooling was the norm. Very little is known about this period in the Arabian peninsula, except that at the very end of it was an intensely humid phase, which extended from c. 3.5 million years ago well into the mid-Pleistocene of 1.2 million years ago (Hotzl *et al.*, 1978; Hotzl, Kramer & Maurin, 1978, Table 3.6). During this phase, many of the major wadis were activated, bringing immense amounts of flood water and eroded material from the western mountains to be deposited as sands, stones and gravels in the

eastern plains: Wadi al-Bahin in the north, Wadi as-Saba in the middle, and Wadi ad-Dawasir in the south were all at flood-fill levels from time to time during this period. The activation of these, and other wadis, also seem to have provided major biogeographical routeways along which 'Sudanian' vegetation species from the old savannas, which had been increasingly confined to western regions during this period, were able to reinvade central areas again, at least to a limited extent. Mandaville (1990) has pointed out that some relicts of these reinvasions still exist. Thus in Wadi al-Batin, *Acacia gerraardi* and the *Cleome* genus may be found; in Wadi as-Sabha, the main representatives are *Acacia ehrenbergiana, A raddiana* and *A tortilis*, along with a selection of species from the *Capparis, Blepharis* and *Cleome* genuses. The unique and solitary stand of *Suaeda monoica* at Jawb al' Asal in the north of Ar Rub' Al Khali may also be explained by its originating from seeds transported from the west by means of water flowing through the Wadi ad Dawasir during the Pliocene, for the plant is located where this wadi cuts through the Tuwayq hills, and before it becomes submerged by the sands of Ar Rub'- al Khali. The biogeographical significance of this situation is discussed later in this chapter.

The Pleistocene period is generally reckoned to have begun some 3 million years ago, to continue through to c. 11,000; from that time, the Holocene runs through to the present day. The Holocene is of course strongly influenced by man's activities, but the entire Pleistocene and Holocene are characterised by major, and sometimes rapid and severe shifts in climate, which parallel those in more northerly altitudes associated with the glacial and interglacial periods. In the Arabian peninsula, the major phases of climatic variability may be categorised as being either hot and wet (interglacials) or cool and dry (glacials); and both induced substantial changes to geomorphological and biological processes, as well as to the floral and faunal compositions of the region. Other major environmental and biological changes are those eustatic features relating to changes in sea-level: dry climatic phases tended to produce a lowering of these, and they may have been higher at times during pluvial, hot wet phases.

Following the markedly wet phase characteristic at the beginning of the Pleistocene, which has been described above, Anton (1984) has suggested that there were five clearly-detectable climatic phases in the Pleistocene/Holocene of the Arabian peninsula. These are:

1. A Middle Pleistocene arid phase
2. A late-Pleistocene humid phase
3. A Late-Pleistocene/Early Holocene arid phase
4. An Early Holocene humid phase
5. The recent arid phase.

Of these, the Middle Pleistocene arid phase appears to have been wide spread, and extreme at times, producing hot dry conditions which were advantageous to the spread of a desert flora in most districts, and, on a more restricted basis, the added dispersal of species such as Chenopodiaceae, which are tolerant of an evaporite environment. The periods of low sea-level during arid phases also indirectly must have added to the general severe dryness: that between 20,000 to 15,000 years before present (3, above), which was certainly not the most severe, lowered levels in adjacent seas by over 100m, and turned most of the Gulf into dry land: some of the sand available at this time from the former sea bed must have contributed to the enlargement of the sand seas, bearing in mind the prevailing north to north-westerly wind systems. Between 12,000 and 8,000 years BP, the sea-level rose rapidly again, reaching its present level by 5,000 years BP (Vita-Finzi, 1978).

The humid (pluvial) phases of the Pleistocene had cooler climates and sufficient precipitation to form and maintain lake water in lake beds, large and small, throughout the peninsula, even within the sand seas (Plate 1). Where they existed, these lakes could also be augmented by water trapped and stored from the wadis that ran into eastern Arabia from the more mountainous areas to the west. Even now, large bodies of water can be formed in the depressions between the dunes, and in desert plateaux, after heavy rain storms, especially in winter when evaporation is much less than in the summer months. Older lake beds have been reported from within the sand seas from time to time. Thus Blunt (1968) recorded the presence of several lake beds during her visit to the region in 1879. While travelling in the northern sand seas, Euting also noted the existence of several lake beds within the northern sand seas in 1883 (Schulz & Whitney, 1986). St John Philby, who travelled widely in both central and northern Saudi Arabia, and in the Ar Rub' Al Khali, further recognised and collected shells from old lake beds throughout the area (Philby, 1933).

More recently, oil geologists from the 1950's and subsequently have described many more such lake beds, and evaluated their significance for the reconstruction of palaeo-environments of the region. McClure (1978, 1984) has indicated convincing evidence for the existence of two series of fresh-water lakes in the central and western Ar Rub' Al Khali, radiocarbon-dated respectively to c 35,000 - 17,000 years BP (Late Pleistocene) on the one hand, and to 9,000 to 6,000 years BP (Early Holocene) on the other. Faunal fossil remnants from these sites included *Bos* and *Hippopotamus*, and a rich assemblage of both aquatic, and adjacent savanna vegetation, apparently of 'Sudanese' affinities.

Similar lakes, from roughly the same periods, also have been identified within the central and northern sand seas (Garrard *et al.*, 1981; Schulz & Whitney, 1986), especially in An Nafud. There, a series of Late Pleistocene lake beds (36,000 to 17,000 years BP) were deposited before the existing sand seas, bearing no relationship to the present sand-sea topography (Whitney *et al.*, 1983). Pollen remains from these lake beds show that the most dominant palaeovegetation types of this period were Gramineae, Cyperaceae and shrubs like *Colligonum*, *Fagonia* and Convolvulus. Herbs from the Compositae, Capparidaceae, Polycarpaceae and Plantagaceae were also common. *Typha* and *Phragmites* were present at lake edges. An over-representation of *Salvadora* pollen in these profiles is interesting, this being a very common species today in the 'Sudanian' biogeographic zone of the south: it is not found in the northern and central sand seas presently, and must have become extinct once the climate changed later, to be come drier. Pollen of *Pinus, Betula, Carpinus, Quercus, Commiphora* and representatives of the Combretaceae may have been transported over long distances, and captured by the surface water. In the Late Pleistocene, the evidence strongly suggests that this area then had a periodically wet, though largely semi-desert environment, with some grass and shrub communities. There is no indication of either Mediterranean woodland or tropical savanna.

Swamps, over very shallow lake beds, of the early Holocene (8,500 to 5,000 years BP) are also found in this region in inter-dune depressions and, unlike the Late Pleistocene situation, appear to have been deposited in alignment with already existing dunes. In consequence, it may be argued that these northern sand dunes have not displayed any major or significant change in their relief or location since the early Holocene. Numerous root and rhizome remains in this period indicate the presence of *Phragmites* and *Typha* swamps in the hollows and depressions between the dunes. Pollen evidence both from An Nafud and Nafud As Sirr (Schulz & Whitney, 1986b) suggests an open-desert vegetation consisting of representatives of Graminacea and Cyperacea, and shrubs including *Artemesia, Convolvulus* and *Cornulaca*, along with herbs like *Moltkiopsis* and *Plantago*. The weak presence of long-distant transported plants such as *Pinus* may be attributed to the much smaller areas of surface water at this time as compared to the Late Pleistocene, which might act as pollen traps. The more common presence of tree pollen, however, of *Acacia, Maerua, Balgnites* and *Hyphaene* suggest that these species were present in the highlands, not far away.

If one may assume from this latter evidence that sand seas in roughly their present form were in existence towards the end of the Late Pleistocene/Early Holocene Arid Phase, their existence was certainly accentuated by the strongly desertic conditions which evolved at the end of the Early Holocene Lake period, at about 6000 years BP. This date correlates with the decrease in humidity recorded in north-western Sudan and southwest Egypt, during which time lakes in these regions, the Sahara, and in other parts of the world, also began to dry out and disappear (Haynes *et al*, 1979; Street & Grove, 1979). The prevailing aridity then must further have severely affected the vegetation cover: many species could not survive, and those that did either adapted generally, or became restricted to small localities in which favourable conditions were available. Either way, they collectively gave rise to a 'Saharo-Arabian-dominated' species group, which prevails in much of the region today.

During the Middle and Late Holocene, aridity deepened, especially during the last 2,000 to 3,000 years, in which most of the sand dunes either were reactivated, or were formed and activated for the first time (Anton, 1984); they then later stabilised, with a subsequent slightly wetter climate recently. Human populations, which have been recorded here since the early Pleistocene (1.5 million years BP: Masry, 1977), expanded during the Holocene, both along the margins of the sand seas and at times inside them: some Holocene environmental deterioration occurred, mainly through overgrazing or woodcutting. This is detailed further in Chapter 6. The landscape and vegetation changes in northern Saudi Arabia which have evolved since the Late Pleistocene are illustrated in Figs. 3.2, 3.3 and 3.4.

3.2 Holocene flora and fauna in rock art and literature

People who lived within, or close to the sand seas of Saudi Arabia left some impression of flora, but especially of fauna, some 4,000 to 5,000 years ago, by means of painting and inscriptions, located mainly on granitic and sandstone rocks (Parr *et al.*, 1978; Gararrd *et al.*, 1981). Dozens of examples of these inscriptions depict animals that were then predominant, including gazelles, ibex and wild oxen, and it may be assumed from these that the environment then probably was less arid than at present, with a somewhat greater semi-arid vegetation cover to support these creatures.

This fits in with the postulation that aridity has intensified during the last three millennia, as noted previously.

More recent clues to the history and environment of the Arabian sand seas may be obtained from the various and scattered Arabic literature. The people who inhabited especially the central and northern sand seas and their vicinity some 2,000 years ago recorded their social life, and described their natural habitat and environment through poetry, which was one of their popular intellectual activities. Species that are common in the sand seas today, such as *Haloxylon persicum, Calligonum comosum, Rhanterium epapposum, Haloxylon salicornicum, Neurada procumens, Anthemis* spp. and *Horwoodia dicksoniae* were mentioned frequently by many poets, in describing different situations, or the desert environment in particular locations. The useful, and harmful uses of these species for humans and animals also were illustrated.

Further, many places such as oases, depressions and high dunes within the sand seas were originally named after the abundant and dominant plant species found around them. Examples are Umm Arta (place of *Calligonum comosum*) in Nafud Ath Thuwayrat and south of Tubarjal in northern Saudi Arabia; and Umm Ghadha (place of *Haloxylon persicum*) near Al Jawf, also in northern Saudi Arabia. These names are still used today, even though the plant species after which they were named now are not abundant, or may even be absent in the location. Large wild animals such as oryx, ibex, wild ass, wolf, cheetah, leopard, hyena and lion further have been mentioned by many poets, under many names (Al-Nafie, 1989).

From this evidence, it is likely that the vegetation cover in the sand seas some 2,000 years ago was largely similar to that of today though, bearing in mind the large number of animals recorded, it is likely to have been of greater density. Walton (1969) suggests that there have been few significant changes in climatic conditions over the last 2,000 years although there is little doubt (see chapter 6) that man's activities have greatly increased the apparent aridity, especially during the last half

of the twentieth century, with an enhanced destruction of vegetation cover.

3.3 The sand seas in the plant geographical regions of the Middle East.

Reference has already been made to the two major biogeographical groupings of vegetation in the Arabia peninsula, one which is 'Sudanian' and largely tropical or subtropical in derivation, and the other being 'Saharo-Arabian', with much more northern affinities.

3.3.1 Biogeographical affinities

The question as to how these two categories originated, and how they may be placed into the broader world and regional biogeographical divisions needs to be considered here.

In recent years, considerable thought has been given to the floristic and other bases for the delimitation of the world into biogeographic regions. Zohary (1973), for example, has indicated that the boundary lines which separate these regions initially must consider the major climatic zones, and the taxa that dominate these zones. Other diagnostic markers are that each region, whether on a world or regional scale, should by preference have a large number of endemics; each should be areas of speciation, with centres of species diversity of certain groups of taxa; and each should display a distinctiveness in the present flora, which might have been gained from a particular vegetation history and past geological events that are unique to the region. On a more local scale, regions might be classified as to whether they are recipients of species from elsewhere, or donors of such species. Within them, plant communities may customarily differ substantially in structure, appearance and species composition, although they may have many common species, and, where it exists, the altitudinally based zonation complex of plants is normally distinctive for each region. Another recent approach is by Ahti *et al.* (1968), who suggest that phytogeographical regions may be classified according to one of three approaches, bioclimatic, edaphic-topographic or floristic.

The bioclimatic approach can be used to delimit the world into broad climatic zones, though for the determination of smaller units which may not be categorised by climatic data alone, other factors such as soil must be considered. This approach often is very useful for understanding past plant distributions from fossil evidence. An edaphic-topographic approach is dependent on ecological similarities, and is accordingly more of an ecological classification *per se*. The floristic approach uses the distribution of plant species more completely, considering the effects of both historical and ecological factors as well.

It is the floristic approach which is used herein. In the recent past, both Walter (1979), invoking both floristics and physignomy, and Takhtajan (1986), taking into consideration floristics and the presence or otherwise of endemics, have suggested that six broad floristic regions, or 'realms' may be distinguished in the world, as follows: the Holarctic (Boreal), the Palaeotropical, the Neotropical, the Australian, the Capensis (South African) and the Antarctic: the Arabian peninsula is split between the first two of these. Each of these six major floristic realms may be divided into several sub-regions, provinces and other smaller units. It can be noted that, with the exception of the Australian and Central Asian deserts, all other desert regions in these classifications are situated between, rather than within, the major world floristic regions: they therefore create difficulties in the precise location and alignment of the frontier of these regions. The desert in the Arabian peninsula is no exception. Some phytogeographers, however, have classified it as falling exclusively in the Palaetoropic region, while others consider it Holartic, or have suggested that the northern parts have clearer links with the Holarctic, while southern areas are more definitively Palaeotropic (Walter, 1979; Zohary, 1973).

On a subregional scale, most authorities now consider that the Arabian peninsula is comprised of parts of two subregions that cover much of the Middle East and North Africa: 1) the 'Saharo-Arabian' (or Sindian) subregion; and 2) the 'Sudanian' (Sudano-Zambezian) subregion. In the 'Jerusalem' School of plant geography, Eig (1931-1933) first defined the Saharo-Sindian subregion as being exemplified by the great desert belt that extends from the Atlantic coast in North Africa through to the Taher desert in India; he considered it to be bordered by the 'Mediterranean' and 'Irano-Turanian' subregions to the north, and by a 'Sudana-Deccanian' (Sudano-Zambezian) subregion to the south. The Saharo-Sindian subregion *per se* was divided further by him into three, western, middle and eastern sections, with the northern part of the Arabian peninsula falling into the middle area, along with Egypt, Sinai, parts of lower Palestine, southern and central Jordan, and lower Iraq. In later investigations, Zohary (1973) also from the Jerusalem School, renamed this broad subregion as the 'Saharo-Arabian', detaching the eastern section from it: he argued that what Eig had defined as 'eastern Saharo-Sindian' is more Palaeotropic than Holarctic in nature, and so should not be included within the 'Saharo-Arabian' subregion. Using the evidence of endemics, this view was later supported by Takhtajan (1986), in his division of the Middle East and adjacent areas into phytogeographic regions. The territories in the south and south-western parts of the Arabian peninsula additionally were classified by Zohary on floristic grounds as being outside the 'Saharo-Arabian' phytogeographic subregion, being more tropical in its floristics, and accordingly 'Sudanian' (Eritreo-Arabian) in definition.

These broad sub-regional divisions are accepted here as forming a good biogeographical basis for present-day floristic realities in Saudi Arabia. However, the boundaries between the Saharo-Arabian and the Sudanian floristic subregions in the peninsula are still ill-defined, and still very difficult to delimit. The main problem is that the southern parts of the Saharo-Arabian subregion are occupied by the very dry, hot and sometimes vegetationless desert of Ar Rub' Al Khali, in contrast to the much more vegetated area of the central and northern sand seas of Saudi Arabia. Zohary (1973) suggested that the hot climate of the Ar Rub'Al Khali should be expected to support Sudanian species, but is too dry to do so: as a result, he extended the southern limits of the Saharo-Arabian subregion to below the Tropic of Cancer in this district. On the other hand, Mandaville (1984) using his own wide floristic knowledge, applied the strategy of Engler (1910) in considering the presence of *Acacia*-dominated plant associations as a key indicator of Sudanian conditions. After many years of careful observation, he concluded that the large wadi systems that cut through central and northern Saudi Arabia, running mainly from the western highlands to the east, all supported some *Acacia*-dominated plant communities (Plate 2). These Sudanian species are believed to be relict from the more humid, pluvial period of the Late Pleistocene and early Holocene. But their very existence was sufficient for Mandaville to suggest a new alignment in Saudi Arabia for the boundary line between the two subregions, in contrast to the views of Zohary. He proposed that the northern boundary of Sudanian territory should be located along the 26th parallel, in the centre of the peninsula. Virtually all of the sand seas of the peninsula, with the exception of An Nafud, accordingly will fall within the Sudanian subregion in this classification. A clear conflict between the relative extents of both subregions within central Saudi Arabia is therefore indicated.

We believe that both these attempts to define the boundary between the two subregions are too simplistic, and do not reflect adequately the floristic realities of the peninsula. It is argued especially that the presence of *Acacia* and other associates in the wadis that cut through central and northern Saudi Arabia can not be considered sufficient reason to include all the centre of the peninsula into the Sudanian subregion, for several important reasons, listed below.

1.   The presence or absence of *Acacia* species and other associates should not be the sole indicator for the definition of such boundaries. Other factors such as the history of the flora, climatic conditions, topography and the presence or absence of other plant communities should also be taken into consideration.

2.   It has earlier (p.26) been noted that this central area of the peninsula has many of the characteristics of being a transitional area between two floristic realms (Palaestropic; Holartic) and three floristic subregions (Saharo-Arabian; Mediterranean; Irano-Turanian). As a result, penetration of species from one of these realms or subregions into another may be expected, causing a good deal of floristic variation; and this in itself emphasises the fact that drawing a single solid line on the basis of the distribution of one species alone, especially if this should prove to be a relict species, is not an adequate means of current delimitation.

3.   In the case of the Arabian peninsula, Sudanian floristics are present in their own type of climate, which is characterised by summer rains and high temperatures in winter. This is found only in the south-western highlands and coastlands of the peninsula, and the interior part of it cannot in any way be included in this category on climatic grounds.

4.   It is clear on environmental and floristic grounds that the wadi systems which support *Acacia* in central and northern Saudi Arabia form a vegetation enclave for ancient thermophilous vegetation. *Acacia* and its associates are likely, from pollen evidence, relict from the Late Pleistocene and early Holocene, when the climate in the northern part of the peninsula seems to have resembled that now prevalent in southern, Sudanian territories. The wadis currently present niches in which the microclimate is hot enough to support such species, and sufficient moisture is available for them, either   after rain when water can accumulate for some time, or from a high water table (Zohary, 1962, 1973; Guest, 1966). But Havely & Orshan (1972, and Kurschner (1986), have reported the presence of *Acacia* spp. and other associates further to the north in several localities in the Jordan valley, south-western Iraq and Sinai, and these are thought to represent their northernmost occurrence. This further, in itself makes the delimitation of the northern Sudanian boundaries in central Saudi Arabia questionable.

5.   Human intervention in recent times must have had a great effect on the distribution of

Acacia species, so that their presence or absence cannot be explained entirely by past or present national environmental conditions. The movement of people and their livestock in the region over millennia has contributed to the wide distribution of many of these species outside their original territories. Mandaville (1984) has suggested that the presence of these species along stations on the Darb Zobaydah pilgrim track, and in south-western Iraq, is attributable to this phenomenon. On the other hand, the continuous burning of trees as firewood, and a lowering of the water table in places, must also have restricted the presence of these species to very remote wadi beds at times. Guest (1966) suggested that the absence of some *Acacia* spp. from southern Iraq was due to their removal by Bedouin populations, who use them for fuel. All this further confuses the validity of the supposition that *Acacia* - dominated plant communities can legitimately be regarded as an indicator of the northern Sudanian subregional floristic boundary today.

6. Dissimilarity between two floristic, or vegetational subregions is normally a result of separation by physical barriers such as very arid deserts, dense humid vegetation, mountains, oceans and wide seas. In the Arabian peninsula, Ar Rub'Al Khali is a very dry, and very extensive sand sea (630,000km^2) that is not hospitable to most Sudanian species today. It is very likely that, after its formation, this very dry desert, in addition to the high mountains that surround the Red Sea, would have acted as an effective barrier to the recent further dispersal of Sudaninan species to the interior parts of Saudi Arabia. On the other hand, barriers between the interior areas and those areas to the north in which Mediterranean and Irano-Turanian species prevail, are almost absent. This major biogeographical phenomenon results in there being a much stronger linkage in floristics and structure between the Saharo-Arabian, and the Mediterranean and Irano-Turanian desert floristics, than with the Sudanian regions.

Taking all these pointers into consideration, we consider that, since the northern part of the Arabian peninsula is more similar in floristics and vegetation type to the Irano-Turanian and Mediterranean subregions, from which it is not separated by any major topographic or climatic barriers, and since species are apparently freely interchanging between them, it is argued accordingly that the interior and northern parts of Saudi Arabia should clearly be included within the Holartic region. Additionally, the Sudanian subregion in the Arabian peninsula could be described as having its northern border to the south of, or within Ar Rub' Al Khali. There is also a floristic case for suggesting that the Sudanian boundary might run to the east of Al Hijaz mountain and the highlands along the boundaries of the Arabian Shield in the central part of the peninsula. Our new representation of the main subregional floristic division is presented in Fig. 3.8; it should be regarded as being tentative only, and more systematic studies to delimit these boundaries more precisely are called for.

3.4 General floristic and vegetation characteristics of the Saharo-Arabian and the Sudanian subregions of the Arabian peninsula: a summary

Compared to the Sudanian subregion, the Saharo-Arabian subregion is very poor in species (Takhtajan, 1969). Eig (1931-32) estimated the number at a maximum of 1500 species, of which about 1200 were steppe or desert plants. Ozenda reported 1200 species for the entire Sahara in Africa (Zohary, 1973). Most of the countries that are occupied largely by Saharo-Arabian flora, such as Iraq, Egypt and the Arabian peninsula territories, also have a low total number of species (Table 3.7). The subregion is further very weak in endemic flora at all taxonomic levels. No endemic families are recorded, and only a few endemic species, such as *Horwoodia dicksoniae* (Mandaville, 1984). This area is also characterised by a very low density of individuals. In the most arid parts, both in the sand seas and surrounding deserts, one might travel for some distance, coming across only a few individuals or perennial species, though in the season there is often a wealth of perennials. Many of the species in this subregion are derived from neighbouring regions, including the Mediterranean and Irano-Turanian to the north and northwest, and the Sudanian subregion to the south (Table 3.8).

The Sudanian subregion in contrast is characterised by hundreds of genera, numerous species and a wealth of plant communities. The main vegetation types generally are open woodland, savanna and grassland. There are a relatively large number of endemics: Takhtajan (1986) indicates that 225 endemic species may be found in the South Arabian Province of the Sudanian Subregion, in the south and southwest of the peninsula, and mainly on the mountainous escarpments of western Saudi Arabia and the Yemen. Within Ar Rub' Al Khali, a few endemic species may be found among dominant subshrubs, such as *Cornulaca arabica* and *Zygophyllum mandavillei*, as well as the bushy herb *Tribulus arabica*.

CHAPTER 4

FLORA OF THE SAND SEAS OF SAUDI ARABIA

The vegetation of the interior sand deserts of the Middle East has not been covered as well in literature as have the geology and geomorphology. Only a small number of botanists and ecologists have been attracted by the sand habitats to conduct research in these territories. On the other hand, coastal dune areas, especially of the Mediterranean, have been intensively studied by many, including Eig (1930), Zohary & Fahn (1952), Tadros (1956) Zohary (1962) and Ayyad (1973). The overlooking of the interior sand seas is probably due to their general past reputation as being 'lifeless', as well the consequence of the difficulties of conducting research in such a harsh environment. Those interior areas that have been examined in some detailed are the limited sand areas in the Negev, and the Wahiba sands in Oman.

Orshan & Zohary (1963) first studied the sand deserts in the western Negev, suggesting that they contained the following three plant associations.

1. An *Artemesia monosperma - Aristida scoparia* association on dunes.

2. An *Artemesia monosperma - Haloxylon articulatum* association on sand-blow, deposited on fluvial loess or calcareous hills.

3. An *Artemesia monosperma - Lolium gaudini* association on sand fields and sandy loess.

The area was classified as Saharo-Sindian, corresponding with most of its species' derivations: the Mediterranean element was of secondary importance.

Danin (1978) further investigated plant species diversity and plant succession in a sandy area of the northern Negev. He concluded that vegetation cover, species diversity, phytomass production and life form diversity were found to increase with sand stability, owing to a parallel increase in available water, as a result of the accumulation of silt and clay in the soil environment. An increased supply of nutrients, and the influence of a crust of blue-green algae and mosses also played a role in enhancing diversity.

From the scientific results of the Royal Geographical Society's Oman Wahiba Sand Project (1985-87), TA Cope (1988) gave a brief phytogeographic background to these sands. He indicated that, although in itself the sand flora was poor in species, it was remarkably diverse. A check-list of 172 plant species in adjacent wadis was compiled from collections taken over the preceding 40 years. The list includes 162 flowering plants, and a selection of microfungi, lichens, macrofungi and ferns. However, Dutton (1978), in the introductory section of this report, determined that only 30 species in this list are found in the sands proper. Munton (1988) agreed that diversity in the sands was low, and he attributed this to low productivity, both long - and short-term climatic and geomorphological instability, isolation from other similar calcium-rich sand seas, a low structural diversity, and the adverse influence of man. Within the sand, *Calligonum comosum* and *Cyperus aucheri* occur mainly on the mobile sand dune tops, while *Heliotropum kotschyi*, *Euphorbia riebackii* and *Prosopis turgidum* were most common in stable sand.

Within Saudi Arabia, the major sand sea of Ar Rub' Al Khali did not attract the serious attention of botanists and biogeographers until 1986, when Mandaville gave the first scientific discussion of the plant life within it. Prior to this study, only very brief floristic descriptions and specimen collections from limited areas in the Empty Quarter had been provided by H St John Philby (1933) and Wilfred Thesiger (1959). The anti-locust officers, Popov and Zeller (1963) also had written a brief review of the vegetation of the Ar Rub' Al Khali margins. In his paper, Mandaville indicated that the vegetation consists of very diffuse shrub communities, three of which were identified:

1. The *Calligonum crinitum* and *Dipterygium glaucum* community

2. The *Haloxylon persicum* community

3. The *Cornulaca arabica* community

Only 20 plant species were recorded from the main body of sand, and 17 species from its margins. Salt flats and gravel floors between the sand dunes were almost devoid of vegetation. Annual species, as well as trees, were almost absent from the inner zones, but might occur in adjacent areas.

Other twentieth-century general descriptions of the interior sand-seas are noted in the Prelude of this work.

Taken altogether, general information on the flora and ecology of the sand seas is still very scanty, and in any case most studies do not include all the sand seas. They are not based on any systematic analysis, and there are no quantitative descriptions or analyses of the vegetation. Nor do they consider, except in the most general terms, the environmental conditions which may affect the vegetation cover. It was with the aim of remedying these several deficiencies that our work on the vegetation of the sand seas initially was conceived.

4.1 The flora of the sand seas.

Excepting Zohary (1973), all recent authorities who have investigated the major vegetation formations of Saudi Arabia (Novikova, 1970; Ministry of Agriculture & Water, 1989) have distinguished between Ar Rub' Al Khali and the remaining central and northern sand seas, on the grounds that the former area has much less vegetation cover

overall, fewer species, and a spattering of Sudanian species, in contrast to the latter, which has a much greater vegetation cover with many more species, in which Sudanian species are extremely rare. The Ar Rub' Al Khali also has a few endemics, while there are virtually none in the central and northern sand seas. This basic division is followed in our analysis.

Still, one of the main characteristics of the vegetation cover of the sand seas in central and northern Saudi Arabia is its relatively low floristic diversity, though this is higher than elsewhere in the deserts of the country. The number of plant species that we collected from the major sand-sea bodies and their periphery in this region is 165 species, which are indicated in Table 4.1. These species comprise approximately 8% of the 2030 species reported by Miller & Nyberg (1991) to be found in Saudi Arabia, most of which of course are located in the wetter areas of the southwest. The number of species recorded in the central and northern sand seas also constitutes approximately 60% of the 300 species reported by Heenstra *et al.* (1990) as being found in the northern parts of the country. Northern and central sand-sea species comprise about 30% of the 565 species reported by Mandaville (1990) to be present in the eastern part of Saudi Arabia: they also account for 40% of the 392 native desert species found in the same area. But the total number of true psammophytes (species that are adapted to, and favour the sand dune habitat), restricted in distribution mainly to deep sand, is limited, amounting to only 22 species (Table 4.2), or approximately 13.3% of the total species within the central and northern sand-sea area. Shallow to deep sand areas have a few more species, 33 in all (Table 4.3) or approximately 20% of the total found in this area. The remaining 110 species are confined to flatter stabilised dunes, and the thin sand sheets found between the major individual dunes. Some of these latter may extend in their distribution far beyond the frontiers and margins of the sand seas, wherever shallow sand sheets are found. Only one Arabian endemic has been noted in this area, *Horwoodia dicksoniae*, the full range of which has not yet been determined, though it is known to extend from the Eastern Provinces of Saudi Arabia across much of the northern, and central parts of the country, southern Iraq and probably parts of Jordan. Overall, however, the flora of the central and northern sand seas of Saudi Arabia is poor in terms of the numbers of species, resulting from the harsh environment to which only a limited number of species have adapted.

In Ar Rub'Al Khali, some at least of the terrain is virtually vegetationless sand, but even where vegetation is present, the number of species is much lower than in the central and northern sand seas. About 20 species are present on deep sand, and a further 17 on sandy flats or on the margins of individual dunes: the full list is given in Table 4.4. There are more endemics, including the dominants *Calligonum crinitum*, which is found on the higher sand-dune bodies, and *Corniculata arabica*, located mainly on sand-dune flanks: and species as a whole are more Sudanian in derivation than is the case further north.

4.2   Biogeographical affinities

Like most plant geographical regions and localities, the central and northern sand seas are covered by species which derive from both the local Saharo-Arabian subregion (uniregional species), and from other subregional areas (biregional and pluri-regional). This is much less the case in Ar Rub' Al Khali, where most of the few species present are endemic or Sudanian alone.

In Table 4.5, it is clear that species from different plant subregions are all represented in the northern and central sand seas. The uniregional species, which are mainly assigned to a single subregion, amount to only 37 species, 34 of which are Saharo-Arabian, 1 Irano-Turanian, 1 Mediterranean and 1 Sudanian. The majority of species *in toto* however (41.8%) belong to either strictly Saharo-Arabian elements (20.06%) or biregional species of Saharo-Arabian and Irano-Turanian derivation (21.2%): there are further high percentages of biregional species, and pluri-regional groups, that originate in part as Mediterranean elements. These confirm the close links that exist between the Saharo-

Arabian subregion and the two subregions to the north. This close link can be explained by the penetration of many of these species, which appear to have dominated the interior parts of Saudi Arabia during the warmer, humid periods of the past. The Irano-Turanian, Mediterranean and Saharo-Arabian elements thus have combined to play a major role in the present floristic composition of the region, comprising together 59.4% of the total species. The close floristic ties between the Saharo-Arabian subregion and the Irano-Turanian and Mediterranean subregions have further been enhanced more recently in the Holocene, due to the lack of geographical barriers between the three areas, and the migration and intrusion of species from the two northern subregions into the south in which recent ecological conditions are now more similar to those farther north than they formerly were.

Sudanian elements are poorly represented in the central and northern sand seas today. Only one Sudanian species (*Morettia parviflora*) is reported. Further, biregional species that belong to both the Sudanian and Saharo-Arabian regions make up only 9.7% of all species in these areas. Sudanian species either are those which are relict (see p.), or those which might have reached these areas more recently from the western highlands of the peninsula by river flow along the wadis that cut through the region from west to east. Such species must have developed effective strategies of adaptation to the new, present-day environmental conditions, and especially those of general moisture scarcity, and changes in the seasonality of precipitation. The small number of Sudanian species which have survived in these areas bears witness to the general lack of sufficient moisture for them, especially during summer, which makes the sand seas of the north and centre of the peninsula an unfavourable habitat, even though temperatures are suitable.

The occurrence and weak presence of species that are present in other continents and subregions such as central and eastern Europe, South Africa, North America, Macaronesia and India are more difficult to explain. Some at least of these suggest that these species once covered a wider range over the Middle East when ecological conditions were more hospitable than at present: others may simply represent chance arrivals in the region.

4.3 Genus and family representation

Within the central and northern sand seas, 64% of the recorded flora belong to six plant families: the Compositae, Gramineae, Cruciferae, Caryophyllaceae, Leguminosae and Zygophyllaceae (Table 4.6). The Compositae have the largest number of genera and species: 22 genera and 29 species. The Gramineae have 17 genera and 25 species. The Cruciferae have 2 genera and 14 species; the Caryophyllaceae 10 genera and 12 species; the Leguminosae 8 genera and 17 species; and the Zygophyllacea 3 genera and 8 species. An outstanding feature of Table 4.6 is that of the 30 families represented, only a limited number are of importance floristically in the northern and central sands seas, most of the families having very few genera and species. 13 families are represented by one genus alone, and nine genera have only one species per genus; thus, the number of genera is very high compared to the number of species. The number of species per genus overall amounts only to 1.4 species. This is a common feature of desert flora, indicating that only a few of the large number of species that belong to the old plant families can adapt and survive in this harsh environment.

Of the 37 plant species recorded in the Ar Rub' Al Khali, most are grouped into four families, three (the Cruciferae; the Gramineae; the Zygophyllaceae) already noted above, with one additional family, the Chenopodiaceae (the 'salt bushes'), representatives of which are particularly well suited to the severely hot and arid conditions. The Chenopodiaceae have 5 genera and 7 species; the Cruciferae three genera and four species; the Zygophyllaceae three genera and four species; and the Gramineae two genera and four species.

4.4 Life forms

Desert ecologists (Zohary, 1962; Kassas, 1966; Mandaville, 1990) have for some time argued that Raunkier's and other life-form classes have only a limited usefulness as a basis for vegetation description in arid regions, due to the morphological plasticity which many desert plants display as an adaptive strategy. However, despite this, Raunkier's system is evaluated here briefly for the desert plants recorded, partly for comparative purposes and also as an aid to questions arising from problems relating to plant geography.

Table 4.7 shows the relative percentages of the five main life-form groups of Raunkier's classification in three environmental areas of Saudi Arabia: the central and northern sand seas; Ar Rub' Al Khali; and (for comparison) the Eastern Province of the country. The high overall proportion of therophytes (annual, or ephemeral plants) reflects that also found in North Africa, and is typical of many hot deserts. However, it is particularly high in the sand seas of the centre and north of the country, where they form 68.4% of the total plant population. Here, annuals bloom and form luxurious growth at the base of individual dunes in hollows, as well as in interdunal depressions, in which moisture accumulates after rain. These annuals are mainly very shallow-rooting herbaceous vegetation. They complete their life cycle within the cool season, when moisture is sufficient and the temperatures are appropriate. At the beginning of the summer, when moisture in the top layer of sand is almost completely exhausted, these species die out very quickly. In years when there is not sufficient rain, annuals might not appear, so that the area then witnesses a complete or partial absence of vegetation.

There is a strong overall decline in the number of therophytes as one moves from north to south within Saudi Arabia, and this reflects the decreasing significance of annuals in the flora of more tropical regions. Thus in Ar Rub' Al Khali they account for only 19% of the flora, mirroring the increased aridity and higher temperatures of this area. Conversely, chamaephytes and phanerophytes are much more significant in Ar Rub' Al Khali, whereas in the northern and central sand seas they are of relatively minor significance in terms of species numbers, although they many be of great ecological importance in the area. The life-form differences of vegetation structure between the two areas, Ar Rub' al Khali on the one hand, and the central and northern sand seas on the other, are striking , and parallel the ecological differences to be discussed in the next chapter. That of Ar Rub' Al Khali is very similar to the life form pattern displayed in Aden, also in Sudanian territory (Shimwell, 1971), except for the lower number of hemi-cryptophytes in the latter.

Within the main body of deep sand in the central and northern sands seas, the 22 species recorded (p.) are divided equally between annuals and perennials (50%-50%). It should be noted that the presence of annuals on these dunes is evidence that they are stabilised. The perennials are present due to their ability to endure occasional movement and burial by sand, as well as the general lack of moisture and nutrition. Water conditions in the dunes are usually favourable for perennial species with long root systems, which are able to reach and extract the required moisture from the water stored in the deeper sand layers.

Perennial species are the main feature of the dunes year-round because of their relatively large size and their beneficial uses: on the other hand, annual species make a showy display and are important for grazing for parts of the year.

4.5 Autecology of sand-sea plants: morphological and physiological adaptations

The main limiting factors for vegetation in sand seas are the high intensity of radiation, resulting in a very high surface temperature and moisture deficiency in summer, nutritional scarcity, and sand movements that might affect seed germination and plant growth. Plant species in the sand dune areas, and especially the true psammophytes, have adopted various morphological and physiological mechanisms to assure their best chances for survival in these circumstances, coping well with the environmental stress. Overall, there are two major contrasting adaptations (along with many minor ones) which serve to resolve the difficulties : one, a minimisation of water use;

and the other, the development of maximum ability to search for, and then utilise any water and nutritional materials available.

4.5.1 MORPHOLOGICAL ADAPTATIONS

Among the numerous anatomical and morphological modifications which plants have adopted in this difficult environment, one general feature is for them to be generally smaller than in other parts of the desert: this is the case, for example, for *Neurada procumbens*, *Anagallis arvensis* and *Silene villosa*. Modifications of their aerial organs and root systems are also common.

Aerial organs

Many sand-sea plants have deciduous leaves, or an absence of leaves for much of the year, as well as a higher proportion of dead tissue than is the case for plants elsewhere, these being attempts to conserve moisture by reducing transpiration, and to counteract the effects of strong winds carrying sand which might create a sand-blast effect, particularly in a zone lower than 1m above the ground surface. Among these species are the perennial dominants *Calligonum comosum, Haloxylon persicum* and *H salicornicum*, all of which appear over most of the year in very poor condition, with little foliage and many dead branches. *Calligonum comosum* and *Ephedra alata* also shed their leaves, at times even in the cooler season, and extend the shedding process to cover some of their branches during the hot dry season.

Species like *Haloxylon salicornicum*, *Rhanterium epapposum* and *Haloxylon persicum* also develop hairs, spines and bristles as a means of protecting themselves from the intense radiation, and to keep the stem and branches in a slightly more humid atmosphere than would otherwise be the case. Branches may further be protected by the formation of a thick waxy layer, which in the dry season may also extend even to some of the subsurface feeder roots, as a means of reducing transpiration. *Rhanterium epapposum* is one species which displays this adaptation during the hot, rainless months, in which only a thread of living tissue may survive within the fibrous rootstock: after the early rains fall, this waxy covering then will be washed off, and the plant will resume its growth (Vesey-Fitzgerald, 1957; Ministry of Agriculture and Water, 1992).

In areas of moving sand, the upper parts of some perennial species, such as the grass *Stipagrostis* spp. and the shrubs *Artemesia monosperma, Calligonum comosum* and *Haloxylon persicum* are flexible so that they can be protected from the sometimes strong winds without breaking their stems and branches. Stems and roots may also be elongated so that the reproductive and photosynthetic organs may be kept above the level of accumulating sand, so as to avoid the very high temperatures of the sand surface. Species like *Artemesia monosperma* further have the ability to merge from a blowing sand cover after a considerable time, after which stems easily become erect and resume their active life.

Root Systems

As in the case of their aerial organs, the root systems of plants growing within the sand seas also display enormous morphological adaptation to potential sand instability, moisture deficiency and the paucity of available nutrient matter. This adaptability is essential to their growth and survival under the prevailing harsh environmental conditions.

Root systems of ephemeral plants

Ephemeral (annual) plants of the sand seas have mainly very superficial and non-extensive root systems, which are mostly stringy, thin and shallow. Some species have a major tap root that penetrates deep into the sand, with a few fine laterals growing horizontally to unusual lengths, all in an attempt to ensure an adequate supply of moisture and nutrition. The length of these roots will also stabilise the plant and protect it from strong winds. Other ephemerals, such as *Cutandia memphitica*, have brush-like roots that allow it to absorb any available moisture

from light rain, before it sinks further into the sand.

It should be noted in general, however, that the root systems of sand-sea ephemerals do not differ greatly from those in other hot deserts, since by and large they form after rain and complete their period of growth during the season of moisture. But one modification seems to be that ephemeral root systems in the sand seas of central and northern Saudi Arabia extend longer and deeper than their counterparts elsewhere. In this context, Migahid (1961) has noted that roots of the most widespread ephemerals in desert near Cairo rarely exceed 10cm in depth. Our observations, however, are that the root systems of some of the most common Saudi ephemerals, such as *Plantago boisserie, Launea mucronata and Anagallis arvensis*, may reach 30-50cm in depth. It is likely that the general plasticity of these roots enables them to extend without any obstruction to moisture which, in the sand seas, is usually available at these depths. On the other hand, roots of similar species in other parts of the desert, including wadis and plains, are predominantly restricted to the uppermost layers of soil, since the rain there does not percolate into the deeper layers.

Root systems of perennial plants

Root systems of perennial plants in this region are very strongly adapted for life in the sand seas. The most dominant perennial species in the sand seas, *Calligonum comosum* and *Haloxylon persicum*, resist the scarcity of moisture and nutrition, and the movement of sand, by means of a large network of roots that can greatly exceed the overall size of the shoot, aerial organs and branch network. It is not uncommon in the sand seas to see the roots of these two phreatophyte species extending downwards to more than 30m, and approaching, or penetrating into the sand water-table. After powerful wind and sand movements, neither is it unusual to see some of these roots partly exposed to more than 20m from the main stem. Such roots remain well protected from the strong radiation, and wind blasts, by a thick coat or crust that covers them.

Species like the perennials *Haloxylon salicornicum, H persicum, Calligonum comosum* and *Rhazya stricta* are sand-binding shrubs, the roots of which gather and intercept sand particles, and fines like clay and silt around their base, forming hillocks (Plate 4), that may cover the leaves and branches of individual plants, which in turn then will provide additional organic material after they die. These hillocks also may play an important role in the interception of moisture, in that numerous adventitious roots may be encouraged which serve in this capacity. Algae also grow and colonise the upper layer of the sand beneath many of these shrubs, allowing more nutrition to be accumulated, and minimising further the potential for sand movement. Some species (like, for example, *Stipagrostis* spp.) need a continuous cover of sand in order that its adventitious roots may survive. The removal of sand can result in the death of this particular species, with the onset of drought in early summer.

4.5.2 PHYSIOLOGICAL ADAPTATIONS

Physiologically, plant species of the sand seas possess many adaptations which help to overcome the adverse conditions of the environment. One general form of adaptation is the capacity of most species to remain metabolically active at very low moisture and nutrition levels, and at very high temperatures. Patterns of evaopotransipiration and photosynthesis may also have been modified, such processes taking place normally only during early morning or at night, when temperatures are relatively low and relatively more moisture is available for the plant: stomata further do not necessarily have to open all day, which would result in major water losses from them. These adaptations occur without endangering the general physiological mechanisms of the plant with surplus photochemical energy (Evenari, 1985). Other species (e.g. *Haloxylon persicum* and *Calligonum comosum*) have additionally an increased capacity to extract any available water present in the soil through a high osmotic pressure.

Seeding and reproduction

Plant species of the sand seas have highly adapted seed and germination mechanisms. In his study of the vegetation of central and eastern Arabia, Vesey-Fitzgerald (1957) suggested that the main adaptive characteristic of ephemeral plants is their ability to germinate, and then survive, as seeds, for several years of drought. Seeds of some species, such as *Calligonum comosum*, have resilient bristles that can be blown for great distances. When they land, these bristles help sand particles to adhere to them, stabilising them, and encouraging seeds to germinate when conditions become favourable. Another adaptation may be seen in *Neurada promcumbens*, a typical herb of the sand seas, which produces only a limited number of seeds per fruit: only one seed might germinate if the conditions are suitable, or they may wait for several years before they do so. Another mechanism is to produce seed early in the season: thus, *Haloxylon salicornicum* releases seeds in the early winter to ensure that they can be transported over a long distance if needs be, and then still germinate during the wet season, before the onset of the high-temperature summer (Vesey-Fitzgerald, 1957; Chaudhary, 1983; Ministry of Agriculture and Water, 1992). Other seed types have hard covers or shells, that protect them from sand blasting, and from high air or sand-surface temperatures.

4.6 Adaptations and the distribution of sand-sea species

Analysis of the sand-sea environment suggests that both individual dunes and inter-dune areas have a variety of broad vegetation types which are closely associated with the topography of the sand seas, and sand movement. Such a distribution reflects the availability of moisture and nutrition, and the wind regime. Thus ephemeral species with shallow roots are restricted to those areas of firmer ground in which moisture levels are enhanced to some extent, and sand movement and temperatures are relatively reduced: additionally, nutritional elements are increased through washing and leaching from the higher areas of the dunes. Such areas appear impressively green after rain and then exhibit a very luxuriant growth, contributing to the sand sea areas being richer floristically than any other desert environment. The presence of ephemeral cover such as this is strong evidence that the individual dunes are stabilised. Once the vegetation cover has been established, it encourages a further stabilisation of the sand, and a greater availability of moisture and nutrition, through the trapping of more organic detritus and fine sediments.

Particular halophytes adapted to a high level of salinisation of the soil are restricted to some sabkhahs, hollows and inter-dunal depressions that are covered with a shallow sheet-layer of sand. These areas are characterised by fine-textured saline soil and a shallow water-table. The intense evaporation of water, when it falls, from such land surfaces increases the concentration of salts in the upper soil layers, emphasising the difficult environment for plant growth. Near Ath Thamireyah in Nafud As Sirr, sabkhahs take a distinctive circular shape between individual dunes, and are often characterised by a dense, pure population of the shrub *Seidlitzia rosmarinus*. Other perennial species are *Haloxylon persicum* and *H salicornicum*, observed on the fringes and edges of these sabkhahs. Ephemerals or other perennials are normally not observed in the sabkhahs; if the salinity is too great, no plant cover at all can of course exist.

On the crests of individual sand dunes, and on windward slopes, *Calligonum comosum* and *Haloxylon persicum* may occasionally be found, but the vegetation cover customarily is only very sparse, and in the mobile area of sand on dune crests may be absent altogether, creating a true vegetationless zone. On the middle and lower parts of sand-dune slopes, on the other hand, especially on the lee sides, on which the sand is relatively stabilised, perennial species such as *Haloxylon persicum, Artemesia monosperma, Stipagrostis* spp. and *Calligonum comosum* are very widely spread. Such shrubs normally grow far apart, at intervals of a few meters, so allowing their long, horizontal roots

to acquire the moisture and nutrition needed for their survival. The customary absence of any form of additional vegetation cover between these perennial shrubs may be accounted for not only by deficiencies of moisture and nutrition, but also by the strong and violent gusts of wind which from time to time prevail on dune slopes, preventing its establishment.

4.7   Phenology

Although few observations have thus been made in Saudi Arabian deserts and sand seas regarding phenological patterns, some general observations may be made. Throughout the entire region, summer is normally (though not exclusively, see below) the unfavourable season for plant growth, which is concentrated in autumn, winter or spring. In the hot summer, dormancy, or the evasion of drought by seed-production, prevails.

The actual time of resumption of active growth, whether of annuals or perennials, depends on the nature of the season, and can vary substantially from year to year. Mandaville (1990) has pointed out that some perennials resume growth in September, a long time before the arrival of the first rains, possibly because of the marginal increase in atmospheric moisture which precedes the rains, especially in coastal regions, a moderation of temperatures at this time, or shortening day length. Once the first Mediterranean depressional storms arrive in the central and northern sand seas, usually in November and December but sometimes earlier, an explosion of annuals may follow, with leafing and flowering rapidly succeeding germination, so that a 'greening' of the lower slopes of dunes may ensue; but if the rains are delayed until December, cold weather in these areas then may prevent germination until early spring. In a year in which the winter rains are minimal, although germination will still occur, plant growth will also be minimalised, so that individuals may only reach a 'dwarf' stage rather than their customary height. Under these conditions, annuals may often reach a peak of biomass, flowering and maturity in March or early April, although the onset of particular phases of growth may vary widely from species to species. Phases of growth in perennials may be somewhat later. By late April or May, depending largely on how long the rains last, most annuals have died back as summer approaches; the perennial's growth may continue to May, or even June, before they enter their dormant phase in the hot season.

Within the summer period, some species may still flower and fruit in June and July. Mandaville (1990) suggests that these are predominantly deeply-rooted Sudanian species such as *Acacia*, *Capparis* and *Ziziphus* spp. Others, mainly small perennials, and including representatives of *Zygopyllum* and *Heliotropium bacciferum* may maintain active growth throughout the summer, though in these cases it is most noticeable during the spring months.

Within Ar Rub'Al Khali, a different phenlogical pattern prevails, since most of the rainfall there arrives in summer from monsoonal origins, and in any case this region supports neither the large number of annuals found farther to the north, nor the relatively large number of species overall. Many of the resident species accordingly are adapted to active vegetation growth in the hottest season, with flowering either in spring or autumn, or just in the latter, during October and November: winter is dry, and a season for dormancy or die-back. Among the more common species to follow this pathway are the saltbushes of the Chenopodiacea family, many of which had their origins in Irano-Turanian lands far to the north.

It is clear that more detailed studies of both the morphological and physiological adaptations of plant species in the sand-sea areas of Saudi Arabia, and their phenological variations, are called for . Meanwhile, new knowledge as to how both annuals and perennials group themselves into the prevailing sand-sea communities, is given in the next chapter.

CHAPTER 5

PLANT COMMUNITIES OF THE SAND SEAS

This chapter investigates, for the first time for any plant communities in Saudi Arabia, the quantitative relationships between species, and their relationships to habitat. It concentrates on the central and northern sand seas, in that these areas have by far the greater number of species present: in any case, there is little one can do quantitatively with the many fewer species, and much larger territory, of Ar Rub' Al Khali, though mention is made of the communities located there where appropriate.

We have recorded 165 species (p.   ) from the sand seas of central and northern Saudi Arabia, but only 37 from Ar Rub' Al Khali. Phytoecological and reconnaissance surveys of the first two of these areas suggested, in the first instance, that three broad ecological groupings of plant species were present, these having a strong relationship with terrain and sand movement, both of which will in turn affect moisture and nutrient availability. These ecological groupings, confirmed by later analysis, are:
1. The communities of sand dune habitats (major sand-dune bodies);
2. The communities of non-dune or shallow-sand habitats;
3. 'Vegetationless' areas.

5.1 Methodologies for sampling and analysis

5.1.1   GENERAL REQUIREMENTS

It is clear from the available literature that there is no established methodology which has been used to sample and analyse the vegetation of inland sand dunes on the scale of the sand seas. One further major complicating factor in the investigation of vegetation in this region is the time and labour required for such work in this rough terrain, which exceeds by far that needed for similar investigations in other parts

of the desert not covered by sand. Our sampling methods accordingly were chosen after careful consideration to suit both the size of the research area, and the difficult physical conditions prevailing in it: they have been applied for the first time in the sand seas, and we consider that they are well worth using elsewhere for comparison in similar sand-sea environments.

In order to examine in a preliminary way the vegetation of the sand seas, a detailed reconnaissance of the central and northern sand seas was first accomplished. In Saudi Arabia, the use of satellite images is strictly limited, and the further unavailability of aerial photographs, as well as the impossibility of organising flights over the research area, both meant that a choice of sampling sites had to be determined by careful survey on the ground by means of using available maps, and aided by the experience of local people in many districts. This reconnaissance took place during the winter and summer of 1992 and 1993, and involved tens of thousands of kilometres of travel within the sand seas, based in part on the previous knowledge of Dr. Nafie.

These reconnaissance surveys revealed a great many irregularities and discontinuities in microhabitat among the several plant communities recognised by the former investigators. In order to clarify these, a system of stratified random sampling was devised, which proved extremely useful in determining all the vegetation elements present over such a large area. The virtues of stratified random sampling in statistical terms as a combination of systematic and random sampling have been outlined by Muller-Dombois and Ellenberg (1974), among others.

Within this general schema, sites were chosen according to the following criteria:

1.   They should cover the main physiographic variations in sand-sea habitats, and

represent as far as possible a reasonable degree of undisturbed vegetation cover in each habitat area;

2. They were chosen in areas in which the several plant communities were most common and best represented;

3. In the areas chosen, plant communities should extend over relatively large tracts of land; and

4. They should be chosen on sites in which the identified plant communities displayed their greatest within-community variation, and the maximum number of species.

Particular efforts were made to select sites in areas that had been protected for some time from intensive human utilisation such as wood-hauling and overgrazing. Private land, and areas that are relatively protected by some town authorities, were especially appropriate for sampling sites for some communities. Once chosen, selected sites for each community then were numbered, and the exact locations where sampling would take place were randomly selected from these sites in advance, before departure to the field.

Time of sampling

On the basis of our own familiarity with the central and northern sand seas, direct observation and field work were undertaken in the periods April to June 1992 (spring to early summer) and January to June 1993 (winter, spring and early summer). In the first of these periods, field work was directed towards evaluating closely the general vegetation cover, and delimiting some probable sites for detailed objective sampling. In the second period, the detailed sampling of plant communities, soils and other environmental elements were undertaken at all selected sites. Fortunately, during the winter and spring of 1992-93, rainfall was exceptionally abundant, so that vegetation cover was particularly rich: annuals were easily recognised in the development and flowering stages, before they completed their life cycle and died. Often, frequent visits were made to the districts in which annuals were

conspicuous, in order to evaluate quickly the rapid changes in vegetation cover over time.

Choice of particular methods of sampling sand analysis

Due to the wide variability in structure and composition of the plant communities found in the sand seas, no single sampling or analytical technique would suffice to fulfil all our analytical and statistical objectives. For this reason, several techniques were applied. For the sake of convenience, it is useful to classify these according to whether they were used for shrub communities, shrubless communities and 'vegetationless' areas.

Shrub communities

The overall objectives of sampling and analysis of the shrub communities were to determine and explain the nature and variation in species and size of shrubs and shrublets within the sand seas. In addition, the measurements of the size and cover of shrubs help also to interpret the effect of biotic and abiotic factors on the ecology and distribution of shrubs from one area to another.

The point-centred quarter method of plotless sampling, which is widely used to sample forest and woodland systems, especially in North America, was used to investigate the shrub communities of the sand seas. At first consideration, this choice may seem to be incongruous, but it works very well in an area in which shrubs are often the only vegetation type and are well spaced. Cottam & Curtis (1956), who devised the technique, highlight its advantages:

'The quarter method gives the least variable results in distance determinations, provides more data on ... species per sampling point, and is least susceptible to subjective bias. The mathematical characteristics are known. It requires no correction factor, the mean of the distance equalling the square root of the mean area'.

The method helped to overcome problems that might have resulted from the sometimes wide distances between species and individuals. These latter also ensured that the use of quadrat sampling was inappropriate.

This method depends on four quarters being established at 20 sampling points randomly located along a transect running through a sampled community in a particular compass direction. The start of each transect also is located randomly, through random-walk procedures. Once begun, the distance between each sample point on the transect and the nearest shrub in each quarter was measured. Due to the use of a random numbers table to determine the location of sample points, the length of the transect differs from one site to another. In addition to distance, the height and crown cover of each shrub also were measured. From these measurements, the density, dominance and frequency of each shrub species for each sample site could be achieved, and also the importance value for each species. For rapid and accurate statistical handling of this vegetation data, the Statistical Package for the Social Sciences (SPSS) was used.

Shrubless communities

For the investigation of the shrubless communities, thirty 1m_ quadrats were randomly sampled in 11 sites (330 in all) in the northern and central sand seas. In these quadrats, vegetation was analysed for floristic composition to determine species abundance, density and importance, thus providing the basis from which precise differences in composition between one location and another could be worked out, as well as the degree of homogeneity or heterogeneity of the several vegetation stands.

Both classification and ordination techniques of analysis were utilised to organise the vegetation data, and also to indicate how they relate to a range of environmental variables. The classification technique was accomplished through the use of two-way indicator analysis (TWINSPAN), which also determined the major shrubless vegetation units in the entire area. The TWINSPAN computer programme devised by Hill (1979) is one of the most widely used in community ecology to analyse raw vegetation data, in that it can categorise quickly and clearly both sample sites and species together, and results in informative hierarchical diagrams. The CANOCO (Canonical Correspondence Analysis) programme was also utilised in order to determine the more precise vegetation-environment relationships and further assert the relationships within the vegetation units produced by TWINSPAN. CANOCO is the most widely applied method of ordination today in community ecology, and can handle most of the multi-variate techniques needed to analyse the complexities of data relating to vegetation and the environment. Full details of these two programmes are given in Hill (1979) and ter Braak (1988). All of the default settings were utilised in both programmes.

Vegetationless areas

Vegetation cover is typically absent from the crests of individual dunes within the central and northern sand seas. For an investigation of these areas, line-transect methods were applied by laying out a transect across individual dune summits in three locations at each site. Twenty sampling points were established randomly on each transect by means of random number tables, with the distance between sampling points and the nearest plant species to each, on both sides of the crest, then being measured, along with identification of the plant species. From these measurements, the floristic composition near dune crests, the frequency of vegetation near the crests, and the average length of the vegetationless area on the sand dune could then be calculated.

Other parameters

From each sample site, soil was collected at three sample depths (to 25cm; 25 to 50 cm; 50 to 75cm) for the analysis of moisture, organic matter, macronutrients, general mechanical and general chemical analysis. Sample analysis was undertaken in the laboratory at the National Agriculture and Water Research Centre in Riyadh.

Identification of the plant species in the first instance was by reference to standard floras, including Migahid (1988), Mandaville (1990), Cole (1985), Heemstra *et al.* (1990) and Daoud (1985). Species which could not be identified in this way were pressed, labelled, and later identified by Dr. S.A. Chaudhary of the National Herbarium at the National Agriculture and Water Research Centre, Riyadh. Vernacular names were obtained by reference to al these sources, and from Dr. A. Nafie. Our general list of plant species and their geographical distributions also was reviewed by Dr. T.A. Cope in Kew Gardens, U.K..

Results from our several analyses are indicated below.

5.2 Communities of the main sand-dune habitats

The main sand-dune habitats of the northern and central sand seas are dominated by five plant communities, the floristic composition of each of which is very simple. In addition to the dominant species, after which the community is named, there are only a limited number of annual and perennial species present. Most of these species can exist in more than one community. The five communities are:

1. The *Calligonum comosum* community.
2. The *Haloxylon persicum* community.
3. The *Artemesia monosperma* community.
4. The *Scrophularia hypericifolia* community.
5. The *Stipagrostis drarii* community.

They are accordingly, in the order above, three shrub communities, one sub-shrub (shrublet) and one grass community. A brief ecological summary of each is given below.

5.2.1 THE *CALLIGONUM COMOSUM* COMMUNITY (PLATE 5)

The *Calligonum comosum* community is the most dominant, characteristic and widespread plant community in the dunes of the northern and central sand seas of Saudi Arabia. *Artemesia monosperma*, *Scrophularia hypericifolia* and *Rhanterium epapposum* are common associates. A few annual grasses and herbs, such as *Neurada procumbens*, *Eremobium aegypticum*, *Stipagrostis drarii* and *Silene villosa* are also found, especially after good rains. On a wider scale, *Calligonum comosum* is a very common species in all areas of the desert belt which extends from Morocco to Pakistan. In the sand seas of central and northern Saudi Arabia, many places have taken their names from the species, as for example *Umm Arta* (the place of *Calligonum comosum*), near Az Zilfi, in Nafid Ath Thuwayrat. In more southern areas of the country (south of 23N in Ad Dahna, and in Ar Rub' Al Khali), the species is replaced by *Cornulaca arabica* as a dominant.

On a more local scale, *Calligonum comosum* is widely distributed on the lower, middle and upper parts of individual dunes. However, in many places in the northern and central sand seas it tends to be limited to deep sand, and the upper parts of dunes. This current distribution often is a result of the cutting and removal of this species elsewhere on dunes for use as a fuel, as well as overgrazing. Table 5.1 confirms the species poverty in this community. In the upper parts of the dunes, often the only associate is an occasional *Artemesia monosperma*. Throughout the community, all individuals are widely spaced, especially in the unstable upper parts of the dunes, where intervening distances might reach 33m. Such enormous spacing, and the general absence of other species, reflects the environmental stresses affecting the *Calligonum* and any other species which may try to establish itself. These intervening spaces mirror of course the length of the lateral roots of full-grown individuals, which may well exceed 30m, a result of the competition for water and nutrients in the upper parts of the dunes. In contrast, competition between plants with long tap roots in negligible, since water is abundant at depth, even in active dunes. In the stable lower and middle parts of dunes, species of *Calligonum* appear to be less widely spaced, and more abundant.

In our survey, individuals were found to be spaced on average at 11.05m to 10.30m. Individual *Calligonum comosum* shrubs grew to 1.63 to 1.67m: however; full-grown shrubs might occasionally reach more than 3.90m. *Calligonum comosum* was by far the most dominant and important species, forming 88.75% to 90% of all shrubs in our sites. Crown diameters ranged between less than 1m and approximately 7m: however, most were between 1 and 5m. The average crown cover accordingly was very low, varying between 4 and 8% per 1000m_. Since these sites were not protected, and are available for all kinds of human activities, it may be expected that individuals might reach a much greater height and size if they were protected from human intervention.

Reference has already been made to the deeply-penetrating root system of *Calligonum comosum*, which can extend downward to more than 30m. This long extension enables the plants to absorb sufficient moisture from the deeper sand layers, as well as serving to anchor them. When the plant dies, both these and the horizontal roots contribute substantially to the organic content of the sandy substrate. Indeed, in many places, especially near permanent settlements and Bedouin camps, this community has been largely destroyed, to be replaced by its associate, *Artemesia monosperma*. This is a direct result of overgrazing, and the removal of the *Calligonum* for firewood and charcoal, a practice which continues today. Low hummocks, which remain where *Calligonum* shrubs have been uprooted, are easily recognised in many places, especially in Ad Dahna and the northern parts of Nafud Ath Thuwayrat. Today, an 'ideal' *Calligonum comosum* community is present in only a few remote and sandy places with rough terrain, where access is difficult.

Soil pH values range between 8.5 and 8.7, indicating a pronounced alkalinity, with no substantive differences between one level and another. Mechanical analysis confirms that all samples are medium sands, again with no appreciable difference between one level and another. The sample sites are poor in organic matter content, with only limited amounts of animal residues and vegetation remains, all of which are burned quickly by the hot, dry climate, and so contribute very little to the extremely low levels of this parameter. It is concluded that the presence and relative abundance of *Calligonum comosum* and its associate species depends largely on the physical properties of the dune sands that affect the dune's stability, rather than on any inherent chemical and nutritional facilities offered by them.

5.2.2 THE *HALOXYLON PERSICUM* COMMUNITY (PLATE 6).

This community is dominant in many places in sand seas of much of the Middle-East and Central Asia, where it has several associate perennial species, including *Scrophularia hypericifolia*, *Artemesia monosperma*, *Stipagrostis drarii*, *Haloxylon salicornicum*, *Calligonum comosum* and *Ephedra alata*. Associate annuals in the dune bodies are few, and mainly confined to stabilised sand and shrub hummocks. Examples include *Eremobium aegypticum*, *Neurada procumbens*, *Plantago boisseri* and *Silene villosa*. When *Haloxylon* shrubs are found in hollows, as in the Al Musafr and Al Gubaydah dunes west and south of Unayzah, as well as in Nafud As Sirr east of Ath Thameriyah, a carpet of winter annuals often is found between the bushes.

The floristic composition of this community within the central and northern sand seas of Saudi Arabia is likely to differ slightly from one area to another, depending on the location and sand-dune topography, as well as human activities in the area. For instance, in An Nafud, *Artemesia monosperma* and *Stipagrostis drarii* are the main associates, especially on those parts of the dune that are not saline. On the other hand, in the Al Musafr and Al Ghubaydah dunes (above) where the sand is moderately saline, *Haloxylon salicoricum* and *Scrophularia hypericifolia* are the major associates in the low hollows.

Haloxylon persicum is a bi-regional Saharo-Arabian / Irano-Turanian species, the centre of the distribution of which is in the latter bio-geographical subregion (Frietag, 1986). A semi-tree or large shrub, it apparently originated in the 'saxaul' deserts of central Asia. It is known to the Arabs as 'Ghadha', and is the most important shrub in Saudi Arabian deserts for use as firewood. It has been mentioned extensively by most of the explorers and travellers who visited the region during the nineteenth century, and the first half of the twentieth century, though it was not identified botanically until 1940 (Zohary, 1940). Despite its undoubtedly former wide distribution in Saudi Arabia, *Haloxylon persicum* now is found only patchily in limited areas. Large stands are found mainly in the central An Nafud, the Al Musafr and the Al Ghubaydah dunes west and south of Unayzah, and in the northern part of Nafud As Sirr east of Ath Thameriyah. In the latter two cases, the plant is protected by the authorities in nearby towns, against such misuses as overgrazing and woodcutting. It is also possible that *Haloxylon persicum* shrubs are scattered elsewhere in the central and northern sand seas where appropriate ecological conditions are found, especially after the general decrease in intensity of wood hauling for fuel in recent years, following the widespread availability of oil. Some *Haloxylon persicum* shrubs also are established on limited sites in Nafud Al Urayq. Mandaville (1990) further reports that the plants are dominant in sand seas that extend to the south of 26 30 N, and also in the western and north-western edges of Ar Rub' Al Khali, as far south as 19 50 N. People interviewed in the southern parts of the sand seas also confirmed these details. But it should also be noted that the shrub is absent from large parts of central Ad Dahna, Nafud Ath Thuwayrat, the southern part of Nafud As Sirr, and Nafud Qunayfithah. Inhabitants in these areas indicated that they had never seen the species. Such an absence may perhaps be attributed to the former destruction of the shrub by Bedouins, and villagers who live in the large number of settlements that intersperse them, though this is by no means clear. It is likely, however, that *Haloxylon persicum* has a low

tolerance for heavy destruction, and cannot re-establish itself under this type of pressure.

Table 5.2 indicates that, from our samples, *Haloxylon persicum* is by far the dominant species in this species-limited community, ranging from 73% to 93.7% of the total number of species. *H. salicornicum* is the most important perennial associate, forming between 5% to 6% of the total number of species. In one site, *Scrophularia hypericifolia* is also a very important associate species, comprising 21% of the total number of species. Both these two associates are found mainly in the inter-dune areas, and on flat bottoms between dunes. A few *Scrophularia hypericifolia* individuals are also scattered in the upper, stabilised parts of the dunes where they can establish themselves, and where they do so, they are usually smaller than lower down on the dune face.

In our sample sites, *Haloxylon persicum*, takes the form of large shrubs, averaging between 1.69 and 2.25m in height: however, some reach 4.13m, mainly in areas of shallow sand between the dunes. When the species grows in wadis with an underground water resource close to the surface, then it can reach a height of 8m, and a diameter of 20m (Musil, 1928). In the sand seas generally, the species grows in clumps that help to protect it from sand accumulation, and to withstand burial from it. Like *Calligonum comosum*, individuals of *Haloxylon persicum* are widely spaced in the upper parts of the dune; and they stand well apart elsewhere, averaging 10.26 to 10.68m between individuals. In areas with shifting sands, close to the dune crests, spaces between the scattered bushes may reach 40m. But the presence of a shrub or a few shrubs in one spot encourages the formation of more individuals, the older shrubs acting as windbreaks to reduce wind velocity. As in the case of *Calligonum comosum*, the wide spacing of individuals reflects the wide spread of lateral roots: vertical roots also can penetrate deeply, exceeding 30m in length, and enabling the plant to extract adequate water and nutrient from the deeper soil layers.

The average crown cover per 1000m_ of this species is very low, at only 5.4 to 16.6%, though it is the case that this is greater than that of the *Calligonum comosum* community, which it resembles, a consequence perhaps of the *Haloxylon* community being better protected from cutting and grazing. The crown diameter of individuals can reach 10m, but on average is much less, at between 2.7m and 4m.

Soil characteristics under *Haloxylon persicum* are quite distinctive. pH values are very alkaline in reaction, between 8.6 and 9.1, with the highest levels on the upper parts of the dunes; there are no significant vertical variations in any one locality. The sand is also clearly more saline than in other parts of the sand seas, with the exception of those covered by *H. salicornicum*. Saline conditions are also confirmed by the presence of salt pans and sabkhahs overlain by and between dunes, as for example near Ath Thameriyah. The suggestion is that *Haloxylon persicum* is a true salt bush. There are several other indications of this. Thus farms that are scattered in those parts of the sand seas in which this species is present tend to have a general problem with salinity. More generally, although the top sand layers are usually low in salts as a result of leaching, the long tap-root system of this species enables it to absorb salt from the deeper sand layers. The presence of *Haloxylon persicum* in this type of habitat might indicate another reason for the absence of this community from those large sand-dune areas in central Saudi Arabia which are less saline.

It should perhaps be noted that, unlike most of the sand seas in central Saudi Arabia, in the Al Musaft and Al Ghubaydah dunes (p.) as well as in Nafud As Sirr east of Ath Thameriyah and in An Nafud, where *Haloxylon persicum* species are abundant, sands are whitish in colour, rather than reddish as elsewhere, and this might be attributed to their higher salt content. Such a difference could lead to a preliminary assumption that the dominant plants of the white sand are different to those of the red sand, a feature first noted in the coastal sands of the Arabian Gulf by Vesey-Fitzgerald (1957).

Mechanical analysis of the sands underneath this community indicates that at all levels they were uniform in texture, being medium to fine sand: however, in interdune communities, percentages of silt accumulation might reach 18%. Clay amounts were negligible. Like other sand seas, this entire area has a very low organic accumulation of less than 1%.

5.2.3 THE *ARTEMESIA MONOSPERMA* COMMUNITY (PLATE 7)

This is another diagnostic plant community of the sand seas of the centre and north of the peninsula, and found especially in parts of the Great Nafud and in Ad Dahna. *Artemesia monosperma* is the dominant species; indeed as Mandaville (1990) points out, it is hardly found outside the community. *Echinops* sp., *Scrophularia hypericifolia*, *Calligonumum comosum*, *Ephedra alata*, *Stipagrostis drarii*, *Haloxylon persicum* and *H. salicornicum* are the main associate perennial species. A wide variety of annuals are also present, the most common being *Silene villosa*, *Polycarpea repens*, *Neurada procumbens*, *Plantago boisseri* and *Anagallis arvensis*.

On a broad scale, *Artemesia monosperma* is found over large areas of Palestine, Sinai and northern Egypt, and many of the smaller dune systems of central Saudi Arabia, including Nafud Ath Thuwayrat, Nafud As Sirr and Nafud Qunayfitah. It becomes less common in the southern part of Ad Dahna, and has not been recorded from Ar Rub' Al Khali, where it is replaced by *Cornulaca arabica*. It is likely that *Artemesia monosperma* does not respond well to the severe drought which it would find in this latter region. Due to its low economic value for grazing or as a fuel, the species is densely spaced in many areas, and may be found even near settlements, standing out when its more useful associates, *Haloxylon persicum*, *Calligonum comosum* and *Stipagrostis drarii*, have been removed. As a result, the nature and composition of the vegetation communities of the deep sand areas have been changed, in that *Artemesia monosperma* scrubs have largely replaced the removed *Calligonum comosum* and *Haloxylon persicum*, and also have occupied wide areas of degraded representatives of these two latter species. When the saline water table comes close to the surface, in areas in which there is only a shallow sand layer, *Artemesia monosperma* does less well, and is replaced by *Haloxylon* species, as in individual dunes west and south of Unayzah, and east of Ath Thameriyah in Nafud As Sirr.

In our sample areas, which were fenced and protected in Nafud Ath Thuwayrat, *Artemesia monosperma* accounted for between 77.5 and 82.5% of all shrubs sampled (Table 5.3). *Scrophularia hypericifolia* formed between 3.7 and 16.2% of the cover, and *Echinops* sp. only 6 to 10%, all other species being minimally recorded. *Artemesia monosperma* individuals are not widely spaced, mean distances between them ranging from 3.0 to 3.3m. Its growth form makes it a very useful species for sand binding, with the average number of individuals ranging from 92 to 113 per 1000m_, this being very high as compared to the *Calligonum comosum* and *Haloxylon persicum* communities. Mean heights were less than 1 metre (0.88 to 0.93m), although some reached up to 1.74m. Average crown diameters were between 1.232 and 1.25m, which are relatively small; and the total vegetation cover per 1000m_ was 11.1 to 11.2%, largely due to the species' very small crowns.

Although *Artemesia monosperma* has the ability to survive in shifting sands, through its elastic branches and bushy form, sand mobility might present some stress during germination, a process which in this species requires a certain amount of light. When seeds are covered with more than 2 or 3mm of sand, establishment of individuals accordingly is limited (Koller *et al.*, 1964). Once established, root systems are both deep and extensive, searching out moisture and nutritious substances in the deep layers of sand, or in other substrates.

Sand sample analyses indicate that this community is characterised by pure medium to fine sand (96 to 100% of sample). A little silt may occur. The sand was poor in nutrients and organic matter, due to leaching and the smaller amount of vegetation cover. Samples were slightly to very alkaline in reaction, pH values ranging from 8.1 to 9.2. Probably because of leaching, salinity is very low, and does not appear to be a problem for plant growth in this community.

5.2.4   THE *SCROPHULARIA HYPERICIFOLIA* COMMUNITY (PLATE 8)

A relatively minor component of the sand-seas flora *in toto*, *Scrophularia hypericifolia*, a small shrublet, nevertheless can achieve dominance in the northern sands, especially in Ad Dahna, where it occupies deep sands. It is part of a somewhat richer vegetation community than that of the dominants noted thus far, with *Haloxylon salicornicum* being the main subordinate, and other perennial components including *Ephreda alata*, *Artemesia monosperma*, *Echninops* spp. and *Rhanterium epapposum*. There are often a large number of annuals in the community as well, the most common of which are *Plantago boisseri*, *Anagallis arvensis*, *Eremobium aegypticum*, *Cynomorium coccineum*, *Monsonia nivea*, *Silene villosa* and *Neurada procumbens*. In some places, the community may represent the remains of a former wider community which then became highly degraded by firewood gatherers and charcoal collectors. It is rarely seen south of the 26th parallel, since it has a low tolerance to severe drought.

In general, micro-topography has an effect on the local distribution pattern of these shrubs, and it is sometimes very difficult to decide where a boundary should be drawn between one community and another. In our samples, *Scrophularia hypericifolia* clearly is dominant (Table 5.4), with values of between 55 - 56.3% of all the species present. But *Haloxylon salicornicum* also shows considerable presence values, at 33-35% of all shrubs, though these tend to be limited to depressions which normally receive slightly more saline water than elsewhere. Other shrubs are present in very small quantities. The community is widely spaced, with the average distance between the individuals reaching between 3.7 to 4.1m. Their heights ranged from 0.6 to 0.56m, although exceptionally they might attain 1.2m. Crown diameters run from 0.72 to 0.86m, and exceptionally 1.9m. A range of animals, including camels, sheep and goats, browse and nibble continuously the individual shrublets, stunting their growth and limiting their size.

The community generally has a low and thin cover, of no more than 5.1 to 7.8% on average.

Unlike other shrubs in the northern sand seas, *Scrophularia hypericifolia* does not have the bush form that is characteristic elsewhere: it has a lean stem which, like the upper parts of the root system, has the ability to swing with the wind. As a result, the stem becomes amazingly twisted, and is deformed under the strong pressure of wind and sand particles. A further consequence is that sand hummocks are unable to build up around it. As is the case in other dominant species of sand-sea communities, it has a massive root system, which both stabilises the plant, and aids its receipt of water and nutrients.

Soil samples indicate that the sand is mildly alkaline, with pH values ranging from 7.9 to 8.5. The soluble salt content is low, but can show a slight increase with depth, especially where *Haloxylon salicornicum* shrubs are abundant. Organic matter, as elsewhere in the region, is low, at less than 1%. There are no substantive differences in chemical or mechanical properties as between one sand layer and another.

5. The *Stipagrostis drarii* community (Plate 9)

A very distinctive and tufted perennial grass, and subendemic to the Arabian peninsula, this species forms the only grass community in the central and northern sand seas, ranging from Sinai in the far north (Tackholm, 1974) to Ar Rub' Al Khali. Although it is very widespread, often covering large areas of individual dunes, it has been much neglected by the botanist, probably due to the popularity of other shrubs, which have appealed so much both to the scientist and the layman. A number of associate perennial species that are also prevalent in other communities are found in this one, but differ from one locality to another in their occurrence, according to sand topography, location and other local environmental conditions. In the central and northern districts, associate species include *Calligonum comosum*, *Haloxylon persicum*, *Scrophularia hypericifolia*, *Ephedra alata*, *Artemesia monosperma*, *Stipagrostis*

plumosa and *Cyperus conglomeratus* spp. Annuals are few, and confined mainly to those that are well adapted to deep sand habitats, such as *Eremobium aegypticum*, *Silene villosa* and *Neurada procumbens*.

Although the community grows in stands over the whole area, and can be found in even the most remote sand-dune fields, it is established best in deep-sand areas in which the sand is stabilised or semi-stabilised. It is found commonly on the shoulders of large sand 'mountains' that are not easily reached by animals, and where vegetation cover accordingly is partly protected and less well grazed. Examples may be seen along the steep slopes of the sand mountains of Ath Thuwayrat, Ad Dahna, As Sirr and An Nafud. *Stipagrostis drarii* apparently germinates on wet sand after a heavy rain. When it becomes established, it has the ability to withstand slow sand movement and accumulation through its flexible and elastic stems, as well as its roots that resist the cutting of loose, surface sand. The species is also capable of sand-binding, tolerating drought and using available moisture. For most of the year, it looks very dry or even dead, but after rain it sprouts new foliage and resumes growth.

In the higher parts of individual dunes, especially on the lee slopes that are well protected from strong winds, the species is clearly and considerably dominant, with presence values from our samples reaching from 75 to 100%. *Calligonum comosum* accounts for up to 25%, and *Artemesia monosperma* only 5%, on one site alone. Farther down the slope, *Stipagrostis drarii* becomes denser in growth, and more associate species are present. In areas that are not influenced by heavy grazing, the species appears to have a wider and richer vegetation cover than elsewhere, sometimes reaching cover values of 50%: the species may also reach 1.50 to 1.60m in height. The community is subject to intense human disturbance, however, in most places. Grazing and cutting of this species for forage has played a major role in helping to determine the precise nature of growth. Extremely high levels of grazing intensity can reduce the shelter afforded by this plant cover to the sand surface, and therefore result in sand movement, which might in turn lead to further reduction in cover. This process may be seen along the sand slopes that bound the small oases, and other settlements in the dunes. Inhabitants traditionally cut and collect the species as fodder within these settlements, where no other alternatives are available.

Most of the sand supporting this community is deep and easily penetrable by roots: sand constitutes 92-98% of our samples, silt and clay comprises only 2-8%. There appears to be a higher percentage of fine sand than elsewhere., which may reach 20% of the total. There is too the customary deficiency in moisture and nutrient materials. Samples, as elsewhere, differ only slightly at different depths in the 'soil' profile.

Calligonum comosum, Haloxylon persicum, Artemesia monosperma, Scrophularia hypericifolia and *Stipagrostis drarii* all form plant communities that provide the main vegetative characteristics of the sand seas of central and northern Saudi Arabia. While each is distinctive in its own right, all intermix to some extent. All species in these communities may be categorised broadly as extreme psamnophytes, whether they are perennial shrubs or sub-shrubs, tall grasses or annuals. Under severe human pressure, all these communities have been severely pushed back into their present areas of distribution, in which they may still establish themselves and develop. In terms of their distribution on a broad scale, the communities may be divided into three: *Stipagrostis drarii*, which is found over the entire peninsula in sand-sea areas, and which can clearly cope with all the harsh environmental variants of the region; *Calligonum comosum, Artemesia monosperma* and *Scrophularia hypericifolia*, all of which are common in the northern and central sand seas but fade away towards the south, for reasons which are not entirely clear; and *Haloxylon persicum*, which is patchily distributed throughout the region, but the precise areas of occurrence of which appear to be controlled by the availability of saline sand rather than by any other factor.

5.3 Communities of non-dune or shallow-sand habitats

Interdunal sand-filled areas, and gaps between the dunes, are occupied by communities that are widely-spread, and often extend far beyond the frontiers and margins of the sand seas. These communities are however important to sand-sea areas, and the communities themselves may also spread over stabilised low dunes, as well as on to the lower parts of the high dunes. A further five communities are important and distinguishable:

6. The *Haloxylon salicornicum* community
7. The *Rhazya stricta* community
8. The *Rhanterium epapposum* community
9. The *Seidlitzia rosmarinus* community
10. Shrubless communities

For sampling communities 6 and 7, identical techniques to those used previously were applied. A different approach was required for community 10. Particular problems attended the analyses of communities 8 and 9, and these will be discussed later as appropriate.

5.3.1 THE *HALOXYLON SALICORNICUM* COMMUNITY (PLATE 10)

This open shrubland probably covers more land than any other community in north-eastern Arabia, extending from Iraq through to the northern edge of Ar Rub' Al Khali. Within the sand seas, it is best developed on inter-dune lows in which fairly deep sand is present, but it also can be found on hard gravels. In the sand-sea habitat, it often forms pure stands, but it may also be found with a few other perennial associates, such as *H. persicum, Scrophularia hypericifolia* and *Rhanterium epapposum*. A considerable number of, and often a dense luxuriant growth of annuals may also occur with it, among which the most common are *Plantago boisseri, Neurada procumbens, Polycarpea repens, Monsonia nivea, Orobanche cernua* and *Cyperus conglomeratus*. Because of the wide ecological range of this dominant, the composition of the annual community will vary widely from place to place. Although the species should perhaps not be classified as an out-and-out halophyte, in that it avoids salt-rich sabkhahs in which *Seidlitzia* is present, nevertheless it does tend to favour slightly salt-rich environments, and often outgrows all other species in the communities which surround such salt-rich lows, as in Nafud Ath Thuwayrat, Nafud As Sirr and Nafud Qunayfithah.

In our samples, *Haloxylon salicornicum* formed between 95 to 100% of the total number of species, with the other three main shrub associates (above) not exceeding more than one or two individuals each (Table 5.5). All growth indicators are rather meagre: individuals are not widely spaced, (3.08 to 3.22m), while individual heights range from 0.88 to 0.97m, although exceptionally they may reach close to 2m. The number of shrubs per 1000m, however, ranges from 91.8 to 109.8, making it one of the most dense and luxuriant shrubs growing in the entire sand sea area, with a crown cover which is also high, at 31 to 33%. Despite this, the species is not regarded particularly highly as a grazing resource, in spite of its high biomass production in summer. Probably, inhabitants prefer *Scrophularia hypericifolia* and *Rhanterium epapposum* as grazing for their animals, where these species are present. For most of the year, usually only the other parts of the top of the branches of *Haloxylon salicornicum* are grazed. Thalen (1979) has suggested that *Haloxylon salicornicum* could well withstand and resist regular grazing, as well as moderate cutting for firewood. But intense grazing, where it exists, takes place mainly during the summer and early autumn, alternative food sources in the form of annuals being available in the spring. Even in early days, the Bedouin classified this species among those that provide the salt needed for grazing animals, especially camels, but they did not allow their animals to use it for long periods, fearing it might have some ultimate adverse affect on them.

The species has adapted well to the harsh environment of the sand seas, and its deep tap-root system extends more than 10m into the soil (Kaul, 1986; Batanouny, 1979), in the search for water and nutrients. Mechanical and chemical analyses of the substrate indicate that this is mainly a medium to fine-sand, but with much more of the latter than elsewhere, reaching in some samples up to 40% of the total. On the other hand, there was also slightly more silt and clay than in many adjacent communities. pH levels, at 7.7 to 9.1, were slightly alkaline to alkaline. There was slightly more salinity than in most other communities nearby, though most salt was present at lower depths than the main root zone. There was little organic material or nutrients at any of the depths measured.

5.3.2 THE *RHAZYA STRICTA* COMMUNITY (PLATE 11)

Rhazya stricta may form a community which is locally dominant in the sand seas, although it is much more common in other regions in Arabia (Migahid, 1988). It occurs within the sand seas in the low depressions which possess fairly deep and sandy soil, where it forms pure or almost pure stands, with few perennial associates. Annual associate species at times grow densely, including species such as *Eremobium aegypticum*, *Plantago boisseri*, *Silene villosa*, *Anagallis arvensis*, *Polycarpea repens* and *Neurada procumbens*, all of which are commonly found on sand dunes. Good representatives of the *Rhazya stricta* community may be found in the vicinity of Ruman, and on the Erg Ath Thimam of the Ad Dahna dunes: in Nafud Qunayfithah, on the way to Al Mushaillah; and in the dunes near Al Quwayiyah. On all these sites, the sand usually has an undulating appearance, with *Rhazya stricta* being established on elevated mounds or hummocks standing 1 to 2m above the general ground surface. The community is especially abundant in those habitats in which the original vegetation cover has been severely degraded and disturbed, through grazing pressure and the cutting of firewood, especially around settlements, the outskirts of towns and along roadsides or desert tracks. In these areas, sheep, goats and camels avoid individuals of *Rhazya stricta*, which accordingly gains a competitive advantage, so much so that they begin to dominate after a while. Mandaville (1990) points out that the plant is generally acknowledged to be somewhat toxic, though since most animals avoid it, it is not regarded as a serious threat.

Our samples (Table 5.6) indicate that the shrub exists in pure stands in the area sampled, with the individuals being widely spaced, the distance between them ranging from 7.2 to 9.4m. Average height was from 1.14 to 3.83m, with exceptional plants reaching 3.83m. Crowns of full-grown individuals can reach a diameter of up to 6.27m, but are on average 2.7 to 3.3m: the crown cover was very thin, ranging from 9.6 to 11.1%, though if environmental circumstances (water, nutrients) were more favourable, it is likely that this would increase substantially, as for example along the Jeddah-Mecca road in western Saudi Arabia, where it reaches 20%.

Mechanical analyses of the substrate indicate that samples are mostly sand, at 96 to 98% of the sample. However, silt and clay are present, albeit it at very low levels (2 to 4%). The chemical analyses show that the sand is slightly alkaline, with pH values of from 8.4 to 9.0. Levels of soluble salts are low, and salinity does not appear to be a problem for the species. As elsewhere in the sand seas, sand at different depths in the profile appeared to be homogeneous, with no significant differences between one level and another.

5.3.3 THE *RHANTERIUM EPAPPOSUM* COMMUNITY (PLATE 12)

This community is found extensively over large areas of the north-eastern plains of Saudi Arabia, Kuwait and the southern desert of Iraq. Mandaville (1990) regards it as being a plant of great economic importance, being the dominant constituent of valuable rangelands, while at the same time stabilising the soil and providing protection for the dense growth of associated annuals. It is also collected for firewood, many individuals being up-rooted for this purpose. It is, however, very vulnerable to overuse, in which case both the rangelands and the species itself are prone to disappear. This seems to have happened in much of the central and northern sand seas of Saudi Arabia. Respondents in Ad Dahna indicated that this species now has been exterminated there. Nor is it present as a dominant any longer in An Nafud (Al Hassan, 1991).

We may have observed that some *Rhanterium epapposum* communities are still present and dominant in certain areas, notably over the Allubah plateau, to the north-east of An Nafud, and on a smaller scale on low sand dunes in Nafud Ath Thuwayrat. Individuals are also scattered here and there in other communities. But it was not possible, from either the extensive reconnaissance surveys, or from interviews with local people, to locate a good site for sampling this community. Some general comments as to its nature and appearance must suffice. Thus in 'normal' conditions, individuals of this species average 0.60 to 0.70m in height and diameter. Mandaville (1990) studied a pure stand of it in the As Suman plateau near Qrayat Al-Ulya in the north-east of the country, and found that the total shrub cover was low, at only 16%. *Plantago boisseri*, *Pieris babylonica*, *Schismus barbatus* and *Neurada procumbens* were the dominant annual associates. Halwagy *et al.* (1982) estimated the ground cover of this community to range between 1 - 25%, and rarely to reach 50%: on the contrary, Gust (1966) reckoned it to be 90% on a site near Umm Qasr, in south-eastern Iraq.

The environments supporting this community in Allubah and the As Summan plateau are of shallow wind-blown sand over limestone, gravel plains. According to Vesey-Fitzgerald (1957), the species was always absent from the high dunes, even when dominant in the region. The autecology of this species, and its extermination from many areas in which it was formerly dominant, needs to be the focus of further research.

5.3.4 THE *SEIDLITZIA ROSMARINUS* COMMUNITY (PLATE 13)

Small sabkhahs, and shallow undrained depressions that are roughly circular, are formed on occasions between individual dunes as a result of the high saline water table and intensive evaporation. These sabkhahs support a very limited and restricted succulent halophyte community dominated by *Seidlitzia rosmarinus*, which is highly adapted to these conditions.

This community is dominant in inland and coastal sabkhahs all over northern and eastern Saudi Arabia and in many neighbouring countries. It dominates all saline depressions, though sometimes when the salt content is very high, the centre of the depression may be entirely bare of vegetation. Annual species and herbs that can be found in surrounding dunes are also absent from the main body of the sabkhahs. Where they contact the surrounding high dunes, the sandy edges of the sabkhahs are usually occupied by *Haloxylon salicornicum*.

A good example of this community may be seen in Nafud As Sirr, close to Ath Thameriyah. The sabkhahs there appear to be part of a series of small sabkhahs that are scattered along Wadi Ar Rumah in the Al Qaseem region. The community can also be found in man-made salt lands in abundant small farms and oases in the dunes, caused by inappropriate use of irrigation water.

In most of these depressions, the community forms a pure, unbroken stand. The total shrub cover is very high, between 80-90%; however, this may vary widely, depending on the degree of salinity and local relief. Measurements of individual shrubs in this community were not possible since several individuals tend to form one clump, a phenomenon also recognised by Vesey-Fitzgerald (1957). The soil supporting the community consists normally of fine sand to gypsiferous silt and clay. Traces of salt can be seen following high evaporation in the summer, which eventually leaves a mantle of salt on the sabkhah surface.

5.3.5 *SHRUBLESS* COMMUNITIES

In general, interdune areas and hollows appear to be less favourable habitats for shrub growth than the sand dune bodies themselves.

This is probably the result of strong grazing and cutting pressures, due to easy access to these areas. Another possible reason is the intense competition for moisture exerted upon these shrubs by annuals, which could prevent the establishment of shrub seedlings, or stunt their growth (Litav *et al.*, 1963).

But it is the case that, during the rainy season, interdune areas and hollows in the sand seas of central and northern Saudi Arabia support a wide variety of annual species, in addition to some perennials that behave as ephemerals, and have an episodic growth pattern. In the rainy season, when undisturbed, this shrubless community forms a luxuriant green carpet between the higher, surrounding dunes. Plant cover might range in winter and spring from 70 to 80% if rainfall is high: on the other hand, in summer during the years with little or no rainfall, cover might drop sharply to as low as 5% or even less, with only a few perennial species which can survive the harsh environment scattered here and there.

Species diversity in any one area might exceed 50. Common and important species are *Plantage boisseri*, *Lotus halophilus*, *Silene villosa*, *Erodium laciniatum*, *Hippocrepis bicontorta*, *Polycarpea repens*, *Cyperus conglomeratus*, *Monsonia nivea*, *Neurada procumbens*, *Eremobium aegyptiacum*, *Cutandia memphitica*, *Moltkiopsis ciliata*, *Dipcadi serotinium* and *Allium ampeloprasum* (Table 5.7).

For the further clarification of relationships between species in the shrubless community, 30 quadrats of uniform size (1m_) were investigated in each of the 11 sites in the sand seas. A total of 330 quadrats were examined, data collected, and then subjected to statistical analysis. 39 species were encountered within the sample sites (Table 5.8). Both quadrats and species were analysed by reference to cluster classification, using the TWINSPAN programme (p. : Hill, 1979). Only the first six levels of analysis were taken, and smaller groups that produced artificial subgroups then were amalgamated, because further subdivision made no ecological sense. The final classification of quadrats and sites resulted in 11 broad groups, illustrated in Fig. 5.4. Table

5.9 indicates that the following groups emerged from the eleven-site classification, using the first and second levels of analysis.

Group A sites:

Nafud Ath Thuwayrat (site 1); Ad Dahna (near Al Artaweyah); Ad Dahna (Khab Ar Redum); Nafud Th Thuwayrat (site 2); Nafud Al Ghamees; Nafud Al Turafayah (sites 1 and 2).

These sites are characterised by the presence of *Lotus halophilus*, *Silene villosa*, *Cutandia memphitica*, *Dipcadi erythraeum*, *Roemeria hybrida*, *Medicago laciniata*, *Launea mucronata*, *Horwoodia dicksoniae* and *Erodium laciniatum*.

Group B sites:

Ad Dahna (Erg Al Hamrani; Erg Ath Thiman); Nafud Qunayfithah (sites 1 and 2).

These have been classified into one group due to the presence of *Arnebia linearifolia*, *A. decumbens*, *Moltkiopsis ciliata*, *Allium sphaerocephalum*, *Parenychia arabica* and *Cyperus conglomerata*.

Certain species have a wide distribution, and are presented in both the two main groups: *Plantago boisseri*, *Launea capitata*, *Stipagrostis plumosa*, *S. drarii*, *Neurada procumbens*, *Hippocrepis bicontorta*, *Polycarpea repens* and *Ononis serrata*.

Group A sites, which are found to the north of the central sand seas, may be further subdivided at level 2 into:

(*Ai*) Ad Dahna (near Al Artaweyah; Khab Ar Redhum); Nafud Ath Thuwayrat (site2)

with the following characteristic species: *Aaronsohnia factorovskyi*, *Anisosciadium lanatum*, *Anthemis hypericifolia*, *Centropodia forsskali*, *Cynomorium coccineum*, *Helianthemum lippii*, *Koelpinia linearis*, *Launea mucronata*, *Medicago laciniata*, *Moltkiopsis ciliris*, *Neurada procumbens*, *Polycarpaea repens*, *Savigyna parviflora*, *Stipagrostis drarii*, *Concolvulus cephalopodus*

and *Horwoodia dicksoniae*, all of which are associated with sites underlain by shallow sand over hard-rock plains (*Jaw*).

(*Aii*) Nafud Al Ghamees; Nafud Al Turafiyah (sites 1 and 2); Nafud Ath Thuwayrat (site 1)

have as diagnostic species those that occupy deep stable sand, that covers depressions between the higher dunes: these are *Astralagus annularis*, *Eremobium aegypticum*, *Roemaria hybrida*, *Rumex pictus*, *Dipcadi erythreum*, *Cynodon dactylon* and *Stipagrostis plumosa*.

Similarly, Group B sites, which lie at the left-hand side of the TWINSPAN diagram, and are found to the south of Group A sites, may also be subdivided further at level 2:

(*Bi*) Nafud Qunayfithah (sites 1 and 2).

These sites lie to the west of Ar Riyadh, and are characterised by species including *Arnebia linearifolia*, *Launea capitata*, *Moltkiopsis ciliata*, *Schismus arabicus*, *Stipagrostis drarii*, *Polycarpea repens*, *Silene villosa*, *Neurada procumbens* and *Plantago boisseri*. These species favour shallow and stable sand in which the clay and salt contents are higher than elsewhere.

(*Bii*) Ad Dahna (Erg Al Hamrani; Erg Ath Thimam).

These sites are distinguished by the presence of *Allium sphaerocephalum*, *Moltkiopsis ciliata*, *Arnebia decumbens*, *Cyperus conglomeratus*, *Hippocrepis bicontorta*, *Ononisserrata* and *Dipcadi erythraeum*, all of which prefer to grow on relatively flat, hard plains between the dunes, that are covered by thin sand sheets.

In order to clarify further the role of environmental factors in the distribution of annual species, canonical correspondence analysis also was undertaken by using the CANOCO computer programme. The CANOCO analysis tended to confirm that floristic composition, and the distribution of the main floristic groups in the shrubless community as a whole reflected the heterogeneous topography, and the physical characteristics of sand and other substrate conditions, which in turn affect the availability and storage of moisture, particularly during the growth period. Slight differences in the chemical properties of the sand appear in general to have only a limited effect on species as indicated by this programme, except for those which reflect an abundance of CaCO3. In general, two main habitats may be inferred from CANOCO analysis: those with deep, loose sand; and those with shallow sand cover. Five different groups may be distinguished as follows:

1. The first is clustered around the meeting points of the two axes, and appear to have a wide ecological amplitude. The major species were present in over a quarter of all sites sampled in each case: *Plantago boisseri*, *Silene villosa*, *Stipagrostis plumosa*, *Lotus halophilus*, *Hippocrepis bicontorta* and *Erobium aegptyicum*. Taken in common, they are abundant in habitats close to the feet of the dunes, with moderately deep and occasionally fine loose sand with a high moisture content.

2. A unispecies group, which nevertheless is distinctive, is present in only two sites, and in 36 of the 330 quadrats sampled. This is represented by *Arnebia linearifolia*, found in Ad Dahna near Erg Al Hamrami. Widespread elsewhere in Saudi Arabia, it is located in the sand seas on the sand in which silt and clay contents are higher than usual, and the sites are also distinguished by the high levels of CaCO3.

3. A third group, consisting of *Ononis serrata*, *Anthemis hypericifolia*, *Erodium laciniatum* and *Medicago laciniata* appears to be characteristic of shallow sand resting on hard-rock plains: it is associated especially with site 2 in Nafud Ath Thuwayrat. All are fairly common species.

4. A group consisting of *Horwoodia dicksoniae* and *Asphodelus tenuifoliuss* is found mainly on well-drained sands or sand-silts with a medium pH.

5. All other species occur in very small numbers on one or two sites, and their presence is not really explicable in terms of current knowledge: their locations may change from year to year, and there may be a strong random element in their distribution patterns for any one time.

Although much remains to be discovered, both TWINSPAN and CANOCO analyses suggest there may be a strong relationship between different groups of species, and both their locations and the physical conditions under which they grow. There may in particular be slight differences in the communities of annuals which are present in the northern, as opposed to the central sand seas, and a suspicion of some significant differences between eastern and western districts of these northern and central sand seas as well.

5.4 Ar Rub' Al Khali

Our detailed survey was not extended to Ar Rub' Al Khali due to the limited number of species reported there. Two perennial communities have been indicated e.g. by Mandaville (1990). One is a Hadh saltbush shrubland, dominated by the endemic *Cornulaca arabica*: its community also appears to be endemic to Ar Rub' Al Khali. This species may appear as pure shrub stands covering thousands of square kilometres or, on the higher and better-drained sands, may have a few associates such as *Calligonum crinitum*, *Limeum arabicum* or *Tribulus arabicus*. *Cyperus conglomeratus* also is usually present. Individuals are customarily spaced at distances of 3 to 20mm or more, depending on the local environmental circumstances. The community is restricted to districts south of 23N.

A second, also widespread community consists of shrubs of *Calligonum crinitum* subsp *arabicum.*, which in this area replaces the *Calligonum comosum* of the northern and central sand seas, and is particularly common on the deep sands. On the huge sand-mountains of the eastern Ar Rub' Al Khali, it is associated with a luxurious growth of *Tribulus arabicus* after rains, and with *Zygophyllum mandavillei* around the edges of the inter-dune salt flats: elsewhere, *Cyperus conglomerata* is a common associate, along with *Stipagrostis drarii* and *Limeum arabicum*.

5.5 'Vegetationless' area

The absence of vegetation cover on parts of sand dunes everywhere may be attributed to three main reasons, namely: 1.) the hyper-aridity; 2.) the dune's type and shape; and 3.) the destruction of plants by human activity. But extreme aridity might affect the presence of a vegetation cover, regardless of other factors, as in the case of many of the southern parts of Ad Dahna, and in Ar Rub' Al Khali. In these areas with very low, or no rainfall, vegetation cover might fail to appear, whatever the dune type or shape (Tsoar & Moller, 1986). Yet the average amount of rainfall in the central and northern sand seas is well within the limits (above 50mm per annum) required to support vegetation, when other requirements are favourable.

Customarily, the density and nature of the vegetation cover here along a dune elevational gradient are determined and controlled by the degree of sand mobility, or stability, and these are influenced by the wind velocities, and by the shape of the dunes. Most areas that undergo high wind velocities, and therefore have a high potential rate of sand movement, show little or no vegetation at all. There are two possible reasons for this: first, there is a continuous loss of sand moisture, and vegetationless active dune sand has the lowest moisture content of all at field capacity (Tsoar, 1990); and second, the sand movement will also expose the deeper sand layers to drying by wind, and solar radiation, leading to further moisture loss.

It is known that all major sand-dune types react differently to the sand movements affecting them. For example, seif dunes are particularly active in crest or near-crest areas, as also are transverse dunes, the most common type of the central and northern sand seas, the crests of which are frequently bare. This is the case too for many longitudinal dunes in Ad Dahna and the central An Nafud. The arms of most star dunes are also frequently bare of all vegetation. Although important locally, the amount of land occupied by bare dunes is really quite small, at 3 to 5% of the whole of central and northern Saudi Arabia (Whitney *et al.*, 1983). Further, there appears to be little difference between the leeward and windward sides of dune crests, no matter what the dune type, though the windward slopes often have more vegetation cover, since their angle of slope is gentler.

From our observations, it is clear that *Stipagrostis drarii* is the most common plant, and at times the only one present in the upper parts of the dunes, and at dune crests, where the slopes are very steep. Other species that sometimes may be found are *Calligonum comosum*, *Haloxylon persicum* and *Artemesia monosperma*, all of which have deep tap roots which can reach the low, subsurface water supplies. In addition, all have the capacity to resist temporary burial by moving sand. These species are first found at an average of 15.4 to 22.5m to the leeward, and from 17.3 to 18.2m to the windward of the sharp dune crests, where the wind velocity and the angle of the slope (30°) cause the greatest sand movement. Annual species are rarely found in these areas, but where they are, they are mainly limited to a few species which are highly adapted to deep sand, such as *Eremobium aegypticum* and *Silene villosa*.

CHAPTER 6

HUMAN USES OF THE SAND SEAS AND THEIR VEGETATION

The Arabian Peninsula has been extensively exploited by human populations from as early as 1.5 M.Y.B.P. (Masry, 1977). More recently it also has been characterised by a large number of settlements and irrigated areas, though nomadic pastoralism has perhaps been the main traditional form of land-use in the area. By piecing together written records, and information provided by elderly inhabitants of the region, through in-depth interviews and questionnaires, it is clear that individual parts of plants, including the fruit, flower, leaves, branches and whole plants were, directly or indirectly, major resources for the livelihood of all these groups. People in this harsh environment have relied heavily on the vegetation to save them and their flocks from starvation and disease. As a result, for these people, the protection of the vegetation cover was a source of pride. Tribal warfare has usually been caused and centred on raids with the aim of gaining vegetation territories, water and livestock.

In order to determine current uses, and attitudes towards the use of vegetation in the sand seas today, a questionnaire was utilised, and distributed to 240 inhabitants, including settlers, farmers and nomads, all of whom were well acquainted with the research area, and had a keen interest in its vegetation. Efforts were made to avoid people who might provide misleading information, such as foreign workers who were based on farms or as shepherds and did not speak Arabic, the language of the questionnaire. The questionnaire was divided into 4 sections in order to achieve its objectives, namely:

- a) a general section for all respondents (17 questions);
- b) a section for farmers in oases, and inside the sand seas (13 questions);
- c) a section for settlers in adjacent villages, towns and cities (2 questions); and
- d) a section for nomads and shepherds (10 questions).

Participant observation, which included observing, listening and friendly casual conversation that created no suspicion or fear was also a valuable method of increasing understanding of these themes.

6.1 Plant uses

Plant species, especially those of the sand dunes, have yielded over time a wide range of productive benefits. Utilisation of these plants has varied to some extent from one area to another, depending on the economic level of the inhabitants. In some cases, exploitation of vegetation resources might be conducted to satisfy limited local demands, but at other times such raw materials could be exported to other surrounding areas. The plants can be divided according to how they are used into the following main groups:-

1. food and beverages for human consumption;
2. industrial materials;
3. medicinal resources;
4. fodder for animals; and
5. fuel.

Food or beverages for human consumption

People interviewed indicated that many parts of the natural vegetation and especially of the annual species within it, provide palatable materials, which can be eaten raw, or cooked with other food products, or utilised for making different beverages and tea substitutes. It should be indicated, however, that these palatable species are not part of the daily diet; they are eaten only during picnic time and for novelty. Species which fall into this category are listed in Table 6.1

Industrial materials

Inhabitants of the region have over time, recognised and used many plant species as raw materials for industrial purposes. There has, for instance, been a long tradition in the use of the wood of *Calligonum comosum* and *Haloxylon persicum* for building houses, fencing farms and building stockades for animal husbandry. These psammophytic shrubs also have been used for reinforcing and afforestation in areas of moving sands. Other uses include application of this timber for making furniture, and farming or industrial implements. Raw materials such as waxes, inks, tannins, alkaloids, dyes, latex, creosote, gums and cosmetics can also be obtained from several different species; an overall list is given in Table 6.2.

Medicinal resources

Folk and traditional medicine, that depends mainly on herbs, has been practised in the region since ancient times.

Despite the availability of modern medicines, some people still use and recommend herbal medicines, derived from local plant species through traditional methods. Most medicines are taken orally, either as fresh leaves, fruits or after boiling in water or added to hot drinks. Others are applied directly over painful areas and infected wounds. Many of these plant species have been tested and approved by pharmacologists, and introduced into modern pharmacopoeia.

Common medicinal uses of plant species found in the sand seas, as stated by questionnaire respondents, are listed in Table 6.3.

Fodder for animals

Grazing has been a traditional form of land use practice in the interior parts of the Arabian Peninsula for thousands of years. The research

area and surrounding regions have been occupied by tribes who consider grazing to be one of their main activities. These tribes roamed the sand seas and surrounding regions in search of rich vegetation cover, which then was their only resource for feeding their animals. In recent years, nomadic people, as well as inhabitants of settlements and scattered oases, still have large numbers of livestock that are raised on farms and are grazed on natural vegetation in the nearby desert. These activities are discussed further later in this chapter.

Fuel

As in the case of grazing, the cutting and uprooting of shrubs for fuel is also a very wide practice in the sand seas. For many years, psammophytic shrubs have been virtually the basic and principal fuel throughout the area and the surrounding region. Inhabitants of this region, like people in many other arid land regions, have relied heavily on wood (especially from *Calligonum cososum, Haloxylon persicum, Haloxylon salicornicum* and *Artemisa monosperma*) to provide fuel for cooking, heating, lighting and fire for other purposes.

6.2 Effects of human activities on the vegetation of the sand seas

Prior to the discovery of oil, the exploitation of the vegetation cover and other environmental components was relatively moderate. All forms of exploitation of the natural vegetation were carried out mainly to satisfy essential human needs, and there was a fair balance between human use, the germination of new vegetation, and the renewal of plant resources. As a result, the overall ecological balance was largely maintained. However, in years of particularly scarce rainfall and severe drought, some degradation of the vegetation cover for several years might ensue, though this was not permanent.

The discovery and exploitation of oil in Saudi Arabia since the 1940's has stimulated considerable and rapid socio-economic changes in the whole country. A rapid transformation of the society from nomadic to settled, and the massive migration of rural populations into urban centres, have been two of the main and obvious consequences of the wealth resulting from the increased oil revenues. Another consequence has been a change in the landscape caused through house building and industrialisation, road construction and the expansion of agriculture. Destruction and degradation of the vegetation cover of the sand dunes can be attributed to the increasing activities of these later developments, including increased wood-cutting, overcultivation, recreation and associated activities that disturb it. Although these several factors are treated here separately, at times they coincide, resulting in severe and cumulative destruction of the vegetation cover.

6.2.1   OVERGRAZING

Overgrazing has been regarded world-wide as a prime cause of desertification and environmental degradation (Goudie,1990). Although livestock, especially camels, sheep and goats, have roamed the sand seas and their surround for thousands of years in search of the sometimes rich vegetation cover, since the establishment of Saudi Arabia, the number of nomads overall has decreased rapidly and most former Bedouins have successfully exchanged desert living for an urban environment. But with these changes, grazing intensity paradoxically has increased, animals being grazed for more multifarious and commercial purposes than formerly, when subsistence was the main aim. Still, inhabitants of many oases, farms, villages and towns in and close to the sand seas raise and maintain herds of sheep and goats and a few camels that are grazed by hired labour (1-2 persons), who take them around the desert. Table 6.4 suggests that 79.9% of respondents use the sand dunes for grazing today; many of the herds are quite large, and levels of grazing are accordingly high.

Table 6.4: Level of grazing use in the sand seas by inhabitants of the region and surrounding areas

Level of grazing	No of Respondents	%
High	111	47.4
Moderate	76	32.5
Seldom	32	13.7
no use	15	6.4

Source: Questionnaire

Before the introduction of motor vehicles, camel herds were larger than those of sheep and goats. People habitually used camels for transportation and took advantage of their ability to survive in the desert without water for a long time. In 1966, camels constituted 43% of livestock in the country, but the number had declined sharply to 16% by 1986 (Al-Hassan, 1991). On the other hand, the numbers of sheep have increased greatly during the same period. The average size of sheep herds now in the northern and central sand seas is 324, while the average size of camel herds is only 43. Goats are also raised, but in relatively small numbers. The multiplication of small livestock herds is the direct result of a new economic stability in the region, the drilling of new water wells, and the continuing availability of forage, as well as of veterinary services. The common use of cars and water tankers also allows livestock owners to bring water and forage to very remote areas in the sand seas, so that an absence of natural water *per se* appears no longer to be a limiting factor in the region for grazing. As a result, the increase of livestock has now begun to exceed the general carrying capacity of the land in many parts of the region. Table 6.5 suggests that 80% of livestock owners who were interviewed indicated that natural vegetation cover in these sand seas is no longer enough to support their livestock all year round. Only 4.7% of respondents indicated (Table 6.6) that they do not need much additional imported forage for their livestock. In contrast, the majority of respondents (95.3%) needed high or moderate levels of additional forage to feed their livestock, except during the spring months. Indeed, most people take their \livestock to graze in the sand seas only in this season. Rainfall, and the growth of the vegetation cover then make the sand firmer, allowing animals as well as cars to move deep into the more remote and grazing-rich areas. Possibly, in these circumstances, sheep then cause more destruction to the vegetation cover than any other animal, in view of their limited movement away from water sources. In addition, they are highly gregarious animals (Goudie, 1990). Camels, which graze and eat the higher stems and branches of larger shrubs such as *Calligonum comosum* and *Haloxylon persicum*, also add to the damage by being able to break down the branches of these shrubs and get access to leaves that are out of the reach of sheep and goats, further reducing and stunting their growth. The main effects of overgrazing, mainly by sheep, camels and goats, can be seen clearly in the vicinity of the small oases that intersperse the sand seas, in which the vegetation cover may be almost absent.

The most desirable plant species for grazing, including both annuals and perennials, are *Plantago boissieri, Cynodon dactylon, Lotus halophilus, Convolvulus cephalopodus, Silene villosa, Hippocrepis bicontorta, Cyperus conglomeratus, Erodium laciniatum, Neurada procumbens, Cutandia memphitica, Allium ampeloprasum, Launaea capitata, Dipcadi serotinum, Scrophularia hypericifolia, Ononis serrata, Stipagrostis drarii, Calligonum comosum, Stipagrostis plumosa, Rhanterium epapposum* and *Haloxylon persicum*. Once these are reduced or removed, the way is then open for an increased use of less palatable grasses and shrubs such as *Rhazya stricta, Eremobium aegyptiacum, Monsonia nivea, Polycarpaea repens* and *Helianthemum lippii*. Clear examples of these changes can be seen near Rumah in Ad Dahna, as well as along the road to Al Mushailah, where *Rhazya stricta* and other less palatable species, which are of little economic value, have largely replaced the more palatable species that are overgrazed or cut. Overgrazing also has contributed significantly to more sand movement and encroachment. The continuous movement and trampling of large numbers of sheep, goats and camels over the relatively soft sand can cause more sand loosening and movement. On the other hand, the effects are not totally negative: livestock wastes serve as an important source of organic matter for sand. In addition, these domestic animals might play the roles of vanishing wildlife by stimulating the growth of some plant species through browsing and by contributing to seed dispersal.

6.2.2   WOODCUTTING

Wood cutting, and uprooting shrubs for fuel, cooking and heating, or for the manufacture of charcoal, is still a common practice, and indeed has increased in recent years. As shown in Table 6.7, 75% of people interviewed indicated that they used wood for heating and cooking, and this practice is expected to continue for the foreseeable future. 82.5% of respondents further indicated that they cut wood intensively or moderately (Table 6.8), though most cut wood usually in small quantities during their movements and journeys in the sand seas. The majority of wood users also buy high-quality firewood such as *Calligonum comosum* and *Haloxylon perciscum* from the nearest woodpile retailers. Other consumers buy loads from pickups and trucks that bring firewood to the market from far away. An insignificant number of respondents indicated that they collect wood for sale.

Only five shrubs were mentioned as preferred firewood species (Table 6.9). *Calligonum comosum* and *Haloxylon persicum* were ranked by the people interviewed as the most preferable and desired species for wood cutting.

Table 6.9: Top firewood species preferred by correspondence (Rankings were based on frequencies of mention; respondents might mention more than one species

Plant	Frequencies of mention	Ranking
Calligonum comosum	214	1
Haloxylon persicum	151	2
Rhanterium epapposum	51	3
Haloxylon salicornicum	50	4
Artemisia monosperma	6	5

Over-exploitation of these shrubs, and the consequent heavy demand on their wood, have affected their availability and presence around cities, small oases and Bedouin camps in the sand seas, near to which loads of firewood of these species can be seen piled up in certain designated wood markets. As with grazing, the use of motor vehicles that can move further into the sand seas than formerly, as well as the use of more advanced saws, has speeded up the destruction of these shrubs. Bedouins and shepherds, during their movement in the sand seas also cut shrubs for cooking and heating. It is very common to see piles of wood in front of Bedouin tents. In oases, towns and cities where alternative fuels are available, such as kerosene, gas and electricity, firewood is used mainly for heating during the very cold winter months, and is still preferred by some people over other alternatives. Wood is used more during the night when the weather is cooler and more people are around. It is also used to boil water for making tea and coffee. Questionnaire respondents indicated that they use wood generally in addition to kerosene and gas, mainly for heating. *Calligonum comosum,* and to a lesser extent *Haloxylon persicum,* are the most popular species used from the sand dunes. These species are usually burned very close to where people sit and gather. They are very desirable because they burn slowly and produce plenty of hot charcoal with few if any sparks, and nontoxic smoke. *Haloxylon salicornicum, Rhanterium epapposum* and dry *Artemisia monosperma,* which burn very quickly, are usually used to light the fire before the slower-burning woods become effective. The use of these latter species is limited to the desert, and near to Bedouin camps, and they are seldom sold in the wood markets.

6.2.3   OVER-CULTIVATION

Over-cultivation and agricultural expansion are two of the major general causes of degradation of the environment in the sand seas. In the past, agriculture was concentrated in the small fertile oases scattered between individual dunes, where water was available. In these small oases, people used traditional methods to tap underground water reserves to grow their crops. But over the course of the last quarter of a century, a massive expansion of agriculture has taken place in Saudi Arabia, in which tens of thousands of hectares have been brought under cultivation. This expansion has been accompanied by the intensive drilling of water wells, which has extended dramatically the area under cultivation. Fertile plains between individual dunes have been utilised for agriculture, especially in Nafud as Sirr, Nafud Qunayfithah, Nafud Ath Thuwayrat and Nafud Ash Shuqayyiquh. The main crops in these farms are grains, palm trees, and different varieties of fruit, alfalfa and vegetables, though most new farms are devoted mainly to grain production. This massive expansion of agriculture has led indirectly to further desertification, for the net result is that Bedouins, villagers and their livestock all have moved deeper in to the sand dunes, looking for replacement pasture, as more and more land is cultivated, so destroying more natural vegetation.

The depletion of underground water resources for agriculture also has had a severe impact on the vegetation cover through continuous loss of habitats. A clear indication of the effect of the ground water depletion can be seen on the palms, tamarisk and other cultivated trees in many oases, some of which have been abandoned as a result of desiccation and salinisation. Abandoned oases and cultivated areas are usually colonised by *Haloxylon salicornicum,* especially on the more salinised land.

6.2.4   RECREATION

Sand seas attract many people from the surrounding regions to enjoy the beauty and unique character of their landscapes, especially in the pleasant weather during spring, with their rich vegetation cover. Some people also visit the sand seas in search of desert truffles and mushrooms, which are very popular foods and have considerable economic value. People may come for the day, for weekends, or sometimes for the whole spring season. 53.8% of respondents (Table 6.10) indicated that they often visited the sand seas for recreational purposes. However, those who inhabit the sand seas or whose occupations involve living in them do not usually use the area for recreational purposes.

Those visiting for recreation normally wander around large areas using powerful four-wheeled drive vehicles, which give them access to places where there are no established roads. This uncontrolled movement of cars and vehicular traffic, which today is the main means of transportation in the sand seas (Table 6.11) has scarred the desert and caused massive environmental destruction in places, with all shrubs and vegetation cover in the way being carelessly knocked down. Recreationists engage also in other activities that have a severe impact on the shrubs of the region, as for instance, commonly cutting wood for cooking and heating during their stay.

6.3 Attitudes of people towards the vegetation cover of the sand seas

Conservation of the environment and its preservation have, since the rise of Islam, had their roots in Islamic belief as one of the bases of the society, law and culture of its followers. Islam allows and encourages people to utilise and benefit judiciously from all aspects of the environment and its natural resources, for reasonable and constructive purposes, such as food and clothing. On the other hand, it warns against and discourages the misuse of natural resources, which would jeopardise the welfare of the majority of the people (Al-Nafie, 1989).

Allah says:

53. He who has made for you the earth like a carpet spread out; has enabled you to go about therein by roads (channels); and has sent down water from the sky. With it have we produced diverse pairs of plants each separate from the others.

54. Eat (for yourselves) and pasture your cattle: verily; in this are signs for men endured with

understanding (The Holy Quaran 20: 53-54)
. . . Eat and drink: But waste not by excess, for God loveth not the wasters. (The Holy Quaran &:31)

Most users of the vegetation cover (77.1%) indicated that they do not normally cut green vegetation, for several reasons such as:-

1. the need to protect it;
2. to allow livestock to graze in it;
3. there is no advantage in cutting most green species; and
4. wood from dead species is more beneficial for most uses.

Only 22.9% of respondents admitted cutting off living branches or whole shrubs and herbs. Reasons given for cutting these living plants were the use of these plants as medicine and to eat them as food.

The great majority of respondents (68%) showed that they understand and sympathise with conservation efforts and the protection of plants and animals, including those in the sand seas. But 31.9% of people, mainly nomads or settlers who have livestock, and are very loyal to their life-style, do not favour the strict protection of sand-sea plants and animals, indicating that it is their only available place for grazing. Others indicated that most wildlife and vegetation have vanished, and there is nothing to protect. A few people, however, appeared to have only a vague idea and limited understanding of the importance and necessity of preserving the natural environment. Generally, such answers, and related misunderstandings are common responses to the idea of conservation in many parts of the world (Mackinnon, *et al*, 1986).

In view of the majority of respondents (92%), there has been a change in the vegetation cover in the last five decades, but nobody thought that it has become denser. There were no differences in the views of older and younger respondents on this matter. However, elderly people stressed repeatedly that vegetation cover during their boyhood was denser, and some shrubs were bigger in size.

87.9% of respondents believed that vegetation cover of the sand dunes is fair (65%) or richer (26%), as compared with vegetation cover in other parts of the desert.   One interesting point is that the majority of respondents (Table 6.12) attributed the degradation of vegetation cover on the sand seas primarily to drought.   Cutting and overgrazing were ranked equally as the second cause of the vegetation degradation. People who practised certain uses also attributed the degradation to others who practised other activities.

The sand seas of central and northern Saudi Arabia are utilised by a considerable number of humans and livestock for many purposes. Such utilisation has had an impact on their vegetation cover. Over-exploitation of some sand-sea systems, as within Ad Dahna, has resulted in a severe degradation of the vegetation cover, especially in terms of the removal of large shrubs.   Praise-worthy conservation measures currently being undertaken in Saudi Arabia should be extended to cover most of these sand seas, such as northern Ad Dahna, northern Nafud Ath Thuwayrat, and the interior parts of An Nafud, in order to protect their fragile but unique terrestrial ecosystem, and limit the economic implications of such severe degradation.

CONCLUSIONS

The interior parts of the Arabian Peninsula are characterised in large measure by the prevalence of 'sand seas', large areas of now largely-stable sand which cover approximately one third of the total region. The harsh environment of these sand seas strongly impacts on all life forms and human activities within the region. However, since sand seas still are commonly thought of as a lifeless environment, many aspects of their vegetation and ecology have been largely neglected by scientists: they have in particular received little consideration and attention from botanists, ecologists, and conservationists, even those who have attempted to investigate the ecology and phytogeography of Saudi Arabia on a wider scale.

Accordingly, this is the first quantitative and qualitative attempt to evaluate the vegetation of the sand seas of Saudi Arabia. Our main findings and conclusions are as follows.

First, the existence and development of vegetation cover on the sand seas are determined by climate, and by the physical, thermal, hydrological and chemical properties of the sand, some of which are favourable to the existence and welfare of vegetation cover on the sand dunes while others are not. Advantages deriving from sand-sea structures are that the extent of water percolation and downward movement in sand is such that it prevents a major loss of water by evaporation. As a result, the sand seas retain a good deal of water beneath the surface layer, from which perennials and shrubs with deep penetrating roots can benefit, allowing such species to be supplied rapidly by enough moisture to make up for losses by transpiration. Further, the general texture of the sand provides good aeration. Disadvantages are that the sand seas *in toto* have a very low water holding capacity. Also, due to the tendency to leaching, sand is very low in nutrients. In addition, the constant movement and erosion of the sand by wind may hinder the establishment of vegetation and may cause physical damage to already established plants.

Bearing this in mind, the present sand-sea flora appears to have originated in the Late Miocene, when the sand seas of the research area began to form and merge. The form of the vegetation currently covering the sand dunes is likely to date from the marked decrease in humidity recorded at the start of the present arid phase, some 6,000 years ago. In the last 2-3,000 years, there has been an acceleration of aridity, such that the sand seas have in part been reactivated. Old literature, travellers' narratives, and pictorial records made by inhabitants and some travellers all reveal that the vegetation cover prevailing during the last 2,000 years has been similar to that present today, though it was possibly greater in density.

Plant species of the sand dunes have adapted to rigorous abiotic environmental factors through various morphological and physical mechanisms. They have also adapted ecologically to this harsh environment. Thus, species with shallow and superficial roots are limited to the more stable and sheltered areas of the sand dunes. Specialised halophytic vegetation has also colonised low-lying depressions between the dunes. In contrast, species with long anchoring roots have established themselves on the more mobile and active parts of the dunes, though where the sand dunes are characterised by extensive movement and shifting, vegetation is entirely absent.

Our biogeographical and floristic analysis of the flora has revealed that floristic diversity is low, though it is higher than elsewhere in the Saudi Arabian desert. 165 plant species have been collected from the main sand seas of northern and central Saudi Arabia and their periphery, constituting some 8% of the 2,030 species which, according to Miller and Nyberg (1991: 265), may be found in Saudi Arabia as a whole, many of which are in much wetter areas as in the mountainous south-west of the country: only 36 species have been noted from Ar Rub' Al Khali. A limited number of psammophytic species were restricted in distribution to the deep sand. These species, which are considered to be true sand-sea species, amount to only 22 in number, or approximately 13.3% of the total species recorded from the main northern and central sand seas and their periphery. Like many plant geographical regions, the sand-seas have a flora comprised not only of species whose distribution is uniregional (Saharo-Arabian), but also a considerable number of biregional and pluriregional species with affinities to other plant geographical regions as well. The uniregional species number 37, as follows: 34 Saharo-Arabian species, 1 Irano-Turanian, 1 Mediterranean and 1 Sudanian. The majority of species (41.8%) belong to the Saharo-Arabian elements (20.6%), and the biregional species of Saharo-Arabian and Irano-Turanian derivation (21.2%). The existence of many Saharo-Arabian species, and their high proportion of the total, confirm the designation of these sand seas as essentially Saharo-Arabian. The northern part of the Arabian Peninsula, however, moves closer in typology to the Irano-Turanian and Mediterranean vegetation. It is almost impossible to draw a clear line between the Saharo-Arabian and these neighbouring plant regions, since species of each region penetrate to the other, where the environments are similar. The interior and northern part of Saudi Arabia should be included initially within the Holarctic rely. On the other hand, the Sudanian floristic frontier in the Arabian Peninsula should be drawn at the northern borders of Ar Rub Al Khali and to the east of Al Hijaz mountain, and high lands along the boundaries of the Arabian Shelf in the central part of the Arabian Peninsula. It should be mentioned that large wadi systems beds that support mainly *Acacia* spp. (Sudanian species) are concentrated in this region. More systematic studies to delimit these biogeographic boundaries more precisely and accurately are called for.

Life form analyses of the flora of the sand seas indicated that 63.6% of the total species reported were therophytes (annuals and biennials). Perennial species accounted for 33.9% of all species. 2.4% of species were those which may behave as annuals, biennials, or short-lived perennials, depending on ecological factors. 21 plant species were recorded from the main sand dune body, of which 52.4% were annuals and 48.6% were perennials.

An outstanding feature of the 30 families present is that only a limited number were of importance regionally, with Compositae, Gramineae, Cruciferae, Caryophllaceae, Leguminosae and Zygophyllaceae predominating both in terms of the number of genera and species. These families account for 64% of the flora recorded in the central and northern sand seas of Saudi Arabia. Compositae have the highest number of genera and species (22 genera and 29 species); Gramineae have 17 genera and 25 species; Cruciferae have 12 genera and 14 species. Caryophyllaceae have 10 genera and 12 species; Leguminosae have 8 genera and 17 species; and Zygophyllaceae have 3 genera and 8 species. But most of the families have very few genera and species. 13 families are represented by only one genus per family, and 9 genera have only 1 species per genus. The number of genera appears to be very high, compared to the number of species, with the average number of species per genus about 1.4. This confirms a common characteristic of desert flora.

Phytoecological surveys, backed up by relevant statistical analyses show that the northern and central sand dunes consist of three plant-community groups, all of which are strongly associated with particular characteristics of the sand-sea terrain. Each individual plant community is dominated by one or more perennial species, after which the community is named. Although the floristic composition of each community is comparable, and repeated with reasonable consistency between one area and another, the floristic composition of each individual might differ slightly from one habitat to another. However, the floristic composition of these communities is very simple. In addition to the dominant species, there are only limited numbers of annual and perennial associate species present in the majority of the sands. Some of these associate species might exist in more than one community. The main characteristic of the plant communities of the sand-sea habitats is that they are distributed in and occupy limited territories. This distribution is due to the terrain and orientation of individual sand dunes, as well as the degree of consolidation of the sand and its movement. Further, in places that are located near to permanent settlements and Bedouin camps, as well as along car tracks and caravan roads, the more favoured and grazed species are less abundant than the least utilised and grazed ones. In general, *shrub* communities are mainly found in the sand dune bodies or around their margins. Interdune depressions and hollows are often covered mainly with a *shrubless* community, of mainly annual vegetation. The absence of shrub communities in these areas favourable for annual species might be the result of competition pressure for water and nutrients exerted by *annual vegetation*. Human intervention might also have caused the absence of shrub communities from these areas. Many places in the research area have taken their names from the species that are or used to be dominant in or around them.

The main plant community groups observed in the northern and central sand seas are as follows:

1. Communities of the true sand sea habitats;
2. Communities of non-dune or shallow sand habitats;
3. 'Vegetationless' areas.

and the individual plant communities associated with each is as follows:

Communities of the sand dune habitats

The sand dune bodies are dominated by five plant communities that occupy the very deep sand. These five plant communities are: 1. *Calligonum comosum* community; 2. *Haloxylon persicum* community; 3. *Artemisia monosperma* community; 4. *Scrophularia hypericifolia* community and 5. *Stipagrostis drarii* community. Plant species of these communities, which are highly specialised as extreme psammophytes, are able to withstand the harsh environmental conditions, particularly the movement of sand and temporary burial by it, as well as the scarcity of water. One of the main characteristics of the plant species of these communities is that they are perennial shrubs or semi-shrubs and tall grasses. All have long roots that anchor them into the sand and enable them to draw water from deep sand layers. These communities can exist also in the shallow hollows between individual dunes and the lower levels of the dunes, but in general, human pressure (cutting and animal grazing) has forced these communities back away from these latter regions.

Communities of non-dune or shallow sand habitats:

Communities of non-dune or shallow sand habitats are common in interdunal sand-filled areas and gaps between the individual dunes and include the following communities: 6. The *Haloxylon salicornicum* community; 7. The *Rhazya stricta* community; 8. The *Rhanterium epapposum community*; 9. The *Seidlizia rosmarinus* community; and 10. A shrubless community.

In addition to the interdunal sand-filled areas and gaps between the dunes, the *Haloxylon salicornicum* and *Rhazya stricta* communities also occur in, and colonise the low stabilised and semi-stabilised sand dunes. They also favour disturbed ground in abandoned farms and oases, or along the fringes of those which are still used. They proliferate where the original vegetation cover has been severely degraded and disturbed through grazing pressure or cutting shrubs for firewood, especially around settlements, the outskirts of towns and along roadsides, as well as desert tracks.

During the rainy season, the interdune areas and hollows in the sand dunes of central and northern Saudi Arabia support a wide variety of both annual vegetation types and some perennial species that behave as ephemerals, and have an episodic growth strategy. These annuals and perennials can not endure and survive in the severe environmental conditions that prevail for most of the year. When undisturbed, this shrubless community forms a luxurious green carpet or lawn between the higher surrounding dunes during the rainy season. The composition and abundance of species in this community depends on seasonal changes, mainly in the time and volume of rainfall. Species composition appears to be relatively uniformly distributed from one area to another. Human disturbance, such as heavy grazing, trampling by animals and traffic vibration might effect the density and composition of this vegetation. Species diversity in these areas is relatively high, with some 50 or more species per 1,000 m^2 in some areas. Common and important species are *Plantago boissieri, Lotus halophilus, Silene villosa, Erodium laciniatum, Hippocrepis bicontorta, Polycarpaea repens, Cyperus conglomeratus, Monsonia nivea, Neurada procumbens, Eremobium aegyptiacum, Cutandia memphitica, Moltkiopsis ciliata, Dipcadi serotinum* and *Allium ampeloprasum.*

Vegetationless areas

When individual sand dunes, or parts of them, are continuously mobile, there is little or no opportunity for plant cover to develop, because of the severe effects of sand movements and moisture deficiency. Consequently, the sand seas also are characterised by vegetationless areas limited to the active small dunes, as well as to the crests and upper parts of the inactive and fixed seif, longitudinal and transverse dunes. The arms of most star dunes are also devoid of vegetation. Human activities might also be a significant factor in the absence of vegetation cover from some parts of the area.

Ar Rub' Al Khali

Two perennial communities have been identified (by Mandaville, 1990) in Ar Rub' Al Khali, with *in toto* a limited number of 36 species present. One is a Hath saltbush shrubland, dominated by the endemic *Cornulaca arabica*; and the other is a shrubland consisting largely of *Calligonum crinitum*. There are however large areas empty of vegetation in this region.

Plant species of sand dunes yield a wide range of products. Utilisation of these plants has varied from one area to another, depending on the economic level of the inhabitants. In some cases, vegetative resources might be exploited sufficiently to satisfy limited local demands only, but at other times, raw materials might be exported to other surrounding areas. The varied uses of plant species can be classified into the following main groups: food and beverages for human consumption; industrial materials; medicinal resources; fodder for animals and fuel.

As a result of these activities the vegetation cover of the sand dunes has been degraded to some extent by over-cultivation, overgrazing, wood cutting, recreation and associated activities, all of which are detailed in the preceding chapters. In consequence we feel there is a growing need to protect sand-sea vegetation before it deteriorates further, as it is a means for encouraging environmental stability in the region.

Indeed, we feel that conservation measures undertaken in Saudi Arabia should be extended to all sand sea areas to preserve their vegetation cover, thereby limiting and minimising their possible future encroachment on nearby farms, oases and towns. In order to facilitate this heightened public awareness concerning the protection of the natural environment, also is needed. Such enhanced awareness can be achieved through all forms of communications, including media, schools and mosques.

Successful conservation measures have been adopted over a very long period of time by people and authorities in Unayzah city and Ath Thameeriyah town to protect adjacent *Haloxylon persicum* shrubs, and these measures have given the local people a source of pride and a better understanding of the advantages of protecting the natural environment. Similar practices elsewhere can be carried out under the supervision of the National Commission for Wildlife Conservation and Development (NCWCD) and the Ministry of the Interior.

Cutting specific conservation measures might include the prevention of the enforcement of laws which prohibit this. Local citizens could be encouraged to report people who violate these laws. However, the collection of completely dead shrubs, especially for firewood and charcoal should be allowed, for the sole domestic use of the Bedouins. Moreover, alternative sources of good quality firewood and charcoal should be provided in the wood markets in the cities, towns and villages in and around the sand seas. The easy availability of such firewood will hopefully satisfy the need of people for firewood that they would otherwise obtain locally from *Calligonum comosum* and *Haloxylon persicum* shrubs. Grazing should also be prohibited in the sand sea areas, at least for a limited period. This measure would allow existing vegetation to recover from the intense overgrazing and trampling by animals that can take place, particularly during the rainy season. Supplementary feed from other sources such as grain agriculture should be provided for large herds to limit their damaging effects on the natural vegetation, in cases when a complete ban on grazing is not possible. Additionally, the movement of cars and off-road traffic should be limited during the rainy season when the natural vegetation is in the growth stage. Such a preventative measure would limit vegetation destruction and allow the vegetation cover to establish itself and return to its normal density. Further, reforestation and the planting of compatible trees and shrubs that are well adapted to the sand seas should be encouraged. Successful attempts of this kind can be seen along roads and around oases and farms in the northern and central sand seas, where *Calligonum comosum* and *Haloxylon persicum*

which play a dominant role in the ecology and economy of the area are the main focus of attention.

The sand-seas of Saudi Arabia are a unique environmental area, on a world scale. It is intended that this work will present at least the beginnings of an understanding of some aspects of their physical, biological and geographical features which is essential, if their main features are to be preserved for future generations.

PLATES

PLATES

PLATE 1

Temporary lakes within the sand seas. These are shallow, formed in a depression between surrounding dunes, after heavy rain storms mainly in winter. Then a cool climate and moderate evaporation help to maintain such pools for a few days. These are the only sources of water for the Bedouin, apart from the few wells, and water transported from nearby towns.

PLATE 2

Acacia-dominated wadi vegetation. Located near Al-Artaweya in central Saudi Arabia, supporting mainly **Acacia ehrenbergia.**

PLATE 3

Root systems of perennial plants. (A) **Haloxylon persicum**; (B) **Tamarix aphylla**; (C) **Calligonum comosum**, extending to more than 30m.

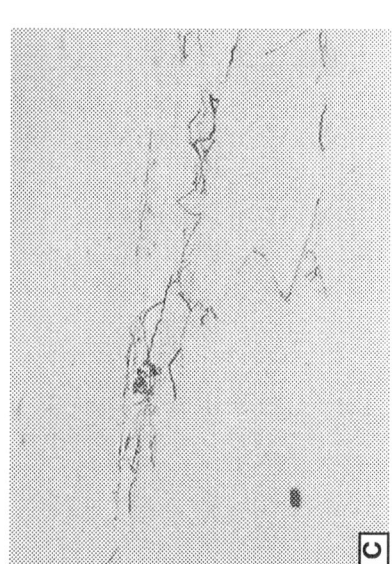

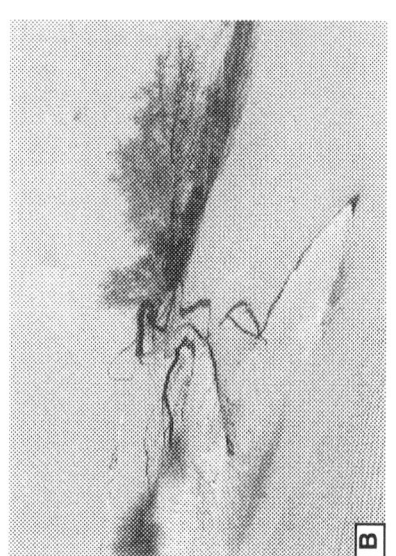

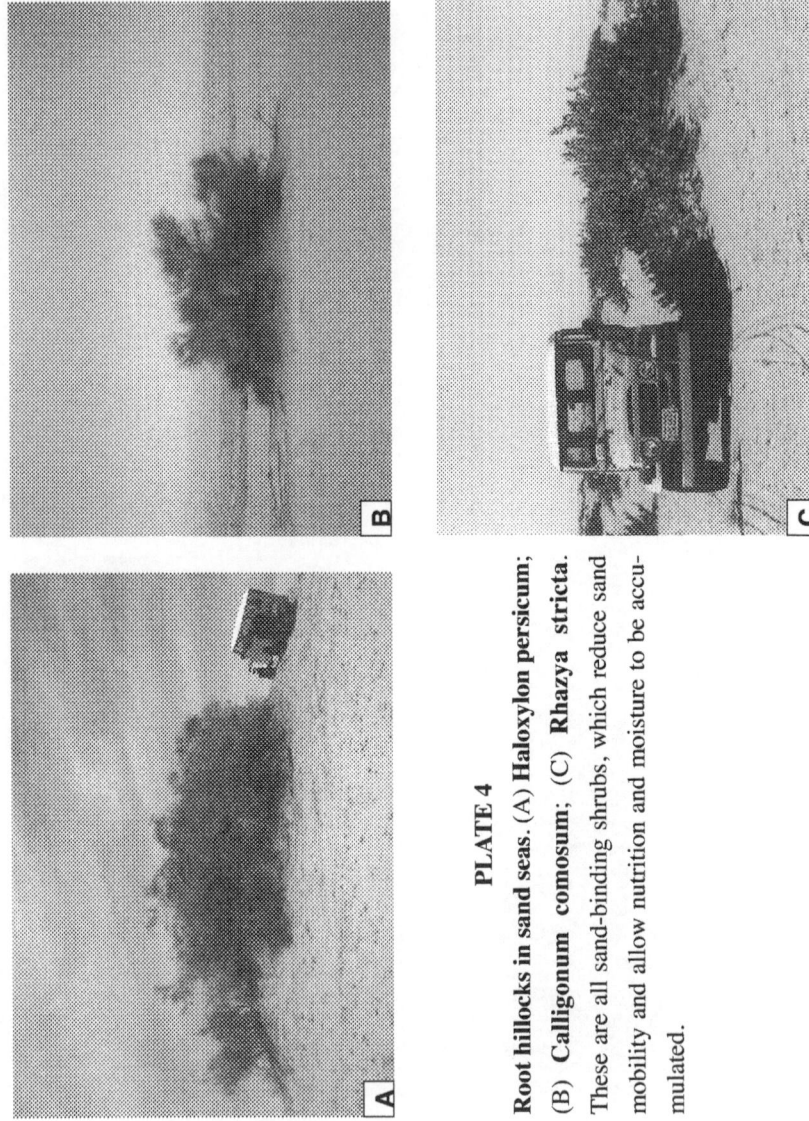

PLATE 4

Root hillocks in sand seas. (A) **Haloxylon persicum;**
(B) **Calligonum comosum;** (C) **Rhazya stricta.**
These are all sand-binding shrubs, which reduce sand
mobility and allow nutrition and moisture to be accumulated.

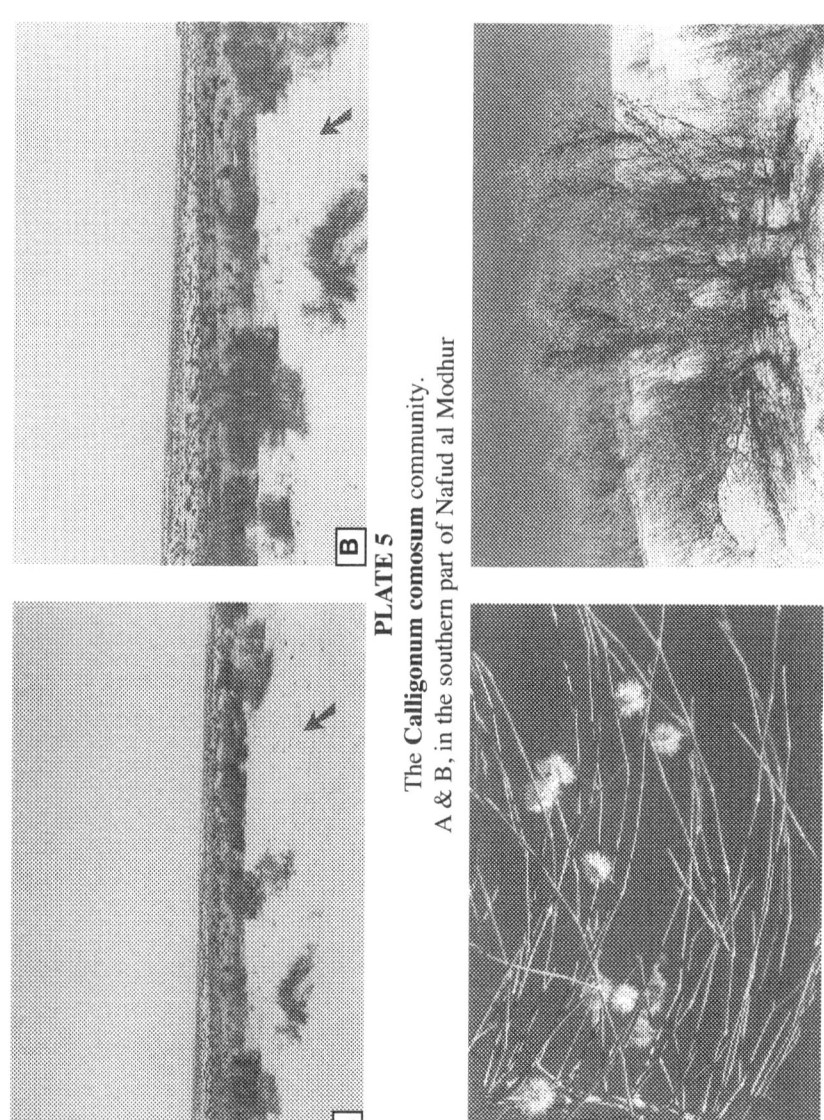

PLATE 5

The **Calligonum comosum** community.
A & B, in the southern part of Nafud al Modhur

PLATE 6

The **Haloxylon persicum** community.

(A) A general view, in An Nafud near Hail; (B)in Al Mufaft dunes west of Unayzah in central Saudi Arabia

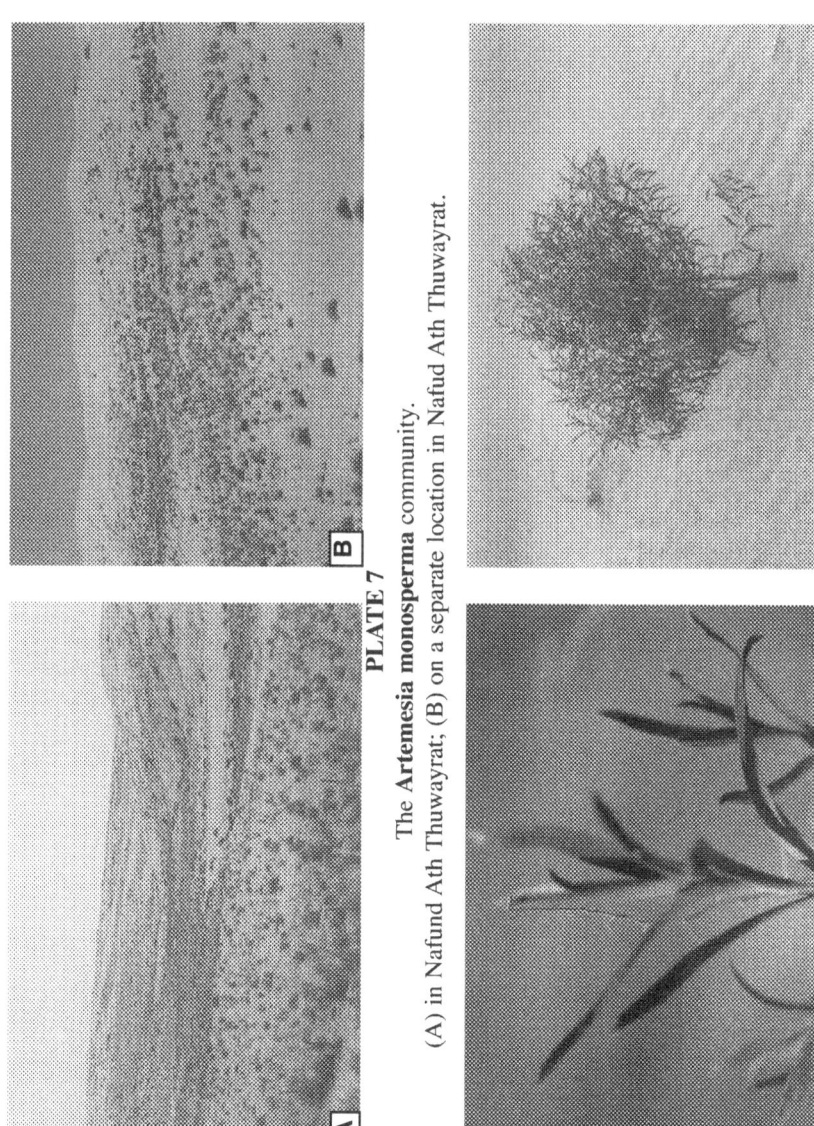

PLATE 7

The **Artemesia monosperma** community.

(A) in Nafund Ath Thuwayrat; (B) on a separate location in Nafud Ath Thuwayrat.

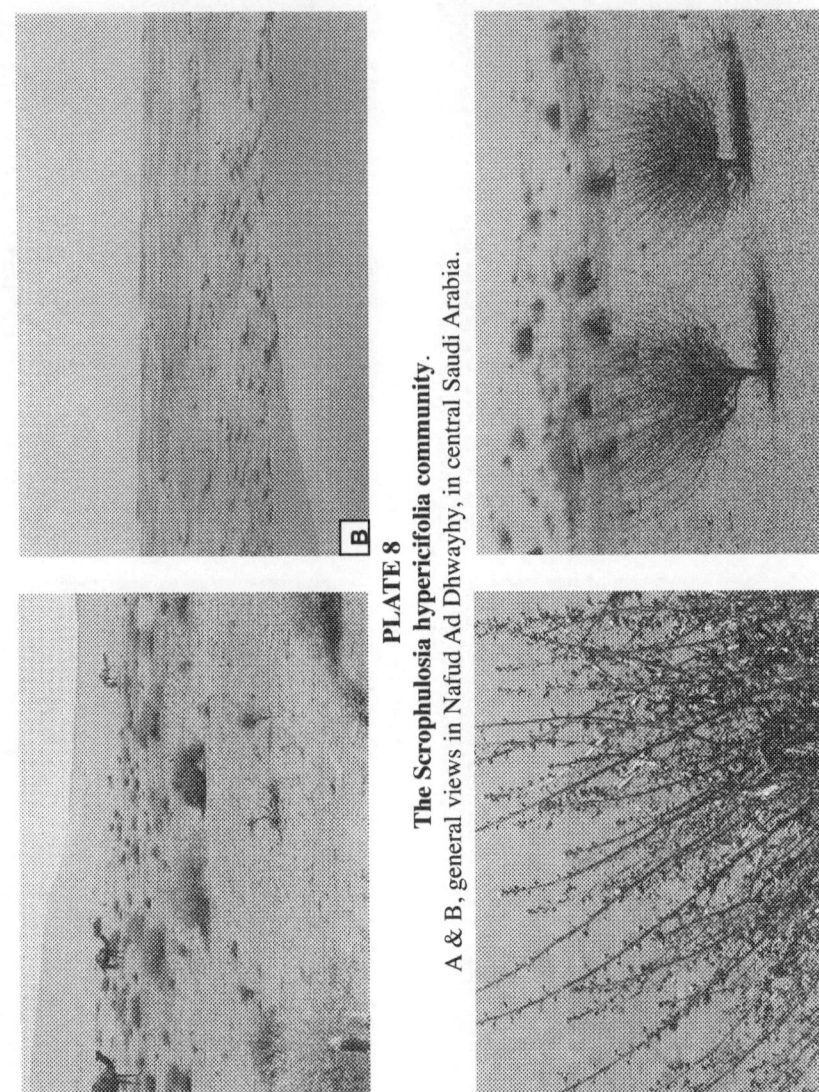

PLATE 8

The Scrophulosia hypericifolia community.

A & B, general views in Nafud Ad Dhwayhy, in central Saudi Arabia.

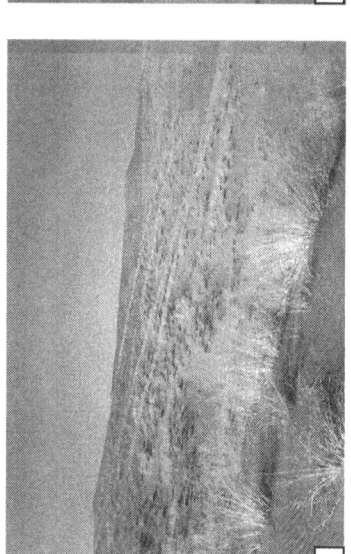

PLATE 9

The Stipagrostis drarii community.

(A) on the sand dunes of Ad Dahna, central Saudi Arabia. Note the barren crest of ever-moving sand.
(B) in Nafud Thuwayrat, central Saudi Arabia.

Vegetation of the Sand Seas of Saudi Arabia

PLATE 10

The **Haloxylon salicornicum** community.

Top photo: a low interdune depression in nafud as Sirr near, nafud Ath Thameriya. Lower photo: an abandoned farm, Nefud Ath Thuwayrat.

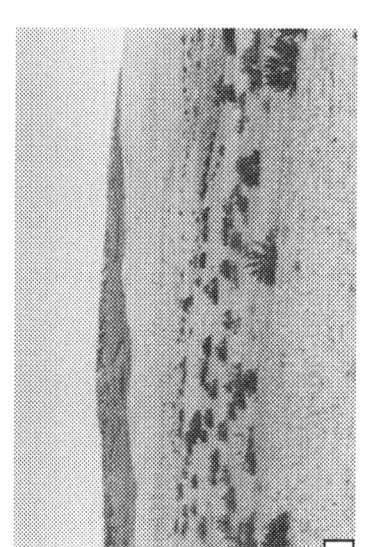

PLATE 11

The **Rhazya stricta** community.
(A) on the fringes of Nafud Qunayfithah; (B) on Erg Ath Thimam (ad Dahna).
The presence of this community is an indication of range degradation.

PLATE 12

The Rhanterium eppaposum community

PLATE 13
The Seidlitzia rosmarinus community. (A) in a sabkhah depression, with
a very restricted community; (B) a pure stand, in Nafud as Sirr.

PLATE 14

Horwoodia dicksoniae.

This striking, largele decumbent endemic is typical of many of the northern shrubless communities in Saudi Arabia. Its full range is not yet mapped, but it is rare south of latitude
24° N.

PLATE 15

Luxuriant green carpets of ephemeral growth.

Vegetation of the Sand Seas of Saudi Arabia

PLATE 16

(A) Ath Thuwayr oasis in Nafud Ath Thuwayrat. Note the absence of the natural vegetation cover from the sand dunes that surround the oasis as a result of overgrazing and woodcutting. (B) Large quantities of firewood of Calligonum Comosum and Haloxylon persicum are brought to the wood markets in towns and cities all over Saudi Arabia to meet high demand.

PLATE 17

Grazing systems. (A) flock of sheep grazing in a stand of ephemerals at the edge of An Nafud near Al Jawf. (B) A herd of camels feeding on mixed vegetation. Note the camels that are feeding on remnants of the shrubs of Calligonum Comosum.

FIGURES

Based on: Harrison, 1964, and Ministry of Communications, 1986

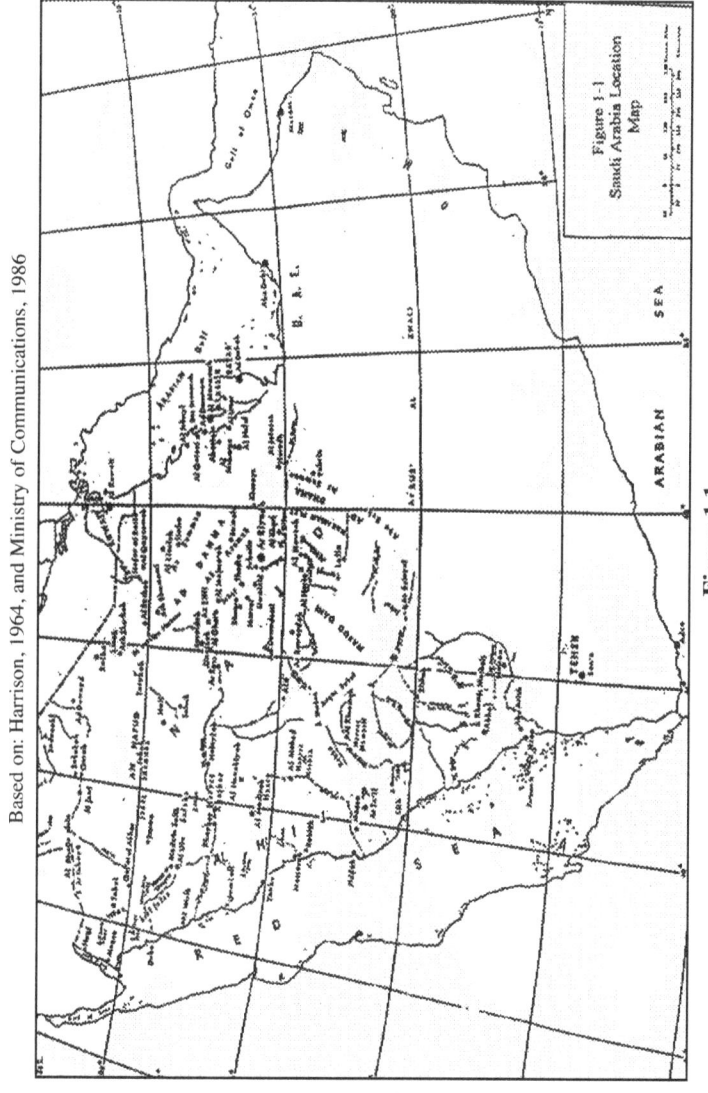

Figure 1.1

Location of Saudi Arabia in its region

Figure 2.1

A structural geological map of the Arabian peninsula

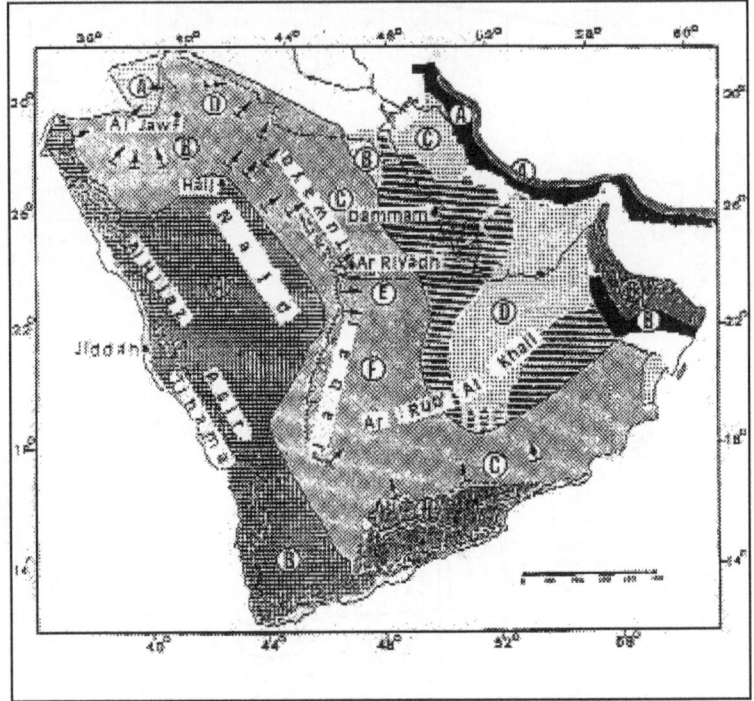

Based on: Powers et al., 1966 and Blume 1976:30

Figure 2.2
Generalised geological map of the Arabian peninsula

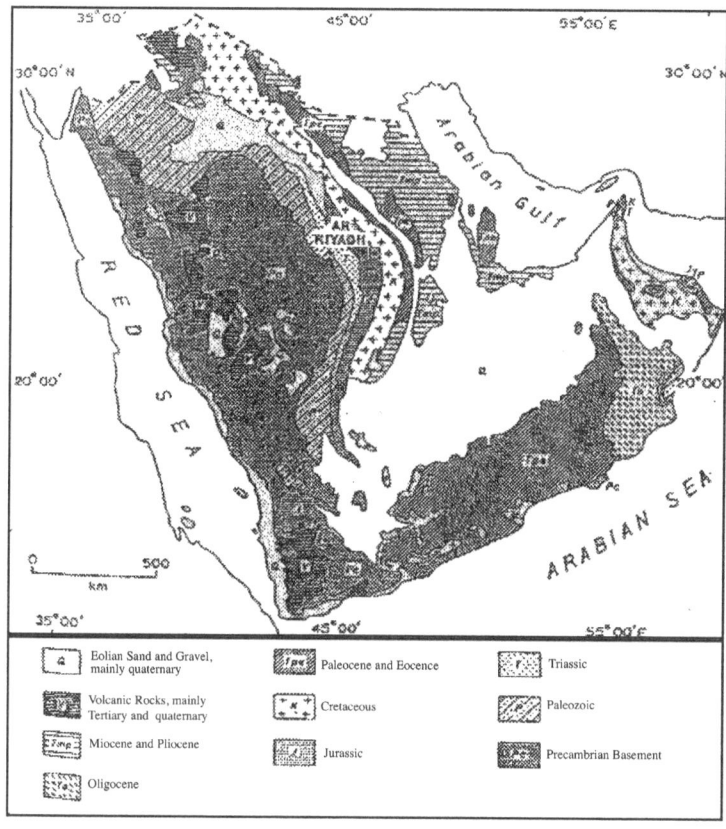

Source: Chapman, 1978:7

Figure 2.3

General geomorphological map of the Arabian peninsula

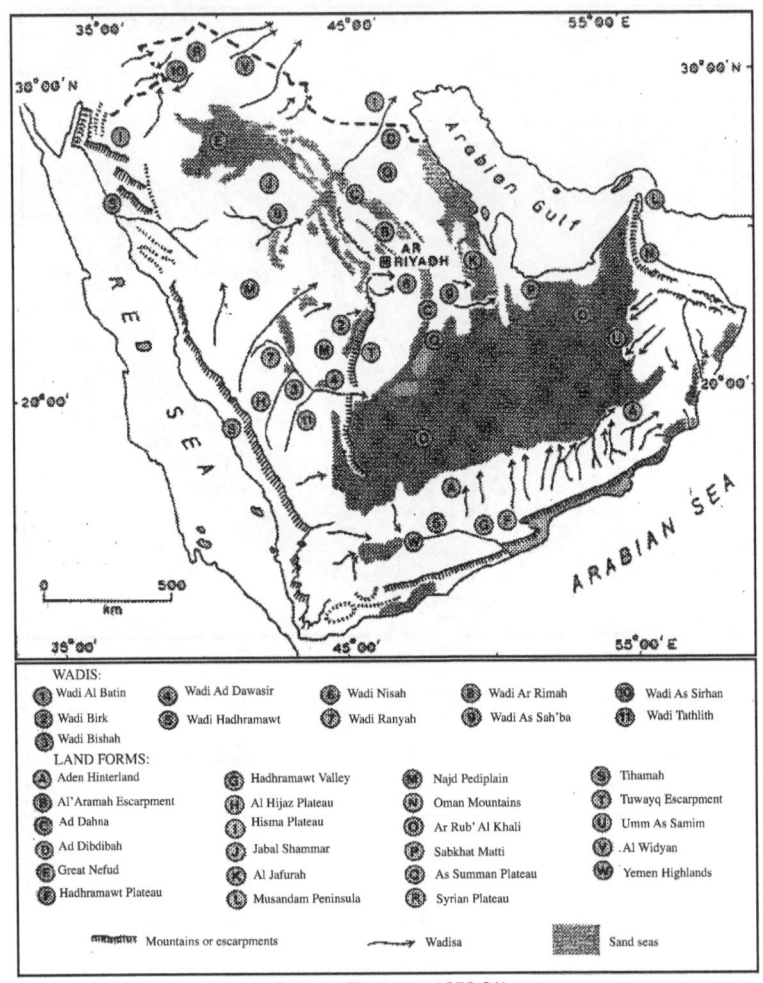

(Source: Chapman, 1978:21)

Figure 2.4a

The distribution of Saudi Arabia's sand seas

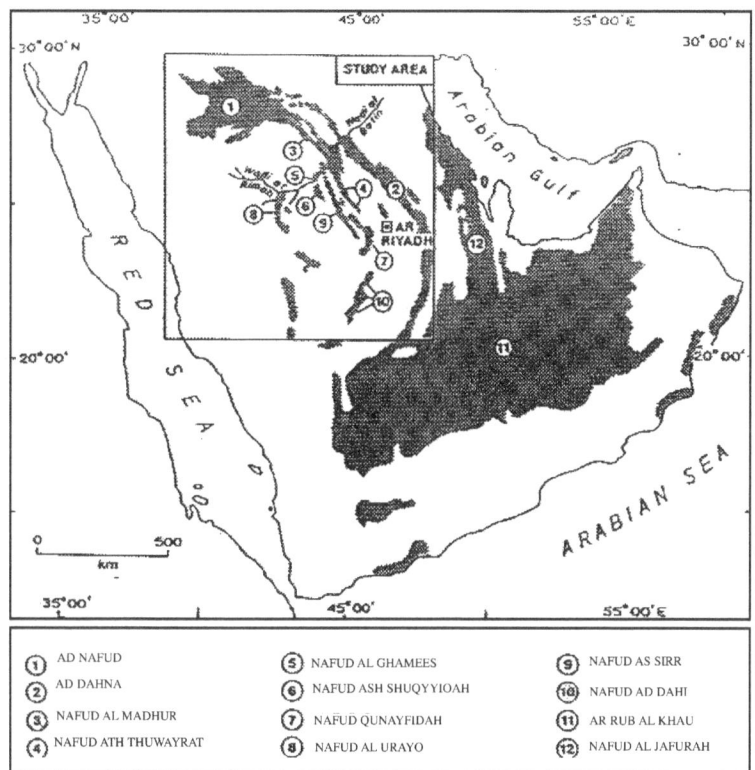

①	AD NAFUD	⑤	NAFUD AL GHAMEES	⑨	NAFUD AS SIRR
②	AD DAHNA	⑥	NAFUD ASH SHUQYYIOAH	⑩	NAFUD AD DAHI
③	NAFUD AL MADHUR	⑦	NAFUD QUNAYFIDAH	⑪	AR RUB AL KHAU
④	NAFUD ATH THUWAYRAT	⑧	NAFUD AL URAYO	⑫	NAFUD AL JAFURAH

Figure 2.4b
The distribution of Saudi Arabia's sand seas
Map showing sample sites

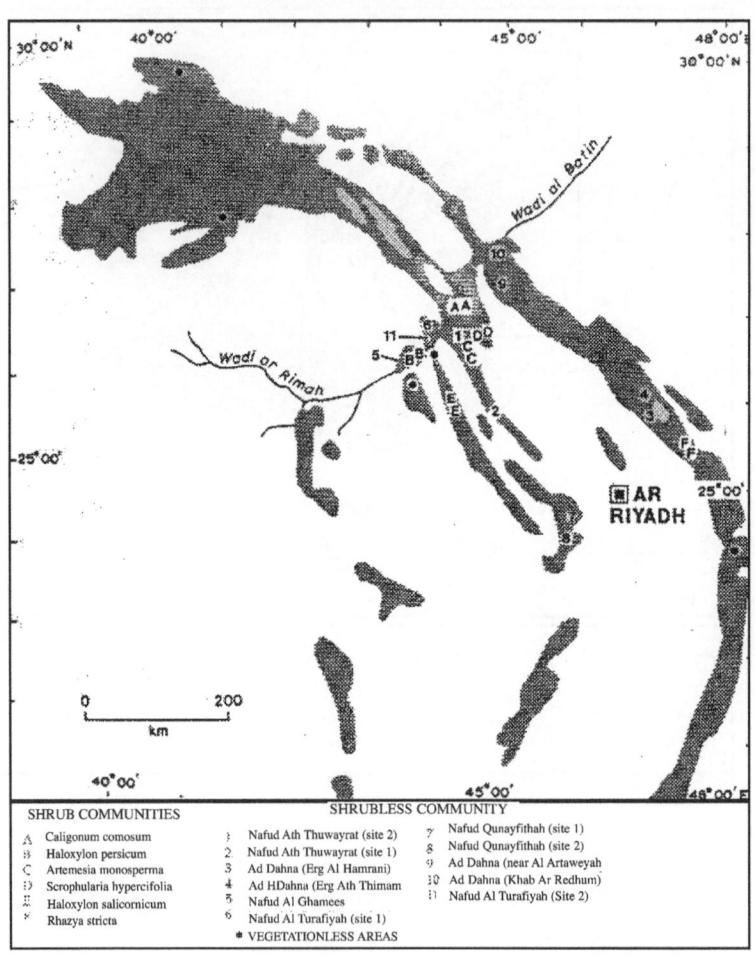

SHRUB COMMUNITIES		SHRUBLESS COMMUNITY	
A Caligonum comosum	1 Nafud Ath Thuwayrat (site 2)	7 Nafud Qunayfithah (site 1)	
B Haloxylon persicum	2 Nafud Ath Thuwayrat (site 1)	8 Nafud Qunayfithah (site 2)	
C Artemesia monosperma	3 Ad Dahna (Erg Al Hamrani)	9 Ad Dahna (near Al Artaweyah	
D Scrophularia hypercifolia	4 Ad HDahna (Erg Ath Thimam	10 Ad Dahna (Khab Ar Redhum)	
E Haloxylon salicornicum	5 Nafud Al Ghamees	11 Nafud Al Turafiyah (Site 2)	
X Rhazya stricta	6 Nafud Al Turafiyah (site 1)		
	● VEGETATIONLESS AREAS		

Figure 2.5

Major sand-dune forms in the sand seas of Saudi Arabia

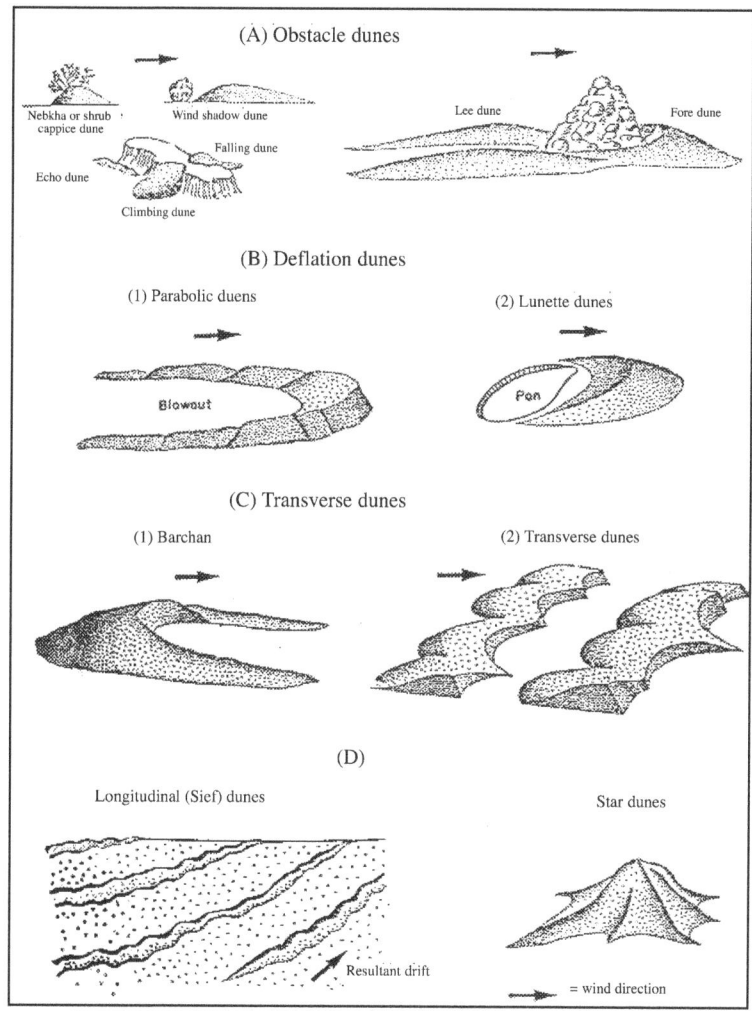

(Source: Modified after Watson, 1990:55, Cooke and Warren, 1973:288-289)

Vegetation of the Sand Seas of Saudi Arabia

Figure 2.7

Major dune types in Saudi Arabian Sand Seas

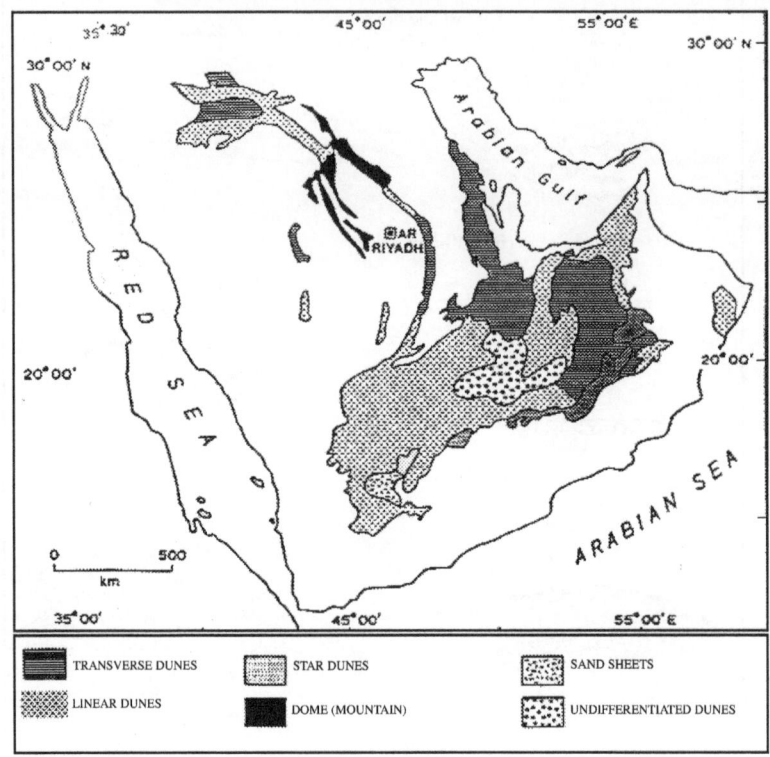

(Source: compiled from: Al-Hinai, 1989:70 and Fairbridge, 1968:977)

Figure 2.8

Diurnal temperature variations in surface sand layers, Ad Dahna

Date	Time	Average of Sand Temperature °C*	Average of Air Temperature °C	Note
25/2/93	9.55 A.M.	13	16	
15/3/93	8.15	16	15	
20/3/93	11.20	23	24.6	
24/3/93	10	13	19.6	
25/3/93	8.20	17	24.7	
2/4/93	9.15	16	21.1	
8/4/93	9	19	21.3	Temperatures are recorded during rain
10/4/93	11.45	23.5	26	
10/4/93	4.30	26.5	27	
14/4/93	2.45	30.5	33.5	
16/4/93	10.20	22.5	27.9	
16/4/93	5.30	29.5	34	
17/4/93	4.30	29.5	27	
19/4/93	8.20	23	30.2	
10/4/93	4	31	38	
25/4/93	8.50	21	21	Temperatures are recorded during rain
24/4/93	10.50	25	32.8	
30/4/93	4.30	22.5	26.9	
2/5/93	1	35	45	
20/5/93	7	28	32.8	
21/5/93	7.20	29	31	
9/6/93	12 noon	31	43	
10/6/93	6.30	22	25.2	
10/6/93	1.30	33	45	

* The measurements of sand temperatures were made by inserting a soil thermometer in the sand after removing the top sand layer. The process was repeated each time many times for each sites and the thermometer readings resulted in the average.

Figure 2.9

Temperature-depth profiles in the dune sand of Ad Dahna

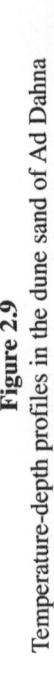

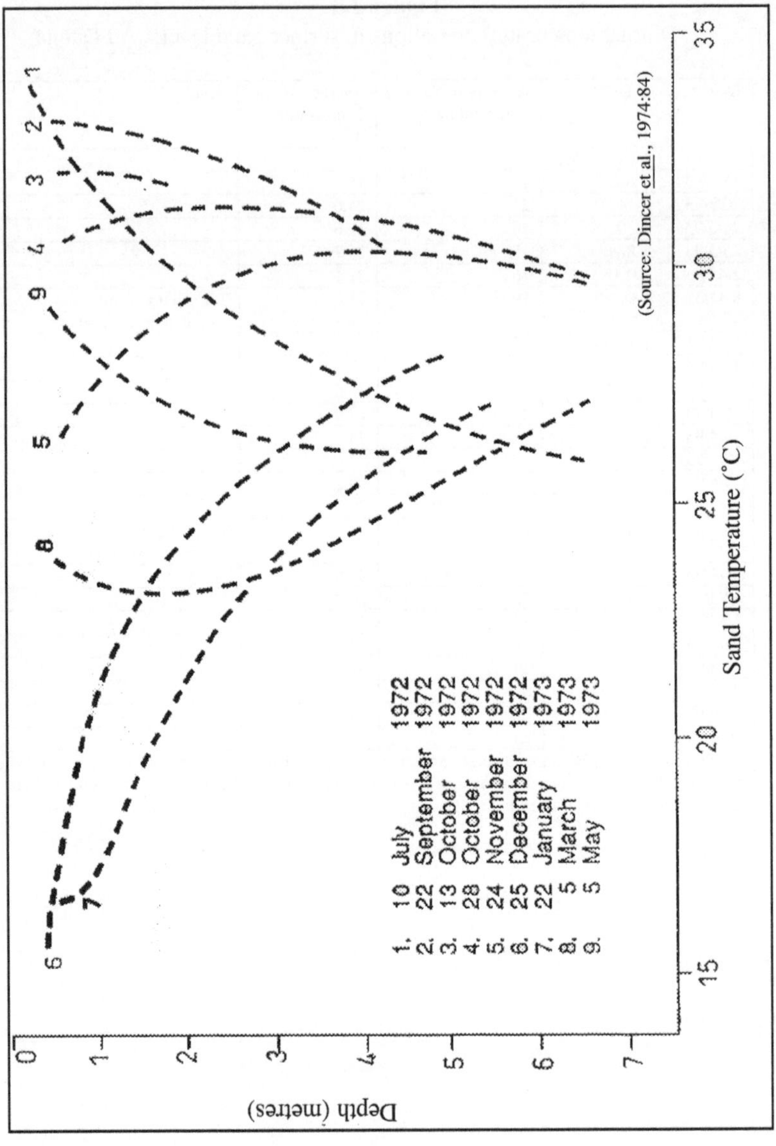

1. 10 July   1972
2. 22 September 1972
3. 13 October   1972
4. 28 October   1972
5. 24 November   1972
6. 25 December   1972
7. 22 January   1973
8. 5   March   1973
9. 5   May   1973

Depth (metres)

Sand Temperature (°C)

(Source: Dincer et al., 1974:84)

Figure 2.10

Meteorological stations located near to the sand seas

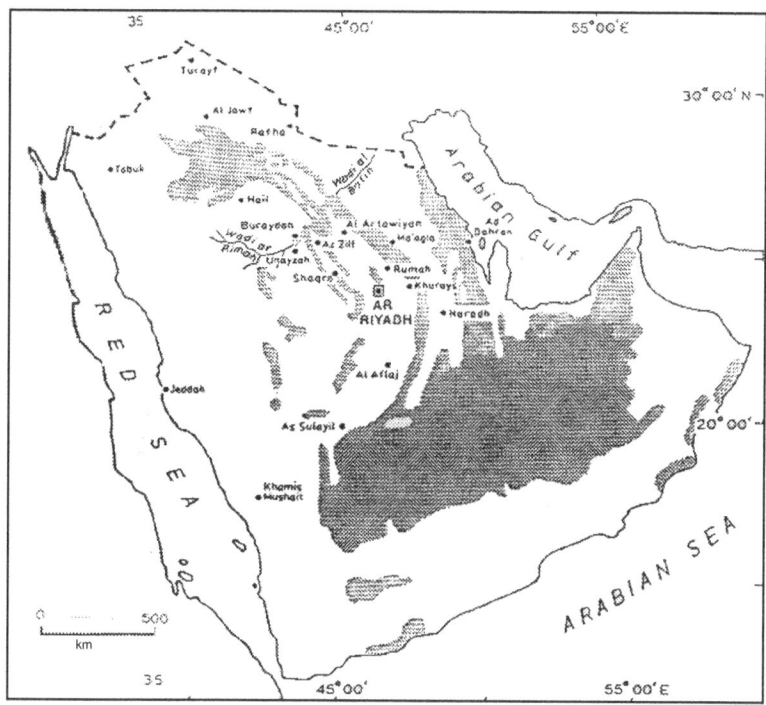

Vegetation of the Sand Seas of Saudi Arabia

Figure 2.11

Prevailing wind directions in the Arabian peninsula

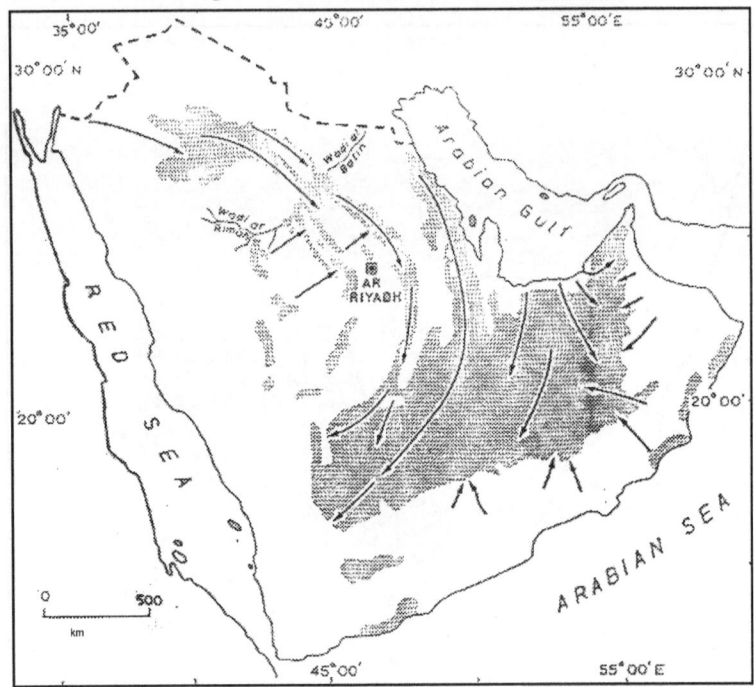

(Based on: Fairbridge, 1968:976)

Figure 2.12

Sand-drift potential in the Arabian peninsula

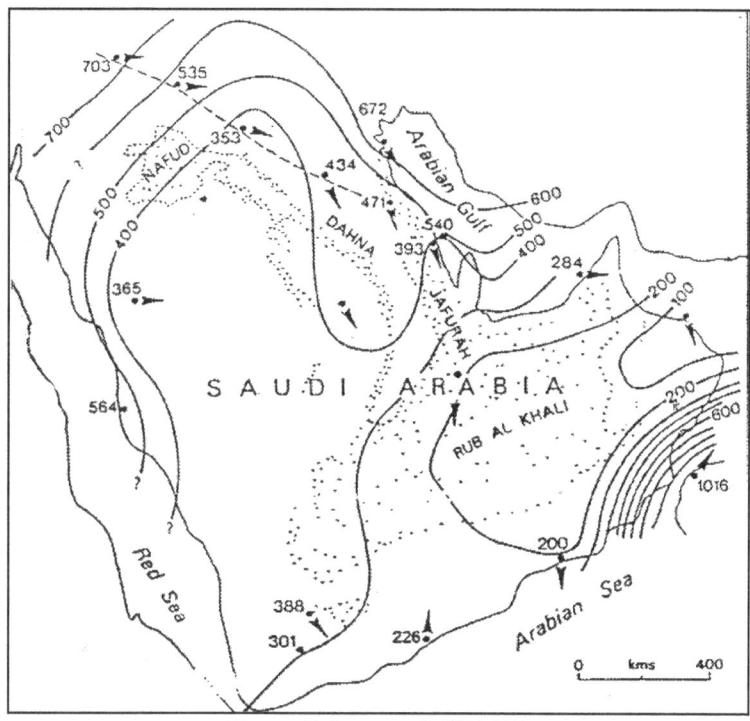

(Source: Fryberger et al., 1984:414)

Figure 3.2

Schematic cross-section in northern and central Saudi Arabia of the
different landscape and vegetation units during the late Pleistocene

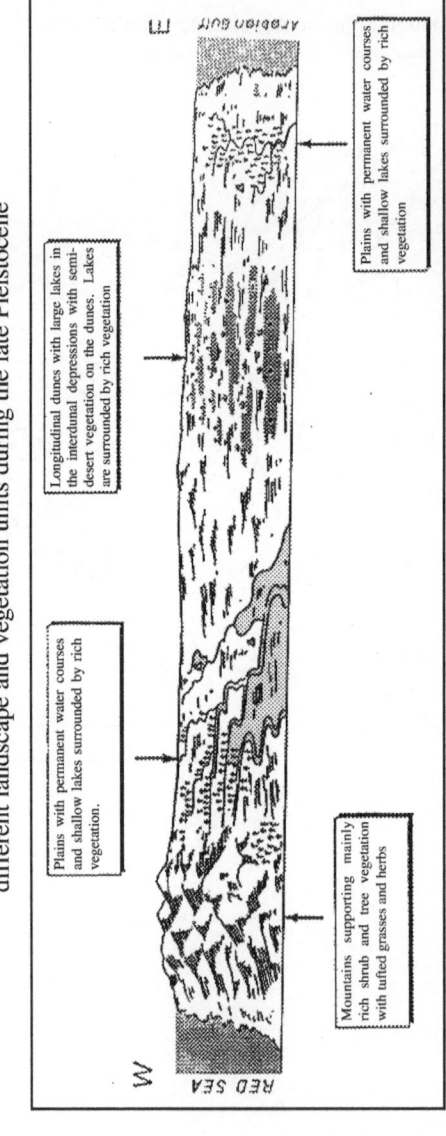

(Based on: Schulz and Whitney, 1986: 175-190; Anton, 1984:275-296; McClure, 1978:252-63; Whitney et al., 1983:1-39 and Garrard et al., 1981:137-148)

Figure 3.3

Schematic cross-section in northern and central Saudi Arabia
of the different landscape and vegetation units during the Holocene.

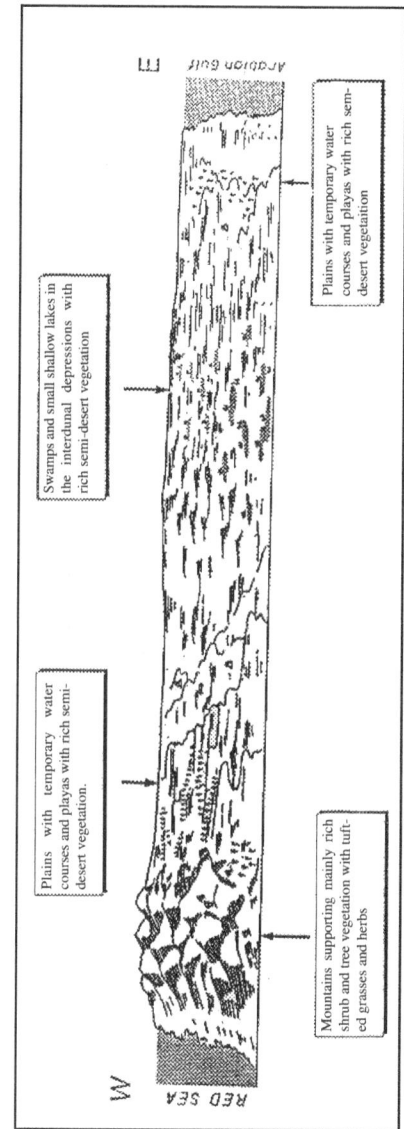

Figure 3.4

Schematic cross-section in northern and central Saudi Arabia
of the different landscape and vegetation units today

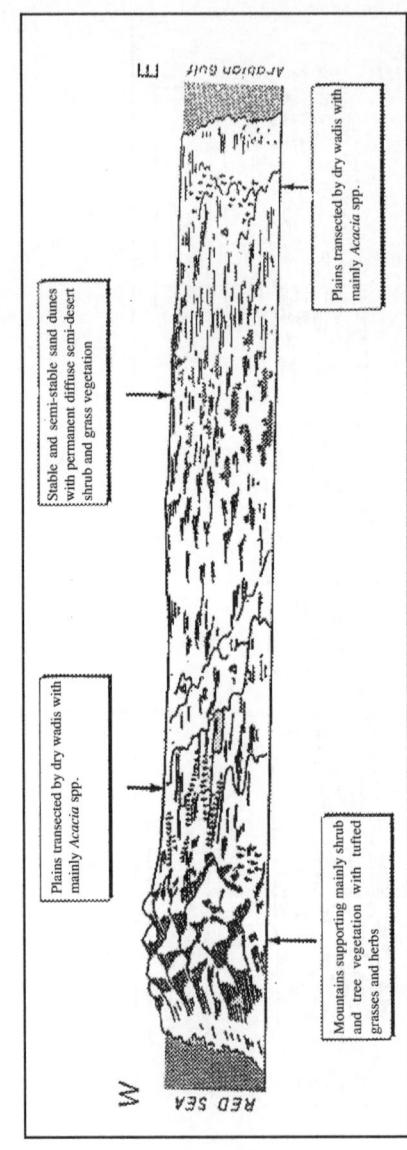

Figure 3.8

A new division of the floristic regions of the Middle East
and neighbouring regions (after Takhtajan, 1986)

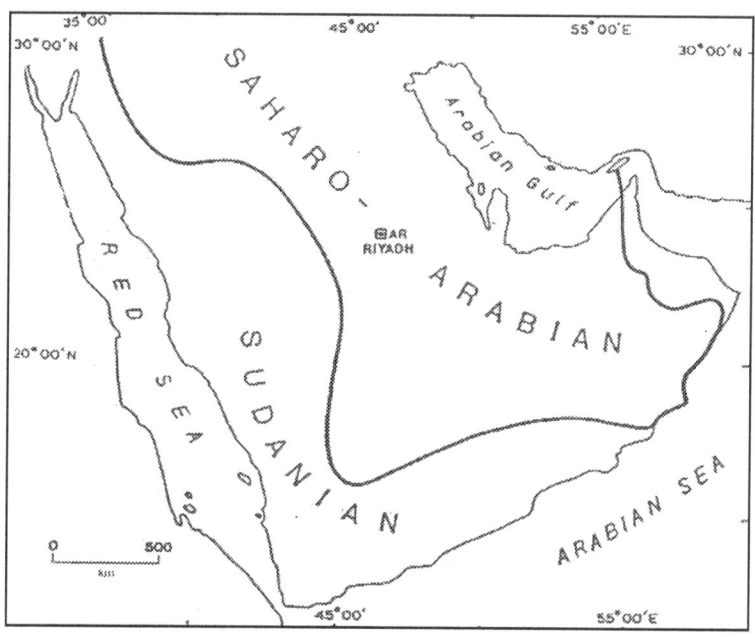

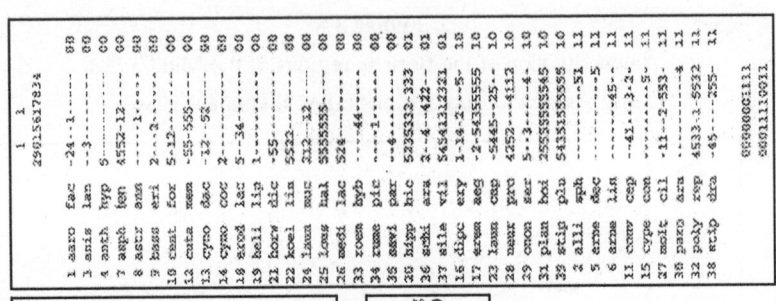

```
                      1  1
                      29015617834
 1  aaro  fac   -24--1-----   00
 3  anis  lan   --3--------   00
 4  anth  hyp   5----------   00
 7  asph  ken   4552-12----   00
 8  astr  anz   ----1------   00
 9  bass  eri   2--3--...--   00
10  cent  fox   5-12-------   00
12  cuta  xem   -55-555----   00
13  cyno  dac   -12--52----   00
14  cyno  coc   2----------   00
18  exod  lac   5-34-------   00
19  heli  lip   1----------   00
21  horw  dic   -55--------   00
22  koel  lin   5532-------   00
24  laxa  mic   212--12----   00
25  loaa  hal   5555555----   00
26  medi  lac   524--------   00
33  roem  hyb   -44--------   00
34  ruma  pic   ---1-------   00
35  saav  par   ---4------0   00
20  hipp  hic   5235332-333   01
36  achi  ara   2--4--422--   01
37  sile  vil   5454123231    01
16  disc  exy   1-14-2--5-    10
17  erem  aeg   -2-54355555   10
23  laga  cap   -5445--25--   10
28  nasr  pro   4252--4112    10
29  onon  ser   5--3-----4    10
31  plan  boi   255555555545  10
39  stip  plu   54315355555   10
 2  alli  sph   ------51      11
 5  arne  dec   -------5      11
 6  arne  lin   ------45-     11
11  carv  cep   -41---3-2-    11
15  cype  cxm   -------5-     11
27  molt  cil   -11--2-553-   11
30  paro  ara   --------4     11
32  poly  rop   4533-1-5532   11
38  stip  dra   -45---255-    11

                      0000000G1111
                      00011110011
```

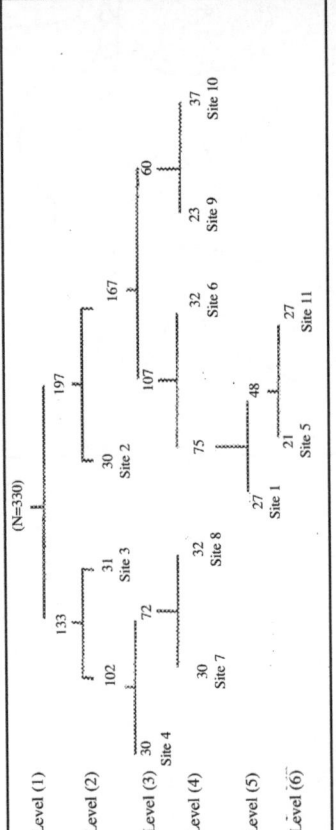

(N=330)

Level (1)

Level (2)

Level (3)

Level (4)

Level (5)

Level (6)

133

197

102   31
       Site 3

30
Site 4   72

30
Site 7

32
Site 8

30   167

107

75

32
Site 6

60

23
Site 9

37
Site 10

27
Site 1   48

21
Site 5   27
Site 11

Site Locations:

1- Nafud Ath Thuwayrat (site 1) 2- Nafud Ath Thuwayrat (site 2) 3- Ad Dahna (Erg Al Hamrani) 4- Ad Dahna (Erg Thimam) 5- Nafud Al Ghamees 6- Nafud At Turafiyah (site 1) 7- Nafud Qunayfithah (site 1) 8- Nafud Qunayfithah (site 2) 9- Ad Dahna (Khab Ar Redhum) 10- Ad Dahna (near Al Artaweyah) 11- Nafud At Turafiyah (site 2)

Figure 5.4

TWINSPAN hierarchy of the shrubless community of floristic data.

TWINSPAN table of the analysis of the shrubless community (right)

Figure 5.5

CANOCO ordination diagram of the shrubless community

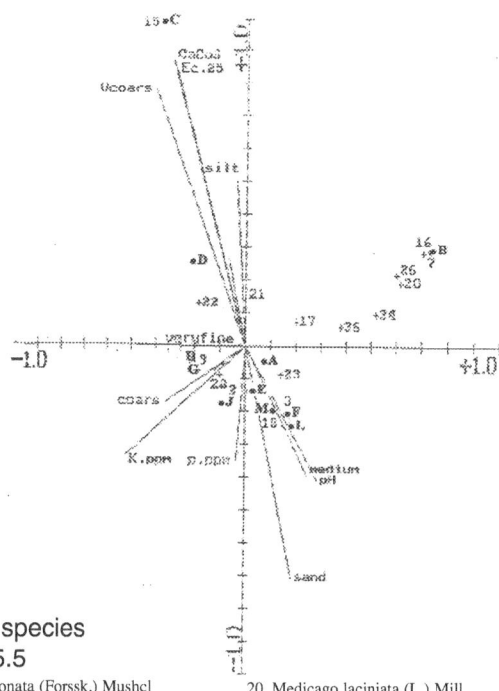

Names of species
in Figure 5.5

1. Launaea mucronata (Forssk.) Mushcl
2. Launaea capitata (Spreng,) Dandy
3. Asphodelus tenuifolius
4. Allium sphaerocephalum L.
5. Roemeria hybrida (L.) DC
6. Anisosciadium lanatum Boiss
7. Anthemis hypericifolia Boiss
8. Savigyna parviflora (Del.) Webb
9. Moltkiopsis ciliata (Forssk.) Johnst.
10. Bassia eriophora (schrad.) Aschers
11. Dipcadi erythraeum Webb and Berth
12. Astragalus annularis Forssk
13. Helianthemum lippii
14. Arnebia decumbens (Vent.) Coss. and Kral
15. Arnebia linearifolia DC
16. Ononis serrata Forssk
17. Hippocrepis bicontorta Lois
18. Horwoodia dicksoniae
19. Polycarpaea repens (Forskk.) Asch. and
Schweinf

20. Medicago laciniata (L.) Mill
21. Stipagrostis plumosa L.
22. Eremobium aegyptiacum (Spreng.) Schweinf and Asch.
23. Lotus halaphilus Boiss. Et Sprun
24. Aaronsohnia factorovskyi War. and Eig.
25. Schismus arabicus Nees
26. Erodium laciniatum (Cav.) willd
27. Convolvulus cephalopodus Boiss
28. Plantago boissieri Hausskn. and Bornm
29. Neurada procumbens L.
30. Stipagrostis drarii Taeckh
31. Cutandia memphitica (spreng.) Benth
32. Paronychia arabica (L) D.C.
33. Cynomorium coccineum L.
34. Koelpinia linearis Pall
35. Cyperus conglomeratus Rottb agg
36. Silene villosa Forssk
37. Cynodon dactylon (L.) Pers
38. Centropodia forsskalii (vahl) Cope
39. Rumex pictus Forssk

TABLES

List of Tables

Table 2.1: Average sand and air temperature in the northern sand seas from February to June

Date	Time	Average of sand Temperature °C	Average of Air Temperature °C	Note
25/02/93	9.55 am	13	16	
15/03/93	8.15 am	16	15	
20/03/93	11.20 am	23	24.6	
24/03/93	10.00 am	13	19.6	
24/03/93	9.50 am	17	24.7	
25/03/93	8.20 am	17	21.5	
02/04/93	9.15 am	16	21.1	
03/04/93	9.00 am	19	21.3	Temperatures are recorded during rain
10/04/93	11.45 am	23.5	26	
10/04/93	4.30 pm	26.5	27	
14/04/93	2.45 pm	30.5	33.5	
16/04/93	10.20 am	22.5	27.9	
16/04/93	5.30 pm	29.5	34	
17/04/93	4.30 pm	29.5	27	
19/04/93	8.20 am	23	30.2	
20/04/96	4.00 am	31	38	
25/04/93	8.50 am	21	21	Temperatures are recorded during rain
29/04/93	10.50 am	25	32.8	
30/04/93	4.30 am	22.5	26.9	
02/05/93	1.00 pm	35	45	
20/05/93	7.00 am	28	32.8	
21/05/93	7.20 am	29	31	
09/06/93	12 noon	31	43	
10/06/93	6.30 am	22	25.2	
10/06/93	1.30 pm	33	45	

Source: Authors' research

Table 2.2: Moisture content of sand at Nafud Al Ghamees, ath Thuwayrat, Adh Dhwayhe and Ad Dahna, February to May, 1992

Sample No.	Site	Depth cm	% Soil Moisture Oven Dried basis	Location of Sample
1-a	Al Ghamees	< 15	3.76	
1-b	=	> 30	4.35	Vegetated rounded crest
1-c	=	> 60	2.41	
2-a	=		2.66	
2-b	=		4.83	Inter-dune vegetated surface
2-c	=		3.13	
3-a	=		3.44	
3-b	=		4.32	Thinly vegetated inter-dune surface
3-c	=		6.12	
4-a	Ath Thuwayrat	< 15	1.54	
4-b	=	> 30	2.17	Stabilised vegetated dune flank
4-c	=	> 60	2.60	
5-a	=		0.52	
5-b	=		1.57	Inter-dune vegetated surface
5-c	=		2.70	
6-a	=		1.42	
6-b	=		2.18	Rounded thinly vegetated surface
6-c	=		2.25	
7-a	Ad Dhwayhe	< 15	0.34	
7-b	=	> 30	1.31	Inter-dune vegetated surface
7-c	=	> 60	3.82	
8-a	=		0.36	
8-b	=		0.83	Sharp bare crest
8-c	=		0.89	
9-a	=		0.31	
9-b	=		1.21	Inter-dune vegetated surface
9-c	=		3.46	
10-a	Ad Dahna	< 15	0.23	
10-b	=	> 30	0.53	Rounded thinly vegetated crest
10-c	=	> 60	0.98	
11-a	=		0.17	
11-b	=		0.72	Vegetated dune flank
11-c	=		1.11	

Source: Authors' research

Table 2.3: Percentage of organic matter in sand samples at three different levels

Sample No	Depth (cm)	O.M. %	Depth (cm)	O.M. %	Depth (cm)	O.M. %
1	> 10	.10	>20	.21	> 30	.21
2		.12		.17		.19
3		.31		.29		.17
4		.12		.12		.17
5		.17		.21		.22
6		.17		.21		.17
7		.08		.11		.08
8		.18		.08		.08
9		.05		.09		.08
10		.07		.05		.05
11		.03		.07		.08
12		.27		.15		.18
13		.11		.10		.08

Source: Authors' research

Table 2.4: Average mean monthly solar radiation in cal/cm^2 at selected meteorological stations

Station+	Jan	Feb	Mar	Apr	May	Jun	Jul	Aug	Sep	Oct	Nov	Dec	Years of coverage
Al Aflaj	347	395	439	479	507	542	530	511	498	448	393	327	81-91
Al Jawl	257	323	383	431	465	501	502	465	416	332	265	227	81-90
Ar Riyadh	290	353	394	434	451	518	498	473	443	376	309	259	81-91
As Sulayyil	219	246	261	292	297	351	342	314	302	271	225	206	81-91
Az Zilfi	231	311	359	403	442	505	503	464	412	334	245	210	81-91
Hail	284	346	403	450	485	541	531	501	436	352	300	261	81-91
Khurais	255	301	317	360	397	421	419	389	369	319	269	246	81-91
Ma'aqla	185	238	295	375	402	430	438	371	331	254	190	164	81-91
Shaqra	297	365	406	444	480	545	534	502	461	392	313	274	81-91
Unayzah	277	364	421	482	515	584	558	530	465	380	302	249	81-91

+ Locations of meteorological stations are shown in Figure 2.10

Primary data for this table has been compiled from the following sources:-

1 - Ministry of Finance and National Economy, *The Annual Statistical Books* for years 1966-1992.
2 - Ministry of Agriculture and Water *Summary of Climatological Data.*
3 - Ministry of Defence and Aviation, Meteorology and Environmental Protection Administration, Climate Directorate (Surface Annual Climatological reports)

Vegetation of the Sand Seas of Saudi Arabia

Table 2.5: Average mean monthly maximum temperatures in degrees centigade at selected meteorological stations

Station+	Jan	Feb	Mar	Apr	May	Jun	Jul	Aug	Sep	Oct	Nov	Dec	Years of coverage
Ad Dhahran*	21	22	26	32	38	41	43	42	40	35	29	23	66-93
Al Jawf	15	18	22	28	34	36	39	39	37	31	23	17	77-93
Al Qaseem	18	21	26	31	37	40	42	41	40	34	26	21	67-93
Al Aflaj	23	25	30	36	41	44	45	45	42	37	31	25	85-93
Ar Riyadh	20	23	27	32	38	41	42	42	39	34	27	22	66-93
As Sulayyil	25	27	32	36	40	43	44	43	41	35	30	25	81-89
Az Zilfi	19	22	26	32	39	42	43	42	41	35	28	22	81-93
Hail	16	19	23	28	33	37	38	38	37	31	23	18	66-93
Jeddah*	28	29	30	34	36	37	38	38	36	36	32	29	66-93
Khamees*	20	22	26	33	39	42	44	43	40	34	27	21	81-93
Khurais	19	22	25	33	38	42	44	44	41	36	28	20	85-92
Ma'aqla	20	21	24	25	28	31	30	31	30	26	24	22	67-93
Shaqra	21	23	27	33	39	43	44	43	41	35	28	23	81-94
Tabouk*	18	20	25	30	34	38	38	38	37	32	25	19	66-93
Turaif*	13	15	19	26	31	34	37	37	35	28	21	15	75-93
Unayzah	19	22	26	32	38	41	43	42	40	34	27	21	81-93

+ Locations of meteorological stations are shown in Figure 2.10
* Stations far from the research area but included for comparison

Data sources:-

1 - Ministry of Finance and National Economy, *The Annual Statistical Books* for years 1966-1992.
2 - Ministry of Agriculture and Water *Summary of Climatological Data*.
3 - Ministry of Defence and Aviation, Meteorology and Environmental Protection Administration, Climate Directorate (Surface Annual Climatological reports)

Table 2.6: Average mean monthly minimum temperatures in degrees centigade at selected meteorological stations

Station+	Jan	Feb	Mar	Apr	May	Jun	Jul	Aug	Sep	Oct	Nov	Dec	Years of coverage
Ad Dhahran*	10	11	15	19	24	27	28	28	25	21	17	12	66-93
Al Jawf	3	5	8	14	17	22	23	24	21	16	9	5	77-93
Al Qaseem	6	8	12	17	22	24	24	25	22	28	12	8	67-93
Al Aflaj	7	9	13	18	22	24	25	25	22	17	12	8	85-93
Ar Riyadh	8	10	14	19	24	26	28	27	24	20	14	10	66-93
As Sulayyil	8	11	16	19	24	25	27	26	22	17	14	9	81-89
Az Zilfi	6	7	12	16	22	24	24	24	21	16	12	8	81-93
Hail	4	6	9	15	20	22	23	22	20	15	10	6	66-93
Jeddah*	19	18	20	22	24	25	26	27	26	24	22	20	66-93
Khamees*	7	9	11	12	14	16	17	17	14	11	8	7	67-93
Khurais	7	8	13	19	23	25	27	26	22	17	13	8	81-93
Ma'aqla	7	10	15	21	24	26	28	28	25	22	17	11	85-92
Shaqra	7	8	13	17	22	24	24	25	21	17	13	8	81-94
Tabouk*	3	5	13	9	18	21	22	22	20	15	9	5	66-93
Turaif*	2	3	7	12	16	17	21	21	18	13	7	3	75-93
Unayzah	6	7	12	17	22	22	24	25	22	18	13	8	81-93

+ Locations of meteorological stations are shown in Figure 2.10
* Stations far from the research area but included for comparison

Data sources:-

1 - Ministry of Finance and National Economy, *The Annual Statistical Books* for years 1966-1992.
2 - Ministry of Agriculture and Water *Summary of Climatological Data.*
3 - Ministry of Defence and Aviation, Meteorology and Environmental Protection Administration, Climate Directorate (Surface Annual Climatological reports)

Vegetation of the Sand Seas of Saudi Arabia

Table 2.7: Average mean monthly rainfall in millimetres at selected meteorological stations

Station+	Jan	Feb	Mar	Apr	May	Jun	Jul	Aug	Sep	Oct	Nov	Dec	Years of coverage
Ad Dhahran*	15.2	14.0	21.5	10.7	3.1	0.3	0.0	0.5	0.1	2.3	4.3	14.4	60-93
Al Artaweyah	23.1	17.3	24.5	25.9	4.7	0.8	0.2	0.0	0.0	2.8	31.1	18.9	66-80
Al Jawf	7.3	5.3	5.7	8.0	2.5	0.7	0.0	0.1	0.0	5.4	4.5	5.8	76-93
Al Qaseem	18.9	12.9	27.1	27.9	16.3	0.0	0.0	0.0	0.0	3.2	17.6	13.1	66-93
Al Aflaj	2.2	9.2	12.1	13.3	3.3	0.0	0.6	0.1	0.5	0.0	0.1	3.4	85-93
Ar Riyadh	10.8	7.2	21.7	28.1	7.4	0.1	0.3	0.7	0.0	1.1	4.6	12.2	61-93
As Sulayyil	1.5	3.1	7.4	13.7	1.3	0.0	0.7	3.1	1.9	0.1	0.0	2.7	78-93
Az Zilfi	19.4	11.4	23.3	27.0	12.3	0.0	0.0	0.0	0.0	4.4	17.3	14.1	66-93
Hail	14.7	12.7	17.6	23.1	8.9	0.2	0.0	0.0	0.1	8.4	27.8	5.8	66-93
Haradh	7.9	11.7	12.0	9.6	1.2	0.0	0.2	0.0	0.0	0.2	0.7	3.5	67-92
Jeddah*	14.4	5.8	1.2	2.3	4.6	0.0	0.1	0.0	0.0	0.3	14.8	12.1	62-93
Khamees*	10.8	14.4	36.5	29.8	30.5	6.2	21.3	26.4	4.7	3.6	9.0	4.2	67-93
Khurais	13.5	14.1	18.2	15.6	1.6	0.1	0.2	0.2	0.0	1.2	2.5	7.6	67-93
Ma'aqla	14.3	12.6	20.5	14.9	1.8	0.2	0.2	0.0	0.0	4.4	8.0	15.0	67-93
Rumah	17.4	9.8	22.7	22.6	1.9	0.1	0.9	0.0	0.0	1.2	1.2	9.3	67-94
Shaqra	15.1	10.7	28.7	27.6	8.4	0.0	0.8	0.0	0.5	0.5	14.5	15.0	66-94
Tabouk*	12.7	3.2	6.7	3.3	2.9	0.0	0.0	0.7	0.0	4.7	7.4	7.7	65-93
Turaif*	16.6	18.3	15.3	11.5	7.0	0.1	0.0	0.0	0.4	9.4	9.0	11.8	72-93
Unayzah	17.9	10.5	19.1	24.2	13.3	1.5	0.0	0.3	0.0	7.2	12.3	11.0	75-93

+ Locations of meteorological stations are shown in Figure 2.10
* Stations far from the research area but included for comparison

Data sources:-

1 - Ministry of Finance and National Economy, *The Annual Statistical Books* for years 1966-1992.
2 - Ministry of Agriculture and Water *Summary of Climatological Data*.
3 - Ministry of Defence and Aviation, Meteorology and Environmental Protection Administration, Climate Directorate (Surface Annual Climatological reports)

Table 2.8: Average mean monthly relative humidities at selected meteorological stations

Station+	Jan	Feb	Mar	Apr	May	Jun	Jul	Aug	Sep	Oct	Nov	Dec	Years of coverage
Al Jawf	66	45	37	39	20	16	15	17	18	29	46	56	76-93
Ar'ar*	60	51	43	34	25	20	19	20	21	34	50	60	77-93
Ad Dhahran*	69	67	61	52	41	34	38	44	52	60	63	67	60-93
Hail	57	49	42	37	26	18	17	17	19	29	50	55	66-93
Jeddah*	59	59	59	57	57	59	55	59	66	66	63	60	59-93
Khamees*	63	61	57	51	46	35	40	47	34	40	55	63	67-93
Khurais	46	41	37	33	26	19	20	22	26	33	45	53	81-91
Ma'aqla	55	50	51	41	30	25	24	27	30	26	48	58	81-91
Al Qaseem	54	45	38	35	25	15	13	14	15	23	41	52	67-93
Ar Riyadh	49	41	38	34	23	13	13	14	16	23	38	47	59-93
Shaqra	50	46	44	40	28	17	14	16	18	26	38	50	81-91
As Sulayyil	39	35	36	29	17	10	10	13	13	17	32	44	81-89
Tabouk*	49	41	35	28	24	22	22	25	27	32	44	50	66-93
Turaif*	67	59	49	38	30	18	27	28	28	38	54	65	75-93
Unayzah	44	35	35	29	18	12	11	12	14	20	35	42	81-92
Az Zilfi	54	45	44	40	24	15	15	16	17	26	41	49	81-92
Al Aflaj	52	47	42	41	32	26	24	23	25	31	42	48	85-93

+ Locations of meteorological stations are shown in Figure 2.10
* Stations far from the research area but included for comparison

Data sources:-

1 - Ministry of Finance and National Economy, *The Annual Statistical Books* for years 1966-1992.
2 - Ministry of Agriculture and Water *Summary of Climatological Data.*
3 - Ministry of Defence and Aviation, Meteorology and Environmental Protection Administration, Climate Directorate (Surface Annual Climatological reports)

Table 2.9: Average mean monthly evaporation from "class A" pans in millimetres at selected meteorological stations

Station+	Jan	Feb	Mar	Apr	May	Jun	Jul	Aug	Sep	Oct	Nov	Dec	Total	Years of coverage
Al Aflaj	147	171	247	286	351	368	373	362	342	293	196	141	3276	81-91
Al Jawf	78	112	181	242	296	311	348	316	305	215	115	76	2596	81-90
Ar Riyadh	107	128	182	212	271	342	356	348	298	227	131	99	2703	81-91
As Sulayyil	194	206	330	355	446	469	520	477	422	306	244	189	4156	81-91
Az Zilfi	96	142	213	281	419	470	485	449	361	266	162	103	3448	81-91
Hail	158	181	258	314	434	479	483	470	378	320	195	147	3819	81-91
Khurais	238	268	352	410	540	585	513	579	439	392	296	287	4900	84-91
Ma'aqla	157	180	272	337	488	643	665	621	493	364	228	162	4611	81-91
Shaqra	155	203	250	322	440	513	489	504	468	355	230	165	4093	81-91
Unayzah	134	173	244	314	406	436	414	427	319	288	204	135	3494	81-91

+ Locations of meteorological stations are shown in Figure 2.10

Data sources:-

1 - Ministry of Finance and National Economy, *The Annual Statistical Books* for years 1966-1992.
2 - Ministry of Agriculture and Water *Summary of Climatological Data.*
3 - Ministry of Defence and Aviation, Meteorology and Environmental Protection Administration, Climate Directorate (Surface Annual Climatological reports)

Table 2.10: Average mean monthly windspeed in knots at selected meteorological stations

Station+	Jan	Feb	Mar	Apr	May	Jun	Jul	Aug	Sep	Oct	Nov	Dec	Years of coverage
Ad Dhahran*	8	8	9	8	9	11	10	9	7	7	7	8	66-93
Al Jawf	7	8	9	8	8	8	8	7	6	6	6	6	76-93
Al Qaseem	5	6	7	7	7	6	6	5	5	5	5	5	67-93
Ar Riyadh	6	7	8	7	7	8	8	7	6	4	5	6	66-93
Ar'ar*	6	7	8	8	7	8	8	6	5	6	5	5	77-93
As Sulayyil	7	8	8	8	7	6	6	6	6	5	6	7	81-89
Hail	6	7	7	7	7	6	6	5	5	6	6	6	66-93
Jeddah*	7	8	8	8	8	8	8	7	7	5	7	7	77-93
Rafhah	7	8	9	9	9	8	8	7	6	7	4	7	66-93
Tabouk*	5	5	7	7	6	6	6	6	5	5	6	4	75-93
Turaif*	7	8	8	9	8	8	8	7	6	6	6	7	66-93

+ Locations of meteorological stations are shown in Figure 2.10
* Stations far from the research area but included for comparison

Data sources:-

1 - Ministry of Finance and National Economy, *The Annual Statistical Books* for years 1966-1992.
2 - Ministry of Agriculture and Water *Summary of Climatological Data*.
3 - Ministry of Defence and Aviation, Meteorology and Environmental Protection Administration, Climate Directorate (Surface Annual Climatological reports)

Table 3.1: Permo-Carboniferous fossil plants identified from the Unayzah Formation

True Ferns and/or seed Ferns:
        Pecopteris candolleana Brongniart
        Pecopteris cyathea (Schlotheim)
        Pecopteris unita Brongniart

Seed Ferns:
        cf. Danaeites emersoni Lesquereux
        cf. Lescuropteris moori (Lesquereux) Schimper
        Neuropteris ovata Hoffman

Sphenopsida:
        Annularia stellata (Schlotheim)
        Calamites sp.

Lycopsida:
        cf. Knoria (xylem core of Lepidodendron sp. after decay of outer tissues)

Cordates:
        Cordaites sp.

Source: Al Laboun, 1987

Table 3.2: The Jabal Midra ash-Shamali and Ad Dabityah fauna of fossil mammals from the Miocene.

A. The Jabal Mira ash-Shamali fauna

Pisces	Lates sp. teeth and bone
Chelonia	Scute fragments
Mammalia	Lagomorpha cheek teeth
	Rodentia

        cf. Cricetodon atlasi cheek teeth Dipodidae
            indet cheek teeth
Artiodactyla
        Bovidae medium-sized species cheek teeth and bone fragments
small species teeth and bone fragments

B. The ad Dabityah fauna

Pisces	Teeth and bones	Perissodactyla
Chelonia	Scutes	Rhinocerotoidea
Crocodilia	Teeth	Brachypotherium sp.
Mammalia		Metapodials and teeth
Primates		Aceratherium/Dicerorhinus

   Hominiodea idet. 2 species   Jaws, cheek teeth, ankle
      Teeth and maxilla   bones
      fragment

Carnivora idet.   Phalange   Artiodactyla
                             Suidae idet. 2 species
Rodentia idet.   Anisociadium   Cheek teeth
Hyracoidea   Tragulidae
     cf. Pachyhyrax championi   DorcAntherium cf. libiensis
        Upper and lower cheek   Jaws and cheek teeth
        teeth   Giraffidae idet.
Proboscidea   Cannon-bone
    platybelodon sp.   Bovidae
        Cheek teeth and tusks   Boselaphinae idet.
                             Lower cheek and
                             horn-core

Source: Hamilton *et al*, 1978

Table 3.3: Preliminary palynological analysis of Miocene pollen collected from Al-Sarrar, eastern Saudi Arabia.

Number of pollen counted: 100	%		%
Gramineae	10	Compositae Artemisia	1
Cyperaceae	1	Plantaceae Plantago	15
Chenopodiaceae/Amaranthaceae	53	Cupressaceae Junipenis	3
Compositae tubuliflorae	8	cf. Vitaceae	1
Compositae liguliflorae	1	cf. Umbelliferae	1
Indeterminate	6		

Source: Thomas *et al*, 1981

Table 3.4: Provisional list of the lower Miocene invertebrate fauna from Al-Sarrar, eastern Saudi Arabia

Madreporaria
　　Poritidae
　　　　Porites sp.

Mollusca
　　Bivalvia
　　　　Crassatellidae
　　　　　　cf. *Indocrassatella*
　　　　　　cf. *Salaputium*
　　　　Anomiidae
　　　　Lucinidae
　　　　　　Gonimyrtea sp.
pseudonilotica
　　　　Ungulinidae
　　　　　　cf. *Diplodonta*
　　　　Veneridae
　　　　　　cf. *Clementia*
　　　　Ostreidae
　　　　　　Ostrea latimarginata

Gasteropoda
　　　　Turritella sp.
　　　　Scaidae indet.
　　　　Naticidae indet.
　　　　Strombus sp.
　　　　Galeodes sp.
　　　　Conus sp.

Arthropoda
　　　　Crustacea
　　　　Thalassiniodea
　　　　　　Callianassa

　　　　　　Callianassa sp.
　　　　Portunoidea
　　　　　　Scylla michelini

Source: Thomas *et al, 1981*

Table 3.5: Provisional list of the lower Miocene vertebrtates fauna from Al-Sarrar, eastern Saudi Arabia.

Selahii

Hemigaleidae
Hemipristis serra
Carcharhinidae
Carcharhinus aff. *priscus*
Carcharhinus aff. *plumbeus*
Galeocerdo cf. *aduncus*
Scoliodon sp.
Negaprion eurybathrodon

Sphyrnidae
Sphyrna sp.
Dasyatidae
Dasyatis sp.
Myliobatidae
Myliobatis sp.
Aetobatus arcuatus
Rhinopteridae
Rhinoptera

Pisces

Mormyridae
Hyperopisus sp
Cyprinidae
Barbus sp.
Labeo sp.
Clariidae
Heterobranchus sp.
Clarias sp.
Centropomidae
Lates sp.
Sphyraenidae
Sphyraena sp
Sparidae indet

Amphibia

Bufoniodea
Ranoidea

Squamata

Sauria
Lacertidae
Amphisbaenia
Amphisbaenidae
Aceratherium sp.

Dicerorhinus sp.

Aves

Threskornithidae
Ciconiidae
Mycteria cinereus
?Mycteria sp.
Scolopacidae
Charadriinae indet.
spp. unidentified

Mammalia

Proboscidea
Deinotheriidae
cf. *Deinotherium*
Gomphotheriidae
Gomphotherium sp
gen. et sp. indet.
Hyracoidea
SaghAtheriinae
Pachyhrax aff. *championi*
Carnivora
Viverridae
Viverra sp.
Mustelidae
cf. *Martes*
mionictis sp.
Felidae
Pseudaelurus tumaue
Artiodactyla
Suidae
Listroidontinae
Listriodon sp
. gen.et sp.indet. (giant species)
Giraffoidea
cf. *Canthumeryx*
sirtensis
Bovidae
Gen. et sp. indet.
Tragulidae
Dorcatherium cf.
libiensis
Perissodactyla
Rhinocerotidae

Contd/...
Table 3.5: Provisional list of the lower Miocene vertebrtates fauna from Al-Sarrar, eastern Saudi Arabia Continued/...

Serpentes
    Scolecophidia
    Boidae
        Python sp.
        Eryx/Gongylophis spp.
    Columbridae
    Elapidae
        Naja/Palaeonaja spp.
    Viperidae

Chelonia
    Pelomedusidae
        cf. *Schweboemys*

        aff. *Stereogenys*
    Trionychidae
        aff. *Cycloderma*
    Carettochelyidae
    Testudinidae
        Geochelone sp.

Crocodylia
    Crocodylidae
        Crocodylidae
            Crocodylus cf. pigotti

Rodentia
    Cricetidae
    Ctenodactylidae
        Metasayimys cf
        Intermadius
    Gerbillidae
    Pedetidae
        Megapedetes cf.
        Pentadactylus
    Dipodidae

        gen. et sp. indet.
        cf. *Protalactaga*
    Tryonomyidae

        Parphiomys sp.
    Lagomorpha
        Ochotonidae
    Insectivora
        Erinacedae
    ? Primates gen. et. sp. indet.

Source: Thomas *et al,* 1981

Table 3.6: Correlation of climatic phases, geomorphologic evolution and geological dynamics, Saudi Arabia

Chronology	Time Scale, Years B.P.	Climatic Phase	Continental Accumulation	Land Forms	Dynamics	Soil	Vegetation
Holocene	6,000	Arid	Eolian sands	Dunes	Eolian	Soils covered by dunes	Mainly open-desert and steppe
	11,000	Semi-arid to humid	Gravels and sands in wadi valleys; lacustrine deposits	Low alluvial plains	Locally torrential erosion		Mainly steppe savanna and desert
Late Pleistocene	17,000	Arid	Eolian Sands	Dunes	Eolian	Soils covered by dunes	Dense opne-desert (N) Steppe and savanna (S)
	35,000	Semi-arid to humid	Gravels lacustrine deposits	Some terraces in the west. Dessication in the eastern fans	Locally torrential erosion	Soils on dunes	Steppe and savanna
Middle Pleistocene	1,100,000	Arid to semi-arid	Alluvial silts	Terraces cover on fans	Erosion on slopes	Soil erosion	Mainly steppe
Early Pleistocene	3,500,000	Semi-arid to semi-humid: very humid at times	Alluvial gravels	Large fans, filling of wadi valleys	Torrential erosion and alluvial accumulation	Red soils	Savanna and forest (S.w)
Pliocene		Semi-arid	Alluvial silts, sands, and gravels	Mainly old fans, pediplains			Tropical and
Miocene		Semi-humid		In plateau position	Erosion on slopes	Soil erosion	subtropical savanna
Oligocene	25,000,000	Humid				Latosols laterites (oxisols)	Rain, tropical forest

Source: Modified from Anton, 1984

Table 3.7: The plant-geographical groups in the floras of the Middle-Eastern countries (percentage of total number of species)

Phytogeographical groups (chorotypes)	Egypt %	Palestine %	Arabian Peninsula Countries %	Syria and Lebanon %	Cyprus %	Turkey %	Iraq %	Iran %	Cret %
Uni-regionals									
Euro-Siberian	0.7	0.6	0.3	1.8	2.3	12.2	1.4	5.0	1.6
Mediterranean	20.2	38.3	2.8	47.0	49.1	32.4	11.0	1.5	69.2
Irano-Turanian	8.0	13.8	5.8	15.7	5.5	36.4	50.5	69.0	1.6
Saharo-Arabian	22.0	13.3	14.0	3.4	1.6	0.2	6.0	1.5	0.6
Sudanian	11.2	0.9	43.6	0.2	0.2	0.1	0.2	5.0	-
Bi-and pluri-regionals									
Euro-Sib-Mediterranean	1.0	0.6	0.1	1.9	2.6	1.3	1.0	1.0	1.6
Euro-Sib-Medit-Irano-Turanian	3.3	4.3	1.5	3.0	5.3	3.2	3.6	2.6	4.3
Euro-Sib-Irano-Turanian	0.5	-	0.2	0.5	0.4	2.7	0.3	2.5	0.6
Mediterranean-Irano-Turanian	13.0	16.5	5.2	19.0	23.3	9.0	18.7	8.5	14.6
Mediterranean-Saharo-Arabian	0.9	0.6	1.1	0.4	0.8	-	0.6	0.2	0.4
Irano-Tur-Saharo-Arabian	2.4	1.4	2.0	0.9	0.3	0.1	1.6	1.3	0.4
Sudanian-Saharo-Arabian	2.0	0.9	2.9	-	-	-	0.4	-	-
Borealo-Trop. & Borealo-sub-Trop.	6.0	3.7	4.0	4.8	6.0	1.9	3.0	1.6	1.4
Tropical & Tropical-sub-Tropical	8.5	4.5	15.2	1.3	0.6	0.2	2.6	1.0	-
Total number of species	**1,700**	**2,400**	**1,800**	**3,000**	**1,300**	**9,000**	**1,900**	**7,000**	**1,80**

Source: Zohary, 1973

Table 3.8: Genera that comprise the flora of the Saharo-Arabian region and are derived from neighbouring regions

Mediterranean derivatives	Irano-Turanian derivatives	Sudanian derivatives	South African derivatives	Endemic
Adonis	*Artemisia*	*Andropogon*	*Aizoaceae*	*Agathophora*
Anthemis	*Astragalus*	*Capparis*	*Gomphocarpus*	*Anastatica*
Bromus	*Ballota*	*Caralluma*	*Ifloga*	*Foleyola*
Erodium	*Calligonum*	*Cenchrus*	*Lotononis*	*Fredolia*
Hypecoum	*Carthamus*	*Citrullus*	*Neurada*	*Gymnarrhena*
Lotus	*Ferula*	*Crotalaria*	*Stipagrotis*	*Gymnocarpos*
Malva	*Glaucium*	*Cucumis*		*Lasiopogon*
Medicago	*Reaumuria*	*Dichanthium*		*Leyssera*
Ononis	*Stachys*	*Lasiurus*		*Leoflingia*
Picris	*Stipa*	*Launaea*		*Lonchophora*
Spergularia	*Tamarix*	*Pancratium*		*Morettia*
Teucrium	*Trigonella*	*Panicum*		*Moricandia*
		Pappophorum		*Muricaria*
		Varthemia		*Nasturtiopsis*
				Neurada
				Nucularia
				Ochradenus
				Oudneya
				Pteranthus
				Reboudia
				Rhanterium
				Savignya
				Sclerocephalus
				Zilla

Source: Compiled from Zohary, 1973; Takhtajan, 1969

Table 4.1: Plant species collected and recorded from the sand dune areas and their margins in northern and central Saudi Arabia

Species Name	General Distribution	Life Form	
1. *Aaronsohnia factorovski* War. and Eig.	SA	An.	H
2. *Aizoon canariense* L.	SAF-SA-SD-MAC	An.	H
3. *Allium sphaerocephalum* L	SA-IT	Per.	H
4. *Anabasis setifera* Moq.	SA-IT-SD	Per.	DS
5. *Anastatica hierochuntica* L	SA-SD	An.	H
6. *Anisosciadium lanatum* Boiss	SA	An.	H
7. *Anthemis deserti* Boiss	SA	An.	H
8. *Anvillea garcinii* (Burmf.) DC	SA	Per.	DS
9. *Aristida adscenionis* Hochst. ex Rich.	SD-SA-SAF-M-IT-TRO	An.	G
10. *Arnebia decumbens* (Vent.) Coss. and Dral	SA-IT	An.	H
11. *Arnebia linearifolia* DC	SA-IT	An.	H
12. *Artemisia monosperma*	SA-M	Per.	SH
13. *Asphodelus refractus* Boiss.	SA	An.	H
14. *Asphodelus tenuifolius*	SA	An.	H
15. *Astralagus annularis* Forssk	SA-M	An.	H
16. *Astralagus bombycinius* Boiss.	IT-SA	An. & Per.	H
17. *Astralagus corrugatus* Bertol.	IT-SA	An.	H
18. *Astralagus hauarensis* Boiss.	IT-SA	An.	H
19. *Astralagus schimperi* Boiss.	SA	An.	H
20. *Astralagus sieberi* DC.	SA	Per.	DS
21. *Astralagus tribuloides* Del.	IT-SA	An.	H
22. *Actractylis cancellata* L.	M-SA	An.	H
23. *Actractylis carduus* (Forssk.) C. Christ.	M-SA	Per.	H
24. *Bassia eriophora (*schrad.) Aschers.	SD-SA-IT	An.	H
25. *Brachypodium distachyon* (L.) P. Beauv	SA-M-IT	An.	H
26. *Bromus danthoniae* Trin.	IT-SA	An.	G
27. *Bromus fasciculatus* Presl	SA-M-IT	An.	G
28. *Bromus madritenis* L.	M-IT-ES	An.	G
29. *Bromus tectorum* L.	SA-M-IT-ES	An.	G
30. *Cakile arabica* Vel. and Bornm.	M-SA-ES	An.	H
31. *Calendula arvensis* L.	M-SA-IT-EUR	An.	H
32. *Calendula tripterocarpa* Rupr	SA	An.	H
33. *Calligonum comosum*	IT-SA	Per.	SH
34. *Cenchrus ciliaris* L.	SD-SA-SAF-IT-M-AUS-NAM	Per.	G
35. *Centaurea pseudosinaica* Czerep.	SA-IT-C,S EUR	An.	H
36. *Centropodia forsskalii* (vahl) Cope.	SA-IT-SD	Per.	G
37. *Centropodia fragilis* (Guinet & Sauvage) Cope.	SA	Per.	G
38. *Chorozophora tinctoria* (L.) Raf.	M-IT	An.	H
39. *Cistanche tubulosa*	SA-IT-SD-E.AFR	Per.	H

Species Name	General Distribution	Life Form	
40. *Convolvulus cephalopodus* Boiss.	SA-IT	Per.	DS
41. *Convolvulus oxyphyllus* Boiss. ssp. *oxycladus* Rech. F.	SA-IT	Per.	DS
42. *Convolvulus pilosellifolius* Desr.	SA-IT	Per.	H
43. *Cornulaca aucheri* Maq.	SA-IT	An.	H
44. *Cutandia memphitica* (spreng.) Benth.	MA-SA-IT	An.	G
45. *Cynodon dactylon* (L.) Pers.	Tropics	Per.	G
46. *Cynomorinum coccineum* L.	MA-SA-IT	Per.	H
47. *Cyperus conglomeratus* Rottb agg.	SA-SD-M-IND-MAC	Per.	G
48. *Dipcadi erythraeum* Webb and Berth.	SA-IND	Per.	H
49. *Diplotaxis acris* (Forssk.) Boiss.	SA	An.	H
50. *Echinops* sp.	SA-IT	Per.	DS
51. *Echium sericeum* Vahl.	M	Per.	H
52. *Emex spinosus* (L.) Campd.	M-SA	An.	H
53. *Enneapogon desvauxii* P. Beauv.	SA-SD	An.	G
54. *Ephedra alata* Dence.	SA	Per.	DS
55. *Eremobium aegytiacum* (Spreng.) Schweinf and Asch.	SA-SD	An.	H
56. *Erodium deserti* (Eig) Eig	SA	An.	H
57. *Erodium laciniatum* (Cav.) Willd.	SA-M	An.	H
58. *Euphorbia granulata* Forssk.	SA-IT-SD	An. & Per.	H
59. *Fagonia bruguieri* DC.	SA-IT	Per.	DS
60. *Fagonia glutinosa* Del.	SA	Per.	H
61. *Fagonia indica* Burm. f.	SA-IT-SD	Per.	H
62. *Fagonia olivieri* DC.	IT-SA	Per.	H
63. *Farsetia aegyptia* Turra	SA-SD	Per.	DS
64. *Farsetia burtonae* Oliv.	SA	Per.	DS
65. *Filago desertorum* Pomel	SA-IT	An.	H
66. *Fumaria parviflora* Lam.	M-IT-ES	An.	H
67. *Gypsophila arabica* Bahoudah.	IT-SA	An.	H
68. *Haloxylon persicum*	SA-IT	Per.	TR
69. *Haloxylon salicornicum*	SA-IT-SD	Per.	SH
70. *Haplophyllum tuberculatum* Forssk.	SA-IT	Per.	H
71. *Helianthemum ledifolium* (L.) Mill.	M-IT-SA	An.	H
72. *Helianthemum lippii.* (L.) Pers.	SA-SD	An.	DS
73. *Heliotropium bacciferum* Forssk.	SA-SD	Per.	H
74. *Heliotropium digynum* (Forssk.) Asch and Schweinf.	SA	Per.	DS
75. *Herniaria hirsuta* L.	M-IT-ES	An.	H
76. *Hippocrepis bicontorta* Lois	IT-SA	An.	H
77. *Hippocrepis unisiliquosa* L.	IT-M	An.	H
78. *Horwoodia dicksoniae* Turrill	SA	An.	H
79. *Hyoscyamus muticus* L.	SA	Per.	H
80. *Hyoscyamus pusillus* L.	IT-SA-SD	An.	H
81. *Hypecoum pendulum* L.	M-IT	An.	H
82. *Ifloga spicata* (Dum.) Nebelek	SA-SAF-M-MAC	An.	H

Species Name	General Distribution	Life Form	
83. *Kickxia aegyptiaca* (Dum.) Nebelek	IT-SA-M-SD	Per.	DS
84. *Koelpinia linearis* Pall.	SA-IT	An.	H
85. *Lasiurus scindicus* Henrard	SA-SD-IT	Per.	G
86. *Launaea angustifolia* (Desf.) Kuntze	SA	An.	H
87. *Launaea capitata* (Spreng.) Dandy	SA-SD	An. or Per.	H
88. *Launaea mucronata* (Forssk.) Muschl	SA	An. or Per.	H
89. *Leysera leyseroides* (Desf.) Maire	SD-SA-SAF	An.	H
90. *Linaria tenuis* (Viv.) Spreng.	SA	An.	H
91. *Lotonois platycarpa* (Viv.) P. Serm	SD-SA-SAF	An.	H
92. *Lotus halophilus* Boiss. Et Sprun.	SA-M	An.	H
93. *Lycium shawii* Roem et Schult	SA-SD	Per.	DS
94. *Malcolmia grandiflora* (Bge.) O. Kuntze.	SA-IT	An.	H
95. *Matricaria aurea* (Loefl.) Sch. Bip	M-IT	An.	H
96. *Matthiola longipetala* (Vent.) DC.	SA-M	An.	H
97. *Medicago laciniata* (L.) Mill	SA-M	An.	H
98. *Mesembryanthemum forsskalei* Hochst.	SA-SD-M-SAF	An.	H
99. *Moltkiopsis ciliata* (Forssk.) Johnst.	SA-M-SD	Per.	DS
100. *Monsonia nivea* (Decne.) ex Webb.	SA-SD	Per.	H
101. *Morettia parviflora* Boiss	SD	Per.	H
102. *Neurada procumbens* L.	SA-SD	An.	H
103. *Notoceras bicornis* (Air.) Amo	SA	An.	H
104. *Onobrychis ptolemaica* (Del.) DC.	SA-IT	Per.	H
105. *Ononis serrata* Forssk.	M-SA	An.	H
106. *Orobanche aegyptiaca* Pers.	M-SA-IT	An.	H
107. *Orobanche ceruaa* Leofl.	M-SA-IT	An.	H
108. *Panicum turgidum* Forrsk.	SA-SD	Per.	G
109. *Parapholis incurva* (L.) C. E. Hubb	M-IT-ES	Per.	G
110. *Paronychia arabica* (L.) D. C.	SA-SD-M	An.	H
111. *Pennisetum divisum* (Gmel.) Henr.	SA-SD-TRO. AFR	Per.	G
112. *Picris cyanocarpa* Boiss.	SA	An.	H
113. *Plantago afra* L.	IT-M	An.	H
114. *Plantago amplexicaulis* Cav.	SA-IT	An.	H
115. *Plantago boissieri* Hausskn. and Bornm.	SA-IT-M	An.	H
116. *Plantago ciliata* Desf.	SA-IT	An.	H
117. *Plantago ovata* Forssk.	SA-IT	An.	H
118. *Plantago psammophila* Agnew and Chalabi-Ka'abi	SA-IT	An.	H
119. *Polycarpaea repens* (Forskk.) Asch. and Schweinf.	SA-SD	An.	H
120. *Pteranthus dichotomus* Forssk.	SA-SD-IT-M	An.	H
121. *Pulicaria arabica* (L.) D. C.	M-IT	An.	H
122. *Pulicaria crispa* (Forssk.) Benth and	SA-SD	Per.	DS

Species Name	General Distribution	Life Form	
Hook. f.			
123. *Pulicaria guestii* Rech. f. and Al-Rawi	SA	Per.	H
124. *Reichardia tingitana* (L.) roth	SA-IT	An.	H
125. *Reseda arabica* Boiss.	SA	An.	H
126. *Reseda decursiva* Forssk.	SA	An.	H
127. *Rhanterium epapposum*	SA-IT	Per.	SH
128. *Rhazya stricta*	SA-IT	Per.	SH
129. *Robbairea dilileana* Milne-Redh.	SA-SD	An.	H
130. *Roemeria hybrida* (L.) D. C.	SA-M-IT-ES	An.	H
131. *Rostraria cristata* (L.) Tzvelev	M-IT-ES-SD	An.	G
132. *Rostraria pumila* (Desf.) Tzvelev	SA-M-IT	An.	G
133. *Rumex pictus* Forssk.	SA-M	An.	H
134. *Rumex vesicarius* L.	SA-M-SD	An.	H
135. *Savigyna parviflora* (Del.) Webb	SA	An.	H
136. *Scabiosa olivieri* Coulter	SA-IT	An.	H
137. *Schimpera arabica* Hochst. ex Steud.	SA	An.	H
138. *Schismus arabicus* Nees	M-SA-IT	An.	G
139. *Schismus barbatus* (L.) Thell.	SA-IT-M-SAF	An.	G
140. *Sclerocephalus arabicus* Boiss.	SA	An.	H
141. *Scorzonera musili* Vel.	SA	Per.	DS
142. *Schrophularia hypericifolia*	SA	Per.	DS
143. *Seidlitzia rosmarinus* Ehren ex Bunge.	IT-SA-SD	Per.	SH
144. *Senecio desfontainei* Druce.	SA-IT	An.	H
145. *Senecio flavus* (Decne.) Sch. Bip.	SA-SD-SAF	An.	H
146. *Silene villosaarabica* Boiss.	SA-IT	An.	H
147. *Silene villosa* Forssk.	SA	An.	H
148. *Spergula fallax* (Lowe) Drause	SA-M-SD	An.	H
149. *Spergularia marina* (L.) griseb.	M-IT-ES	An.	H
150. *Spergularia rubra* (L.) J. and C. presi.	M-ES-NAM	An.	H
151. *Stipa capensis* Thunb.	M-SA-IT-SAF	An.	G
152. *Stipagrostis drarii* Taeckh.	SA	Per.	G
153. *Stipagrostis obtusa* (Del.) Nees	SA-SAF-SD-TRO, AFR	Per.	G
154. *Stipagrostis paradisea* (Edgw.) De Wint.	SA-SD-IT	Per.	G
155. *Stipagrostis plumosa* L.	SA-M-SD-IT	Per.	G
156. *Tamarix aphyla* (L.) Karst.	SA-SD-SAF	Per.	TR
157. *Tribulus longipetalus* Viv.	SA-SD	An.	H
158. *Tribulus macropteris* Boiss.	M-IT-SA	An.	H
159. *Tribulus terrestris* L.	M-IT-SD-ES	An.	H
160. *Trigonella anguina* Del.	SA-IT-M	An.	H
161. *Trigonella hamosa* l.	SA-IT-SD	An.	H
162. *Trigonella seidlitzia* Forssk.	SA-IT	An.	H
163. *Tripleurospermum auriculatum* (Boiss.) Rech. f.	IT	An.	H
164. *Zilla spinosa* (Turr.)	SA	Per.	DS

Species Name	General Distribution	Life Form	
165. *Zygophyllum simplex* Forssk.	SD-SA-SAF	An.	H

General distribution:	**SA** = Saharo-arabian:	**SD** = Sudanian	**IT** = Irano-Turanian
	M = Mediterranean	**SAF** = South African	**MAC** = Macaronesia
	ES = Euro-Siberian	**NAM** = North American	**Trop** = Tropics
	IND = India	**EUR** = Europe	
Life-forms	**H** = Herb	**G** = Grass	**D** = Dwarf shrub or shrublet
	SH = Shrub	**TR** = Tree	**An** = Annual
Per = Perennial			

Source: Authors' research

Table 4.2: Plant species collected and recorded from the deep sand areas in northern and central Saudi Arabia

Species Name	General Distribution	Life Form	
1. *Artemisia monosperma*	SA-M	Per.	SH
2. *Asphodelus refractus* Boiss.	SA	An.	H
3. *Calligonum comosum*	IT-SA	Per.	SH
4. *Centropodia forsskalii* (vahl) Cope.	SA-IT-SD	Per.	G
5. *Centropodia fragilis* (Guinet & Sauvage) Cope.	SA	Per.	G
6. *Cyperus conglomeratus* Rottb agg.	SA-SD-M-IND-MAC	Per.	G
7. *Echinops* sp.	SA-IT	Per.	DS
8. *Eremobium aegytiacum* (Spreng.) Schweinf and Asch.	SA-SD	An.	H
9. *Haloxylon persicum*	SA-IT	Per.	TR
10. *Hippocrepis bicontorta* Lois	IT-SA	An.	H
11. *Lotus halophilus* Boiss. Et Sprun.	SA-M	An.	H
12. *Moltkiopsis ciliata* (Forssk.) Johnst.	SA-M-SD	Per.	DS
13. *Monsonia nivea* (Decne.) ex Webb.	SA-SD	Per.	H
14. *Neurada procumbens* L.	SA-SD	An.	H
15. *Plantago boissieri* Hausskn. and Bornm.	SA-IT-M	An.	H
16. *Polycarpaea repens* (Forskk.) Asch. and Schweinf.	SA-SD	An.	H
17. *Rostraria pumila* (Desf.) Tzvelev	SA-M-IT	An.	G
18. *Schismus arabicus* Nees	M-SA-IT	An.	G
19. *Schismus barbatus* (L.) Thell.	SA-IT-M-SAF	An.	G

Species Name	General Distribution	Life Form	
20. *Silene villosa* Forssk.	SA	An.	H
21. *Stipagrostis drarii* Taeckh.	SA	Per.	G
22. *Stipagrostis plumosa* L.	SA-M-SD-IT	Per.	G

General distribution: **SA** = Saharo-arabian   **SD** = Sudanian   **IT** = Irano-Turanian **IND** = India

M = Mediterranean   **SAF** = South African   **MAC** = Macaronesia

Life-forms   **H** = Herb   **G** = Grass   **D** = Dwarf shrub or shrublet

SH = Shrub   **TR** = Tree   **An** = Annual **Per** = Perennial

Source: Authors' research

Table 4.3: Plant species collected and recorded from the shallow to deep sand in northern and central Saudi Arabia

Species Name	General Distribution	Life Form	
1. *Aaronsohnia factorovski* War. and Eig.	SA	An.	H
2. *Aizoon canariense* L.	SAF-SA-SD-MAC	An.	H
3. *Allium sphaerocephalum* L	SA-IT	Per.	H
4. *Anabasis setifera* Moq.	SA-IT-SD	Per.	DS
5. *Anthemis deserti* Boiss	SA	An.	H
6. *Arnebia decumbens* (Vent.) Coss. and Kral	SA-IT	An.	H
7. *Arnebia linearifolia* DC	SA-IT	An.	H
8. *Astralagus annularis* Forssk	SA-M	An.	H
9. *Astralagus hauarensis* Boiss.	IT-SA	An.	H
10. *Astralagus schimperi* Boiss.	SA	An.	H
11. *Actractylis carduus* (Forssk.) C. Christ.	M-SA	Per.	H
12. *Cakile arabica* Vel. and Bornm.	M-SA-ES	An.	H
13. *Cistanche tubulosa*	SA-IT-SD-E.AFR	Per.	H
14. *Convolvulus cephalopodus* Boiss.	SA-IT	Per.	DS
15. *Cutandia memphitica* (spreng.) Benth.	MA-SA-IT	An.	G
16. *Cynomorinum coccineum* L.	MA-SA-IT	Per.	H
17. *Dipcadi erythraeum* Webb and Berth.	SA-IND	Per.	H
18. *Emex spinosus* (L.) Campd.	M-SA	An.	H
19. *Ephedra alata* Dence.	SA	Per.	DS
20. *Erodium laciniatum* (Cav.) willd.	SA-M	An.	H
21. *Fagonia indica* Burm. f.	SA-IT-SD	Per.	H
22. *Haloxylon salicornicum*	SA-IT-SD	Per.	SH
23. *Heliotropium digynum* (Forssk.) Asch and Schweinf.	SA	Per.	DS
24. *Ifloga spicata* (Dum.) Nebelek	SA-SAF-M-MAC	An.	H
25. *Koelpinia linearis* Pall.	SA-IT	An.	H
26. *Medicago laciniata* (L.) Mill	SA-M	An.	H
27. *Ononis serrata* Forssk.	M-SA	An.	H
28. *Orobanche aegyptiaca* Pers.	M-SA-IT	An.	H
29. *Rhanterium epapposum*	SA-IT	Per.	SH
30. *Rhazya stricta*	SA-IT	Per.	SH
31. *Savigyna parviflora* (Del.) Webb	SA	An.	H
32. *Schrophularia hypericifolia* Del.	SA	Per.	DS
33. *Silene villosaarabica* Boiss.	SA-IT	An.	H

General distribution:	**SA** = Saharo-arabian:	**SD** = Sudanian	**IT** = Irano-Turanian
	M = Mediterranean	**SAF** = South African	**MAC** = Macaronesia
	ES = Euro-Siberian	**NAM** = North American	**Trop** = Tropics
	IND = India	**EUR** = Europe	

Life-forms	**H** = Herb	**G** = Grass	**D** = Dwarf shrub or shrublet
	SH = Shrub	**TR** = Tree	**An** =
Annual			
	Per = Perennial		

Source:	Authors' research

Table 4.4: Plant species noted from Ar Rub' Al Khali (collated from Mandaville, 1990)

Species Name	General Distribution	Life Form	
1. *Limeum arabicum* Friedr.	SA-SD	Per	DS
2. *Silene villosa* Forssk.	SA	An. or Per.	H
3. *Polycarpea repens* (Forssk.) Asch. & Schweinf.	SA-SD	Per.	DS
4. *Saueda monaca*	SD	Per.	SH/TR
5. *Siedlitzia rosmarinus* Ehren ex Bunge.	IT-SA-SD	Per.	SH
6. *Salsola cyclophylla* Bak.	SA-SD	Per.	DS
7. *Haloxylon salicornicum* (Moq.) Bge.	SA-SD-IT	Per.	SH
8. *Haloxylon persicum* Bge.	SD	Per.	SH/TR
9. *Cornulaca arabica* Botsch.	End	Per.	SH
10. *Cornulaca monocantha* Del.	SA-SD-IT	Per.	DS
11. *Calligonum crinitum* Boiss. subsp. arabicum (Sosk.) Sosk.	SD	Per.	SH
12. *Maeru crassifolia* Forssk.	SDF	Per.	SH/TR
13. *Dipterygium glancum* Dence.	SA-SD	Per.	DS
14. *Savignya parviflora* (Del.) Webb.	SA-SD	An.	H
15. *Fsrsetia burtonae* Oliv.	SA	Per.	DS
16. *Farsetia longisiliqua* Decne.	SA-SD	Per.	SH
17. *Eremobium aegyticum* (Spreng.) Boiss.	SA-SD	An.	H
18. *Neurada procumbens* L.	SA-SD	An.	H
19. *Prosopis cineraria* (L.) Druce	SD	Per.	SH/TR
20. *Cynomorinum coccineum* L.	M-SA-IT	Per.	H
21. *Fagonia indica* Burm. f.	SA-SD-IT	Per.	H
22. *Fagonia ovalifolia* Hadidi	SA-SD	An. or Per.	H
23. *Zygophyllum mandavillei* Hadidi	SA-SD	Per.	SH
24. *Tribulus arabicus* Hosni	SA-SD End?	Per.	H
25. *Monsonia nivea* (Decne.) ex Webb.	SA-SD	Per.	H
26. *Heliotropum ramosissimum* (Lehm.) DC	SA-SD	Per.	DS
27. *Heliotropum digynum* (Forskk.) asch. & Schweinf.	SA	Per.	DS
28. *Moltkiopsis ciliata* (Forssk.) John st.	SA-SD-M	Per.	DS
29. *Arnebia hispidissima* (Lehm.) DC.	SA-SD	An. or Per.	H
30. *Plantago boisseri* Haussk. & Bornm.	SA-IT-M	An.	H
31. *Cistanche tubulosa* (Schrenk) Wight	SA-SD	Per.	H
32. *Stipagrostis drarii* Taeckh.	SA	Per.	G
33. *Stipagrostis plumosa* L.	SA-SD-M-IT	Per.	G
34. *Centropodia forsskali* (Vahl.) Cope	SA-SD-IT	Per.	G
35. *Centropodia fragilis* (Guinet & Sauvage) Cope.	SA	Per.	G
36. *Cuppesus conglomeratus* Rotth. agg.	SA-SD-M-IND-MAC	Per.	G

Table 4.4: Plant species noted from Ar Rub' Al Khali (collated from Mandaville, 1990) Cont/....

General distribution:	**SA** = Saharo-arabian: **M** = Mediterranean **End** = Endemic	**SD** = Sudanian **IND** = India	**IT** = Irano-Turanian **MAC** = Macaronesia
Life-forms	**H** = Herb **SH** = Shrub **Per** = Perennial	**G** = Grass **TR** = Tree	**D** = Dwarf shrub or shrublet **An** = Annual
Source:	Mandaville (1990) and authors' research.		

Table 4.5: Distributional types of sand dune flora of the central and northern sand seas

No	Distribution type	No of species	%	No	Distribution type	No of species	%
1	IT	1	0.6	17	SD	1	0.6
2	M	1	0.6	18	TRO	1	0.6
3	M-ES-NAM	1	0.6	19	IT-M-SD-ES	2	1.2
4	SA-IND	1	0.6	20	SA-IT-M-ES	2	1.2
5	SA-IT-C,S-EUR	1	0.6	21	SA-IT-M-SAF	2	1.2
6	SA-IT-M-EUR	1	0.6	22	SA-IT-SD-M	3	1.8
7	SA-IT-SD-E-AFR	1	0.6	23	SA-SD-M	4	2.4
8	SA-IT-SD-M-SAF-AUS-NAM	1	0.6	24	IT-M-ES	5	3
9	SA-IT-SD-M-SAF-TRO	1	0.6	25	SA-SD-SAF	5	3
10	SA-M-ES	1	0.6	26	IT-M	7	4.2
11	SA-MS-AF-MAC	1	0.6	27	SA-M	10	6.1
12	SA-SD-M-SAF	1	0.6	28	SA-IT-SD	11	6.7
13	SA-SD-MAC-IND	1	0.6	29	SA-IT-M	12	7.3
14	SA-SD-SAF-MAC	1	0.6	30	SA-SD	15	9.1
15	SA-SD-SAF-TRO, AFR	1	0.6	31	SA	34	20.6
16	SA-SD-TRO, AFR	1	0.6	32	SA-IT	35	21.2

General distribution:

SA = Saharo-arabian: **SD** = Sudanian   **IT** = Irano-Turanian
M = Mediterranean   **SAF** = South African   **MAC** = Macaronesia
ES = Euro-Siberian   **NAM** = North American   **Trop** = Tropics
IND = India   **EUR** = Europe   **C,S EUR** =

Central and

Southern Europe
Source: Author's research

Table 4.6: Family, genus and species representation in the sand dunes' flora in northern and central Saudi Arabia

Family	Number of genera	Number of species	Family	Number of genera	Number of species
Aizoaceae	2	2	Geraniaceae	2	3
Apocynaceae	1	1	Gramineae	17	25
Boraginaceae	4	6	Leguminosae	8	17
Caryophyllaceae	10	12	Liliaceae	3	4
Chenopodiaceae	5	6	Orobanchaceae	2	3
Cistaceae	1	2	Plantaginaceae	1	6
Compositae	22	29	Polygonaceae	3	4
Convolvulaceae	1	3	Resedaceae	1	2
Cruciferae	12	14	Rosaceae	1	1
Cynomoriaceae	1	1	Rutaceae	1	1
Cyperaceae	1	1	Scrophulariaceae	2	2
Dipsacaceae	1	1	Solanaceae	2	3
Ephedraceae	1	1	Tamaricaceae	1	1
Euphorbiaceae	2	2	Umbelliferae	1	1
Fumariaceae	3	3	Zygophyllaceae	3	8
			TOTALS	115	165

Source: Author's research

Table 4.7: The main life-form groups of plants (in percentages) in the central and northern sand-seas; in Ar Rub' Al Khali; and the eastern province of Saudi Arabia; and the absolute number of annual species in the same areas

	Life-form groups %		
	E. & N. Sand Seas	Ar Rub' Al Khali	E. Province
Phanerophytes	5.0	32.0	18.0
Chamaephytes	11.4	36.0	23.0
Hemi-cryptophytes	7.6	7.0	6.0
Cryptophytes	7.6	6.0	7.0
Therophytes	68.4	19.0	46.0
N. of annual species	165	8	145

Source: Author's research & Mandaville (1990)

Table 5.1: Floristic composition of two transects representing the *Calligonum comosum* community

Species	Transect No. (1) No. of species	%	Transect No. (2) No. of species	%
Calligonum comosum	72	90	71	88.75
ArtemisIa monosperma	4	5	8	10
Scrophularia hypericifolia	3	3.75	1	1.25
Rhanterium epapposum	1	1.25	-	-

Table 5.2: Floristic composition of two transects representing the *Haloxylon persicum* community

Species	Transect No. (1) No. of species	%	Transect No. (2) No. of species	%
Haloxylon persicum	58/80	73	75/80	93.75
Haloxylon salicornicum	5/80	6	4/80	5
Calligonum comosum	-	-	1/80	1.25
Scrophularia hypericifolia	17/80	21	-	-

Table 5.3: Floristic composition of two transects representing the *Artemisia monosperma* community

Species	Transect No. (1) No. of species	%	Transect No. (2) No. of species	%
Artemisia monosperma	62/80	77.50	66/80	82.50
Scrophularia hypericifolia	13/80	16.25	3/80	3.75
Echinops sp.	5/80	6.25	8/80	10
Calligonum comosum	-	-	1/80	1.25
Ephedra alata	-	-	1/80	1.25
Haloxylon salicornicum	-	-	1/80	1.25

Table 5.4: Floristic composition of two transects representing the *Scrophularia hypericifolia* community

Species	Transect No. (1)		Transect No. (2)	
	No. of species	%	No. of species	%
Scrophularia hypericifolia	44/80	55	45/80	56.25
Haloxylon salicornicum	28/80	35	27/80	33.75
Ephedra alata	5/80	6.25	2/80	2.50
Artemisia monosperma	1/80	1.25	5/80	1.25
Rhanterium epapposum	1/80	1.25	1/80	1.25
Echinops sp.	1/80	1.25	-	-

Table 5.5: Floristic composition of two transects representing the *Rhazya stricta* community

Species	Transect No. (1)		Transect No. (2)	
	No. of species	%	No. of species	%
Rhazya stricta	80/80	100	80/80	100

Table 5.6: Floristic composition of two transects representing the *Haloxylon salicornicum* community

Species	Transect No. (1)		Transect No. (2)	
	No. of species	%	No. of species	%
Haloxylon salicornicum	76/80	95	80/80	100
Rhanterium epapposum	2/80	2.5	-	-
Scrophularia hypericifolia	1/80	1.25	-	-
Haloxylon persicum	1/80	1.25	-	-

Table 5.7: Numbers and percentages of quadrats in which shrubless-community species occurs

Species Name	No. of quadrats	%	Total No. of individuals	Abundance	Density
1. *Aaronsohnia factorovskyi* War. and Eig.	12	3.6	16	1.3	0.0
2. *Allium sphaerocephalum* L.	15	4.5	27	1.8	0.1
3. *Anisosciadium lanatum* Boiss.	3	0.9	5	1.7	0.0
4. *Anthemis hypercifolia* Boiss.	21	6.4	68	3.2	0.2
5. *Arnebia decumbens* (Vent.) Cross. and Kral.	30	9.1	322	10.7	1.0
6. *Arnebia linearifolia* DC	36	10.9	167	4.6	0.5
7. *Asphodelus tenuifolius*	69	20.9	354	5.1	1.1
8. *Astragalus annularis* Forssk.	1	0.3	1	1.0	0.0
9. *Bassia eriophora* (Schrad.) Aschers	3	0.9	5	1.7	0.0
10. *Centropodia forsskalii* (Vahl) Cope.	18	5.5	46	2.6	0.1
11. *Convolvulus cephalopodus* Boiss.	24	7.3	27	1.1	0.1
12. *Cutandia memphitica* (Spreng.) Benth.	95	28.8	382	4.0	1.2
13. *Cynodon dactylon* (L.) Pers.	29	8.8	75	2.6	0.2
14. *Cynomorium coccineum* L.	1	0.3	1	1.0	0.0
15. *Cyperus conglomeratus* Rottb agg.	16	4.8	31	1.9	0.1
16. *Dipcadi erythraeum* Webb and Berth.	37	11.2	53	1.4	0.2
17. *Eremobium aegyptiacum* (Spreng.) Schweinf and Asch.	179	54.2	2041	11.4	6.2
18. *Erodium laciniatum* (Cav.) Willd.	39	11.8	141	3.6	0.4
19. *Helianthemum lippii*	1	0.3	1	1.0	0.0
20. *Hippocrepis bicontorta* Lois.	84	26	139	1.7	0.4
21. *Horwoodia dicksoniae* Turrill	45	13.6	100	2.2	0.3
22. *Koelpinia linearis* Pall.	47	14.2	132	2.8	0.4
23. *Launea capitata* (Spreng.) Dandy	82		161	2.0	0.5

		24.8			
24. *Launea mucronata* (Forssk.) Muschl	8		10	1.3	0.0
		2.4			
25. *Lotus halophilus* Boiss. Et Sprun.	198	60	2433	12.3	7.4
26. *Medicago laciniata* (L.) Mill.	27		71	2.6	0.2
		8.2			
27. *Moltkiopsis ciliata* (Forssk.) Johnst.	70		571	8.2	1.7
		21.2			
28. *Neurada procumbens* L.	36		54	1.5	0.2
		10.9			
29. *Ononis serrata* Forssk.	45		504	11.2	1.5
		13.6			
30. *Paronychia arabica* (L) D.C.	13		19	1.5	0.1
		3.9			
31. *Plantago boissieri* Hausskn. and Bornm.	271		5752	21.2	17.4
		82.1			
32. *Polycarpaea rapens* (Forskk.) Asch. and Schweinf.	83		173	2.1	0.5
		25.2			
33. *Roemeria hybrida* (L.) D.C.	16		22	1.4	0.1
		4.8			
34. *Rumex pictus* Forssk.	1		1	1.0	0.0
		0.3			
35. *Savigyna parviflora* (Del.) Webb	6		15	2.5	0.0
		1.8			
36. *Schismus arabicus* Nees	26		34	1.3	0.1
		7.9			
37. *Silene villosa* Forssk.	73		180	2.5	0.5
		22.1			
38. *Stipagrostis drarii* Taeckh.	56	17	129	2.3	0.4
39. *Stipagrostis plumosa* L.	179		548	3.1	1.7
		54.2			

Table 5.8: Vegetational composition of the shrubless community collected from 11 sites in the central and northern sand seas

Species Name	Sites and number of species											No of sites occurance	%
	1	2	3	4	5	6	7	8	9	10	11		
1. *Aaronsonia factorovskyi* War. and Eig						1			2	13		3	27
2. *Allium sphaerocephalum* L.			26							5		2	18
3. *Anisosciadium lanatum* Boiss.												1	9
4. *Anthemis hypericifolia* Boiss.		68										1	9
5. *Armebia decumbens* (Vent.) Cross. and Dral.				322								1	9
6. *Armebia linearifolia* D.C.							10	157				2	18
7. *Asphodelus tenuifolius*	4	11				1			194	144	2	6	55
8. *Astragalus annularis* Forskk.						1						1	9
9. *Bassia eriophora* (Schrad.) Aschers.		2			3							2	18
10. *Centropodia forsskalii* (Vahl.) Cope.	2	43								1		3	27
11. *Convolvulus cephalopodus* Boiss.	1		4				7			15		4	36
12. *Cutandia memphitica* (Spreng.) Benth.					53	135			85	25	84	5	45
13. *Cynodon dactylon* (L.) Pers.						69			1	2	3	4	36
14. *Cynomorium coccineum* L.		1										1	9

Species Name	1	2	3	4	5	6	7	8	9	10	11	No of sites occurance	%
15. *Cyperus conglomeratus* Rottb. agg.												1	9
16. *Dipcadi erythraeum* Webb. and Berth.	17	1	31			3						5	45
17. *Eremobium aegyptiacum* (Spreng.) Schweinf and Asch.	150		460	218	14	5	423	676	2		93	9	82
18. *Erodium lacinatum* (Cav.) Willd.	6	117			18							3	27
19. *Helianthemum lippii*		1										1	9
20. *Hippocrepis bicontorta* Lois	56	37	8	6	5	9		7	4	5	2	10	91
21. *Horwoodia dicksoniae* Turrill.									53	47		2	18
22. *Koelpinia linearis* Pall.	3	82							44	3		4	36
23. *Launaea capitata* (Spreng.) Dandy	19				31		3	46	43	19		6	55
24. *Launaea mucronata* (Forssk) Muschl		3				1			1	3	2	6	55
25. *Lotus halophilus* Boiss. et Sprun.	417	367			128	304			81	204	992	7	64
26. *Medicago*		57							4	10		3	27

Species Name	Sites and number of species											No of sites occurance	%
	1	2	3	4	5	6	7	8	9	10	11		
liciniata (L.) Mill.													
27. Moltkiopsis ciliata (Forssk.) Johnst.	2		6			4	275	284	1	1		6	55
28. Neurada procumbens L.		11	1				11	1	2	23		8	73
29. Onois serrata Forssk.	8	485	11									3	27
30. Paronychia arabica (L) D.C.				19								1	9
31. Plantago boissieri Hausskn. and Bornm.	225	4	12	92	1196	43	1388	1308	102	277	1105	11	100
32. Polycarpaea repens (Forskk.) Asch. and Schweinf.	7	15	6	2		1	35	79	22	6		9	82
33. Roemeria hybrida (L.) D.C.					11	11						2	18
34. Rumex pictus Forssk.						1						1	9
35. Savigyna parviflora (Del.) Webb.										15		1	9
36. Schismus arabicus Nees	16	2	3				3	3			10	5	45
37. Silene villosa Forssk.	10	84		1	1	6	3	8	16	47	1	11	11
38. Stipagrostis drarii Taeckh.			51				3	27	15	33		5	45

+ Species Name	Sites and number of species											No of sites occurance	%
	1	2	3	4	5	6	7	8	9	10	11		
39. *Stipagrostis plumosa* L.	21	63	42	96	1	42	44	69	18	8	144	11	100

Site locations:1 - Nafud Ath Thuwayrat (site 1) **2** - Nafud Ath Thuwayrat (site 2) **3** - Ad Dahna (Erg Al Hamarain) **4** - Ad Dahna (Erg Ath Thimam)**5** - Nafud Al Ghamees **6** - Nafud At Turaifiyah (site 1) **7** - Nafud Qumayfithah (site 1) **8** - Nafud Qumayfithah (site 2) **9** - Ad Dahna (Khab Ar Redhum) **10** - Ad Dahna (near Al Arraweyah) **11**- Nafud At Turaifiyah (site 2)

Table 5.9: TWINSPAN table of the analysis of the shrubless community

			1 1 29015617834	
1	aaro	fac	-24--1-----	00
3	anis	lan	--3--------	00
4	anth	hyp	5----------	00
7	asph	ten	4552-12----	00
8	astr	ann	-----1-----	00
9	bass	eri	2---2------	00
10	cent	for	5-12-------	00
12	cuta	mem	-55-555----	00
13	cyno	dac	-12--58----	00
14	cyno	coc	2----------	00
18	erod	lac	5--34------	00
19	heli	lip	1----------	00
21	horw	dic	-55--------	00
22	koel	lin	5522-------	00
24	laun	muc	212--12----	00
25	lous	hal	5555555----	00
26	medi	lac	524--------	00
33	roem	hyb	----44-----	00
34	rume	pic	----1------	00
35	savi	par	--4--------	00
20	hipp	bic	5235332-333	01
36	schi	ara	2--4--422--	01
37	sile	vil	54541312321	01
16	dipc	ery	1-14-2---5-	10
17	erem	aeg	-2-54355555	10
23	laun	cap	-5445--25--	10
28	neur	pro	4252---4112	10
29	onon	ser	5--3-----4-	10
31	plan	boi	25555555545	10
39	stip	plu	54351555555	10
2	alli	sph	---------51	11
5	arne	dec	----------5	11
6	arne	lin	-------45--	11
11	conv	cep	--41---3-2-	11
15	cype	con	---------5-	11
27	molt	cil	-11--2-553-	11
30	paro	ara	----------4	11
32	poly	rep	4533-1-5532	11
38	stip	dra	-45----255-	11
			00000001111	
			00011110011	

Site numbers and locations

1 - Nafud Ath Thuwayrat (site 1)   2 - Ad Dahna (near Al Artaweyah)   3 - Ad Dahna (Khab Ar Redhum)
4 - Nafud Arth Thuwayrat (site 2)   5 - Nafud Al Ghamees   6 - Nafud Al Turafiyah (site 1)
7 - Nafud Al Turafiyah (site 2)   8 - Ad Dahna (Erg Al Hamrani)   9 - Ad Dahna (Erg Ath Thimam)
10 - Nafud Qunayfithah (site 1) 11 - Nafud Qunayfithah (site 2)

Table 6.1: Sand-sea plant species utilised as food or beverages for human consumption

Plant	Comments
Allium sphaerocephalum	The bulb is edible, its seeds used as spicces
Anisosciadium lanatum	Leaves are edible raw
Astragalus annularis	
Cathamus persicus	
Cynomorium coccineum	Roots are edible raw. Used in making iqt (Dried cakes of boiled curdled milk)
Cyperus conglomeratus agg	
Dipcadi erythaeum	The bulb is edible
Diplotaxis acris	
Emex spinosa	Roots and petioles are edible
Mesembryanthemum forsskalei	Its seeds can be ground into flour to make bread
Koelpinia linearis	
Launaea capitata	
Matricaria aurea	Make tea substitute
Medicago laciniata	
Neurada procumbens	Young fruits are edible raw
Asphodelus tenufolius	Used in making iqt (Dried cakes of boiled curdled milk) to make it softer
Roemeria hybrida	
Rumex pictus	Leaves are edible raw
Rumex vesicarius	Leaves are edible raw or cooked with meat
Savignya parviflora	
Schimpera arabica	
Scorzonera musilii	

Source: Questionnaire

Table 6.2: Sand-sea plant species utilised for industrial purposes

Plant	Industrial uses
Calligonum comosum	Tanning leather, making packsaddles, construction material for building houses and furniture as well as fences. Making candy and molasses.
Haloxylon persicum	Making farming and industrial implements, making packsaddles, construction materials for building houses and furniture as well as fences.
Rhanterium epapposum	Manufacturing dying, roofing houses.
Seidlitzia rosmarinus	Dried pounded leaves as a soap substitute.
Haloxylon salicornicum	Soap substitute.
Stipagrostis drarii	Stuffing pillows and cushions.
Artemisia monosperma	Roofing houses to prevent water leaks and leather tanning.
Farestia burtonae	Wax for making gum.
Horwoodia dicksoniae	Making perfumes.
Cynomorium coccineum	Drying clothes.
Cyperus conglomeratus agg	Making ropes.
Anthemis deserti	Making perfumes.
Arnebia decumbens	Used as cosmetic; red dye is made from the surface of its roots.
Rhazya	Tanning leather.

Source: Questionnaire

Table 6.3 Sand-sea plant species used medically.

Plant	Main medicinal uses
Calligonum comosum	Root decoction used for gum sores and toothache. A decoction of the leaves is used for treating wounds, interior ulcers and diabetes. It is also used as a laxative.
Artemisia monosperma	Leaves boiled in water and drunk to cure cold, sore throats and fevers. It is also used for the treatment of infertility.
Rhanterium epapposum	Used as a purgative and for treatment of sore wounds and headache.
Rhazya stricta	Used to treat ulcers and skin desease. Leaf infusions are also used to treat diabetes, sore throat, fever and as a purgative.
Cynomorium coccineum	After drying and grinding, used for diabetes treatment.
Heliotropium bacciferum	Boiled water of the shoot is drunk as a remedy for snake and scorpion bites. Crushed fresh shoot is applied to relieve the pain of these bites as well as skin irritations.
Scrophularia hypericifolia	Used to treat diabetes, and as a purgative.
Mesembryanthemum forsskalei	Used for stomach disorders.
Cynodon dactylon	Treatment of eye infection.
Polycarpaea repens	Rheumatism treatment.
Euphorbia granulata	Toothache treatment, as well as intestinal parasites.

Source: Questionnaire

Table 6.4: Level of grazing use in the sand seas by inhabitants of the region and surrounding areas

Level of grazing	No.	%
High	111	47.4
Moderate	76	32.5
Seldom	32	13.7
No use	15	6.4

Source: Questionnaire

Table 6.5: Vegetation sufficiency level in the sand seas as indicated by livestock owners

Answer	Number of Respondents	%
Yes	17	20
No	68	80

Source: Questionnaire

Table 6.6: Use level of forage by livestock owners in the sand seas

Level of forage usage	Number of Respondents	%
High	42	49.4
Moderate	39	45.9
Seldom	4	4.7

Source: Questionnaire

Table 6.7: Sources of energy for Bedouins and other inhabitants in the sand seas

Energy Type	Number of users	%
Firewood only	15	6.5
Kerosene, gas or electricity	55	23.5
All the above	162	69.2
No answer	2	–

Source: Questionnaire

6.8: Level of wood cutting in the sand seas by inhabitants of the region and surrounding areas

Level of wood cutting	No	%
High	117	50.0
Moderate	76	32.5
Seldom	27	11.5
No use	14	6.0

Source: Questionnaire

Table 6.9: Top firewood species preferred by correspondents (Rankings are based on frequencies of mention; respondents might mention more than one species.

Plant	Frequencies of mention	Ranking
Calligonum comosum	214	1
Haloxylon persicum	151	2
Rhanterium epapposum	51	3
Haloxylon salicornicum	50	4
Artemisia monosperma	6	5

Source: Questionnaire

Table 6.10: Level of recreational use of the sand seas by inhabitants of the region and surrounding areas

Level of recreational use	No	%
High	49	20.9
Moderate	77	32.9
Seldom	78	33.3
No use	30	12.8

Source: Questionnaire

Table 6.11: Means of transportation in the sand seas

Means of transportation	No of users	%
Feet	5	2
Animals	24	11
Cars	152	67
Cars and animals	45	20
No answer	8	-

Source: Questionnaire

Table 6.12: Main causes of desertification indicated by correspondents (Rankings are based on frequencies of mention, respondents might mention more than one cause).

Cause of desertification	Frequencies of mention	Ranking
Cutting	85	2
Overgrazing	85	2
Drought	182	1

Source: Questionnaire

INDEX OF PLANT NAMES

	Species Name	Arabic Names	
1.	Aaronsohnia factorovskyi War.and Eig.	QARRAS	قراص
2.	Aizoon canariense L.	DU'AA'	دعاء
3.	Allium sphaerocephalum L.	KURRATH	كراث
4.	Anabasis setifera Moq.	SHA'R	شعر
5.	Anastatica hierochuntica L.	KAFF MARYAM	كف مريم
6.	Anisosciadium lanatum Boiss.	BASBAS	بسباس
7.	Anthemis deserti Boiss.	QAHWIYAN	قحويان
8.	Anvillea garcinii (Burmf.) DC	NUQD	نقد
9.	Aristida adscensionis Hochst. ex Rich.	GHAFAH	غفة
10.	Arnebia decumbens (Vent.) Coss. and Kral.	KAHIL	كحيل
11.	Arnebia linearifolia DC	KAHIL	كحيل
12.	Artemisia monosperma	A'THER	عذر
13.	Asphodelus refractus Boiss.		
14.	Asphodelus tenuifolius Boiss.	BARWAQ	برواق
15.	Astragalus annularis Forssk	ABU KHAWAITEM	بو خويتم
16.	Astragalus bombycinus Boiss.		
17.	Astragalus corrugatus Bertol.		
18.	Astragalus hauarensis Boiss.		
19.	Astragalus schimperi Boiss.	KRAIDON ASWAD	كريدون أسود
20.	Astragalus sieberi DC.	MISHT ATH THEEB	مشط الذيب
21.	Astragalus tribuloides Del.	QAFA'A	قفعا
22.	Atractylis cancellata L.	UMM DHIRS	ام ضرس
23.	Atractylis carduus (Forssk.) C.Christ.	SHUWAYKAH	شويكة
24.	Bassia eriophora (schrad.) Aschers.	HAYTAMAN	هيتمان
25.	Brachypodium distachyon (L.) P. Beauv		
26.	Bromus danthoniae Trin.		
27.	Bromus fasciculatus Presl		
28.	Bromus madritensis L.		
29.	Bromus tectorum L		
30.	Cakile arabica Vel. and Bornm.	SALIH	صبح
31.	Calendula arvensis L.	HANWAH	حنوة
32.	Calendula tripterocarpa Rupr	A'SHB AL GHWORAB	عشبة الغراب
33.	Calligonum comosum	ARTA	أرطى
34.	Cenchrus ciliaris L.	KHADIR	خضير
35.	Centaurea pseudosinaica Czerep.	MARAR	مرار
36.	Centropodia forsskalii (vahl) Cope.	ZAREA'	زريع
37	Centropodia fragilis (Guinet & Sauvage) Cope.	QASBA	قصب
38	Chrozophora tinctoria (L.) Raf.		
39	Cistanche tubulosa	THANUN	ثنون
40	Convolvulus cephalopodus Boiss.	RUKHAMAH	رخامة
41	Convolvulus oxyphyllus Boiss. ssp. oxycladus Rech. F.	ADRIS	عدرس

Vegetation of the Sand Seas of Saudi Arabia

INDEX OF PLANT NAMES

42. Convolvulus pilosellifolius Desr.		
43. Cornulaca aucheri Maq.		
44. Cutandia memphitica (spreng.) Benth.	SAYSFAN	سيسفان
45. Cynodon dactylon (L.) Pers.	THAYYIL	ثيل
46. Cynomorinum coccineum L.	TURTHUTH	طرثوث
47. Cyperus conglomeratus Rottb agg..	A'NDAB	عنداب
48. Dipcadi erythraeum Webb and Berth.	A'SANSAL	عصصل
49. Diplotaxis acris (Forssk.) Boiss.	JAHAQ	جهق
50. Echinops sp.	KHRFASH	خرفش
51. Echium sericeum Vahl.		
52. Emex spinosus (L.) Campd.	A'MBASIS	عبيسص
53. Enneapogon desvauxii P.Beauv.		
54. Ephedra alata Decne.	A'LANDAH	علنة
55. Eremobium aegyptiacum (Spreng.) Schweinf and Asch.	GHURAYRA	غريراء
56. Erodium deserti (Eig) Eig	RAQAM	رقم
57. Erodium laciniatum (Cav.) willd.	RAQAM	رقم
58. Euphorbia granulata Forssk.		
59. Fagonia bruguieri DC.	JANBAH	جنبة
60. Fagonia glutinosa Del.	UMM AT TURAB	أم التواب
61. Fagonia indica Burm. f.	DURAYMA	ضريماء
62. Fagonia olivieri DC.	DURAYMA	ضريماء
63. Farsetia aegyptia Turra	HAMAH	حمة
64. Farsetia burtonae Oliv.		
65. Filago desertorum Pomel	QUTTAYNAH	قطينة
66. Fumaria parviflora Lam.		
67. Gypsophila arabica Bahoudah.		
68. Haloxylon persicum	GHADHA	غضا
69. Haloxylon salicornicum	RIMTH	رمث
70. Haplophyllum tuberculatum Forssk.	MUSAYKAH	مسيكة
71. Helianthemum ledifolium (L.) Mill.	RAQRUQ	رقروق
72. Helianthemum lippii. (L.) Pers.	RAQRUQ	رقروق
73. Heliotropium bacciferum Forssk.	RAMRAM	رمرام
74. Heliotropium digynum (Forssk.) Asch and Schweinf.	KARY	كري
75. Herniaria hirsuta L.		
76. Hippocrepis bicontorta Lois	UMM KHWAYTIM	أم خويتم
77. Hippocrepis unisiliquosa L.		
78. Horwoodia dicksoniae Turrill.	KHOZAMA	خزصي
79. Hyoscyamus muticus L.		
80. Hyoscyamus pusillus L.		
81. Hypecoum pendulum L	UMM ATH THURAYB	أم الثريب
82. Ifloga spicata (Dum.) Nebelek	TARBAH	تربة
83. Kickxia aegyptiaca (Dum.) Nebelek		
84. Koelpinia linearis Pall.	THA'LUQ	ثعلوق

INDEX OF PLANT NAMES

INDEX OF PLANT NAMES

128. Rhazya stricta	HARMAL	حرمل
129. Robbairea dilileana Milne- Redh.		
130. Roemeria hybrida (L.) DC.	BAKHATRI	بغزوي
131. Rostraria cristata (L.) Tzvelev		
132. Rostraria pumila (Desf.) Tzvelev	SHU'AYYIRAH	شعيرة
133. Rumex pictus Forssk.	HAMBASIS	حميصيص
134. Rumex vesicarius L.	HUMAYDH	حميض
135. Savigyna parviflora (Del.) Webb	QULAYQILAN	قليقلان
136 Scabiosa olivieri Coulter	WUBAYRAH	وبرة
137. Schimpera arabica Hochst. ex Steud.	SUFFAR	صفار
138. Schismus arabicus Nees	SUMAYMA	صميماء
139. Schismus barbatus (L.) Thell.	SUMAYMA	صميماء
140. Sclerocephalus arabicus Boiss.	HARAS	حراس
141. Scorzonera musili Vel.	THA'LUQ	ذعلوق
142. Scrophularia hypericifolia	A'LQA	هلقى
143. Seidlitzia rosmarinus Ehren ex Bunge.	SHNAN	شنان
144. Senecio desfontainei Druce.	ZUMLUQ	زملوق
145. Senecio flavus (Decne.) Sch. Bip.		
146. Silene arabica Boiss.		
147. Silene villosa Forssk.	TURBAH	تربة
148. Spergula fallax (Lowe) Krause		
149. Spergularia marina (L.) griseb.		
150. Spergularia rubra (L.) J. and C. presl.		
151. Stipa capensis Thunb.	SAMA'A	صمعاء
152. Stipagrostis drarii Taeckh.	SABAT	سبط
153. Stipagrostis obtusa (Del.) Nees	SULAYLAH	صليلة
154. Stipagrostis paradisea (Edgw.) De Wint.		
155. Stipagrostis plumosa L.	NASI	نصي
156. Tamarix aphyla (L.) Karst.	ATHEL	أثل
157. Tribulus longipetalus Viv.		
158. Tribulus macropteris Boiss.		
159. Tribulus terrestris L.	SHIRSHIR	شرشر
160. Trigonella anguina Del.	NAFAL	نفل
161. Trigonella hamosa L.	DARJAL	درجل
162. Trigonella stellata Forssk.	NAFAL	نفل
163. Tripleurospermum auriculatum (Boiss.) Rech. f.		
164. Zilla spinosa (Turr.)	SHUBRUM	شبرم
165. Zygophyllum simplex Forssk.	QARMAL	قرمل

REFERENCES

Ahlbrandt, T. 1979. Textual parameters of aeolian deposits. In: McKee, E. E. (Ed). *A study of global sand seas*, 21-51. Prof. Pap. U.S. Geological Survey, No. **1052**.

Ahti, T., Hamet, A. & Jalas, J. 1968. Vegetation zones and their sections in north-western Europe. *Ann. Bot. Fenn.* **5**, 169-211.

Al-Hamawe, Y. 1955. *Mu'a iam Al Buldan* (in Arabic). Beirut: Dar Suder, Das Beirut.

Al-Hassan, H. 1991. *Range-lands condition, and ways to their improvement in the Widyan of northern Saudi Arabia.* (in Arabic). Unpublished M.A. Thesis, Arabian Gulf University.

Al-Laboun, A. 1987. The Unayzah formation: a new Permian-Carboniferous unit in Saudi Arabia. *Am. Ass. Pet. Geol. Bull.* **71**, 29-38.

Al-Laboun, A. 1990. Scientific research reveals extensive detail of Al Qaseem fossilised forest and its vegetation. (in Arabic). *Al Majallah Al Arabivah* **154**, 14-18

Al-Nafie. A. 1989. *Large mammals of central and northern Saudi Arabia.* Unpublished M.A. thesis, University of New Mexico.

Al-Nafie, A. 1995. *Natural vegetation of the sand seas of central & northern Saudi Arabia: a biogeographic study.* Unpublished Ph.D. dissertation, University of Hull.

Al-Tubrak, A. & Al-Hasson, S. 1992. Infiltrometer tests in the Ad-Dahna sand dunes. *The Arabian Journal for Science and Engineering.* **17**, 121-129.

Anton, D. 1984. Aspects of geomorphological evolution: palaeosols and dunes in Saudi Arabia. In: A Jado & J. Zotl (Eds). *The Quaternary period in Saudi Arabia*, pp. 275-296. New York: Springer Verlag.

Arab League Organisation of Agricultural Development (AOAD). 1955. *The propagation of endangered species in Saudi Arabia.* (in Arabic). Khartonum: AOAD.

Axelrod, D. 1952. A theory of angiosperm evolution. *Evolution* **6**, 29-60

Ayyad, M. 1973. Vegetation and environment of the western Mediterranean coastal land of Egypt: the habitat of sand dunes. *J. Ecol.* **61**, 509-523.

Bagnold, R. 1954. The physical aspects of clay deserts. In: Cloudsley-Thompson, J. (Ed). *The biology of hot and cold deserts.* pp. 7-12. London.

Baierle, H. & Frey, W. 1986. A vegetation transect through central Saudi Arabia. In: H. Kurschner (Ed.) *Contributions to the vegetation of south-west Asia.* pp. 25-66 Wiesbaden.

Bashour, L., Al-Mashhady, A., Deviprasad, J., Miller, T. & Mazroa, M. 1983. Morphology and composition of some soils under cultivation in Saudi Arabia. *Geoderma* **29**, 327-340.

Batanouny, K. 1979. Vegetation along the Jeddah-Mecca road: pattern and process as affected by human impact. *J. Arid. Environments* **2**, 21-30

Blunt, Lady Anne. 1881, 1968 reprint. *A pilgrimage to Nejd* (2 vols). London: Murray.

Breed, C., Fryberger, S., Andrews, S., McCauley, C., Lennartz, F., Gebel, P. & Horstmann, K. 1979. Regional studies of sand seas, using Landsat imagery. In: McKee, E. D. (ed.) *A study of global sand seas* 305-398. U.S. Geological Survey.

Brown, G. 1960. Geomorphology of western and central Saudi Arabia. *Proc. 21st. Int. Geol. Cong.,* 150-159.

Carruthers, D. 1935. *Arabian adventure to the Great Nafud in quest of the oryx.* London: Weatherby.

Chapman, R. 1978. Geology & geomorphology of the Arabian peninsula. In: Al-Sayari, S. & Zotl, J. (Eds.) *The Quaternary period in Saudi Arabia.* pp. 31-44. New York: Springer-Verlag.

Chaudhary, S. 1983. Vegetation of the Great Nafud. *J. Saudi Arabian Nat. Hist. Soc.* **2**, 32-37.

Cope, T. A. 1985. A key to the grasses of the Arabian peninsula (Studies in the flora of Arabia XV). *Arab Gulf Journal of Scientific Research* Special Pub. **1**.

Cope, T. 1988. The flora of the sands. *J. Oman Studies, Special Report* **3**, 305-312.

Cottam, G. & Curtis, J. 1956. The use of distance measures in phytosociological sampling. *Ecology* **37**, 451-460.

Danin, A. 1978. Plant species diversity and plant succession in a sandy area in the northern Negev. *Flora* **167**, 409-422.

Daoud, H. 1985. *Flora of Kuwait: Dicotyledonae* London: KPI.

Dincer, T., Al-Mugrin, A. & Zimmerman, U. 1974. Study of the infiltration and recharge through the sand dunes in arid zones with special reference to the stable isotopes and thermonuclear tritium. *J. Hydrology* **23**, 79-109.

Dregne, H. 1976. *Soils of arid regions.* Amsterdam: Elsevier.

Dutton, R. 1988. Introduction, overview and conclusions. *J. Oman Studies, Special Report* **3**, 1-17.

Eig, A. 1931-32. *Les elements et les groupes phytogeograpique auxiliares dans la flora palestinienne* 2 pts. Beirut.

Eig, A. 1939. The vegetation of the light soil belt of the coastal plain of Palestine. *Palest. J. Bot.* **1**, 255-312.

El-Khayal, A., Chaloner, W. & Hill, C. 1980. Palaeozoic plants from Saudi Arabia. *Nature* **285**, 33-34.

Engler, A. 1910. *Die Pflanzenwelt Afrikas insbesondere seiner tropischen Gebiets.* Leipzig.

Evenari, M. 1985. The desert environment. In: M. Evenari, I. Noy-Meir & D Goodall (Eds) *Hot deserts & arid shrublands A,* 1-19. Amsterdam: Elsevier.

Farsi, Z. 1991. *National guide and atlas of the Kingdom of Saudi Arabia.* Jeddah: Zaki Farsi Office.

Freitag, H. 1986. Notes on the distribution, climate and flora of the sand deserts of Iran and Afghanistan. *Proc. Roy. Soc. Edinburgh.* **89B**, 135-146.

Frey, W. & Kurshner, H. 1989. *Die Vegetation imvorderen Orient*. Tubingen: Atlas Vorderen Orient.

Fryberger, S., Al-Sari, A., Clisham, T., Rizvi, S. & Al-Hinai, K. 1984. Wind sedimentation in the Jafurah sand sea, Saudi Arabia. *Sedimentology* **31**, 413-431.

Garrard, A., Harvey, C. & Switzer, V. 1981. Environment and settlement in the upper Pleistocene and Holocene at Jubbah in the Great Nafud, Saudi Arabia. *Atlal* **5**, 137-148.

Goldsmith, F., Harrison, C. & Morion, A. 1986. Description and analysis of vegetation. In: P. D. Moore & S. B. Chapman (Eds.) *Methods in plant ecology*. Oxford: Blackwell Scientific.

Goudie, A. S. 1990. Desert degradation. In: A.S. Goudie (Ed.) *Techniques for desert reclamation*. Chichester: John Wiley.

Gray, J., Massa, D. & Boucot, A. J. 1982. Caradocian land plant microfossils from Libya. *Geology* **10**, 197-201.

Guest, E. 1966. *The flora of Iraq*. Baghdad.

Gupta, J., 1979. Some observations on the periodic variations of moisture in stabilised and unstabalised sand dunes in the Auton desert. *J. Hydrology* **41**, 153-156.

Halwagy, R., Moustafa, A. & Kamel, S. 1982. On the ecology of the desert vegetation in Kuwait. *J. Arid Environments* **5**, 95-107.

Hamilton, W., Whybrow, P. & McClue, H. 1978. Fauna of fossil mammals from the Miocene of Saudi Arabia. *Nature* **274**, 248-249.

Halevy, G. & Orshan, G. 1972. Ecological studies on *Acacia* species in the Negev and Sinai. *Isr. Journal Bot.* **21**, 197-208.

Haynes, C., Mehringer, P. & Zaghloul, E. 1979. Pluvial lakes of north-western Sudan. *Geographical Journal* **145**, 437-445.

Heathcote, R. L. 1983. *The arid lands, their use and abuse*. London & New York: Longman.

Heemstra, H., Al Hassan, H. & Al Minwer, F. 1990. *Plants of northern Saudi Arabia: an illustrated guide* Al Jawf, Saudi Arabia: Ministry of Agriculture & Water.

Hill, M. 1979. *TWINSPAN: a fortran program for detrended correspondence analysis and reciprocal averaging*. Ithaca: Cornell University.

Holm, D. 1953. Dome-shaped dunes of the Central Nejd, Saudi Arabia. *19th Int. Geol. Cong. Algiers, Comptes Rendus* **7**, 107-112.

Holm, D. 1960. Desert geomorphology in the Arabian peninsula. *Science* **132**, 1369-1379.

Hotzl, H., Kramer, F. & Maurin, V. 1978. Summary and general conclusions. In: S. Al-Sayari & J Zotl (Eds.) The *Quaternary period in Saudi Arabia*, 264-311. New York: Springer Verlag.

Kassas, M. 1966. Plant live in deserts. In: E. Hills (Ed.) *Arid lands, geographical appraisal* pp. 145-180. London: Methuen.

Kaul, A. 1986. *Haloxylon salicornicum* - an arid-land shrub: its ecology and potential. *Annals of Arid Zone* **25**, 31-43.

Kent, M. & Coker, P. 1992. *Vegetation description and analysis: a practical approach*. London: Bellhaven Press.

Koller, D., Sachs, M. & Negbi, M. 1964.Germinating-regulating mechanisms in some desert seeds. VIII. *Artemesia monosperma*. *Plant & Cell Physio*. **5**, 85-100.

Kurschner, H. 1986. A physiognomic-ecological classification of the vegetation of southern Jordan. In: H. Kurschner (Ed.) *Contributions to the vegetation of south-west Asia*, 45-74. Weishaden: Ludwig Reichert Verlag.

Leachman, G. 1911. A journey in north-eastern Arabia. *Geographical Journal* **37**, 265-274.

Litav, M., Kupernik, G. & Orshan, G. 1963. The role of competition as a factor in determining the distribution of dwarf shrub communities in Mediterranean territory. *J. Ecology* **51**, 467-486.

Lorimer, J. 1908, 1970 reprint. *Gazeteer of the Persian Gulf, Oman and Central Arabia*. Farnborough: Gregg International.

MacKinnon, J., MacKinnon, K., Child, G. and Thorsell, J. 1986. *Managing protected areas in the tropics*. Gland: IUCN.

Mandaville, J. 1984. Studies in the flora of Arabia XI: some historical and geographical aspects of a principal floristic frontier. *Notes, Royal Bot. Gdn. Edinburgh* **42**, 1-15.

Mandaville, J. 1986. Plant life in the Rub'Al Khali (the Empty Quarter). *Proc. Roy. Soc. Edinburgh, Section B,* **89**, 147-157.

Mandaville, J. 1990. *Flora of eastern Saudi Arabia*. London: Kegan Paul.

Mann, H., Lahiri, A. & Pareek, O. 1976. A study on the moisture availability and other conditions of unstabalised dunes. *Annals of Arid Zones* **15**, 270-284.

Masry, A. 1977. Introduction: the historical legacy of Saudi Arabia. *Atlal* **1**, 9-20.

McClure, H. 1984. *Late Quaternary environments of the Rub' al Khali*. Unpublished Ph.D. Dissertation, University of London.

McClure, H. 1978. Ar 'Rub al Khali. In: S. Al-Sayari & J. Zotl (Eds.) *The Quaternary period in Saudi Arabia,* 252-263. New York; Springer Verlag.

Migahid, A. 1961. The drought resistance of Egyptian desert plants. *Arid Zone Res.* **16**, 213-231.

Mighaid, A. 1980. Natural vegetation of Saudi Arabia (in Arabic). *Al Majallah Al Arabivah* **5**, 32-43; **6**, 40-47.

Mighaid, A. 1988. *Flora of Saudi Arabia, 3rd Edit*. 3 vols. Riyadh: King Saud University.

Mighaid, A. & El-Sheikh, A. 1977. Types of desert habitat and their vegetation in central and eastern Saudi Arabia. *Proc. Saudi Biol. Soc.* **1**.

Miller, A. & Nyberg, J. 1991. Patterns of endemism in Arabia. *Flora et Vegetatio Mundi* **9**, 263-279.

Ministry of Agriculture & Water. 1988. *Water Atlas of Saudi Arabia*. Riyadh: Ministry of Agriculture and Water.

Ministry of Agriculture & Water. 1992. *Natural history of Saudi Arabia: an introduction*. Riyabh: Ministry of Agriculture and Water.

Mueller-Dombois, D. & Ellenberg, H. 1974. *Aims and methods of vegetation ecology*. New York: Wiley.

Munton, P. 1988. An overview of the ecology of the Wahiba sands. *J. Oman Studies, Special Report* **3**, 231-240.

Musil, A. 1927. Arabia deserta. *Oriental explorations & studies, American Geographical Society*, **5.**

Musil, A. 1928. Northern Negd. *Oriental explorations and studies, American Geographical Society*, **5**.

Novikova, N. 1970. Drawing up a preliminary vegetation map of Arabia. *Geobotanicheskoe Karo-Gratifovanie,* 61-71.

Noy-Meir, I. 1973. Desert ecosystems: environment and producers. *Ann. Rev. Ecol. Syst.* **4**, 25-51.

Orshan, G. & Zohary, M. 1963. Vegetation of the sand deserts in the western Negev of Israel. *Vegetatio* **11**, 112-120.

Palgrave, W. 1871. *Personal narrative of a year's journey through central and eastern Arabia* London and New York: MacMillan.

Parr, P., Zarins, Ibrahim M., Waachter, J., Garrard, A., Clarke, C., Bidmead, H. & Al-Bodr, H. 1978. Preliminary report of the Northern Province survey. *Atlal* **2**, 29-50.

Petrov, M. 1976. *Deserts of the world.* New York: Wiley.

Philby, H. St. J. B. 1933. *The Empty Quarter* London: Constable.

Philips, J. 1882. The red sands of the Arabian desert. *Geol. Soc of London, Quarterly Journal* **38**, 110-113.

Popov, G. & Zeller, W. 1963. *Ecological survey report on the 1962 survey in the Arabian peninsula.* Rome: FAO.

Powers, R., Ramirez, L. Redmond, C. & Elberg, E. Jr. 1966. *Geology of the Arabian peninsula: sedimentary geology of Saudi Arabia.* U.S. Geological Survey. Washington D.C.

Prill, R. 1968. Movement of moisture in the unsaturated zone in a dune area, south-western Kansas. *U.S. Geol. Survey Prof. Pap. 600-D,* 1-9.

Pye, K. & Tsoar, H. 1990. *Aeolian sand and sand dunes.* London: Unwin Hyman.

Richards, L. 1956. *Diagnosis and improvements of saline & alkaline soils.* U.S. Dep't Agriculture, Washington D.C.

Robinson, M. & Seely, M. 1980. Physical and biotic environment of the southern Namib dune ecosystem. *J. Arid Environments* **3**, 183-203.

Schulz, E. & Whitney, J. 1986. Upper Pleistocene & Holocene lakes in the An Nafud, Saudi Arabia. *Hydrobiologia* **143**, 175-190.

Shimwell, D. W. 1971. *The description and classification of vegetation.* London: Sidgwick & Jackson.

Street, F. & Grove, A. 1979. Global maps of lake-level fluctuations since 30,000 B.P. *Quat. Res.* **12**, 83-118.

Täckholm, V. 1974. *Student's flora of Egypt,* 2nd. edit. Cairo: Cairo University.

Tadros, T. 1956. An ecological survey of the semi-arid coastal strip of the western desert of Egypt. *Bill. Inst. Desert Egypte* **6**, 28-56.

Takhtajan, A. 1969. *Flowering plants: origin and dispersal.* Edinburgh: Oliver & Boyd.

Taktajan, A. 1986. *Floristic regions of the world.* Berkeley & Los Angeles: University of California Press.

Ter Braak, C. 1988. *CANOCO-a Fortran program for canonical community ordination* Wageningen: Agricultural Mathematical Group.

Thesiger, W. 1959. *Arabian Sands.* London:

Longmans Thomas, H., Sen, S., Khan, M., Battail, B. & Ligabue, G. 1981. The Lower Miocene fauna of Al-Sarrah *Atlas* 5, 109-136.

Thornthwaite, C.W. 1948. An approach towards a rational classification of climate. *Geographical Review* 38.

Tsoar, H. 1990. The ecological background, deterioration and reclamation of desert dune sand. *Agriculture, ecosystems and environment* 33, 147-170.

Tsoar, H. & Moller, J. 1986. The role of vegetation in the formation of linear sand dunes. In: W. Nickling (Ed) *Aeolian geomorphology,* pp. 75-95. Boston: Allen & Unwin.

Van Couvering, J. 1976. Evolution of Old World grasslands fauna. *25th Int. Geol. Congr. Abstracts* 1, 320-321.

Van Wijk, W. & de Vries, D. 1963. Periodic temperature variations in a homogeneous soil. In: W. Van Wijk (Ed.) *Physics of the plant environment,* 102-143. Amsterdam: North Holland.

Vesey-Fitzgerald, D. 1957. The vegetation of central and eastern Arabia. *J. Ecol.* 45, 77-98.

Vita-Finzi, C. 1978. Recent alluvial history in the catchment of the Arabo-Persian Gulf. In: W. C. Brice (Ed.) *The environmental*

history of the Near and Middle East since the last Ice Age, 255-261 London: Academic Press.

Wallen, C. & Stockholm, S. 1966. Arid zone meteorology. In: E. Hills (Ed.) *Arid lands: a geographical appraisal.* Paris: UNESCO.

Wallin, G. 1848. Narrative of a journey from Cairo to Medina and Mecca. *J. Royal Geog. Soc.* 24, 115-207.

Walter, H. 1979. *Vegetation of the earth, and ecological systems of the geobiosphere.* New York: Springer-Verlag.

Walton, K. 1969. *The arid zones.* Chicago: Aldine.

Whitney, J., Faulkender, D. & Rubin, M. 1983. *The environmental history and present condition of the northern sand seas of Saudi Arabia.* Saudi Arabian Deputy Minister of Mineral Resources Open File Report USGS-OF-03-95.

Whybrow, P. & McClure, H. 1980/81. Fossil mangrove roots and palaeoenvironments of the Miocene of the eastern Arabian peninsula. *Palaeogeography, Palaeoclimatology, Palaeoecology* 32, 213-225.

Wilson, L. 1973. Ergs. *Sedimentary Geology* 10, 77-106.

Zohary, M. 1940. On the Ghadha Tree of northern Arabia and the Syrian desert. *Palestine J. Bot., Johnsalem Series* 1, 413-416.

Zohary, M. 1962. *The plant life of Palesting.* New York: Ronald Press.

Zohary, M. 1973. *Geobotanical foundations of the Middle East.* 2 vols. Stuttgart: Gustav Fischer Verlag.

Zohary, M. & Fahn, A. 1952. Ecological studies on east Mediterranean dune plants. *Bull. Res. Counc. Israel* **1**, 38-

VALUING HEALTH IN PRACTICE

H0234823

Valuing Health in Practice
Priorities, QALYs, and Choice

DOUGLAS McCULLOCH
University of Ulster

Routledge
Taylor & Francis Group

LONDON AND NEW YORK

First published 2003 by Ashgate Publishing

Reissued 2019 by Routledge
2 Park Square, Milton Park, Abingdon, Oxon, OX14 4RN
52 Vanderbilt Avenue, New York, NY 10017

Routledge is an imprint of the Taylor & Francis Group, an informa business

Publisher's Note
The publisher has gone to great lengths to ensure the quality of this reprint but points out that some imperfections in the original copies may be apparent.

Disclaimer
The publisher has made every effort to trace copyright holders and welcomes correspondence from those they have been unable to contact.

A Library of Congress record exists under LC control number:

ISBN 13: 978-1-138-72172-2 (hbk)
ISBN 13: 978-1-138-72170-8 (pbk)
ISBN 13: 978-1-315-19419-6 (ebk)

Contents

List of Tables and Figure

Preface

Social priorities tend not to be of interest to physicians, possibly because they are trained to focus on the health needs of individuals, not groups, and they can be reluctant to examine prioritisation issues. The pages that follow tease out some of the complexities, particularly those identified by economists.

The pharmaceutical companies are spending millions on the making of value judgements by economists, because governments have begun to require evidence that new drugs and other health technologies give "value for money". This term is often imprecisely defined, and the evidence, when collected, is not always used as the basis for action. Their commercial interests should not prevent pharmaceutical companies from greater engagement in prioritisation debates, and the issues explained here are also relevant to them.

Perhaps economists do not often enough explain the importance of trying to get the most from the resources available. Most people are involved in health care as either patients or carers, so that they become focussed on one condition, to the exclusion of all others. Just what it means to think socially about health is new to most people, as some of the experience reported here has shown, but it is not impossible, nor even difficult, if the ideas are carefully presented.

In the richest societies, there continues to be an interest in social mechanisms for resource allocation which are beyond the market and the centrally planned economy. Health care provision has a high political priority in most countries; it also involves the requirement to provide basic care as well as advanced technological solutions, in a manner which respects basic human values. While strategies for valuing health in practice cannot be described as templates for dealing with other modern problems, an understanding of these particular issues may provide lessons which have wider relevance.

Acknowledgements

I would like to thank Professor Charles Normand, of the London School of Hygiene and Tropical Medicine.

Thanks are also due to:

Dr. M. Barry, Director, and Dr. M. Ryan, Senior Pharmacist, Irish Centre of Pharmacoeconomics, Dublin; Dr. R. Cookson, London School of Economics and Political Science; Dr. E. Kula, University of Ulster; Professor A. Maynard, London School of Economics and Political Science; Dr. D. McDaid, London School of Economics and Political Science; Ms. P. McKee, University of Ulster; Mr. H. O'Kane, Cardiac Surgeon, Royal Victoria Hospital, Belfast; Dr. C. O'Neill, University of Ulster;

Patricia McKee, at the University of Ulster, was indispensable to all aspects of the computing work required to get this book written and into print.

The errors and omissions that remain are mine.

Dr. Kind's permission to reproduce material derived from the MVH Project investigation of EuroQol 5-D, the Rosser-Kind collaboration, and the Health Measurement Questionnaire, Professor Patrick's permission to reproduce the statements from the Functional Limitations Profile, and Dr. McKenna's permission to reproduce the statements from the Nottingham Health Profile, are all gratefully acknowledged.

Abbreviations

ASTEC	Analysis of the Scientific and Technical Evaluation of Health Interventions
CBA	Cost-Benefit Analysis
CEA	Cost-Effectiveness Analysis
CMA	Cost-Minimisation Analysis
CUA	Cost-Utility Analysis
EPMST	Extended Post-Marketing Surveillance Trial
EHI	Evaluation of Health Interventions
EQD	Expected QALY Deficit
FLP	Functional Limitations Profile
HMQ	Health Measurement Questionnaire
hrqol	health-related quality of life
MEQI	Mean Expected QALY Indicator
NHP	Nottingham Health Profile
PBMA	Programmed Budgeting and Marginal Analysis
QALY	Quality Adjusted Life Year
RCT	Randomised Controlled Trial
SIP	Sickness Impact Profile

Chapter 1

Priorities, QALYs, and Choice

Introduction

During a research project valuing health states, a heart bypass candidate expressed suicidal intent during two separate interview sessions. This patient had been waiting months for the procedure; he could barely get out of his chair without help, he was unable to read or talk for more than a few minutes at a time, and his responses to the questionnaires registered zero quality of life. The surgeon was told of the researcher's fear that the patient might kill himself; a few weeks later, the patient received the bypass.

Without the two research interviews, this patient might have died before the operation took place; this chance occurrence probably prolonged his life, and improved its quality. Clearly, it would have been better if his quality of life and survival prospects had been assessed on some routine, consistent basis, and compared with the health of other patients who were waiting for the same procedure. This would have brought his very poor quality of life to the surgeon's notice, without the need for a consultation; it might also have caused the procedure to have gone to someone with the same quality of life, and a better chance of survival. But in either case, his quality of life and survival prospects would have been taken into account as a matter of routine, rather than by chance. This is possible because reliable questionnaires have been developed, which can determine patient quality of life, and measure health outcomes; for a variety of reasons, they have not been routinely applied in health services.

Even when formal measures are not being used, health sector choices imply health valuation. Suppose a hospital can, for the same cost, increase either the number of neo-natal intensive care places, or the number of hip joint replacements; selecting one and not the other values its outcomes more, whether or not quality of life information are available. Similarly, the allocation of respite days between carers, when not all can have a break, effectively values the need of some carers more than others. Health valuation is thus the consequence of scarcity and the need for choice.

Purpose

The purpose of this book is to explain health valuation in practice, that is, the different methods of making choices in the health sector, particularly the main measure of health outcome, the quality-adjusted life year, or QALY. The rest of this chapter explains three methods of choice-making, Programmed Budgeting and

Marginal Analysis (PBMA), Cost-Effectiveness Analysis (CEA), and Cost-Benefit Analysis (CBA), as a prelude to the examination of health priority-setting which constitutes the rest of the book.

The development of the QALY has been one of the success stories of economics in the past twenty years; the concept illustrates what choice means in the health sector, and it has generated a large literature in the fields of medical ethics, decision analysis, and health policy, as well as in health economics. This is not to say that a QALY measure should invariably be used to compare   medical interventions, though (in my view) QALY measures could and should be used more often. The arguments surrounding the QALY are important, and in exploring them, we are investigating the dimensions of the problem of health valuation.

Outline

With the aim, then, of exploring the valuation of health in practice, chapter 2 explains the QALY idea, and the main approaches to developing QALY values, while chapter 3 examines the development of two particular measures, the EuroQol, and the Rosser-Kind Index. The first is a relatively widely used and well-tested QALY measure, while the use of the second to produce measured outcomes began the QALY debates in the United Kingdom in the early 1970s. The contrast is necessary because the choice between QALY measures remains a matter of judgement; we have no choice but to choose between health interventions and patients, and hence to value health, but judgement can and should be exercised over the method employed for determining the alternatives and the data collected.

The issues involved in QALY development are illustrated by chapter 4, which explains and discusses the statistical testing of the Rosser-Kind measure, while chapter 5 explains how procedures may be compared using a QALY measure. Chapter 6 examines three problems of getting the "right" evidence for applying a QALY measure, and develops a different basis for prioritisation, which permits a more scientific approach to be taken to resource allocation in health services than is possible using only CEA and evidence from randomised controlled trials.

The collection of statistical evidence is a necessary part of valuing health outcomes; the question is, what is the best means of collection? The Randomised Controlled Trial (RCT) has its limitations, even when diseases and procedures are relatively well understood; when the disease is not understood, when the operation of the available drugs is uncertain, and when non-disease factors, such as accommodation type, proximity of family members, and other health variables, have a significant effect on outcome, getting statistical control can be expensive. Alzheimer's Disease is an example of a condition which, for these and other reasons, is not easily susceptible to analysis using RCT evidence. In chapter 7, we explain how the drug companies have coped with these difficulties, and present two possible methods for valuing health, that is, for making the difficult choices which resource allocation within the AD sector involves. These are offered and discussed as part of the exposition of what valuing health means, in practice; neither they nor the QALY approach are simple solutions to the problems of health prioritisation.

What valuation of health occurs in practice, and how successful is it? This seems an impossibly large question, but attempting to answer it provides important information about the health sector, particularly the way that research results are actually applied. Broadly speaking, this question was the remit of the ASTEC project (Analysis of the Scientific and TEChnical Evaluation of Health Interventions), which completed its work in April 2000. Chapter 8 reports the salient findings, as part of our exploration of what health valuation means, in practice; it indicates some of the structural problems in the way of what appear to be obvious innovations and developments in the adoption of cost-effective medicines.

Approaches to Health Valuation

The theme of choice runs through all of this book. The basic idea is familiar; as consumers, we often weigh the features of different items against their prices, and make a decision which is intended to get the best value from our expenditure. The same applies to health care, except that the aim is to improve health to the greatest possible extent (usually, on behalf of society as a whole), given the available resources, and the definition of both costs and outcomes is explicit and may be complex, as the following outline of Programmed Budgeting and Marginal Analysis demonstrates.

Programmed Budgeting and Marginal Analysis (PBMA):Making Judgements on the Evidence

The steps of PBMA may be described as follows:[1]

- Identify and describe the programme (cardiac care; children's hospital services; etc.), including all its components, or sub-programmes;
- Set out the programme budget, showing the expenditures allocated to the sub-programmes, and the activities of each programme;
- Decide which services are to be introduced / expanded / contracted;
- Measure, or assess, as accurately as possible, the costs and benefits of the possible changes which emerge from the previous stage;
- Make recommendations, based on a judgement which weighs the costs and outcomes of each alternative.

There may be costs which cannot be allocated to different parts of the programme; whether they are important depends on the structures of care delivery, in the sense that the proposed changes may or may not have an effect on the size or incidence of these totals. It should also be considered whether objectives of the programme have been specified which have had no resources allocated to them, and whether (strange as this may seem) money amounts exist which are not actually being spent on any part of the programme.

In the assessment of benefits and costs, groups of purchasers, providers, and patients should be asked what the effect of the proposed changes (more funds / less funds) would be on their particular service. Local knowledge should be accessed, and the literature should be examined for suitable potential changes, or for reasons for doubt about value for money in particular areas.

PBMA may be described as a non-prescriptive approach to the structure of healthcare choice; value judgements do enter, in the definition of the budget, its sub-budgets, and their associated activities These will have been defined on the basis of a particular view of how a service should be structured. It is possible to question the division of the budget into its sub-headings; the decisions examined in the PBMA concern amounts which may be allocated to one sub-heading or another, and it follows that the accounting system is important. If we can identify different classifications, and reliably determine the allocation of the budget between these headings, then a PBMA based on new definitions of the budget is possible. The choice is between different incremental (or marginal) alterations to the sub-budgets; each change is expected to have different merits and drawbacks, and the changes have to be compared, by weighing these impacts, and exercising judgement between them.

Cost-Effectiveness Analysis: Measuring to Maximise

In PBMA, incremental changes are compared, and a judgement reached, without necessarily measuring costs and outcomes. By contrast, the decision model underlying Cost-Effectiveness Analysis (CEA), is that of a consumer allocating a budget between alternatives which are comparable in cost per unit of outcome terms, such as the cost per QALY or the cost per year of survival. To take one possible example, the decision-taker is saying "Will one more hip replacement give us more health per unit cost than one more bypass?" The idea is that the maximum impact on health will be achieved by going down the list of alternatives ranked in these terms until the budget is exhausted.

This model of the decision-taking process comes from welfare economics (for a definition, see the next section, on Cost-Benefit Analysis). As a representation of health services; it leaves something to be desired. Numbers of procedures are increased in steps, not one at a time; costs depend on definitions which can vary, and data is not often available regarding the health impact of the procedures to be compared. (The development of the quality-adjusted life year, or QALY, is an attempt to facilitate such comparisons; CEAs which use QALYs as outcome measures are "Cost-Utility Analyses".)

Conclusions about the relative cost-effectiveness of procedures depend on the assumptions made, particularly about costs; it follows that a clear CEA can be more important in terms of its method than in its actual quantitative results, because it shows which factors determine the value of the cost per unit of outcome measure, providing a guide to similar calculations in other contexts.

It is important to distinguish between the average cost of an intervention and the marginal cost; briefly, the latter is the cost of additional interventions, added to an existing programme, while average cost is simply total costs divided by the number of interventions undertaken. For example, the capacity of a unit might be 200 cases a year; if it is treating 180 cases, with (say) total running costs of £720,000, the average cost per case is £4,000. Treating a further 20 cases could cost less or more than £80,000 (20 x 4,000), depending on what resources were necessary to treat the extra cases. If the existing staff had to work overtime, at a higher rate per hour, then the additional cost would be greater than £80,000, so that the marginal cost would be greater than the average cost. If existing staff were not already fully employed, then the marginal cost of the new cases would be less than the current average cost. Analyses do sometimes make the assumption that average cost and marginal cost are identical; it is important that this assumption is made evident.

Cost-Effectiveness Analysis (CEA) has been widely applied to health alternatives; the importance of assumptions can be shown by the following example. It is possible that Paget's Disease (which affects the strength of bones) could be treated by a pill taken daily; currently, treatment consists of an intensive procedure in hospital, which lasts two days every six months. Suppose that clinical trials show that the two treatments are equally effective; also suppose that, for the health service, six months of taking the pill is cheaper. Should the daily pill be substituted for the two-day procedure every six months?

The answer is not obvious; will patients who are not in a clinical trial actually take the pill every day? If they do not, is the decline in health effect (and the waste of resources) the responsibility of the physician or of the patient? In a health service which is free at the point of delivery, the health service always has responsibility for improving the patient's health, and if the treatment does not actually have the impact expected, the liability to expend resources remains, regardless of where lies the fault for the patient not getting better. This liability does not appear on the balance sheet, but it is nonetheless real, and proposals have recently been formulated for taking it into account (Hughes et al (2001)).

The CEA approach defined below is widely used (recent examples include Gyrdhansen et al (1998), and Whynes et al (1998)), and examples are provided on the UK National Health Service Database (www.nhs.crd.co.uk), as well as, commercially, by the London Office of Health Economics (www.ohe.org). The approach is not free from controversy, particularly in respect of the costs which should be included (Johannesson and Metzler (1998)), but it is widely accepted as an approach to valuing health in practice.

The important steps in cost-effectiveness analysis may be defined as follows:

1. Clearly specify the interventions to be compared - this means identifying the patient groups to be treated, as well as the actual interventions.
2. Identify and measure the relevant costs - these are usually the direct medical costs, such as nursing time, drugs, or scanner use, but may also include the time of carers and patients, as well as earnings foregone for both as a result of the interventions.
3. Identify and measure the relevant outcomes - generally these include the health improvement, including relevant quality of life effects, plus

"negative benefits", such as adverse side-effects (hair loss in chemotherapy), and income, if the ability to work is restored. Health impacts can be added if they are measured in the same terms, using for example survival changes, or a QALY measure.

4.   Account for uncertainties - all analyses rely on assumptions, such as the expected length of survival, or the expected average age of patients, and the vulnerability of the results to possible changes in these assumptions should be explicitly examined. Altering such assumptions to see their effect on the treatment comparison is referred to as *sensitivity analysis* (see chapter 5 for an example).

The point of view matters; society's costs will be wider than those of the health service or the insurer. In cost-effectivness analysis, an arbitrary line has to be drawn around the subject for investigation (Drummond et al (1987)) if any analysis at all is to be completed. Determining which procedure is cost-effective might, on an idealistic view, require a theory of value, or an estimate of the effect on resource costs of a firm's monopoly power. The researcher has to make assumptions, and proceed, to get any results which might be useful within the time or resources available.

It is also possible, of course, that researchers do not include all the costs that others might consider reasonable. In our chapter on Alzheimer's Disease, we see that the cost of unpaid carers' services were not included in all the studies calculating drugs' costs and benefits; from the point of view of health services finance, this might be justifiable, but, if carers are regarded as a health service asset (because they prevent health budget expense), such costs should be included.

Also, specifying the monetary value of resource costs can be difficult; drug prices are sometimes subsidised, and administration costs may have to be divided between different specialties. When there are costs or benefits occurring in the future, a discount rate is often applied to convert all costs into present-day terms; this is not a straightforward matter (see Kula (1997)), though the issues involved need not detain the present discussion.

Cost-Benefit Analysis (CBA): Maximising Utility

This is the technique of choice for most economists, when they want to appraise a project (in either the public or the private sector) from a communal viewpoint; it is the application of welfare economics (also known as the "welfarist", or "Paretian", approach, see Culyer (1989)) to economic evaluation. The central assumption is that markets are perfectly competitive, with many buyers and sellers, perfect price information, and a homogeneous good, among other conditions. Different situations are evaluated under the assumptions that:

- individuals are the best judges of their own welfare;
- total social welfare depends on the value (or "utility") to individuals of goods and services, and nothing else; and
- total social welfare, and nothing else, should be the maxim.

All the effects of the project (both positive and negative) on the individual welfare of everyone in the community are identified, and measured in money terms, so that aggregate effects can be compared to aggregate costs. The decision rule is that a project provides a potential improvement if the total money amount that gainers are willing to pay, to ensure the project is implemented, is greater than the total money amount which losers from it are willing to accept, to persuade them to tolerate it. (This is known as the "Kaldor-Hicks" criterion (Little (1965)); actual compensation does not have to be paid). When there are several projects competing for finance, then the one which offers the greatest potential improvement should be chosen.

When the CBA approach is applied to the health sector, the setting of money values on health outcomes, however defined, is a necessary feature. There is a reluctance to value health in money terms, which has been noted by Sloan (1995), and Coast et al (1996), in their discussions of health evaluation and CBA. The approach has also been criticised (Coast et al (1996), Rheinhardt (1998)) on the grounds that it will value more highly those interventions which are particularly desired or needed by those with greater wealth or income, and this is regarded as unacceptable in regard to health care production. There is also the question of the choice of discount rate (see above), to equalise the value of future outcomes with present ones, taking into account the greater preference of individuals for present outcomes. The view taken here is that discounting on behalf of society is different from discounting by individuals (as measured in the financial markets from which government discount rates are usually taken).

Further, the requirement to include all welfare effects of the different alternatives requires some means of capturing all, or most, of these effects; this means is usually the theory of perfect markets ("perfect competition"). Given its assumptions, this theory shows that the operation of perfect markets reduces prices to the level of the per unit cost of production, so that consumers pay only for the resources required to produce the good. If consumers are rational and well-informed, these prices will be equal to the social value of the item produced. According to Sugden and Williams (1978), there is a "working assumption" that prices measure social costs and social values. When this assumption does not hold, "shadow" prices must be applied, with the aim of reflecting social opportunity costs and/or marginal social benefits.

CBA Applied to Health

The health care domain has important features which are good reasons to conclude that the required assumptions are incorrect. First, consumer ignorance regarding both the nature and effects of treatments and procedures implies that the social value of an intervention cannot be determined from observing market transactions, or their near-equivalents. In health terms, patients frequently understand neither what they want nor what they need; the same may apply to other important goods, such as pension plans, computer systems, and genetically modified food. Whatever the product, when its important features are not understood, consumer choice may be defective, and markets cannot achieve economic efficiency, that is, the maximum (least-cost) possible output of the goods which consumers value most.

Given this ignorance, it may also be a mistake to assume that in all cases doctors will act in the patient's best interests, as "perfect agents". Doctors have interests of their own which may conflict with the health and the welfare of the patient, or with the aim of governments to get the most health from the health budget. Over-prescribing of drugs, or "Supplier-Induced Demand" for procedures or tests, are examples of this; doctors may treat patients more, either more frequently or more intensively, in order to maintain their incomes. The "perfect" agent would identify perfectly with the patient, using his or her knowledge to treat the patient as him- or herself.

It seems to be widely accepted that health care is different from the commodities traded in the perfect markets from which CBA derives its shadow prices (Santerre and Neun (1996), Folland et al. (1993), Williams (1992)). In the 1970s, these considerations, plus the increasing political importance of health service efficiency in times of budgetary restriction, led to the development of cost-effectiveness analysis, described above. CEA is the technique of choice for what have been called the "extra-welfarist" economists (Culyer (1989)), who accept health as the maximand, rather than utility or welfare. The QALY permits the comparison of procedures and treatments between health sectors and not just within them, so that, in principle at least, meaningful choices between health sectors (as well as within the same sector) can be defined.

Conclusion

Ever present, scarcity implies choice, and when health choices are made, valuations result; in practice, valuing health is inescapable, so that the question is not whether to have health valuations, but how best to make them. This requires an understanding of health sector choice, to which the QALY, in all of its aspects, is central. In what follows, arguments for and against QALYs will be discussed; these are part of the problems of health valuation, and should not be interpreted to imply that QALYs cannot or should not be used, because in many contexts, a QALY measure will be useful and appropriate. Since we must choose, QALY data will often be the best basis for such a choice.

The QALY, and all the aspects which relate to it, does not entirely define the area of health valuation, and other aspects are considered towards the end of the book. The essential problem, which faces the members of all health systems, is the valuation of health in practice; all the other considerations are only part of the journey to that destination. Since the QALY is central, the next chapter introduces and develops this idea.

Note

1. Donaldson et al (1995) is a useful introduction to PBMA; recent contributions to the
   literature include Mitton et al (2000) and Miller et al (2001).

Chapter 2

The Quality-Adjusted Life Year

Introduction

Should health choices just happen, or should we have a clear idea about what the choices are, and debate them? This issue began to be raised in the 1950s, and the QALY is the latest in a series of attempts to measure health outcomes. Developers have drawn on and contributed to the emerging discipline of psychometrics, as well as the work done to produce health profiles, which are briefly described in the next chapter. In QALY development, reliability and validity have proved to be important, and this chapter examines these, before discussing some of the main points from the literature, and outlining the important approaches to the development of QALY measures. First of all, however, the QALY approach is described.

The QALY Approach

> We can define the full range of health states that describe patients before and after all the interventions between which resources are to be allocated. These states can be valued on a cardinal scale, from zero (death) to unity (full health). If H1 and H2, and S1 and S2, respectively, are the average health state values and expected years of survival before and after a particular intervention, then the value in QALYs of the intervention is: (H2 x S2) - (H1 x S1).

Source: McCulloch (1998)

The following fictional example shows how the QALY could work, given a reliable and valid QALY measure.

Example

Two cancer drugs are the same in every respect except their impacts on survival and health-related quality of life (hrqol). On the average, Drug A increases hrqol from a health state valued at 0.6, to one valued at 0.8, and increases survival from 2 years to 3 years; therefore, it produces:

$$(0.8 \times 3) - (0.6 \times 2) = 1.2 \text{ QALYs.}$$

Drug B increases hrqol from 0.6 to 0.7, and increases survival from 2 years to 4 years; it produces:

$$(0.7 \times 4) - (0.6 \times 2) = 1.6 \text{ QALYs.}$$

If A and B cost the same, the QALY measure indicates that B gives more health per unit of resources; if the prices were different, A would be preferable on cost grounds if the ratio P_A/P_B was less than 1.2/1.6, i.e., 0.75.

Discussion

The QALY approach is ambitious, particularly if it is intended to provide the basis for allocating resources between specialisms (such as cancer and heart disease treatments), rather than between procedures within the same specialism. The complete range of health states is wide, and the measuring process has to be able to identify both small and large changes in hrqol.

Also, a process for identifying health states and measuring their values is required. In the design of that process, there is a tension between the number of states identified for valuation, which determines the sensitivity of the QALY measure, and the complexity of the valuation task. The sensitivity of the scale depends on the number of health states, and the greater the number of health states, the more complex valuation will be.

In principle, then, a QALY measure, based on a cardinal scale, could be applied to all medical interventions, in order to value them all on a single basis. This would permit value for money comparisons throughout a health service, on the basis that resources could be re-allocated from high incremental cost per QALY procedures to those with low incremental cost per QALY. This is the economist's ideal, as it would enable the achievement of an identifiable maximum health impact per unit of expenditure; however, it appears that most of the interest in QALYs comes from people who want to know whether one treatment or procedure is better than another, usually within the same sector (for example, cardiac disease).

Here, we explain the general criteria for QALY measures, and problems of the QALY in principle, before going on to explain the different QALY approaches.

General Criteria for hrqol Measures: Reliability and Validity

Reliability

This feature is described in many places in the literature (see Patrick et al (1993), and many different aspects have been considered, such as internal consistency (inter- and intra-observer), sources of bias, and random error. For our purposes, it is sufficient to note that a reliable instrument delivers the same or similar results from its administration on different occasions, or by different observers, to the same or similar individuals (Streiner and Norman (1989)). We would expect a hrqol measure to be reliable, or consistent, according to this definition, but the subjectivity of health state valuation may give rise to problems.

Suppose a sample numbering 10 per cent of the UK population is chosen, in such a way that it represents all the UK's age, sex, and disease groups. A set of health states is specified, and a valuation exercise is carried out, to determine the sample's mean valuation of each health state, on a scale from zero to one. While these values would be representative of the values of the population at the time of the sample, there is no good reason to suppose that the values would be reliable, in the sense that a repetition of the exercise would find the same values. The fact that individuals can change their minds implies that we are not observing an unambiguous variable, like the number of cars sold, but recording the outcome, on one or more occasions, of individuals' judgement processes. Only when the factors determining such outcomes are better understood may reliability be estimated; the extensive testing of the EuroQol instrument (EuroQol Group (1990)) will have the result that its reliability will be better understood.

It is worth emphasising again that health valuation is inescapable; this aspect of reliability will apply to all health valuation methods.

Validity

An instrument is valid if it can be shown to measure what it purports to measure, usually by comparing its results with another measure. "Criterion" validity is present when an instrument has been validated by a "gold standard" measure. It is widely accepted that there is no "gold standard" measure of hrqol, which is applicable to either profile or QALY measures (Richardson (1994), Whynes and Neilson (1993), Nord (1992), and Kind (1988)). In principle, therefore, criterion validity for a hrqol measure cannot be found.

"Construct" validation means investigating one measure, and identifying another, which purports to measure the same or a closely related phenomenon. Validity is tested by specifying a theory to explain the relationship between the components of one measure and those of another (Patrick and Erickson (1993)), and using data gathered by the relevant instrument(s) to test the hypotheses suggested by the theory. "Convergent" validity is found when two measures agree as expected, and "divergent" validity is found when two measures disagree as expected. One relevant example in the QALY field, discussed in chapter 4, is Whynes and Neilson (1993), which uses the Nottingham Health Profile to determine the "convergent" validity of the Rosser QALY values.

It follows that validity is a more elusive concept than reliability. At a minimum, we expect an hrqol measure to show construct validity, in that its score should be systematically related to another measure, which purports to measure the same or similar concepts.

Conclusion

However large the sample of respondents and whatever the research method, the statements and values established cannot have objective status. At best, one can say that a set of values has been established in a rigorous and (as far as possible) scientific process, with each part of the process explicitly defined and followed. Even given such conditions, how is the chosen process to be justified? It seems that every possible process could be criticised, because there is no objective basis on which to stand the method adopted.

As our opening chapter indicated, however, while health valuation is unavoidable, it cannot be objective; the question is not how can objectivity be achieved, but what subjective measure is the best? Some of these issues arise in our brief review of some points from the literature.

Problems of the QALY Approach: A Selection from the Literature

A full review of the relevant literature would take several books. However, the main difficulties which QALYs involve are problems intrinsic to the development of health valuation methods, and we consider in turn health maximisation, equity, health state valuation, and Nord's empirical work.

Health Maximisation

In mainstream economics, the convention is that only personal satisfaction (utility), or proxy measures of it, can be used to value social states. The health maximisation pursued by CEA is a relatively new departure, though the use of non-utility information is endorsed, as being permissible under some circumstances and in accordance with particular criteria, by Sen (1979). Also, Culyer (1989) identifies the general idea of individuals' personal characteristics as relevant to the allocation of health care resources.

Members of the "extra-welfarist" school (Williams (1985), Sugden and Williams (1978), Drummond et al (1987), Torrance (1976)) usually assume that health can be defined in terms of total life expectancy and hrqol (Torrance (1976), Williams (1985)). It follows that when QALY values are developed and applied, only the chosen aspects of health and the values expressed by the original respondents are taken into account. The weighing of other (non-health) aspects of consumers' choices with the health dimension is not possible with a QALY approach, as it is (for example) in the Willingness to Pay approach (Carlin and Sandy (1991), Zethraeus (1998)), though it is possible to argue that health decisions often take precedence over ordinary consumption decisions. However, maximising health, defined in QALY terms, does mean that every individual counts at least once, equally, and independently of his or her income and wealth.

An economist might expect physicians to approve of the QALY maximisation objective, but Williams' introduction of it to a British Medical Association conference (Williams (1985)) aroused controversy (for example, Smith (1987)). Scarcity is an uncomfortable idea in the health sector, for obvious reasons. Attempts to identify doctors' choices between categories of patient have met with resistance, often based on the view that the physician is responsible for individual patients, not for groups. At the least, this suggests a need for care on the part of economists, when they propose measures which rely on medical data, because the generalisations required from physicians for a cost per QALY assessment may not be readily available. (See chapter 6 for a discussion of some of these issues.)

Equity

Torrance (1985) advocates QALYs because the approach is egalitarian, that is, each individual's health, measured by survival and hrqol, counts the same, as does each year of an individual's life, whenever it occurs in the life span. Such an approach ignores the differences that income might make to the value of a health state, as well as the different meanings which "full health" might have at different stages of the lifespan.

One example of such an argument is where Broome (1993) notes that the QALY maximisation approach "ignores equality", in that 10 QALYs for 5 people are identical to 2 QALYs for 25, regardless of the pre-existing QALY distribution. The fact is that the QALY data, if available, would define the opportunity cost of health care alternatives. We can only proceed to *any* kind of reasonable and fair decision (that is, reasonable and fair in the eyes of the decision-makers) if the QALY data exist. When the data are known, the decision taken may or may not follow the QALY maximisation rule, but until they are known, the choice cannot be described.

Similarly, Broome (1993) and Harris (1985) argue that QALYs are "ageist", because (for example) a 65-year old person can only gain a maximum of about 10 years, on the average, while a 25-year old has a potential gain of more than four times this amount. However, it seems clear that the demands we make of a policy approach should not exceed the given bounds of the problem, that is, the limits of the power to effect a solution. Since society has the ability to affect only the number and quality of future life years, not those that have been, birth dates are not relevant to the distribution of health care resources. The limits to health policy are given by the birth dates of the population, and the (realistic) life expectancy of its different age groups.

Loomes and Mackenzie (1989) attack the "equal weight" idea also, on the grounds that health has a different value at different stages of the life span; they offer an equality rule based on equal weights for particular years of life, between individuals, and on weights including individual's preferences between years, which, in their view, is at least as egalitarian as the QALY maximisation rule. The idea that health may be differently valued over the life span is intuitively plausible; it may or may not follow that the planning of health care for the whole of society should reflect this.

There is also the question of the equality between persons of the zero to unity scale between death and full health. According to Broome (1993), it is "quite implausible" to assume that the distance between full health and death is the same for all, on the grounds that "good health is plainly not equally good for everyone" (page 160), given different levels of happiness in different lives. However, the search of the "extra-welfarist" economists is for a rule to allocate resources so that health, not happiness or welfare, is maximised. Equal length for the unity to zero scale is simply equal treatment for all persons regarding their health prospects.

Next, are health states equal, over time, for the same person? The QALY maximisation model implies that they are, while Broome (1993) raises the possibility of interdependence, in that (for example) three years in a health state followed by perfect health would be valued differently from three years in the same state followed by death. From society's viewpoint, equal treatment implies that the pursuit of QALY maximisation should be independent of individual values; every year should count the same, and should be quality-adjusted on the same basis, that is, depending on the health state of the individual, but regardless of whether the health state is followed by death.

Finally, there is the question of inter-generational equity: do we (the current generation) seek to maximise QALYs from this point in time (our "point of view"), discounting potential future QALYs at an appropriate rate? Equity implies that each generation, and each person, should count for the same; if every person, now and in the future, counts for the same (from society's point of view), does this imply a zero discount rate? Without subscribing to any specific doomsday scenario, it is realistic to assume that society's survival is uncertain, if only because of its relatively short duration in the earth's millenia (Leakey (1995)). Society should therefore adopt the principle of discounting, though what the rate should be depends on some estimate of the risk of the extinction of the human race. While patients may not typically discount with respect to their own health states, as Reinhardt (1998) indicates, they might be prepared to discount on behalf of society, given the uncertainty affecting society as a whole. This means that conventional discount rates, taken from financial markets (or from government treasuries which raise money there), may set too high a value on present-day costs and benefits, compared to costs and benefits in the future. (See Kula (1997) for a comprehensive treatment of discounting.)

Health State Valuation

Carr-Hill (1989) focuses on the process of comparing health states, particularly their comparison with death, which he regards as an event, not a state. He casts doubt on whether respondents have either the same understanding or even any adequate understanding of what they are being asked to do when comparing health states. Similarly, Mulkay et al (1987) contrast the ordered valuation of artificially designed health states in the Rosser-Kind research with normal choices in everyday life; they suggest that it would be wrong to assume that the Rosser-Kind valuations correspond to ordinary judgements by real people. This is echoed by Johanesson,

Jonsson, and Karlsson (1996), who note that no-one ever makes the kinds of choices found in health state valuation exercises, for example, between *x* years in "full health", and *y* years in some less well state.

Of course this is true, and as Nord (1992) points out, health states are not compared systematically, or even at all, in everyday life, unlike (possibly) the states of being with or without a particular consumer product. The question is, what does this signify? The degree of resemblance between health state choices and other choices is simply not relevant; as a society we do not know what our health sector choices are. The creation of health state values is an attempt to structure society's problem of health care prioritisation. This is an "unnatural" or "artificial" problem, precisely because medicine intervenes in nature. In the QALY maximisation approach, we have a decision rule that treats every person and every year of every person's life the same; if we are defining health policy choices on behalf of society as a whole, this seems to be appropriate.

Nord's Empirical Work

Nord's approach (Nord (1999)) is unusual, in that his work over the last decade has identified important value judgements which empirically raise reservations about the simple "minimise the cost per QALY" objective of many studies. He is mainly concerned with the assumption of distributive neutrality, summed up as "a QALY is a QALY is a QALY, no matter who gets it." Nord's main concerns can be illustrated by using a table to represent hypothetical average QALY gains, for three patient groups, A, B, and C, as follows:

Table 2.1 Hypothetical QALY Gains

Patient Group	Initial Health State	Health State After Treatment	Gain
A	0.2	0.6	0.4
B	0.3	0.7	0.4
C	0.3	1.0	0.7

If only one group can get treatment, and if all three treatments cost the same, then the QALY approach means that group C should be treated.

This conclusion runs counter to the view that those worst off deserve treatment more (the "rule of rescue"), most prominently discussed by Rawls (1972), and more recently by Callahan (1994). On this view, group A should be treated, but Nord (1999) notes that government commissions in Norway, Holland, New Zealand, and Sweden have concluded that severity of illness continued to be the most important basis for prioritisation, though effectiveness also had to be taken into account. Evidence in support of the importance of severity to the population at large is reported from the United States, Norway, England, Spain, and Australia. While this cannot be assumed to be a universal value judgement, it at least gives grounds for caution before assuming that the minimising of the cost per QALY is a universally acceptable healthcare objective.

A second issue raised by Nord concerns the comparison between groups B and C; just because group B cannot benefit as much as group C, is this a sufficient reason for group C to be preferred? Evidence (from Spain, Australia, and Norway) suggests that many people hold the view that those who are equally ill have equal rights to treatment; it appears that, provided the treatment effect is sufficiently large, differences in the actual sizes of these effects will not receive much weight (Nord, personal communication, (2002)).

Is the measurement of population values a scientific task? We have to accept that the questions and the statements used have more or less the same meaning to all of the respondents. Given this reasonable assumption, a rigorous and scientific approach can be taken, and a body of scientific knowledge developed.

Conclusion

These then are the main problems of principle affecting the acceptance of QALY measures; if we accept that hrqol and survival are the main dimensions of health outcome, they appear to be inescapable aspects of health valuation. While they are important, they do not diminish at all the importance of QALY information to the prioritisation of health services. It should not be a question of "Why the QALY?", but more a question of "Why not a health outcome measure?", of which the QALY is the outstanding example. Health valuation is inescapable, and it appears that the QALY is the best approach to health valuation; in what follows here, the main QALY approaches are explained.

The Main QALY Approaches

Introduction

In terms of the QALY definition above, the intention of each approach is to determine a set of values so that H1 and H2 can be determined, and the value of a procedure measured. (It is assumed that S1 and S2 can be determined from medical research; the problems this can involve are discussed in chapter 6.) We consider Rating Scale and Magnitude Estimation, Trading Off Time and Persons, and the Standard Gamble, all of which have drawn on the development of health profiles (discussed in the next chapter), which have also been applied to health outcome comparison.

Rating Scale and Magnitude Estimation

These are the simplest approaches; they lack an explicit theoretical base, but they are the easiest for the respondents creating the values to understand.

Rating Scale In the Rating Scale procedure, the respondent places all the chosen health states on a scale with the best at one end and the worst at the other; a variation might include full health at one end and death at the other. For example, we might ask respondents to set the following health states on a scale:

A: Confined to bed; moderate distress
B: Fully mobile; mild pain
C: Mobile, but unable to climb stairs at all; moderate pain
D: Wheelchair-bound; mild pain.

The respondent might set these on a zero to one hundred scale as shown:

```
0   10  20  30  40  50  60  70  80  90  100
-----X---------X------------------X------------ X----------
     A         D                  C             B
```

This is an example of what is known as a "visual analogue" scale, which is also used in the EuroQol and the Health Measurement Questionnaire of the Rosser-Kind Matrix, examined in the next chapter. (A vertical version is sometimes referred to as a "thermometer" scale.)

While the valuation task appears simple to the respondent, the values which result are difficult to interpret. Do respondents place states on the scale without reference to previous choices, or do they carefully ensure consistency? How much can be asked of respondents, and how much guidance should be undertaken? Nord ((1990) and (1992)) indicates that individuals are unable to construct explanations of their responses, though what this means, itself, remains debatable.

Magnitude Estimation This is the valuation approach used in the development of the Rosser-Kind QALY, which is fully examined and discussed in the next chapter. Briefly, respondents are asked a question such as "On the basis of these descriptions of health states A and B, how many times worse is A than B?" Again, this task is fairly clear to respondents, although Richardson (1994) notes that, because there is no accepted scale for health states, the meaning of such a question, and therefore of its answer, is "deeply obscure" (page 16). Nonetheless, Nord (personal communication, 2002) finds the results of Rosser-Kind magnitude estimation approach understandable, because the questions were expressed in terms of the resources required to remedy the different health states, that is, the questions were based on health prioritisation choices, rather than abstract examples of different health states.

Trading-Off Time and Persons

These approaches are closer to economic theory, but also resemble health care choices as they actually occur.

Time Trade-Off The health state to be valued, S, is described fully; the respondent is asked the following question:

> The survival for health state S is t years; if you could have years of full health instead, how many years of full health would be equivalent to t years in condition S?

A response of r years implies that the respondent values the health state at r/t years, that is, V_S (the value of health state S) = r/t.

In principle, the value of t should make no difference to the approach; this is contrary to the usual assumption that, for the individual, future gains are less attractive than present ones, and this criticism is made by Broome (1993). It seems arbitrary to pick a discount rate, and apply it to a person's time trade-off preferences, but the alternative is to establish an individual's discount rate. This seems likely to be complex and difficult.

McNeil et al (1981) suggest that years of life are only traded for health status improvement when (in their research) the absolute length of time with less than perfect speech is over 5 years. It may also be that the value of a health state changes as the time in question increases. For example, a person may be indifferent between 4 years in state A and 5 years in state B; at the same time, she might be indifferent between 7 years in A and 10 years in B, when consistency with the previous valuation would require indifference between 8 years in A and 10 years in B. The Person Trade-Off approach avoids some of these difficulties, and appears to be more related to a health policy context.

Person Trade-Off (also known as "equivalence") The health states to be described, P and Q, are described in detail. The question put to respondents is:

> Suppose you can cure (restore to full health) only one of two groups: Group A, which comprises n people in health state P, and Group B, which contains (for example) 20 people in health state Q; which would you choose?

The value of health state P in relation to health state Q may be found by altering the number in the first group until the individual is indifferent between the two groups.

The key problem of the Time Trade-Off method is that it is affected by the normal assumption in economics that future gains are less attractive than present ones. The Person Trade-Off approach avoids this difficulty, and, as Sloan (1995) points out, the information sought is similar to that required for health policy. By contrast, the standard gamble approach has the strongest theoretical base, though it presents choices which are relatively remote from the health policy context.

The Standard Gamble

The health state to be valued, H, is described in detail, and is used to describe two alternatives, A and B:

Alternative A: 10 years in state H;

Alternative B: A gamble of 10 years in full health or immediate death, with a probability of full health = p (and of immediate death = 1-p)

The value of H is estimated by altering p until the individual is indifferent between A and B.

Indifference means that the values of A and B are the same, that is,

$$V_A = V_B.$$

By definition, B contains two possibilities; its value comprises the value of each, times the relevant probability, that is,

$$V_B = p.V(10 \text{ years in full health}) + (1-p).V(\text{immediate death}).$$

Given that the health state is to be measured on a scale from 0.0 (Death) to 1.0 (Full health), the value of full health is 1.00 and the value of immediate death is zero, so the second term is zero. It follows that

$$V_B = p,$$

so that

$$V_A = p.$$

This approach is based directly on indifference analysis and conventional utility theory [(Boyle at el (1983), Torrance et al (1972), Torrance (1976)(a), and (1976(b))], and has been discussed extensively. However, standard gamble comparisons are fairly difficult for respondents to understand, despite the ingenuity which researchers have shown in providing visual analogues for utility values. Also, because it focuses entirely on the value of a health state to an individual, not its value to society, the approach presents alternatives which are somewhat different from those involved in real health policy choices.

Conclusion

We cannot choose not to choose between health priorities; the status quo is a choice, and the discussion above is only an introduction to the problems which priority-setting involves. Those who reject the economist's proposed solutions are required to come up with valuation mechanisms of their own; as the arguments so far have made clear, these seem just as likely to be contestable, because of the nature of the subject matter.

What cannot be disputed is the urgency and the import of the health choices societies make, with or without discussion, analysis, or reliable data. There cannot be many areas of academic discussion which have such potentially serious and widespread implications for so many people, as the determination of procedures for valuing health in practice. In the next chapter, we explain two QALY measures which have achieved some success, in terms of their acceptance and use.

Chapter 3

Two QALY Measures

Introduction

Early markers in the search for a suitable basis for health prioritisation include World Health Organisation (1957) and Sullivan (1966); Torrance (1976) may be described as the earliest clear statement of the approach which is necessary for QALYs to be used. Since then, substantial development work has been undertaken, both on the principles of an acceptable QALY approach, and on the empirical testing of different instruments suggested by the theory (Nord (1999)).

The theories of several measures were outlined in the last chapter; this one examines the EQ-5D developed by the EuroQol Group, and the Rosser-Kind Index, two multi-attribute utility instruments (MAUIs), developed using the time trade-off and magnitude estimation approaches respectively. While in principle there can be no "gold standard" QALY measure, the EQ-5D is probably the most widely used QALY measure, and has been subjected to substantial empirical testing (Agt, van, H.M.E., et al (1994), Brooks et al (1996), Dolan et al (1995), Dorman (1997), Jenkinson et al (1997), Wolfe (1997)). While the Rosser-Kind Index is older, and has received less empirical testing, its use as a QALY measure made it the first QALY to receive substantial attention, and it remains interesting, in particular because of its basis on resource allocation from the point of view of society, rather than on the valuation of health states as if they were experienced by respondents.

The EQ-5D

Introduction

The diversity of health-related quality of life (hrqol) measures, and the absence of a "gold standard" against which measures could be tested, led a group of researchers (meeting in 1988) to develop a measure which would compare outcomes on the basis of a defined common set of hrqol features (Dolan et al (1995)). The EuroQol Group's EQ-5D instrument combines a tested theoretical foundation, the very large (over 3000) respondent sample, who determined the health state values, and ease of use. We consider in turn the classification of health states, the valuation process, and validation and reliability testing.

Classification of Health States

After a review of existing instruments, the developers defined the dimensions "Mobility", "Self-Care", "Usual Activities", "Pain / Discomfort", "Anxiety / Depression", and classified health states so that respondents indicate levels 1, 2 or 3, on each; the health states resulting are shown in Table 3.1. (This classification is used to compare five health-state valuation methods in Krabbe et al (1999)).

These dimensions and levels give a five-digit number for each health state, depending on the response to each dimension; for example, "21312" would be: Some problems walking about (2); No problems with self-care (1); Unable to perform usual activities (3); No pain or discomfort (1); and Moderately anxious or depressed (2). Adding the states "unconscious" and "dead" to the 3^5 health states implied by the above dimensions gives a total of 245 health states.

Table 3.1 EQ-5D Dimensions and Statements

Mobility
1 - No problems walking about
2 - Some problems walking about
3 - Confined to bed

Self-Care
1 - No problem with self-care
2 - Some problems washing or dressing self
3 - Unable to wash or dress self

Usual Activities
1 - No problems with performing usual activities
2 - Some problems with performing usual activities
3 - Unable to perform usual activities

Pain/Discomfort
1 - No pain or discomfort
2 - Moderate pain or discomfort
3 - Extreme pain or discomfort

Anxiety/Depression
1 - Not anxious or depressed
2 - Moderately anxious or depressed
3 - Extremely anxious or depressed

Source: Dolan et al (1995), p. 2-3.

The Valuation Process

The problem is to establish a workable valuation process for all of these 245 health states, so that they are located on a continuum from zero ("death or unconsciousness") to one ("full health").

Forty-five states were selected so that they were "evenly" spread through the set of states; respondents' direct valuations of these were obtained with the time trade-off method, and the response data were used to create a model which would best predict all the 245 values. What "evenly" means is open to question, though the reliability of the selection is likely to be high, given the availability of psychometric literature and other sources of data regarding health states. Each respondent was asked to value:

Full health - state 11111,

Immediate Death - 33333, plus

2 from 5 "very mild" states (for example, 11112),
3 from 12 "mild" states (such as 21133),
3 from 12 "moderate" states (22122), and
3 from 12 "severe" states (32223).

The criteria for the model are:

- Goodness-of-fit, i.e., the quality of the model's explanation of the differences in the valuations given to those states for which there is direct data;
- Simplicity; and
- Consistency, i.e., states which are better by definition must have higher predicted values.

It follows that the value assigned to each health state should depend on the level of score in each of the five dimensions; the model's general definition is:

$$V = f (M_i, S_i, U_i, P_i, A_i).$$

V is the value of the health state, M, S, U, P, and A refer to the five dimensions, and i is the level of each dimension. The form of the function (f) is to be determined by statistical anlaysis of the responses.

Full health is defined as 11111, and is given the value of unity; the move from level i to the level i+1 means a reduction in value, and the purpose of the model is to estimate the size of this reduction. The actual health state value is thus (1 - R), where R is this reduction; R's value will increase as the value of i increases.

The values were based on data from 3395 respondents, from 2997 of whom complete sets of time trade-off data were obtained. The best model, in terms of the above criteria, was found to be a "main effects" model, in which each of the five dimensions was independent of the others, which the data fitted, and which could be reasonably interpreted. There are 12 independent variables, whose co-efficients are shown in Table 5.2; an intercept associated with any move away from full health, two variables for each of the five dimensions, one to represent the move from level 1 to level 2, and one to represent the move from level 2 to level 3, and a term referred to as "N3", an intercept term which registers whether any of the dimensions is at level 3.

Table 3.2 EQ-5D Coefficients for Time Trade-Off Tariffs

(All "Level 1" coefficients are zero)

DIMENSION COEFFICIENT

Constant	0.081	
Mobility		
Level 2	0.069	
Level 3	0.314	
Self-care		
Level 2	0.104	
Level 3	0.214	
Usual Activity		
Level 2	0.036	
Level 3	0.094	
Pain/discomfort		
Level 2	0.123	
Level 3	0.386	
Anxiety/depression		
Level 2	0.071	
Level 3	0.236	
N3	0.269	Adjusted $r^2 = 0.46$

The valuation of a particular health state is carried out by subtracting appropriate amounts from 1.0, as the following table shows.

Table 3.3 Calculating the Value of Health State "11223"

Full Health = 1.0; from this value, subtract:

Constant Term (for any dysfunctional state)	0.081
Mobility (for level 1)	0.0
Self-care (for level 1)	0.0
Usual Activities (for level 2)	0.036
Pain or discomfort (for level 2)	0.123
Anxiety or depression (for level 3)	0.236
N3 (level 3 occurs within at least one dimension)	0.269
Total Subtractions:	0.745
Health State Value (= 1.0 - 0.745)	0.255

Source: Dolan et al (1995) page 12.

Validation and ReliabilityTesting

The EQ-5D has been shown to be a practical method of measuring a population's health, and of distinguishing sub-groups within it (Kind et al (1998)). The instrument has recently been used in two randomised controlled trials, in one to measure hrqol after angioplasty and stent replacement (Bosch et al (1999)), and in another (Wilson et al (1999)) to compare the effectiveness of patient care in hospital and at home. It is accepted as valid by Richards et al (1997), and was found to have acceptable concurrent and discriminant validity by Dorman et al (1997a), who also suggested that careful use of the measure with proxy respondents could produce useful results for stroke patients (Dorman et al (1997b)).

Conclusion

The EQ-5D is the outcome of a sophisticated and rigorous process of development, which has been successful in establishing the instrument. One reservation is that the respondents assessed health states independently of the resources allocated to their treatment, unlike the Rosser-Kind approach, which is examined in the next section.

The Rosser-Kind QALY

The Rosser-Kind instrument is the original example of the direct approach endorsed by Broome (1993), and it is the instrument tested in the next chapter. We examine here its development, reliability and validity.

Development

Health states were valued in a hospital output measurement project (Rosser and Watts (1972)), first identifying two dimensions of a health state matrix, using medical expertise, and then asking lay and medical respondents to value the health states using magnitude estimation (see the last chapter).

Doctors in a London hospital were asked to describe the criteria they used to decide on the severity of illness in hospital patients, ignoring the patient's prognosis. Discussions led to the emergence of two dimensions of illness severity, observed disability (loss of function and mobility), and subjective distress; all other aspects of patient conditions were thought to be subsumed within this framework, which was refined into eight levels of disability, and four levels of distress, shown in Table 3.4. The dimensions were tested with non-medical subjects, and a study involving 2120 patients rated on admission by 50 doctors in a wide variety of specialisms (such as Gynaecology, Urology, Ophthalmology, General Medicine) showed that doctors were able to use the system reliably and quickly.

Table 3.4 Health State Dimensions, and their Levels

DISTRESS: A. None; B. Mild; C. Moderate; D. Severe

DISABILITY LEVELS
1. No disability.
2. Slight social disability.
3. Severe social disability and/or slight impairment of performance at work. Able to do all housework except very heavy tasks.
4. Choice of work or performance at work very severely limited; housewives and old people able to do light housework only, but able to go shopping.
5. Unable to undertake any paid employment; unable to continue any education. Old people confined to home except for escorted outings and short walks, and unable to do shopping. Housewives able only to perform a few simple tasks.
6. Confined to chair or wheelchair, or able to move around only with support from an assistant.
7. Confined to bed.
8. Unconscious.

Source: Rosser and Kind (1978) p. 349.

These dimensions imply 29 different health states which have to be placed on a continuum between 0 and 1; the method of magnitude estimation was used, in the following procedure:

- 6 marker states were chosen for their (perceived) wide dispersion over the categories of disability and distress, namely 1C, 2D, 5C, 7B, and 7D.
- 70 judges (lay people, patients, and doctors) were asked to rank the marker states in order of severity, on the assumptions that all states can be cured, that the states refer to people of the same age, about middle age, and that the states will remain static if untreated.
- The next task was to place all the marker states on a scale, by asking the question: "How many times more ill is a person described as being in state A as compared with state B?" It was emphasised that the ratio would define the proportion of resources that the judges would consider appropriate to allocate to each case.
- The other 23 cases were then ranked, and the ranks were similarly expressed in ratio terms.
- The judges were asked to adjust the marker state ratios, that is, to resolve any contradictions that might have arisen.
- The judges were asked to review their valuations on the new assumption that the health states were permanent, and to place death on the scale, assigning a value to it.

Contradictions between valuations were resolved, in an interview process lasting between 1.5 and 4.5 hours per subject; this is what Nord refers to as the achievement of reflective equilibrium, and it is a unique feature among QALY measures (though it was also part of the Sickness Impact Profile development).

The respondents were:

- 10 patients from medical wards
- 10 psychiatric in-patients
- 20 experienced state registered nurses
- 20 healthy volunteers
- 10 doctors who were members of at least one Royal College

This is not a large sample, but the median values of the health states from these respondents, shown in Table 3.5, have generated wide interest, from the British Medical Association (CABG Panel (1984)) to the Department of Health (1995).

Table 3.5 Rosser-Kind Matrix of Health State Values

Disability Level

Distress	A	B	C	D
1	1.000	0.995	0.990	0.967
2	0.990	0.986	0.973	0.932
3	0.980	0.972	0.956	0.912
4	0.964	0.956	0.942	0.870
5	0.946	0.935	0.900	0.700
6	0.875	0.845	0.860	0.000
7	0.677	0.564	0.000	-0.486
8	0.000			

Source: Kind (1990)

For example, a patient's health might improve from 5C to 3A; this would be valued at 0.980 - 0.900 = 0.080 of full health. If survival altered from 5 years to 8, the QALY impact would be:

(8 x 0.98) - (5 x 0.90) = 3.34 QALYs.

Health states 6D and 7C are as bad as death, while 7D is found to be worse than death, since its value is negative. (The respondent who threatened suicide, mentioned in our opening chapter, was in health state 6D.)

Originally, the matrix was used to ask physicians what health state they believed applied to a particular patient (Williams (1985)). Researchers at the University of York Centre for Health Economics developed a questionnaire for use by patients, to determine which of the health states applied (Williams (1988a), Kind and Gudex (1991)). The Health Measurement Questionnaire (HMQ) is short and easily completed; testing against the Nottingham Health Profile (NHP) and the General Health Questionnaire (a screening test for psychiatric disorder) found it to be both viable and valid (Kind and Gudex (1991)). The HMQ, and a worked example in which Rosser-Kind values are determined, is shown in Appendix 2.

The development of the values seems to have been a complex process, and its detailed explanation and justification would require a great deal of exposition. It is therefore relatively inaccessible, because, as was the case for the EQ-5D, there is no theoretical or objective basis for constructing a health state valuation procedure. It is important that care was taken to resolve contradictions between valuations; this seems to be a desireable feature of any health state valuation procedure, particularly given the strangeness to most people of the valuation process, noted by Carr-Hill (1989), and Mulkay et al (1987).

Also, the exercise was firmly located in a health policy context, because of the emphasis on resources. By covering the whole range of health states, albeit using only 29 identified states, the resolution of contradictions between values brought the valuation process further towards the real difficulties of health care prioritisation than any of the procedures so far described. On the other hand, a 29-cell matrix must be crude, compared to the range of possible health states which can occur before and after medical treatments.

Reliability and Validity

Kind, Rosser and Williams (1988) state that their matrix health state values are median values, that the data from which they were calculated had a high degree of variation, and that the values were not normally distributed. As Leu (1988) points out, this makes reliable inference difficult, assuming one wishes to use these values as estimates of society's values.

Test-retest reliability was measured in a separate experiment (also reported in Rosser and Kind (1988)) using the six marker states with 50 volunteers in full health, with the two interviews (as specified above) separated by mentally distracting exercises; the percentage agreement was 97.2 per cent.

An external test of validity would compare the Rosser-Kind values with scales obtained by wholly other methods; in the Health Measurement Questionnaire development work, tests against the NHP and the General Health Questionnaire produced evidence for convergent validity at a descriptive level (Kind and Gudex (1991)). More significantly, of all the QALY approaches, only the Rosser-Kind approach includes the pursuit of reflective equilibrium as part of value determination, and we could expect that the values might perform well in a test against a person trade-off approach. Nord (1993) reports that the Rosser-Kind index has a good fit with person trade-off data, unlike the EQ-5D. Lastly, Whynes and Neilsen (1993) found "convergent" validity between the Nottingham Health Profile and Rosser-Kind values developed from the HMQ. One further endorsement of the values comes from their use by Launois (1994), in a cost-effectiveness analysis.

Donaldson et al (1988) express concerns that the adoption of Rosser-Kind values would discriminate against procedures which deliver only small increments of hrqol. Suppose a minor low-cost intervention improves hrqol by an amount which is undetectable by the Rosser-Kind measure, amounting to 0.02 QALYs. If this improvement continues for 30 years (for instance, between the ages of 55 and 85), the total QALYs generated per person would be 0.02 x 30 = 0.6 QALYs. Also suppose that a more dramatic intervention improves quality of life in 55-year-old men, by an amount the Rosser-Kind measure can detect, 0.5, but on the average this improvement lasts only 1 year, yielding 0.5 QALYs per person. If the two interventions cost about the same, in total, the one with the unmeasurable impact is better value per unit of resources.

The main value of the Rosser-Kind QALY is as a measure of hrqol from a social viewpoint. Loomes and Mackenzie (1989) point out that the valuation process abstracted from prognosis by asking subjects to assume initally the same prognosis, for all the states, and then to adjust their values on the assumption that the states were permanent. According to these authors, this means that the value of each state is assumed to be independent of its duration, and of any states preceding it, while (as noted above) evidence suggests that duration matters (McNeil et al (1982), Sackett and Torrance (1978)), and a priori it would seem that prognosis must affect values; Broome (1993) raises similar issues.

This is to confuse the requirements of a social approach with the summation of individual values. Clearly, when individuals make their own health choices, they will be influenced by the prognoses of the alternatives which they face; social choices are different. Necessarily, they must be taken by individuals who have not experienced more than a few of the health states which resource allocations will affect; if we are aiming for equal treatment, from the viewpoint of society as a whole, a-temporal and a-prognostic valuation of health states is unavoidable.

Similar arguments have been applied to the Rosser-Kind team's implicit assumption about risk and uncertainty, particularly in Williams (1985), where health state values assumed to be certain are applied to the outcomes of bypass surgery so that their value in QALYs is multiplied by their respective probabilities. As Loomes and Mackenzie (1989) point out, this assumes "risk neutrality" on the part of the individuals involved. The argument is that the very prospect of taking a risk may itself be appealing or repellent, depending on preferences regarding risk, not health states, and that this will affect valuations. It seems obvious that the choices made by society between numbers of different treatments, to maximise overall health, are different from an individual's choices about whether to have a particular intervention or not. The survival of society is not involved in these choices, and we may therefore exclude risk preferences from the remit of health maximisation, with all the other aspects of consumer preferences which "extra-welfarist" economists are prepared to ignore.

In sum, the Rosser-Kind values remain comparable with those from other QALY methods; this is certainly the view of one distinguished commentator (Nord (1999)). This is surprising, given the development of the values from a hospital output measurement project, with no basis on economic theory as such, and their age, 30 years (at time of writing) since first publication. For the purpose of setting health priorities, the key features are the emphasis on social, not individual, choices, and the opportunities which were offered in the original research process for the correction of inconsistencies.

Conclusion

The EQ-5D appears to be gaining acceptance as a QALY measure, as a consequence of its extensive and thorough testing for validity and reliability. The development and use of the Rosser-Kind Index have been explained, as a contrast with the EuroQol, and the next chapter examines the empirical testing of this instrument in two separate studies, as an illustration of what such testing involves. This is another example of exploring the problem of health valuation, which includes criticising the methods adopted, on scientific grounds, without retreating from the important task of valuing health in practice.

Chapter 4

Testing a QALY Measure

Introduction

There is a large array of instruments designed to measure outcomes using health-related quality of life (hrqol) variables; they are of two main kinds, health profiles and QALY measures. The difference between profile and QALY approaches is that profile measures create one or more ordinal scales, with no starting point common to all of the respondents putting values on health states, while all QALY measures aim to achieve cardinality and a single scale, that is, to develop a single measuring scale from zero (death or unconsciousness) to unity ("full" health) on which all health states can be located, and in which zero and unity are common to all valuators. It is the cardinal nature of the QALY measure which provides a basis for resource allocation; ordinal measures do not have an empirical basis for the zero which is often used to assess procedures using profile data.

The obvious method for testing a QALY measure is to make a comparison between its data and data from a profile measure, because both measures should rank patients in the same order. Two sets of results are outlined here, those of Whynes and Nielsen (1993) and McCulloch (1998); both compare the rank ordering of patient health states by a health profile with the sequence produced by the Rosser-Kind (R-K) measure.

In principle, it would be preferable to test the R-K instrument's *criterion* validity, that is, to assess its validity by comparing its results with those of an established "gold standard" measure. Since no such standard exists, "construct" validity must be tested, by specifying hypotheses to explain how one measure is expected to relate to another, and using data gathered by the relevant instruments to test these hypotheses. "Convergent validity" is found when two measures agree as the hypotheses predicted, and this is the approach taken here.

This requires the assumption that the two instruments measure the same social phenomena; health profiles measure hrqol, without weighing quality of life against survival, while QALY measures compare health states, and establish a zero point, as well as a "full health" point at unity, so that QALY units can be compared on a ratio scale. It seems clear enough that in this case the assumption is reasonable, though the approaches of their developers to hrqol measurement are different.

Both Whynes and Neilsen (1993) and McCulloch (1998) used the Health Measurement Questionnaire to derive Rosser-Kind (R-K) values; they compared these data with results from the Nottingham Health Profile and the Functional Limitations Profile respectively, to assess the convergent validity of the R-K QALY. While the profiles resemble QALY measures, in that health states are described and valued, it is important to explain profile development, and to outline the two profiles referred to here, before going on to explain the two sets of empirical results. This also completes the discussion of the principles of health valuation.

Development of Health Profiles

Definition

Profiles began to be developed in response to the deficiencies of existing measures, such as mortality, consultation rates, and morbidity (Hunt et al.(1980)) as measures of health for policy purposes. The aim was to measure changes in health status, reliably and with validity, defining health to include social, emotional, and physical dimensions. The method may be specified as:

1) Identify the dimensions of health (such as "Mobility", "Social Interactions", or "Emotional Items");
2) Define or obtain statements (from experts, patients, or carers) describing all the significant points along these dimensions;
3) Value these statements within each dimension;
4) Value the statements between dimensions, so that each statement has a value on a common scale (this step was part of the development of the Sickness Impact and Functional Limitations profiles; it is omitted for most health profiles);
5) Test the instrument for validity and reliability.

Having established the value of each statement in the initial research process, a questionnaire comprising the statements is used to determine which apply to the respondent, and the values of the applicable statements are added, within each dimension, to obtain a numerical value for the respondent's health status on that dimension. The higher the score, the worse the health state on that dimension. If statements have been valued between the dimensions, as in step 4 above, all the values can be added, to obtain a single figure measuring overall health-related quality of life. A zero score means full health; as the score increases, hrqol declines.

Application

Since all such instruments measure only hrqol, treatment outcomes which include both survival and hrqol effects have to be described using at least two numbers, as the following fictional example demonstrates.

Two angina treatments, X and Y, cost the same; their effects on the average patient may be described as follows:

> X reduces the Functional Limitations Profile score by 210 points (an improvement in hrqol), and increases survival from 1 to 5 years, and Y reduces the FLP score by 500 points (ditto), and increases survival from 1 to 4 years.

Since the two treatments cost the same, a person who chooses X is valuing (-210, + 4 years) more than (-500, + 3 years); in the case of treatments which affect survival, the profile approach does not attempt the task of weighing quality of life against survival, which is left to the decision-maker. The two profiles used in the studies to be examined below were the Functional Limitations Profile, and the Nottingham Health Profile, and they are now briefly described.

The Functional Limitations Profile

The Functional Limitations Profile is the United Kingdom version of the Sickness Impact Profile; apart from minor language modifications, the two instruments have been shown to be identical in use (Peach et al (1981), Patrick et al (1982, Patrick et al (1985)). The dimensions of the FLP are:

Physical dimension: Statements 1 - 55, comprising sections "Walking", "Body Care and Movement", "Mobility", and "Household Management";

Psychosocial dimension: Statements 56 - 109, comprising "Recreation and Pastime Items", "Social Interaction Items", "Emotion Items", "Alertness Items", and "Sleep and Rest Items";

Eating and drinking dimension: Statments 110 - 118, corresponding to a single section of the questionnaire;

Communication dimension: Statements 119 - 127, again corresponding to a single section of the questionnaire;

Work dimension: Statements 128 - 136.

Examples of statements and their weights are shown in Table 4.1.

Table 4.1 Statements and Weights from the Functional Limitations Profile

Because of my health:

	Weight
(Walking Section)	
1. I walk shorter distances or often stop for a rest	54
2. I do not walk up or down hills	64
3. I only use stairs with a physical aid...	82
4. I only get up and down stairs with assistance...	87
5. I get about in a wheelchair	121
(Emotional Section)	
84. I say how bad or useless I am; for example, ...	89
85. I laugh or cry suddenly	58
86. I often moan or groan because of pain or discomfort	67
87. I have attempted suicide	141
88. I behave nervously or restlessly	48
89. I keep rubbing or holding areas of my body...	59
90. I am irritable and impatient with myself	79

The total of all the weights is 10154, though it is logically impossible to suffer all the dysfunctions at once. Suppose a respondent identifies statements numbered 89, 58, 48, and 79, above, as applying to her; the section score would be 89+58+48+79, = 274. This is a measure of her hrqol in the Emotional Life dimension; the sum of all the dimension scores is thus a measure of the respondent's total functional limitation.

The FLP is an evidence-based instrument; there is no explicit recognition of pain or distress, which were regarded as subjective, and significant only as they have an impact on behaviour. The SIP, on which the FLP is based, is recognised as a "widely used, highly respected measure", by Pollard et al (2001), which has been translated into nine languages. Patrick and Erickson (1993) report 27 studies using the SIP, and the examination of studies using the SIP by de Bruin et al (1992) found that it is a reliable and valid measure of functional status, performing best when overall scores are used to compare groups. More recently, the SIP has been used to assess the hrqol impact of lung volume reduction surgery (Cranshaw (2001)), to compare patient hrqol between hospital and home care (Wilson et al (1999)) and to assess the multiple sclerosis functional composite measure (Miller et al (2000)), and the Sydney Psychosocial Reintegration Scale (Tate et al (1999)).

The Nottingham Health Profile

The example used above refers to the Functional Limitations Profile, which measures hrqol on a single scale. Most profiles – such as the Nottingham Health

Profile – use several dimensions, which are kept separate, so that several scores are produced, not just one. If a profile had four separate dimensions, the above choice might read as follows:

> Treatment X reduces the four dimension scores by 200, 75, 80, and 230, and increases survival from 1 to 6 years, while treatment Y reduces dimension scores by 290, 50, 150 and 240, and increases survival from 1 to 4 years. Treatment X is thus better than treatment Y by 2 years in survival terms, and by -90, +25, +30 and –10, on each dimension

Clearly, if we assume all the dimensions have some importance, without actually stating the relative value of the scores between the dimensions, then the profile data may deliver unclear results if there are improvements on some dimensions and not on others. This may or may not inhibit the use of profiles; perhaps the most widely-known application of the NHP was the successful demonstration of the cost-effectiveness of the heart transplant programme in the United Kingdom (O'Brien et al (1988)).

Turning to the Nottingham Health Profile, suppose a respondent identified the statements shown in Table 4.2 as applying to her.

Table 4.2 A Selection of NHP Statements

I'm tired all of the time	39.20
I'm in constant pain	20.86
I'm in pain when I walk	11.22
I wake up feeling depressed	12.00
It takes me a long time to get to sleep	16.10
I sleep badly at night	21.70
I find it hard to reach for things	09.30
I find it hard to bend	10.57

The NHP is intended to be a set of six scores, one on each of its dimensions; since there are two "Pain" statements, above, and two statements on the "Sleep" and "Physical Mobility" dimensions, the above numbers are expressed as the six-dimension set of individual scores shown in Table 4.3.

Table 4.3 A Set of NHP Dimension Scores

Energy		39.20
Pain	11.22 + 20.86	32.08
Emotional Reactions		12.00
Sleep	16.10 + 21.70	37.80
Social Isolation		00.00
Physical Mobility	9.30 + 10.57	19.87

Without a "gold standard", validity cannot be shown, except by inference, for example, if all of the profile dimension scores move in the expected directions with clinical measures, such as blood pressure, or resting heart beat rate. The NHP is widely accepted and used, as a valid health impact measure; applications include a study of patients with Parkinson's Disease (Karlsen et al (1999)), of obesity (Gemert et al (1998)) and of hip replacement (Garellick et al (1998)), as well as the effectiveness of stroke unit treatment (Indredavik et al (1998)), and the health status of patients in methadone maintenance treatment (Torrens (1997)). The acceptance of the NHP is also demonstrated by its translation into other languages (Alonso et al (1980), and Wiklund et al (1988)).

Testing the Rosser-Kind (R-K) QALY

Introduction

Does the R-K QALY rank the health of different patients in the same order as the profile does? We describe the datasets, before outlining the results.

The Patient Datasets

The respondents in the Whynes and Neilsen study (W&N) were 188 patients who had suffered from colorectal cancer, who had been discharged from hospital after in-patient treatment, and who were attending a routine follow-up clinic. A further 33 patients who had not yet had an operation were also included, a total of 221 patients. W&N found no significant difference, in the mean scores of the NHP dimensions, between the patients they studied and the population generally. The study collected data of these patients' hrqol in a "snapshot" approach; there was no comparison of health states to determine a treatment impact.

The McCulloch (1998) dataset assessed the impact on hrqol of heart disease procedures, the routine bypass, the emergency bypass, and the angioplasty. There were data before and after treatment from 12 routine bypass and 31 angioplasty patients, data from 14 "waiting" routine bypass patients who did not have the procedure during the project, and data recorded after the procedure from 48 emergency bypass patients. To compare the FLP and R-K data, it was necessary to create a data set of patients before a procedure (14 + 12 + 31), Group A, and another, of patients after a procedure (12 + 31 + 48), Group B. This avoided bias from including some patients twice, while at the same time getting the most information from the dataset.

Given the well-recognised debilitating nature of heart disease, it seems clear that the mean hrqol of the heart disease patients is likely to be less than the mean hrqol of the patients in the W&N study, because the NHP scores of the latter patients did not differ significantly from those of the general population. Since there were heart disease patients with hrqol close to or at 1.00 (full health), this means that the McCulloch (1998) test of convergent validity is more rigorous, because there is a wider range of hrqol states among these respondents than among those of W&N.

W&N used the number of NHP statements identified as an overall measure of health impact, and McCulloch (1998) used the FLP total score for the same purpose. As these values increase, hrqol falls, so there should be a negative correlation between these hrqol measures and R-K QALY values; also, since R-K Disability and Distress levels (from 1 to 7 and from 1 to 4 respectively) increase as hrqol falls, there should be a positive correlation with the overall measure of health impact in each study.

Bringing together the relevant figures from both studies, we have Table 4.4.

Table 4.4 Profile Correlations with R-K measures

	R-K Disability	R-K Distress	R-K Value
Group A (n=57) Total FLP Score	0.62	0.43	-0.61
Group B (n=91) Total FLP Score	0.54	0.60	-0.65
W&N (n=188) No. of NHP responses	0.68	0.54	-0.46

All of these co-efficients are significant at the 1 per cent level, and it is clear that convergent validity is demonstrated.

The McCulloch (1998) study data permit one further analysis, given the measurement of hrqol before and after the bypass and the angioplasty. We would expect that, for these two groups combined, the change in R-K health status will be significantly and negatively correlated with the change in FLP score, and that the change in Distress and Disability levels will be significantly and positively correlated with the change in FLP score. For the purpose of generating QALY values, one could argue that this is one of the more important aspects of the analysis, because ultimately, the intention is to compare the (marginal) cost per (marginal) QALY of different interventions. These results are presented in Table 4.5.

Table 4.5 Correlation of FLP Changes with R-K Changes

Change in	Correlation with change in FLP score
Disability Level	0.55
Distress Level	0.38
Rosser-Kind Value	-0.54

All of these coefficients are significant at the 1 per cent level (n=43), and these findings add to the weight of the evidence in favour of the convergent validity of the Rosser measure.

Discussion

The correlations found are not large, though they are statistically significant; are they important?

They are certainly important in terms of the conventionally accepted testing of convergent validity, and according to current standards, convergent validity has been demonstrated. However, our focus is the prioritisation of health interventions; it may be that the Spearman test is not rigorous enough. The rank-ordering of health cases means taking decisions about who shall live (longer), and who shall suffer (less); only a Spearman co-efficient of 1.00 would mean identical orderings of patients, and therefore identical sets of opportunities for life- and hrqol-enhancing treatments, for the patients involved.

It is hard to see that a Spearman co-efficient of 1.00 would be possible in a study of this kind, given that the NHP, FLP and Rosser measures are designed differently, from different premises and contexts, and therefore may be different in their rankings, even if respondents are 100 per cent accurate in their replies. The Spearman test for significance works by comparing the correlation found with what could have been expected to result from chance; it might be more appropriate to compare the correlation with complete agreement plus a margin of error – for instance, "our results are consistent with complete agreement plus or minus 5 per cent average error in the responses". When health priorities are being decided, and rankings are being compared, the distance of our results from complete agreement seems more important than their distance from complete randomness.

We are not discussing the testing of scientific hypotheses, such as the objectively measurable effect of a drug on blood pressure, or of smoking on perinatal mortality. The basic project is to arrive at more acceptable value judgements and decision-making procedures for health prioritisation. Either we allow values to be determined by chance (including the operation of lobbying through contacts of one kind or another), or we attempt to be reasonable about the determination of health priorities, and use science to help us determine what they should be.

The QALY appears to be the most reasonable approach to the determination of health priorities, because it encapsulates all the essential information about health impact; without QALY information, it is not possible to define health choices at all, whether or not the decisions taken actually follow the "minimum cost per QALY rule".

On the basis of two studies covering a wide range of health states, it is clear that the R-K measure has covergent validity, and that this is an important contribution to the discussion of health valuation. The next chapter uses the data from McCulloch (1998) to compare procedures, on the assumption that the QALY figures found in that study are accurate and reliable measures of health outcome. This is part of an exploration of what valuation in practice means; as is becoming clear, while the problem is important, its solution is complex.

Chapter 5

Comparing Procedures Using QALY Values

Introduction

Chapter 1 explained the decision model of health economics; in cost-effectiveness analysis which uses QALYs, prioritisation involves measuring the costs of procedures, and comparing procedures in terms of the cost per QALY delivered by each. Given a limited budget, procedures are ideally "bought" down a list, from least cost per QALY down, until the budget is exhausted. The decision model is that of the consumer maximising the impact on health.

To explore more fully the implications of the QALY approach, this chapter assumes that there are no problems about applying it in cost-effectiveness analysis (CEA), and explains the comparison of two procedures using Rosser-Kind QALY values from the data provided as Appendix 2 (collected as part of the project described in McCulloch (1998)). Chapter 1 also mentioned the alteration of key assumptions and the analysis of their effects in a "sensitivity analysis" of CEA results; a technique for clarifying the sensitivity analysis of such comparisons is presented.

Comparing the QALY values of procedures

In conventional CEA, the aim is to produce a comparison of medical interventions, of the form:

> A's cost per QALY is £2,000, and B's cost per QALY is £1,800. Other things equal, the finance available should be spent on procedure B, to maximise the impact of the budget on health.

We begin with a comparison of the angioplasty and the CABG.

Comparing the CABG and the Angioplasty

Table 5.1 Rosser-Kind Data

	Pre-CABG	Post-CABG	Pre-PTCA	Post-PTCA
Mean	0.861	0.986	0.957	0.986
Median	0.942	0.990	0.972	0.995
Standard deviation	0.270	0.010	0.050	0.010
Number	12	12	31	31
per cent scoring 1.00	0	25	13	36

(1.00 represents "full health".)

We can see that the mean health gain from the Routine CABG was 0.986 - 0.861 = 0.125, while the mean gain from the PTCA was 0.986 - 0.957 = 0.029.

These data show that the mean gain from the Routine CABG was about four times the mean gain from the PTCA, and that PTCA patients have the same mean hrqol, after their procedure, as Routine CABG patients. It is noticeable that the standard deviation of the Rosser values reduces after the CABG and PTCA, from 0.27 to 0.01 for the former, and from 0.05 to 0.01 for the latter; the numbers of patients in full health increase respectively from zero to 25 per cent, and from 13 per cent to 36 per cent. This appears to be a "ceiling effect", in that variations in hrqol are concealed because the instrument does not measure beyond 1.00. The question of whether QALY values are normally distributed is an important one for research purposes. It could be argued that we would expect human hrqol, like height and weight, to be normally distributed; if hrqol was measured positively, as well as negatively, perhaps a normal distribution might be found.

For comparison, Table 5.2 shows the FLP data for the same variables:

Table 5.2 FLP Data

	Pre-CABG	Post-CABG	Pre-PTCA	Post-PTCA
Mean	2593.2	789.3	1227.0	588.9
Median	2014.0	496.5	972.0	361.0
Standard deviation	1528.9	744.0	235.4	610.6
Number	12	12	31	31
per cent scoring zero	0	8	6	23

(For the FLP, zero represents "full health".)

The mean gain from the CABG was 2593.2 − 789.3 = 1803.9, while the mean gain from the PTCA was 638.1, so that the CABG, on this measure, also has a larger health impact.

The Routine CABG group sample size (12) is particularly small. Fourteen patients were on the waiting list for the CABG, but did not get the procedure during the project; also, 48 patients had Emergency CABGs, and could not be interviewed before the procedure. The hrqol values from the first group are estimates of pre-CABG hrqol, while the values of the second are estimates of post-CABG hrqol; it follows that we can create two larger groups of pre- and post-CABG hrqol, Group I, comprising those who did not get the CABG during the project ("Waiting" patients) and the Pre-procedure CABG patients, and Group II, made up of the Post-routine CABG patients and the Emergency CABG patients.

Table 5.3 Groups I and II

	Number	Mean QALY	Mean FLP
"Waiting"	14	0.965	1637
Pre-CABG	12	0.861	2593
Group I	26	0.917	2078
Post-CABG	12	0.986	589
Emergency	48	0.979	677
Group II	60	0.980	659

This calculation estimates the QALY impact of the CABG as 0.980 − 0.917, or 0.063. This value has been reduced, relative to the previous CABG QALY estimate, by the higher QALY values for the "Waiting" patients, and the same applies to the FLP data, with a gain of 1419, compared to 1804. This appears to call into question whether the patients left on the waiting list were in fact likely to get the procedure. Clearly, getting accurate QALY values from different categories of patient is not a straightforward matter; surgeons tend to focus on curing patients, not collecting statistics, and some of the problems this can throw up are examined in the next chapter.

Leaving these difficulties on one side, we now proceed to a graphical technique, which permits the comparison of procedures in terms of the cost per QALY, and the sensitivity analysis of such comparisons.

Graphical Analysis

Introduction

The assumption is that we can use the above QALY data as reliable and valid measures of health outcome, in a prioritisation exercise which can be subjected to "sensitivity analysis", to demonstrate the impact on its conclusions of changes in costs or QALY outcomes. We begin by using algebra to explain the approach, in a general statement regarding the variables, and go on to illustrate it graphically. This is followed by an explanation of sensitivity analysis.

The Approach

Assume there are two procedures, X and Y, whose benefits, in QALYs, are Qx and Qy, and whose marginal costs, in £s (Cx and Cy) are known. If we represent Qx and Qy, in QALYs, on the horizontal and vertical (x and y) axes, respectively, we can represent the additional QALYs available from the two procedures by a single point on the diagram, described by the (x,y) co-ordinates Qx; Qy. Further, if the cost of X is Cx, and the cost of Y is Cy, then the cost per QALY of each procedure is Cx/Qx, and Cy/Qy.

A useful benchmark for comparing the two procedures is equality between the fractions, when the costs per QALY of procedures X and Y are the same. For these two fractions to be equal,

$$Cx/Qx \ = \ Cy/Qy, \text{ or}$$

$$Qy \times (Cx/Qx) = Cy, \text{ or}$$

$$Qy = (Cy \times Qx) / Cx \qquad \text{(Equation 1)}.$$

That is, if $Qy = (Cy \times Qx) / Cx$, the costs per QALY of the two procedures are the same.

In the proposed diagram, Cy and Cx will be constants, because the axes measure Qy and Qx. The line representing Equation 1, above, shows all the points for which the cost per QALY is the same for the two procedures.

If the actual QALY values for X and Y happen to result in a point located above the line, this means that the cost per QALY of Y is less than the cost per QALY of X. Similarly, if the QALY values result in a point below the line, the cost per QALY of Y will be more than the cost per QALY of X.

An Illustration

Assuming for the sake of exposition that our data accurately represent mean cardiac patient health gains from the PTCA and CABG, we can compare the PTCA and routine CABG in cost-per-QALY terms, using the average Rosser-Kind values, and making reasonable assumptions about survival and cost. So far, we have only the hrqol increments, not survival, and we have not yet discussed cost figures; consider survival and cost in turn.

Survival Estimates of survival times are hard to obtain because physicians are naturally reluctant to provide them; an estimate implies a promise to every patient about the outcome of treatment, which the physician may or may not have the power to fufil. As chapter 6 explains, the meaning of a particular estimate of survival, in a specific context, is a matter of clinical judgement, not of scientific estimation.

Since anecdotal evidence from physicians suggests that neither the PTCA nor the CABG affect survival, we may assume that the procedures affect only quality of life. Making a reasonable estimate (based on Williams (1985), among others), we also assume that CABG and PTCA patients have mean life expectancies of 5 and 10 years respectively, regardless of whether or not they have a procedure. The QALY gains from each procedure can be calculated as the quality of life increment multiplied by the years of life expectancy; using our hrqol gain figures, calculated from Table 5.1 above, we have Table 5.4.

Table 5.4 The Value of Each Procedure in QALYs

Procedure	Hrqol Gain	x Life Expectancy	= QALY Value
CABG	0.125	x 5	= 0.625
PTCA	0.029	x 10	= 0.290

Representing the CABG gains on the vertical axis (procedure Y), and the PTCA gains on the horizontal axis (procedure X), we have a point R, which has the co-ordinates y = 0.625, x = 0.29.

Cost For ease of exposition, we assume throughout that marginal and average costs are equal; cost assumptions are more easily stated, though like survival, cost figures are difficult to determine accurately in practice. According to Gunnell and Smith (1994), the respective costs of the CABG and the PTCA were approximately £4,000 - £7,000, and "over £3,000". For the purposes of illustration, let us assume figures of £5,500 and £3,500 for the CABG and PTCA respectively.

Taken together, these results enable us to calculate the cost per QALY of each procedure, in terms of the Rosser and FLP QALYs. If $Cy = £5,500$, and $Cx = £3,500$, equation 1, given above as:

$$Qy = (Cy \times Qx) / Cx,$$

now reads:

Qy = £5500 x Qx / £3500, or

Qy = (11 x Qx) / 7.

This is the graph of all the QALY yield combinations which would equalize the cost per QALY of the two procedures, given the particular ratio indicated by the costs given. Figure 1 shows the point R, and the line representing the equation; we noted above that if the combination of QALY values was above the line, then the cost per QALY of Y, Cy/Qy would be less than the cost per QALY of X, Cx/Qx.

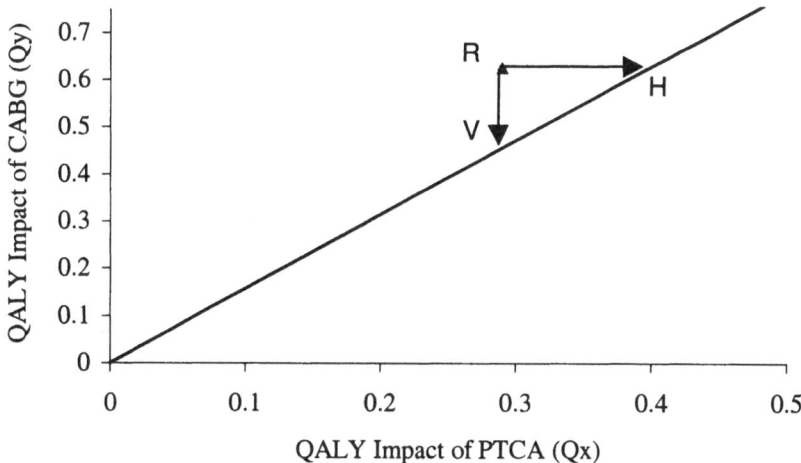

Figure 5.1 The Cost Per QALY of two procedures

The cost per QALY of each procedure, under our assumptions, are calculated as follows:

Routine CABG: £5,500 / 0.625 = £8,800 per QALY
PTCA: £3,500 / 0.290 = £12,069 per QALY

R shows a combination of QALY values above the line, implying a lower cost per QALY for the CABG.

As an example of sensitivity analysis, we now consider the changes in the procedure costs, and in the Rosser QALY components, required to produce equal costs per QALY for both the CABG and PTCA.

Sensitivity Analysis

If our aim is to maximise health, we have a preference for a procedure with the lowest cost per QALY, and we are interested in the sensitivity of this conclusion to change, particularly to changes in the incremental hrqol value established by a QALY measure.

We know that, in our example, for the cost per QALY of X and Y to be the same,

$$Qy = 11 \times Qx / 7,$$

and our data have given us a point, R, where

$$Qy = 0.625 \text{ and } Qx = 0.290.$$

The changes that could bring about equality between Cx/Qx and Cy/Qy are changes in costs, and changes in either Qx or Qy.

Changes in costs Currently, the line has a gradient of 11/7; for such a line to pass through the point R, it would have to rotate left, increasing its gradient until the gradient was 0.625 / 0.290, or 2.155; this is the value of the ratio of the money costs of the two procedures required to produce equal costs per QALY, given QALY values for the CABG and PTCA respectively of 0.625 and 0.290. Leaving the cost of the PTCA unchanged at £3,500, the cost of the CABG would have to rise to 2.155 x 3,500, that is, to £7,543, from £5,500, an increase of £2,043, or 37 per cent.

Changes in Qx and Qy Arguments developed in respect of Qx will also apply to Qy. Decreasing Qy to equalise the procedures' costs per QALY (in the diagram) means moving vertically from R to V, on the equal cost line (increasing Qx, horizontally, for the same purpose, means moving from R to H). Since Qy is the product of a hrqol increment and survival, the change in the hrqol increment required to produce equality in the cost per QALY of two procedures will be in proportion to the length of survival. Here survival length is 5 years; changes to the hrqol increment will matter only one quarter as much as if the survival figure had been 20 years.

If life expectancy remains at 5 years, the hrqol gain required to produce a CABG cost per QALY of £12,000 can be found from:

$$£12,000 \text{ (new CABG cost per QALY)} = £5,500 / \text{(hrqol gain x 5 years), or}$$

$$\text{(hrqol gain x 5)} = 5500 / 12000, \text{ that is,}$$

$$\text{hrqol gain} = 1100 / 12000 = 0.092.$$

The hrqol increment would thus need to fall from 0.125 to 0.092, a reduction of 0.033, or 26.4 per cent, to make both the costs per QALY equal to £12,000.

On the other hand, what change in survival would be required, leaving the hrqol increment the same, to bring the two costs per QALY into equality? Using the same equation, we have:

£12,000 = £5,500 / (hrqol gain x life expectancy);

if the hrqol gain remains unchanged at 0.125, we have:

£12,000 = £5,500 / (0.125 x life expectancy), or

£12,000 x (0.125 x life expectancy) = £5,500,

that is,

life expectancy = £5,500 / (£12,000 x 0.125) = 3.06 years.

CABG life expectancy would have to fall by about 2 years, from 5 to 3.06, a decline of about 40 per cent, to equalise the costs per QALY of the procedures.

Conclusion

If the cost per QALY comparison is to be part of health policy, it is important to present the comparison as clearly as possible; it is argued that the diagrammatic approach explained here sets out in detail the different dimensions of the QALY choices, and makes their sensitivity analysis clearer.

Our exploration of the QALY approach continues in the next chapter, with an examination of three problems identified in the research project which produced the values used above.

Chapter 6

Using QALYs in Practice

Introduction

The QALY measure has to be applied with care, but given the right evidence, it permits the comparison of procedures in terms of the impact of each upon health for a given quantity of resources. The question is, how easy or difficult will it be to find the right evidence? This chapter examines one particular research project (McCulloch (1998)), and the next considers the same issues in respect of Alzheimer's Disease; chapter 8 then takes a European view of actual economic evaluation, to consider practice by health sectors, universities, and health technology industries.

In this chapter, three points arising from the project are explained; they appear to be of general relevance, and they lead to the development of the "Mean Expected QALY Indicator", as an alternative basis for prioritisation. Instead of maximising health from a limited budget, in a decision analysis model, a specific sector of the health economy (such as the "Cardiac sector") might be managed on the basis of scientific evidence; the suggestion is that, given similar evidence from the health economy as a whole, resources could be allocated similarly between all of the health sectors. This would be a type of strategic management, based on scientific evidence which would be more open to discussion than consultants' survival estimates.

Finding The Right Evidence In Practice

The following issues are intrinsic to the use of QALY measures: measurement and accountability, the representativeness of any particular sample, and the use of randomised controlled trial evidence to estimate survival.

Measurement and Accountability

Originally, the project was to consist of a before and after assessment of the routine Coronary Artery Bypass Graft (CABG), using the Health Measurement Questionnaire to establish a QALY measure, and the Functional Limitations Profile for comparison. Patients on the CABG waiting list were to be interviewed every six weeks until they had the operation, and then interviewed six months afterwards. The original estimate of the numbers of routine CABG cases was 24 per month, so that a seven month period would generate 168 cases; this was judged to be enough for the purposes of the project.

After the first three months of the project, 72 patients should have had the procedure and been interviewed; in fact, only 3 of the identified patients had had the procedure, 2 had died, and 1 had been admitted for urgent surgery before an interview could be arranged. It appeared that the definition of what was and what was not a routine CABG had altered, with the effect that the project sample size would take years, not months, to accumulate. With the agreement of the Cardiologists, the project was extended to include Angioplasty patients, who were interviewed similarly; again, there were not enough cases in this group to achieve the target within a reasonable timespan, and the project was further extended to include patients who had had an Emergency CABG. In the resulting group, all of the patients had heart disease, and all were or had been candidates for invasive treatment.

The diagnosis of heart disease appears to be an art, more than a science; it depends in part on the interpretation of angiogram (X-ray) pictures taken of the heart, and there is variation both between observers, and between observations of the same observer, in the symptoms detected from the same angiogram pictures (Bertrand et al (1993), and Kleiman et al (1992)). The criteria for deciding between CABG, Angioplasty, and drugs-only treatment are not well-defined; cardiologists in Northern Ireland have differed by as much as 300 per cent in their rates of referral of patients for an emergency CABG (DHSS (1992)). That this is normal is confirmed by Gunnell and Smith (1994), who note (page 35) that the "emergency" CABG has many different definitions in the literature.

It follows that cardiac surgery requires the exercise of a given level of skill under conditions which are, to a degree, unknown and unpredictable. While accountability is desirable, and implies some method of measuring outcomes, the CABG and the Angioplasty are not homogenous products. For unknown reasons, some patients' procedures will involve more health outcome, more skill, and/or more resources than others, and it is in principle difficult to predict which patients will require what resources or "deliver" what health outcomes. In terms of the project under discussion, revisions to the expected figure may be understandable, if they occurred on a case by case basis. It is possible that the surgeons were not deciding "I will lower the criteria", but "this patient is too uncertain to be included". On this interpretation, there were many more uncertain patients than had been expected.

This problem is as general as its source, uncertainty; in practice, strategies for valuing health will have to respect the interests of the practitioners involved, while at the same time attempting, in a situation of uncertainty, to achieve the greatest impact on health from the available resources.

The Representativeness of the Sample

Given enough resources, we might have proceeded in the project under discussion (McCulloch (1998)) by selecting at random one patient from every successive group of ten on the CABG waiting list, generating (say) one hundred respondents from a thousand cardiac patients. Would this have been a representative sample? It would have been an unbiased selection from the population at the time, but its representativeness changes over time, and not just because of the variability in diagnosis already discussed.

As clinical opinion, scientific understanding, and technology develop and change, so does the selection of particular types of cardiac patient for different treatments. The basis for that selection is ill-defined, and is subject to unmeasurable change. Also, since the data were collected, an additional cardiac surgeon has been appointed to the Northern Ireland cardiac surgery team. Other things equal, one would expect the average "need" of the cardiac patients receiving a CABG to fall, after such an appointment, thereby reducing the representativeness of our sample in relation to the current Northern Ireland population of cardiac patients.

Part of the problem is the lack of a valid and objective definition of "patient need" for surgery, or indeed for any other kind of medical intervention. This is a general difficulty in the economics of health services, noted by Culyer (1995). As "need" varies, and as the ability of physicians to meet it (using new technologies) increases, so will the benefit gained by patients from the procedure, as they are selected on different bases, for technically changing treatments. Over the past 10 years, there have been large and small changes in medical practice in respect of cardiac treatment, from the inclusion of patients over 75 years old, to the routine use of aspirin at the onset of symptoms. As medical practice continues to change, it follows that conclusions drawn from our data may be true only temporarily, though they may serve as benchmarks. The size of the effects of particular changes on such marks may be judged, but may not be determined scientifically. This is not a problem which can be solved by holding larger or more frequent clinical trials, even if resources were available for this purpose. Similar difficulties arise in the estimation of survival impacts, using clinical trial evidence.

Clinical Trial Evidence for Survival Estimation

Chapter 2 explained that both survival and hrqol estimates are required for the measurement of health impacts in terms of QALYs. Here, the problem of survival estimation using the only available scientific approach, the Randomised Controlled Trial (RCT), is discussed. It is a cardinal principle of evidence-based medicine that procedures should be assessed using an RCT, and it is to be expected that procedure survival impacts should be available and applicable to QALY estimation.

Detsky (1995) specifies three requirements for the scientific comparison of treatments in an RCT:

- For each set of patients treated, the distribution of known and unknown prognostic factors must be similar, so that all the sets have the same or similar prognoses. This explicitly recognises that unknown prognostic factors may be present, and may affect results in unforeseeable ways.
- All the outcomes must be assessed in the same way for each set of patients; observers recording outcomes should not be aware of which treatment has been applied to which patient, and (ideally) neither should any patient be aware of which treatment has been administered. This is obviously problematic in the case of bypass surgery versus angioplasty, since the former, and not the latter, involves opening the chest.
- The only difference between the sets of patients must be the application of the new or of the control treatment(s), strictly defined; there must be no "co-interventions", such as heightened interest and care given to patients receiving the new treatment, and the two groups must be identical in terms of clinical conditions. This can be difficult to achieve; in the cardiac sector, it might mean, for instance, including only patients with 1-vessel disease, and ignoring those with 2-, 3-, and 4-vessel disease.

Estimating Survival

In principle, the RCT approach could be used to determine the survival values of established treatments, for the purpose of QALY estimation. However, this raises an ethical problem. By definition, an established procedure is the recommended treatment for certain categories of patient; anyone who falls into these categories should have it, on medical grounds. In an RCT to determine the procedure's impact on survival, we would have to select at random, from a group comprising patients in those categories, those who would get the procedure, and those who would not. Denying the procedure to the second group, the control group, would mean leaving their survival at a level below what the treatment is known to be able to deliver.

According to the Declaration of Helsinki, "concern for the interests of the subject must always prevail over the interests of science and society" (18th World Medical Assembly, June 1964, quoted in Adami et al (1994)). If a particular treatment is the recognised medical response to the condition of a well-defined group of patients, we cannot set up a trial in which a control group would (according to medical opinion) die sooner than necessary in order to determine the treatment's value in survival terms. Interestingly, this seems to be true even if there is no definite scientific rationale for either the treatment's acceptance, or for the diagnostic procedures which determine each patient's category.

The implication is that we cannot determine, scientifically, what the QALY impact of an established treatment is, because we cannot, for this purpose, reduce patient survival below what (medical opinion believes) it otherwise would be.

In any case, there seems to be agreement in the medical literature that RCT evidence is unrepresentative; each trial involves a selective protocol, designed to isolate the effects of the procedure(s) of interest. Protocols vary between trials, because of variations in the procedures and patient groups compared.

Herman (1995) notes the importance of differences between trial and routine clinical practice, and warns of the placebo effect, which may be present even for active treatments. Bailey (1994) (quoted in Fayers and Hand (1997) page 1025) goes as far as to say "there is simply no logical basis on which to generalise quantitative results from a trial", and similar points are made by Rothwell (1995), Davis (1994), and Rubins (1994). One response is that there is no alternative to RCT evidence; at least RCT results have an estimated level of uncertainty.

As an example, consider the clinician's estimation of the survival impact of the CABG and PTCA in Northern Ireland, using RCT evidence from studies carried out elsewhere. An examination of the literature on heart disease treatments by Gunnell and Smith (1994) makes the following points:

- Those patients included in the cardiac procedure trials were only a small proportion of those referred for angiogram (that is, for an invasive cardiac procedure); in the Coronary Artery Surgery Study, for instance, only 12.7 per cent conformed to the trial's inclusion criteria, and of these only 37 per cent were randomised, amounting to only 4.7 per cent of all cardiac referrals.
- RCTs tended to be carried out by the best practitioners, in excellent treatment centres, which are unrepresentative of the service generally provided.
- As explained above, in relation to hrqol impacts, the meaning of RCT results may also be affected by the impact of small and large technical changes, so the average CABG of 1982 is likely to have been different, in terms of its impact on survival and hrqol, from the average CABG of 2002.

The physician's judgement must allow for:

- the unrepresentative character of the trial cases;
- differences in the patient inclusion criteria, between different trials;
- differences between trial centres' diagnostic protocols and the region's protocols;
- the trial hospitals' relative excellence; and
- the impact of technical change on procedure success since the completion of the trial.

Clearly, a large degree of judgement is necessary, which is not open to scientific analysis. Rather like the prioritising surgeon in the first paragraph of chapter 1, physicians have to make life or death decisions based on evidence which appears to be capable of many interpretations. The allocation of resources must either rely on such judgements, or develop an alternative method for prioritisation.

Physicians are entrusted with life or death judgements about patient treatments; a resource allocation based on the cost per QALY ranking of procedures requires that they should also assess the value of their treatments in survival terms. This seems undesirable, on a number of grounds, not least fairness to the physicians. In the next section, a proposal for the strategic management of a cardiac sector develops a solution which permits the scientific analysis of health outcomes, so that some kind of objective appraisal can be made of the value of health outcomes, without requiring physicians' estimates of survival.

Managing a Health Sector to Maximise Health

Why "manage" a health sector (such as cardiac care) at all? Briefly, because estimating the cost per QALY of particular procedures involves a degree of judgement that cannot be analysed scientifically. In practice, even given QALY hrqol data, surgeons still have to determine survival impacts by interpreting the results of a trial or trials carried out elsewhere. Only in this way can they assess what survival would be in their specific locality, in order to reach a conclusion about the value of treatments in terms of QALYs.

The alternative proposed here appears to be more attractive, because it would enable the managers (whoever is effectively in charge, if anyone) of a particular sector in a region (such as renal care, or orthopaedics) to determine the relative efficiency of the service in both costs and outcome terms, on grounds which are open to scientific analysis, rather than dependent on judgements which are (and must be) private to the professionals concerned. Data definition is considered before the Mean Expected QALY Index is explained.

Data Definition

The Randomised Controlled Trial is not the only method of collecting clinical data which is relevant to the measurement of procedure impacts on health. Mega-trials (described by Charlton (1995)) and database analysis (Knaus (1995)) are possible alternatives, of which the latter is the most relevant to our present purpose.

Knaus (1995) was concerned with factors determining the success of anti-sepsis drugs for patients in intensive care; these patients were typically on life-support machines, and were acutely ill. Knaus observed that there were multiple risk factors, demonstrated by different clinical trials, which affected patient survival when these drugs were used. The trials involved unrepresentative patients (to achieve control), and did not generate enough data or comparisons for risk factor estimation. It followed that examination of the trial data could not determine the weighting of risk factors, on which treatment combinations would be based.

Knaus' response to this problem is the database approach, which involves collecting data from every patient, rather than from a random sample, establishing patient categories, and using multi-variable statistical techniques to determine the risk factors for each category of patient from the population studied.

We can apply this approach to the treatment sectors of a region, so that they can be compared in terms of their health outcomes and costs, and so that scentific techniques can be used to establish the effectiveness and cost-effectiveness of treatment delivery.

The Proposal

The proposal is to collect QALY data, at regular intervals, from each patient in a particular sector, up-dating relevant patient characteristics at the same time, and recording the date of decease if appropriate. This would permit the construction of the Mean Expected QALY Indicator (MEQI); the next section describes this proposed measure, applied (as an example) to a cardiac sector, and explains its interpretation as a basis for maximising the health impact of cardiac procedures. This is followed by the application of the same approach to the comparison of sectors within a region using the "Expected QALY Deficit", as an indicator of the need for treatment of the patients in a particular health sector.

The Mean Expected QALY Indicator (MEQI) in the Cardiac Sector

Key Assumptions

- Heart disease patients (for example, in Northern Ireland) can be reliably identified, and registered as "cardiac sector" patients;
- The costs of such a sector can be identified, for both its diagnoses and treatments;
- QALY and clinical data can be collected from every such patient at least once a year.

The mean expected QALYs of these patients might be calculated as shown in the fictional example of Table 6.1.

Table 6.1 Mean Expected QALY Indicator (MEQI) Calculation

Mean survival of cardiac patients	59 years
Mean age of cardiac patients now	50 years
Mean patient life expectancy (1 - 2)	9 years
Mean patient QALY health state value	0.88
MEQI (= 9 x 0.88) in QALYs	7.92

As survival fluctuates, and the mean age changes, so the MEQI value will alter; its value will depend on treatment effectiveness, and on the incidence and severity of the disease. From the accumulated database, statistical analysis could determine what the trends in incidence are, and establish the case mix of patients (for example, between "mild" and "severe" angina, and between "low" and "high" risk of a fatal heart attack), so that the expected change in the MEQI over time can be calculated. Given the trends established by publicly accessible findings, the MEQI value (adjusted as necessary) over time would indicate whether treatment effectiveness was rising or falling. After allowance had been made for changes in the case mix, and their effects on the MEQI value, increases in the adjusted MEQI would indicate greater effectiveness, and vice versa.

Such a measure would of course require judgement by experts in the interpretation of the database to discern the factors affecting the MEQI value. In particular, it would involve the application of econometric techniques, to analyse the time series of the value of the MEQI.

A serious possible obstacle to the database approach is that clinicians might not be willing to permit the collection of survival and hrqol data from every single patient (see chapter 5). There is evidence that the publication of CABG surgery outcome data in the United States may have reduced the number of surgeons willing to treat seriously ill patients (Schneider and Epstein (1996), Hannan et al (1997)). Also, if the principle of competition (Maynard (1993), Malcomson and Chalkey (1995)) was followed to its logical conclusion, there might be direct assessment of each surgeon in terms of his or her average QALY outcome, or average MEQI. In such a situation, surgeons would be vulnerable to an unexpectedly large proportion of difficult cases, the outcomes of which might adversely and unfairly affect a surgeon's performance. These cases might not be predictable, given the problems of diagnosis indicated above.

A sector-wide MEQI would conceal the performance of individual surgeons; observers of sector performance would have no reason to be concerned with the performance of individuals, being focussed on the issues related to the trends in the incidence and severity of the disease, and the performance of the sector as a whole. Given the availability of the data proposed, and the physicians' common interest in a high MEQI value, senior clinicians might be more willing (than seems to have been the case hitherto, according to DHSS (1992)) to agree treatment criteria.

More positively, the use of the proposed MEQI as a cardiac sector performance indicator might give additional importance to those patients who are not eligible for an invasive procedure, because the MEQI would include data from all cardiac patients. Data from 1991 show that, in the average English health district, with a population of 500,000, there were 5700 patients presenting genuine angina symptoms to their General Practitioners, and, in the same year, there were (in the district) 150 CABGs, and 75 PTCAs (Gunnell and Smith (1994)). It may be the case that nothing, apart from a drug regime, could be done for the 5475 patients who were not eligible for an invasive procedure. However, the use of the MEQI might encourage more searching for symptom remedies, such as exercise tailored to individual patient requirements, or more interest by clinicians in general health promotion.

The definition of the sector to include diagnosis formally recognises the significance of diagnosis to treatment success. Not only would the database be important for improving diagnosis, but the inclusion of diagnosis in the same unit of management implies that overall management of the sector would have to take into account all of the factors affecting treatment success, as well as the actual costs of diagnosis.

Cost-Effectiveness

If the incidence and severity of cardiac disease remain unchanged, the value of the proposed MEQI variable should be constant over time; if it increases, and expert (epidemiological and public health) opinion agrees that it should have remained constant, we can say that the sector's effectiveness is increasing. The logical next question is, what has been happening to cost-effectiveness? If the cost per patient, that is, the total cost of the sector, divided by the number of patients, is also constant, then a rise in the value of the MEQI implies that cost-effectiveness has also increased.

The MEQI in Other Sectors

On the same assumptions, a similar survey could be carried out in other sectors, such as arthritis and renal failure; the first sector treats a disease which has a large impact on hrqol, but is not life-threatening, while the second, like the cardiac sector, aims to prevent death from a chronic illness. As an illustration, fictional MEQI calculations for such patients are shown in Tables 6.2 and 6.3.

Table 6.2 MEQI Calculation for Arthritis Patients

Mean survival of arthritis patients	70 years
Mean age of arthritis patients	42 years
Mean patient life expectancy (1 - 2)	28 years
Mean patient QALY health state value	0.90
MEQI (= 28 x 0.90) in QALYs	25.2

Table 6.3 MEQI Calculation for Kidney Disease Patients

Mean survival of renal patients	29 years
Mean age of renal patients	25 years
Mean patient life expectancy (1 - 2)	4 years
Mean patient QALY health state value	0.60
MEQI (= 4 x 0.60) in QALYs	2.4

MEQI values could be analysed in the same way as the value for the cardiac sector; similarly, an accessible judgement could be reached about the trends in each MEQI value, so that an overall assessment of each sector's treatment performance could be made. Also, given the calculation of a sector's average cost, the changes over time in the cost of treatment could be related to the value, over time, of the MEQI, and conclusions drawn regarding the cost-effectiveness of the sector.

Given the information proposed, then, it is possible for individual sectors to be managed with the aim of maximising MEQI per unit cost, taking into account all the influences on this value. We have a within-sector efficiency measure, based on analysis which is accessible to criticism and discussion. There is a resemblance to the "continuous improvement" approach advocated by O'Connor (1996), though the latter is less formal, based as it is on professional practice and its informal criteria of effectiveness.

We consider, next, how a basis for resource allocation between sectors might be developed, if MEQI values were available for all the sectors of a health service, managed on a regional basis.

Resource Allocation Between Sectors - the Expected QALY Deficit (EQD)

Chapter 5 noted the problem of the absence of a verifiable and objective definition of "patient need" for cardiac surgery. Here, the proposal is to develop a MEQI value for the population as a whole, for comparison with sector MEQIs, so that an indicator of "need" can be produced for each sector, which takes into account the number of patients treated. The calculation of a fictional population MEQI is shown in Table 6.4.

Table 6.4 A Population MEQI

Mean survival	72 years
Mean age	37 years
Mean life expectancy (1 - 2)	35 years
Mean QALY health state value	0.98
MEQI (= 35 x 0.98) in QALYs	34.3

Here, we are not interested in identifying risk factors, or informing diagnosis and treatment; it follows that a representative sample would be appropriate, rather than a survey of every individual in the region, to determine the QALY health state and mean age. The survival figure could be obtained from mortality statistics.

The need for a sector's services might be measured by the difference between a sector's MEQI value, and the MEQI value for the population as a whole, multiplied by the number of the sector's patients. The difference between the average MEQI for the population, and the average MEQI for the patients of a particular health sector, may be called an "Expected QALY Deficit" (EQD). The aim of each sector might be defined as the reduction of this deficit; this aim is clear and unambiguous, and its achievement can be measured in an accessible way. From the fictional examples set out in Tables 6.1 to 6.4, we have the data for Table 6.5.

Table 6.5 Measuring "need": the Expected QALY Deficit (EQD)

Sector	MEQI	Population MEQI	Difference	Number of patients	EQD
Cardiac	7.9	34.3	26.4	3,000	79,200
Arthritis	25.2	34.3	9.1	20,000	182,000
Renal	2.4	34.3	29.9	500	14,950

The health budget might be distributed in proportion to the sectors' different EQD figures; this could be a basis for prioritisation. The argument here is that it is a better basis than the cost per QALY, given the reliance of the latter on survival estimates made by physicians, and the other difficulties associated with QALYs, such as the very large quantities of data which would be necessary for system-wide resource allocation.

Comparison with Culyer's Definition of "Need" (Culyer (1995))

It is interesting to compare this measure of need with the requirements proposed by Professor Culyer; paraphrasing slightly, they are:

- The measure's value content should be evident, and easily interpretable;
- The measure should be capable of empirical application in issues of horizontal and vertical distribution;
- The measure should be service- and person-specific;
- The measure should enable a straightforward link to be made to resources;
- The measure should not, if acted upon as a distributional principle, produce manifestly inequitable results.

The EQD appears to fulfil conditions 1, 3, 4, and 5. Regarding horizontal equity, it seems clear that all those suffering in the same way receive equal weight; as suffering (measured by the QALY measure) increases, the individual's weight increases, so that vertical equity is also taken into account.

However, someone suffering from two diseases, such as arthritis and heart disease, would be counted twice, because some of the same "QALY Difference" would be included for each sector. One response might be to allow such a patient to count twice, but only for the lower of the two life expectancy values (if different); in both sectors, the lower hrqol would then count twice, and strict equity would not be followed. It does not seem likely that the greater equity which might be achieved would be worth the resources required to develop and apply formulae for dividing the "QALY Deficit" of the relevant patients between different sectors.

It may be, then, that the database described would permit the measurement of individuals "needs", in relation to the population MEQI value. The patient categories and expected disease patterns made possible by the database might permit accessible analyses to be made of the MEQI for well-defined groups of patients.

Conclusion: Incremental QALYs and MEQI Values

The MEQI measure is intended to open prioritisation to scientific analysis, without having to rely on the judgement of the physicians whose performance is to be measured. The proposed value, for a particular sector, would be an indicator of the sector's performance; over time, the changes in the cost per patient, as the MEQI altered, would be an accessible indicator of the sector's cost-effectiveness. Also, it seems that the difference between each sector's MEQI value, and the same value calculated for the population as a whole, multiplied by the number of patients treated by the sector, would provide a measure of "need", in terms of the "Expected QALY Deficit", or EQD, for that sector. If appropriate, resources could be allocated in proportion to the EQD figure for each sector.

There remains the problem of the resources required to collect the information, though of course this problem would exist for any attempt to base health choices on hrqol data. We saw above that, according to Gunnell and Smith (1994), more than 1 per cent of practice patients (5,700 out of 500,000) presented genuine angina symptoms; if their mean life expectancy is 5 years, then at any given time 5 per cent of the population would be included in the cardiac sector's list of patients. With Northern Ireland's population of 1.5 million, our proposal would mean performing the survey every year on 75,000 patients. There is also the cost to the patients of completing the necessary forms, in terms of both time and effort; the surveys could disrupt the coping strategies of people trying to maintain an ordinary lifestyle in the face of crippling illness.

We may be forced back to some kind of sampling regime, in which we select at random 1 patient in every 10, though this is still 7500 patients. On the other hand, it seems likely that both data collection and analysis will be less costly as the prices of electronic media continue to fall, and their technical effectiveness continues to improve.

The concluding question is this: when determining the allocation of health care resources within a health service, should we trust physicians' judgement, or spend resources on monitoring patient hrqol and survival? From society's viewpoint, it is desirable to make judgements about prioritisation both accessible *and* objective, that is, independent of any professional interest in the number of procedures performed. It seems unfair to expect individuals to be objective about the value of their work, particularly when that work directly affects the chances of others' survival and hrqol. One could argue, further, that any serious attempt at prioritisation by a physician, over any substantial case load, would effectively prevent the physician from practising, such is the volume of scientific information that would have to be considered. Finally, it is surely part of the essential health infrastructure that physicians should be provided with fully comprehensive monitoring of the impact of their work on patient hrqol and survival, at no cost to their practice, that is, at no cost to the well-being of their patients.

The fact remains, however, that the main obstacle to the use of the EQD is not a question of principle, but the practical one of where the data are to be found, not just in the sense of collecting it, but in the sense that by no means all conditions are as understood as heart disease is, and by no means all conditions have effective remedies. Many psychiatric illnesses, conditions of the third age, such as Alzheimer's Disease, and some genetic disorders, are examples; the "rule of rescue" dictates that even when there is no remedy for their disease or condition, sufferers deserve care.

In the next chapter, we continue to explore the valuation of health in practice, by examining the example of patients suffering from Alzheimer's Disease; this is taken as an example of a condition for which treatment is difficult, and for which data collection in randomised controlled trials is also problematic. Lessons are learned from the experience of pharmaceutical companies, which have been required, despite these problems, to demonstrate the "value for money" of their products.

Chapter 7

The Case of Alzheimer's Disease

Introduction[1]

Chapter 1 explained how scarcity requires choice, and choice implies valuation; in practice, therefore, health valuation does not just cover the valuation of actual health states, but the making of choices. Comparing alternatives may not be straightforward, and this is particularly the case for patients suffering from Alzheimer's Disease.

Conventional approaches to economic evaluation (Gold et al (1996), Sloan (1995)) assume that choices have to be made between distinct alternatives. Given clear distinctions, and (for preference) data from Randomised Controlled Trials (RCTs), cost-effectiveness analysis can identify a rank-ordering of the alternative interventions, in terms of the cost per unit of outcome measure. The rational allocation of resources to maximise their impact on health therefore means spending the budget on the interventions in that order. However, not all interventions or programmes of care lend themselves to the RCT approach, or to CEA, for a variety of reasons. If the condition has no cure, is defined as much culturally as clinically, or if scientific control of interventions is expensive, then CEA may not be possible, or not adequately cost-effective, and other approaches to prioritisation may be required.

In Alzheimer's Disease (AD), care takes place in a large variety of contexts, from nursing homes to extended families; these contexts, and the presence of other conditions and diseases, make it difficult to achieve scientific control, or to measure costs. For example, a 20 per cent difference in a caregiver quality of life index was found (Drummond (1991)) between a group of carers receiving a Caregiver Support Programme, and a control group supported by conventional community nursing care, but this result was not statistically significant, because the sample was small. The study found 146 caregiver-relative pairs in southern Ontario, of which only 60 were eligible for the study; eligibility criteria mainly consisted of excluding confounding from other illnesses, which would affect quality of life. In each group, 178 subjects would have been needed, a total of 356, to demonstrate statistical significance.

In addition, the general problems of evaluating mental health treatments (Chisholm (1996), Chisholm (2000)) also apply to AD; treatment and care of the mentally ill improves patient quality of life, rather than its length, and there is "intrinsic uncertainty" surrounding the nature of the disease and the efficacy of treatment.

Despite these difficulties, prioritisation is still important, and this chapter explains three attempts to deal with the problems of valuing health in the AD sector. Pharmaceutical companies have had to justify the adoption by health services of their AD drugs; this has led to literature which has adopted a common approach to health valuation. While the approach has its merits, not least economy and ingenuity, it does leave some questions unanswered. Secondly, the "extended post-marketing surveillance trial" (McCulloch et al (2000)) is examined, as possibly a better method for collecting information (in the case of AD) than the randomised controlled trial, given what is known about the disease. Finally, the application of the "lattice approach" to choice-making in AD is explained; it makes choice possible without the measurement of health state values or economic impacts.

The Approach of the Pharmaceutical Companies

Introduction

Evidence[2] was presented to the Irish Centre for Pharmacoeconomics, supporting the adoption of two drugs (donepezil and rivastigmine) for funding by the Irish health service. The basic proposition was that adoption of the relevant drug would reduce health service costs by more than the cost of the drug. This conclusion rested on the idea that the drug would increase, or prevent the decline of, the Mini-Mental State Examination score (a clinical measure of outcome), which had been shown elsewhere to be inversely related to institutional care costs. (A score of 30 means that all faculties are intact; as the disease progresses, the score declines.) Clinical outcome measures such as the MMSE can be useful in economic studies, but their reliability requirements may be different from those of QALY measures.

The articles used data from existing empirical studies which had tested the drug to provide outcome estimates; they relied on the multi-national randomised controlled trials which had been carried out to demonstrate the efficacy of the drugs. Separate studies of cost-effectiveness were not undertaken. The following common pattern could be identified in the studies:

- Data collection: The drug is tested in a multi-national randomised controlled trial, lasting six months; MMSE data is collected, so that the impact of treatment between the beginning and end of the trial can be determined.
- Cost Relationships: The relationship between the MMSE score and the cost of caring for AD patients can be determined from a secondary data source, generated in only one country, which is based on the proportions of patients institutionalised, and on the cost of care in institutions and in the community. (Expecting the same relationship to apply in a country which is not the one where the data was collected is problematic.)

- Modelling: Extrapolations beyond the six-month trial, to between two and five years, are made, based on the RCT data, using survival functions or Markov analysis to determine the total time, during the period modelled, spent by each patient at a particular MMSE level.
- Conclusion: Cost-effectiveness is demonstrated, because, given the assumptions made, the drug reduces the amount of time spent in an institution, and increases the amount of time spent in the community, so that there will be a reduction in the costs of care to the health service, or to society.

The UK National Institute for Clinical Excellence recommended (on 19 January, 2001) that donepezil and rivastigmine should be made available to patients a) with mild-to-moderate AD b) who have an MMSE score of >=12 points, and c) who are likely to take their medication regularly. (The press release is available on http://www.nice.org.uk.) There is no comment as to the access or otherwise of physicians to every patient's MMSE score; the decision of the Irish Centre for Pharmacoeconomics was that the evidence for cost-effectiveness in the Irish setting was not sufficiently strong. It is important to note that one set of studies relied on the relationship between the MMSE and costs discovered in empirical work carried out in England, while the other set relied on similar work in Canada. (There is a detailed discussion of the "balance of care" – between different types of institutional settings and programmes – with reference to Dementia in the United Kingdom, in Kavanagh et al (1995).)

A detailed weighing of all the arguments presented, and the Irish Centre's response, would require another chapter at least; for the purpose of an examination of the problems of prioritisation in respect of Alzheimer's Disease, we may focus on the questions associated with the Mini-Mental State Examination Scale, modelling, and resource identification and measurement.

The Mini-Mental State Examination Scale

It tends to be assumed that clinical outcomes can be used when value for money is to be demonstrated. This may be a convenient assumption, because clinicians are familiar with such measures, and datasets are likely to be available for comparison; in particular, the acceptance of the clinical measure means that resources are not required for an economic study. The MMSE is the clinical instrument of choice, and the one used for the clinical trials, to test the effectiveness of the drug. As we shall see later, it may not be the most appropriate outcome measure, if the objective is to achieve value for money, even given a fairly simple definition of "value".

Assuming the MMSE is an appropriate instrument, is it valid? According to Almqvist (1998), while there is high test-retest reliability, the MMSE does have a high rate of false positives, and there is low discrimination between normal ageing and very mild dementia, and there is no patterning of deficits in varying cognitive domains.

While the MMSE has been found to be valid for moderate to severe dementia, Tombaugh et al (1992) also report that validity was less for cases of mild dementia, mainly because of its sensitivity to variations in age, education, and cultural background. This is important, because recorded cost is proportional to the time between initial diagnosis and death; when the diagnosis is mild, that time will be greater.

The problems of determining health outcomes in AD are considered by Busschbach et al (1998), in respect of multi-national clinical trials. Since the disease is manifest through behavioural disturbances, its diagnosis and progression are heavily influenced by cultural factors, which is one of the main problems of the MMSE; the authors' proposal, of the development of a hrqol questionnaire seems not to escape this difficulty.

Part of the problem is the use of international RCTs, and the attempt to economise on research effort. We examined the problems of extending the results of controlled trials to routine practice in chapter 6; it seems likely that the reliance of the approach upon the RCT methodology may be misplaced. If studies were undertaken in one country, greater reliability could be achieved, though the obvious problems of using questionnaires to assess the quality of life of severely handicapped AD patients would remain. One alternative is the assessment of the quality of life of the carer, for instance in the ACQLI measure used by Drummond (1991). While the patient has to be respected, the carer's quality of life is intimately related to that of the patient, and may reasonably be taken to be a proxy for the patient's quality of life.

Modelling

The trial data come from a period of six months, but costs and benefits over the longer term are likely to be important. It follows that a modelling approach (Maynard et al (1998), Nuitjen et al (1998), Buxton et al (1997), Beck et al (1983)) is appropriate. However, it remains the case that all models based on trial results still leave us ignorant of what actually happened to patients in the months and years that followed the trial. Also, we only have one model of what actually happened; errors in the original data may be undetected, and if they exist, extrapolation continues and may compound them.

Resource Identification and Measurement

When seeking the impact of a treatment on the budgets of health services, it is perhaps to be expected that most of the work ignored the costs borne by carers; as indicated in chapter 1, the point of view matters. A more sophisticated view might have taken the carers' input as a contribution to the reduction of costs (the avoidance of institutional care); carers are assets the value of which could be jeopardised by over-use. In any case, the studies do not resolve the problems of valuing carer time; one study (O'Brien et al (1999)) values carer time at two-thirds the minimum wage in Canada, while the others ignore it. Patients with AD are cared for either at home or in institutions; if the drug reduces hospital care, it must increase informal care, to achieve its cost reductions. Other things equal, then, the greater the value placed on home care, the less cost-effective the drug will be. When the funding of institutional care comes from the government, carers' interests are directly opposed to those of taxpayers in an analysis of this kind.

Conclusions

There is at least a question mark against the validity of the MMSE, and its validity within a particular country, as well as between countries, should be tested. Also, the assumptions necessary to extrapolate from a six-month trial need careful consideration, and the valuation of informal care has to have explicit and careful examination.

Because efficacy is difficult to establish, it seems unlikely that prioritising drugs, on the basis of the balancing of effect against per unit cost, will be feasible using international RCTs. Given the sample size problems found in Drummond (1991), it seems likely that RCTs will be expensive even in a relatively homogeneous population, such as that of Ireland. The basic problem is the lack of understanding of the disease; without a basic understanding, the sample cannot be controlled to achieve generalisable results, and unknown factors such as accommodation type, or the proximity of family members, intervene in unexpected and unpredictable ways.

The RCT is part of a hypothesis-testing approach, which involves the verification of a hypothesis through statistical evidence, and then its interpretation by practitioners in each particular context. The assumption is that a body of professional scientific knowledge is being increased, and that the results obtained will have value universally, because they are capable of application in every context, once local factors have been taken into account. The care of patients with Alzheimer's Disease is not based on definite scientific understanding of the disease; drugs to relieve symptoms exist, but they do not work for all or even most of this patient group.

The approach adopted by the pharmaceutical companies was ingenious; they made the most of existing data and a secondary dataset, but they did not carry out additional studies. Given the difficulties identified, and also the problems of inter-country cost comparisons, this reluctance to fund research for governments is understandable, but it gets us no further forward in the development of choices in the case of Alzheimer's Disease.

The Extended Post-Marketing Surveillance Trial (EPMST)

Definition

This term has been coined (McCulloch et al (2001)) for a study which describes a disease sector, rather than tests a hypothesis. Some of the problems discussed would remain, but such a trial might provide a set of data which would not only prove to be beneficial in the evaluation of these drugs in the study country, but could be adapted for other countries if cultural differences could be mediated, using some further research on the translation process necessary between countries.

In brief, the trial proposed is designed to be as close to routine practice as possible; it has the following features:

- *Patient selection* Probable AD diagnosed, and an MMSE score of 30 or less, plus the presence of dedicated carer also willing to participate in the trial.
- *GP role* Normal treatment and care, including the freedom of the physician to alter the prescription if necessary.
- *Duration* Up to 24 months.
- *Treatment arms* One arm per licensed AD drug, plus no treatment.
- *Initial data collection* Patient MMSE score; current AD treatment details; history of previous AD treatment; approximate date of diagnosis of AD; details of participation in any other trials in the last 12 months; carer questionnaire including qol, medications, own GP visits, and health treatments
- *Every 2 months* (by physician visit or by telephone contact): Patient MMSE Score, carer questionnaire, and (if appropriate) the date of institutionalisation, date of death, or reason for withdrawal from project.
- *At study end* Calculation of: duration of home care (time from diagnosis to institutionalisation), survival time, MMSE scores profile, carer well-being profile from questionnaire scores.

The cost of care would be measured with reference to the number of patients in institutions, expected survival rates, the number of respite care places, and the consumption cost of care (that is, annual purchasing power minus subsistence cost, to represent satisfactions forgone), and the consumption of other health services, such as visits to GP by carers and patients.

Possible problems: There is some evidence that drugs do benefit some patients; therefore, a placebo arm would not be ethical, and it would also be unethical to randomly control the treatment groups, or to introduce drugs blind. The AD patient's expected survival is approximately five years, of which a trial participation of two years is a fairly large proportion. It follows that the patient, GP, and/or carer should not be constrained from changing the treatment if they wish to do so, and that a bias could be introduced in favour of a known treatment, so that there could be significant differences in the number of patient receiving each treatment. Patients might also change between treatment arms, or move to a new licensed therapy, if a product was introduced during the course of the trial. As a result, it would be necessary to have sufficiently large numbers of patients participating in the trial to try to ensure that any of the problems mentioned above would not have a significant impact on the trial results.

This approach might be a better basis for resource allocation decisions aiming to achieve maximum health, than conventional cost-effectiveness analysis. It seems likely that, in this particular area, useful lessons are more likely to be drawn from detailed and rigorous description than from hypothesis testing, particularly given the large variety in the arrangements for the care of the elderly, even within one health service. Such data could also provide the basis for a Programmed Budgeting and Marginal Analysis, as outlined in chapter 1; they would permit the comparison of patient groups, and the delineation of choices, which is not otherwise possible. Generally speaking, PBMAs are carried out from within care services; given the data suggested, a PBMA could be carried by an independent observer, using publicly available cost figures to determine the size of the budget allocated to the AD sector.

The EPMST and the MEQI

The question arises, is the MEQI approach developed in the last chapter applicable to AD?

The carer's health-related quality of life (hrqol) could be used as a proxy for that of the patient, and as in chapter 6, and in the "extended post-marketing surveillance trial", above, the relevant patient characteristics could be up-dated at the same time as QALY data, recording the date of decease if appropriate. For a MEQI approach to work, it seems likely that all of the AD patients in a particular region would need to be surveyed, if patterns of rersource allocation were to be determined on the basis of this evidence.

One problem is sustaining the assumption that AD patients can be reliably identified, because AD is often indistinguishable from the ageing process or from other types of dementia. Kavanagh et al (1995) include all patients with dementia, and it seems probable that any practical system for allocating resources would have to do the same. Identifying costs may be easier, though as above, the valuation of carer time is a difficult issue. However, at the least, data collection should pose no additional problems with these patients, if the carer's hrqol is accepted as a measure of the patient's hrqol.

Once collected, such data would make possible tables like 7.1 and 7.2, on the next page.

Table 7.1 Mean Expected QALY Indicator (MEQI) Calculation

Mean survival of Dementia patients:	80
Mean age of Dementia patients now:	75
Mean patient life expectancy:	5
Mean Carer QALY health state value:	0.80
MEQI (= 5 x 0.8) in QALYs:	4.00

Table 7.2 Some Expected QALY Deficits

Sector	MEQI	Pop. MEQI	Difference	No. of patients	EQD
Cardiac	7.9	34.3	26.4	3,000	79,200
Arthritis	25.2	34.3	9.1	20,000	182,000
Renal	2.4	34.3	29.9	500	14,950
Dementia	4.0	34.3	30.3	20,000	60,600

Our measure of need implies that Dementia patients should have a priority approximating to that of cardiac care, which contrasts with the substantial differences between the resources allocated to the two diseases. Even if these figures were taken from a real region, this would not "prove" that cardiac wards should be closed and new dementia units opened. It does show the balance which has to be struck between the needs that can be remedied, and those which cannot. A choice which is normally evaded has been made explicit, and discussion about the choices we are making can begin.

Without suitable evidence, such discussions are not possible; it is always easier to ignore choices, and to avoid the hard comparisons, so that choices just happen, rather than being based on reason. The QALY approach is probably the most powerful method of generating evidence, but reasonable choices can still be made, even when QALY evidence is not available. The next section examines a technique for defining choices, which avoids the difficulties of valuing dementia health states and carer costs, though for a limited number of carer-patient pairs.

The Lattice Approach to Decision-Making

Sector-level resource allocation requires the comparison of patient groups within a total population. At the level of management, however, choices arise between carer/patient pairs, which are difficult to rationalise successfully because of the nature of AD. The approach of Hirst (1990) appears to offer a meaningful definition of choices, without measuring health states.

In his analysis of the health states of severely disabled children, Hirst represents disablement using binary descriptors, that is, a set of statements which either do or do not apply to a particular individual. The rationale is that summary measures (or summarising techniques) consider individuals as only statistical units, included in ways which can sometimes have inequitable results. Also, summative measures lose information, or at least rely on the low value of any information they omit, so that the picture given by the data may not reflect important complexities in the situation. Lastly, deciding the relative weights of different aspects of disablement should be transparent, as it would not be when indices, or summary outcome measures, are created. The binary statements describe subjective experience, which is multi-dimensional; they convey information while at the same time maintaining its complexity. Whether the dataset is complete "enough" depends on the decision-makers' requirements, which will be determined by the context.

Following Hirst's method, a cohort of Alzheimer's patients might be described in the following way, to assess the need for respite care provision:

Feature A:	Is not able to dress unaided
Feature B:	Is not able to feed unaided
Feature C:	Does not have own room
Feature D:	Is unable to converse normally
Feature E:	Has had to be restrained in the last four weeks
Feature F:	Has wandered off in the last four weeks

Asking these questions of a group of 20 carer-patient pairs, to record a "1" for "Yes", and a "0" for "No", might produce the matrix, or "lattice", shown in Table 7.3, on the next page. This array preserves the data relevant to each patient, and assuming that all of the important features (A-F) have been identified, we have a complete description of the patients, without making any summary measures or assumptions.

Table 7.3 Describing a Cohort of Patients with Alzheimer's Disease

Patient	A	B	C	D	E	F
1	1	1	0	1	1	1
2	1	1	1	1	1	1
3	0	0	1	1	1	1
4	1	1	0	0	1	1
5	1	1	1	1	1	1
6	1	1	0	1	1	1
7	1	1	1	1	1	1
8	0	0	1	1	1	1
9	1	1	0	0	1	1
10	1	1	0	1	1	1
11	0	0	1	1	1	0
12	0	0	1	1	1	0
13	0	0	1	1	1	0
14	0	0	1	1	1	1
15	1	1	0	0	1	1
16	1	1	0	1	1	1
17	1	1	1	1	1	1
18	0	0	1	1	1	0
19	1	1	1	1	1	1
20	0	0	1	1	1	1

For decision-making purposes, the data can be summarised by arranging the feature combinations to identify the patients suffering from the same features together. In the table, we have:

ABCDEF	2, 5, 7, 17, 19
ABDEF	1, 6, 10, 16
CDEF	3, 8, 14, 20
ABEF	4, 9, 15
CDE	11, 12, 13, 18

As an example, suppose there are respite care episodes to be allocated between carers, and that the carers of all the above patients have requested respite care. The calculation of a general algorithm for determining priorities would be time-consuming and complex, and would not be transparent or justifiable. Given the information above, a discussion can take place, and a decision can be reached, without formally specifying, once and for all, the decision rule for allocating scarce respite resources.

While the lattice approach has limited uses, because it can realistically deal with a maximum of about twenty patients, it does illustrate that, while scarcity implies choice, getting reasonable conclusions about choices need not require formal measurement.

Conclusion

Science searches for knowledge that will be true as far as possible in space and in time. In practice, science has its limitations, because of resource constraints on data collection, and because the collection of data on a controlled basis is costly in the complexity of a particular healthcare context, where many different variables may have a serious impact on the outcome of interest. This is the case for many situations in which the socially dependant have to receive care, such as stroke, or AD. At least, alternative approaches to data collection, besides the randomised controlled trial, should be considered.

We have examined the problems of health valuation in some detail; we now turn to the actual practice, that is, health valuation as it is carried out in universities, research centres, and pharmaceutical firms. While hard statistics are difficult to get, a review of the activities of this multi-million dollar business should provide some general insights to the practice of health valuation, and its importance in the development of healthcare technologies.

Notes

1 Some material in this chapter is based on an article, "Alternative Approaches to the Economic Evaluation of a Drug for Patients with Alzheimer's Disease", McCulloch D.,

Barry M., Ryan M., Heerey A., (2000) published by *European Hospital Pharmacy*, 6(2) pp 64-68. We are indebted to the European Hospital Pharmacy Journal for permission to use material from it.

2 The evidence was in the form of articles submitted for publication, such as O'Brien et al. (1999), Stewart (1998), and Fenn (1999).

Chapter 8

The ASTEC Evidence

Introduction

What valuation of health occurs, how much, and how successful is it? If the valuation of health in practice is to be fully understood and developed, it is important to have some idea about what evaluation is occurring, and what effect (if any) it is having. This question is not as large as it sounds, because health valuation remains small, in relation to the vast field of medical practice, to all of which, in principle, valuation techniques could be applied.

Roughly speaking, the question defines the brief of the ASTEC (Analysis of the Scientific and Technical Evaluation of Health Interventions) project. Funded by the European Commission, and led by Professor Alan Maynard of the London School of Economics, the 29 members of a Europe-wide network studied the evaluation of health interventions (EHI) in all 15 countries of the European Union (EU). A report was produced for each country, and case studies were developed in respect of evaluation initiatives in the USA, Japan, Canada, and Australia. The permission of the ASTEC team for the inclusion of material from the project reports is gratefully acknowledged; unless otherwise indicated) a new form of words is used throughout, while contributions which belong to the present author alone are given in italics. The overall report (Cookson et al (2000a)) is available from the London School of Economics website; the chapters on which we rely here are: McDaid, D., Cookson, R. and the ASTEC group, "Evaluation activity in Europe", Cookson, R. "The role of industry in the evaluation of health care interventions", and Maynard, A. and McDaid D. 'The implications for policy makers'.

In full, the project research questions were:

- who commissions health evaluations in the public, private, and charitable sectors?
- what are the current initiatives for evaluating health interventions?
- what evaluation topics receive most attention and why?
- what evaluation methods are used by researchers and why?
- what mechanisms are used to control the quality of evaluations?
- what incentive mechanisms are used to implement evaluation evidence in decisions?
- what influence does evaluation evidence have on decisions, and why?

The term "health intervention" is defined as: "any activity which is primarily aimed at improving people's health". This includes health promotion, medical devices, and different organisation and delivery systems, as well as drugs and clinical procedures. Given such a definition, we have also to define "evaluation": "the assessment of such an intervention compared to other interventions or doing nothing" in terms of safety, efficacy, effectiveness, or cost-effectiveness. Given our emphasis on CEA so far, it is important to note that EHI is general evaluation, and is broader than CEA or economic evaluation. The broader category was necessary because of the practical difficulties in the way of separating economic evaluation from other kinds.

The chapter opens with a description of the context in which both "non-commercial" and industrial EHI take place, including the introduction of "Guidelines" for health evaluation evidence, and the proposed Irish Guidelines, as an example. The nature and types of both "non-commercial" and industrial EHI are then explained, and the final section examines the policy implications of the project's findings.

Unavoidably, many of the findings are impressionistic and anecdotal, but they make up the best available information about valuing health in practice, and they do raise important issues about health evaluation information and technology development criteria. We consider the context, the proposed Irish Guidelines, Non-commercial EHI activity in EU countries, and Industrial EHI, before looking at two challenges raised by the ASTEC authors.

The Context

In the countries of Western Europe, as well as in North America and Australasia, the rising expectations and performance of medicine, and ageing populations, have caused pressures to obtain value for money from health budgets. There are also increasing demands from better-informed patients, who have generally become more critical of treatment and care standards. All of these factors are related to the substantial increase in the evaluation of clinical interventions over the 1990s in EU countries, including the evidence-based medicine "movement" (and its associated Cochrane Centres), though the quantity and types of EHI activity show a large degree of variation.

The most significant developments have been the changes in the regulatory frameworks applied by governments to the licensing and approval of new technologies, mainly drugs, but also medical devices. Licensing laws require evidence of product quality, safety, and efficacy, that is, whether the new product is safe, and whether the claims made for it are true. Until recently, evidence has not been required regarding whether, in normal use, the product is better in its effect on health than alternatives (comparative effectiveness) or better value for money than the available alternatives, given the impacts on the costs and resources involved for the purchaser (cost effectiveness).

Evidence for cost-effectiveness is now being demanded by some governments, and cost-effectiveness is widely termed the "fourth hurdle" which new products are required to surmount (in addition to quality, safety, and efficacy). Since 1997, official procedures (or "guidelines") asking for or requiring economic evidence have been introduced by Denmark, England and Wales, Finland, the Netherlands, and Portugal; the proposed Irish Health Technology Guidelines are provided, below, as a (relatively brief) example.

Outside the EU, Australia and Canada use guidelines; France, Germany, Italy, Norway, Ireland and Spain are considering similar developments (see the ASTEC country reviews). Also, the European Medicines Evaluation Agency has begun to seek evidence of safety, tolerability, and efficacy in comparison with other drugs, to provide an improved basis for comparative- and cost-effectiveness.

The Proposed Irish Guidelines

(Prepared by the National Centre for Pharmacoeconomics in Ireland; the actual wording is used, and comments are shown in italics.)

1. Purpose

The purpose of the pharmacoeconomic guidelines is to provide the Department of Health, the GMS payments board, and prescribers, with information on the cost effectiveness of a health care technology. The aim is to ensure that only those interventions will be adopted by the Irish Health Service which, according to the best available evidence, add more to health outcome, per unit of cost, than existing interventions. In short, the aim is to achieve "best value" from expenditues on health technologies. *The term "technology" includes any distinct practical method of delivering health care, including drugs; an alternative term is "health intervention".*

It is important to note that "best value", or greater cost-effectiveness, is consistent with an increase in health impact achieved with an increase in the drug budget, as well as with the same health impact achieved with fewer resources. It follows that increasing the cost-effectiveness of Irish health technologies may or may not reduce health service expenditures, though it should result in greater health impact per unit of expenditure.

2. General Approach

Following instruction from the Department of Health and Children, it is envisaged that the first stage in the process of an economic evaluation would consist of a preliminary discussion between the Centre and representatives from the relevant pharmaceutical company, to determine information requirements.

When a formal submission of evidence is made, it is expected to weigh the benefit of a new technology against its costs in the Irish context and/or in a similar health service setting, using one of the approaches described in the appendix.

(These are the approaches described in chapter 1.) It is important that the submission specifies, addresses, and answers a specific study question. This does not mean that data collection in Ireland (such as a randomised clinical trial) will always be necessary; previously existing work, supplemented if possible by studies specific to Ireland, may be used to estimate the cost-effectiveness of the technology in question. Reasonable inference (by the standards of the medical and pharmaceutical literature) from populations studied elsewhere will be acceptable. *Compare with the evidence presented in the last chapter, and the reaction of the Centre of Pharmacoeconomics to it.*

However, an examination of the cost dimension in Ireland may be required, because of differences in unit costs, the pattern of resource use, and in the extent and practice of health sector funding, between the Irish context and the context of other studies. *Ireland remains, to a large extent, an economy of small towns dominated by the captial; agriculture is of relatively large importance economically, though the Dublin conurbation is introducing the megalopolis associated with larger countries, with implications for the organisation of health care. This should also affect the relevance to Ireland of findings in other countries.*

Any existing evaluation may be supplemented by new data; all data supplied by the pharmaceutical industry will be treated in a confidential manner. Finally, in the interests of fairness and transparency, companies will have access to the Centre's response to the submission, to discuss it, and if necessary, to appeal it. Evaluations will be carried out by the staff of the Centre and external consultants, under conditions which respect the necessary confidentiality requirements.

3. The Guidelines

The requirements that should be considered may be described under the headings of study design, data analysis, and result presentation.

3.1 Study Design

3.1.1 Study Question

- The question being addressed should be clearly stated.
- The economic importance of the research question should be explained.
- The perspective adopted (health care system, society) for the analysis should be clearly stated and explained.

These features appear to be straightforward, but they are by no means universal in empirical studies.

3.1.2 Selection of Alternatives

- The rationale for the particular comparison (of specific alternative treatments) should be given.
- The alternative treatments should be described in sufficient detail to enable the reader to assess their relevance.

3.1.3 Type of Study

Generally cost effectiveness analysis (CEA) is appropriate. Cost utility analysis (CUA) should be applied when quality of life is the sole or major output of the therapy. If treatment options have been demonstrated to be equivalent, cost minimisation analysis (CMA) is appropriate. In certain circumstances, cost benefit analysis (CBA) is the best available means of clarifying the choices present. *See the definitions given in chapter 1.*

3.1.4 Benefit Measurement and Evaluation

- The primary outcome measure(s) for the economic evaluation should be clearly stated, such as cases detected, increased survival, or quality-adjusted life years (QALYs).
- If the measure involves the use of any psychometric instrument, such as a QALY or cognitive function questionnaire, its derivation, validation, and relevance should be briefly explained, and details given of the published evidence supporting it.
- If changes in production (an indirect benefit) are included, they should be reported separately, and their relevance to the study question discussed.
- There is an understandable tendency to treat QALY data like readings on a thermometer; they certainly may be used, but care should be exercised regarding their meaning.
- It is the custom in academic journals to take as much as possible for granted, because space is scarce, and the aim is to add to the sum of knowledge; here, the guidelines are trying to pull in the opposite direction, so that explanations are at least adequate.

3.1.5 Method of Data Capture

- High quality randomised trials, supplemented by information from other sources including meta analysis, observational data, and modelling, are acceptable.
- Other data sources and approaches should be discussed with the Centre before substantial resources are committed to them.

3.1.6 Costing

- Quantities of resources (drug amounts, or staff time) should be reported separately from the prices (unit costs) of those resources.
- Methods for the estimates of both quantities and prices (unit costs) should be given.

3.1.7 Irish Cost Data

As yet, there are no agreed Irish cost models, such as those produced by the Personal Social Services Research Unit at the University of Kent, and much work needs to be done to generate valid Irish cost data. It follows that flexibility is required in applying the requirement that studies should consider the cost dimension in Irish terms. Where costs are applied from other contexts, there must be an explanation of the assumptions necessary to translate these costs to the Irish health economy.

In a small economy like Ireland, a map of the facilities of the country might be more useful than a model; in large economies, models may be necessary because of the size and complexity which needs to be summarised.

3.1.8 Modelling

- Details should be given of any modelling used in the study - for example, a decision tree model, epidemiology model, or regression model - especially the assumptions on which the model is based, and the methods used to obtain data, other than conventional data collection in a trial.
- The model and its assumptions should be justified.

3.1.9 Time Horizon

The study period should be clearly described and appropriate to the disease and treatment. Long term effects should be emphasised and a need for modelling discussed as above.

3.2 Data Analysis

3.2.1 Adjustments for the timing of costs and benefits

- The time period over which costs and benefits are measured should be given.
- The discount rate should be given, and the choice of rate(s) explained.
- If costs and benefits are not discounted, an explanation should be given.

3.2.2 Allowance for uncertainty

> When appropriate, details should be given of the statistical tests performed and the confidence intervals around the main variables.
> When a sensitivity analysis is performed, the choice of variables to be altered, and the ranges over which they were altered, should be justified.

It is not possible to be more precise than this; the choice will usually be clear enough from the context.

3.3 Results Presentation

> Major outcomes - for example, treatment impact on quality of life - should be presented in disaggregated as well as summary form, by patient groups.
> Any comparison with other health care interventions - for example, in terms of relative cost-effectiveness - should be made only when close similarity in study methods and settings can be demonstrated.
> The answer to the original study question should be given; any conclusions should follow clearly from the data reported, and should be accompanied by appropriate qualifications or reservations.

4. Conclusion

The fundamental test of all healthcare technology studies is: "what is a *reasonable* balancing of costs against health outcomes in the context given?" Important features of the "given context" include the inherent difficulties of measuring outcomes and costs, and the nature of the choices being investigated. The appropriate choice of evaluation approach is usually clear from the context, and from the existing literature.

The test of what is "reasonable" is more demanding than it might sound; given that the aim is to compare the cost-effectiveness of technology alternatives, there are definite limits on the variations in the assumptions that can be made.

That concludes our inspection of the proposed Irish Guidelines; they are more brief than most, but they convey the basic approach, of requiring economic analysis (CEA, CUA, CBA) to be completed before a medical technology is adopted for funding by a government. Whether not the "guidelines movement" has been successful in containing health sector expenditure is difficult to determine, in principle, though George et al (2001) have produced evidence to show that the Australian use of guidelines has produced decisions which are consistent with economic efficiency. There is no means of determining what drug expenditures would have been without guidelines; it is not possible to know, either, what drugs have not been developed because of the cost-effectiveness requirement.

Lastly, notice that the the cost of the study is left with the developer of the technology. In principle, it would appear that there should be some sharing of the cost of data collection, especially in respect of health service resource cost measurement. Medical device manufacturers in particular might find it difficult to bear the costs of economic evaluation (see below). Also, the figures for the resource impacts of different treatment alternatives will have to come from Irish health service accounting systems.

Non-Commercial EHI Activity in EU countries

We consider the overall picture, and common themes emerging from the country reports.

The Overall Picture

Many countries have created organisations for the prioritisation, quality assessment, and communication of EHI, such as Cochrane Centres and Health Technology Assessment units. Generally speaking, these developments have been common across most of the developed world, though the rate of change has varied. Evidence-based medicine and health technology assessment also grew in the United States, Australia, and Canada, though not (interestingly) in Japan.

Overall, however, much the largest proportion of non-commerical evaluation work assesses the safety, efficacy and effectiveness of single products. Rather less is being done to determine whether an intervention is better than its alternatives ("comparative effectiveness"), or whether an intervention is cost-effective, that is, better value for money than its alternatives, given the full range of impacts on the funding organisation's costs. (This reflects industrial practice, described below.)

It is almost impossible to measure the quantity of non-commercial EHI activity across the EU, mainly because of difficulties in determining what fraction of national research funds are targeted at EHI rather than at other types of health research. However, based on the country reports, and on feedback from other colleagues, the countries can be grouped as follows:

Group 1: Portugal, Ireland, Luxembourg, Belgium, Austria, Greece.
Group 2: Italy, Germany.
Group 3: Spain, Finland.
Group 4: United Kingdom, Netherlands, Sweden, Finland, Denmark, France.

Group 1 contains countries where EHI activity has only recently begun to develop. While individual projects and examples of economic evaluation have been undertaken, this work has been relatively limited and ad hoc compared to other EU countries. In Germany and Italy, the second group, research activity has been more substantial, and Cochrane centres have been established, but the dominant focus has been clinical research; neither non-clinical interventions nor cost-effectiveness have received much attention, possibly because of the comparatively low status within those health services of non-clinical research.

By contrast, Spain and Finland, group 3, have relatively small amounts of clinical research, but they have begun to develop EHI activity; some of the provinces of Spain, for example, have established HTA Agencies, and there is a Finnish Office of Health Technology Assessment. However, the budgets of EHI groups in both countries are small.

The fourth group contains countries in each of which there is considerable evaluation of clinical interventions, covering both comparative and cost effectiveness; also, there are EHI institutions which prioritise EHI, apply quality control, and disseminate results. The focus of activity in France is clinical evaluation, with some emphasis on other health service research, including economic evaluation. In the remaining countries there is both clinical research and greater emphasis on other kinds of research into health services. However, even in the last group, there are few examples of the impact of evidence on practice.

In the scientific model informing the ASTEC approach, findings are expected to have an identifiable impact on practice. This view seems to ignore the importance of medical judgement, and the nature of medical evidence, discussed in chapter 6. It is entirely possible for an RCT to prove that a drug is more cost-effective or beneficial, and for doctors to continue to prescribe its rival; the typical physician may judge that the trial evidence does not apply to his or her patients. On this ground alone, we should not expect too much in the way of identifiable impacts from EHI work. It is a major conclusion of the ASTEC study that there is a general lack of incentives and mechanisms for the translation of robust evidence into practice.

In addition, health services are run (often) by intelligent and thoughtful people, who are aware of costs, and health systems do adapt to cost changes. In any particular specialty, it may be that few comparisons with obviously uneconomic practices are possible because internal action by the health system has changed the accepted practice.

Non-commercial EHI work in the EU is done mainly by universities, research units, and the health care sector, rather than by government departments or government institutions. It has not been possible to project a figure for total EHI research spending, and it is difficult to separate out EHI funding from total health research funding or funding for health services research in general. These institutions usually have no direct link to the decision-making process, unlike the operation of institutions concerned with determining whether products are safe, effective, or cost-effective (see the section on the role of industry, below).

Policy Themes Emerging From Country Reports

Decentralisation In practice, is health valuation work to be done centrally, or locally? There is wide variation in the extent of decentralisation in EU health services, which also applies to the funding and development of EHI. At one extreme, county councils in Denmark regard EHI activities as a priority, and as part of the councils' responsibility for health services, so that each county has a health services research policy and a specific research unit. In Spain, responsibility for health care is being devolved to the provinces, so that seven autonomous regions look after the health care of about 60 per cent of the population. By contrast, the health services in Ireland are heavily centralised, and the main (funded) evaluation activities take place in Dublin, though Cork is developing as a centre of EHI expertise. A still different picture is that of England and Wales, where about 70 per cent of research funding comes from the NHS Research and Development Programme, but this is allocated in regions according to local criteria.

Cultural differences For historical reasons, the frequency of systematic reviews and meta-analyses is variable across the EU; Sweden, France, the Netherlands, the UK and Spain make much use of these techniques, but in Greece, Austria and Germany, systematic reviews are uncommon. Language may be a factor, because the English-speaking countries tend to dominate the development of EHI; the relative lack of progress of evidence-based medicine in France may be in part the result of its identification with anglophone countries.

Health care organisation and financing Overall, countries with social insurance systems tend to spend a higher proportion of GNP on health care than those with tax-funded systems. The converse seems to be true for EHI spending; most of the countries with tax-funded systems (UK, Denmark) have larger volumes of EHI than those with social insurance systems (France, Germany). *It may be that when health budgets are not ring-fenced, as they are in social insurance systems, then pressures on public spending are greater, and there are greater political incentives to use evaluation evidence. It is interesting that in the United States, cost effectiveness data is largely used in managed care organisations or publicly funded programmes such as Medicare.*

Research capacity EHI depends on a mix of disciplines, such as epidemiology, statistics, and medicine, as well as economics. It follows that there is no single discipline structure in which individuals can make progress, which could be reflected in promotion prospects. This lack of structure is reflected in the limited number of training courses for EHI researchers; some countries have very few courses in health economics or public health. Also, throughout Europe, potential EHI researchers have poor status and limited career prospects compared to medical professionals and core-funded academics; in Italy, for example, health services research does not enjoy a favourable status in the medical and research community, although bio-medical training is excellent.

Industrial EHI

Introduction

The European pharmaceutical industry has a budget for EHI which is larger than that of all the EU's other private, public, and voluntary bodies put together. Most of it is spent during the development stage of new drugs, and is aimed at initial licensing, and at marketing immediately after the launch into a market which is often world-wide in scope. Much less is spent on the evaluation of medical devices, for reasons examined below, though according to industry experts (UK ASTEC report) the larger firms have begun controlled trials of new products which have a potentially large impact on healthcare expenditure and/or potential safety risks.

We consider pharmaceutical EHI, the evaluation of medical devices, the strengths and weakenesses of industrial evaluation, and challenges in the development of industrial EHI.

Pharmaceutical EHI

Most industrial EHI is carried out by the large drug companies, because the development and marketing of a compound requires large clinical and distribution networks. Much EHI is contracted out to specialist academic consultants, to reduce salary overheads and to add to the acceptability of the evidence produced. This was the case for the Alzheimer's Disease drugs discussed in chapter 7; in general, the EHI work in industry is of the same standard as "non-commercial" studies. For cultural reasons, the universities tend to set the standard and define the academic context of industrial evaluation in general.

The focus of the activity tends to be the expected time of the product launch; sales have to be maximised while the drug is still new (and priced accordingly), and purchasers of the drug want the evidence as early as possible, to meet clinician requests with the right answer, based on the best evidence. The "fourth hurdle" has affected clinical trials in several ways; patient quality of life outcomes have been measured (instead of just bio-medical outcomes, such as cholesterol levels), resource costs have been measured alongside trials, and outcomes have been compared between alternative drug therapies (instead of only between a drug and a placebo).

As a result, Phase III trials have increased in sample size, though duration has not altered; also, multi-disciplinary pharmacoeconomics departments have been set up by all the large drug firms, to give advice on the design of trials, and to perform an evaluation of clinical and cost effectiveness from trial data. Phase II trials are being designed to inform the decision about which drugs to develop from Phase II to Phase III, by generating data in respect of both comparative- and cost-effectiveness. As the ASTEC report states, "a good safety and efficacy profile is no longer sufficient to guarantee market success, and the prospect of marketing failure due to evidence of poor comparative or cost effectiveness can be enough to kill compounds."

If this is happening, the new drugs already coming to market may be more cost-effective than would otherwise have been the case, but there may be no means of telling, because the drugs ruled out are not there to be tested. It follows that the effects of EHI on health sector resource allocation may not be visible. Also, it would be interesting to know how widely companies defined cost impacts; a focus on minimising health service expenditures might appeal to the administrators of most centralised health services, but a Health Maintenance Organisation which aimed to minimise all health-related costs for all of its patients would include different cost items for measurement.

The Evaluation of Medical Devices

Because medical devices have much shorter development times (usually between 1 and 3 years, compared to 10 to 12 years for drugs), the need to recoup large development costs is less, and hence less is spent on their evaluation. Also, devices are less extensive in their physiological impact than pharmaceuticals, and there is less concern over safety on the part of licensing authorities, which (in Europe, and unlike the US) do not require clinical trial data to demonstrate efficacy. In addition, there are (even) more confounding factors to affect the conduct of trials of devices, which are generally used in a complex and variable series of activities carried out by clinicians, and lower utilisation rates, so that trials are simply more difficult to carry out. Finally, new devices have relatively minor effects on health budgets, compared to new drugs, so that purchasers are relatively less concerned about cost-effectiveness.

Where safety and expense are important, however, large firms are carrying out randomised controlled trials, though even where these features are common to different specialties, EHI development has been uneven. For example, there is a greater likelihood of economic evaluation for cardiological devices than for costly and potentially dangerous radiological technologies. It remains true, however, that the small- or medium-sized firms which make the vast majority of devices in the EU do not carry out clinical trials of their products. These firms are concerned that the implementation of a "fourth hurdle" for medical devices could result in the merging of most of the firms in the EU device industry, because of the costs of carrying out evaluations. (In the United Kingdom, there is provision, under the National Institute for Clinical Excellence arrangements, for the government to fund such research for firms with a small turnover.)

Strengths and Weaknesses of Commercial Evaluation

There is general agreement that new pharmaceutical products are evaluated rigorously and comprehensively, and that the adoption of the controlled trial approach has prevented the repetition of disasters such as thalidomide. It is less obvious that EHI has helped to increase the health impact per unit of resource of health interventions. There are concerns about the scientific validity of evidence, and about its use by regulatory authorities, which may be unclear or inconsistent. In the industry, the accepted limitations of EHI evidence include the relatively short duration of trials, which may not be long enough to detect important outcomes, and the frequent comparison with placebo, rather "head to head" against the best alternative therapy. It is also accepted that there has been limited evaluation of drugs in everyday use, and that particular groups (such as the elderly, and children) tend to be under-represented in clinical trials.

It is in their routine use by patients in everyday life that drugs achieve or do not achieve their health impacts. Pragmatic trials (such as the one proposed in McCulloch et al (2000)) are sometimes carried out, but usually only when a new drug is entering an existing class of drugs, and has to out-perform the market leader. It follows that there is a general shortage of evidence about the actual impact of drugs on the health of patients routinely using them. There may also be an inherent conflict between the need for generalisations robust enough for policy purposes, and the need to reflect patient realities.

Finally, there is disagreement over whether the full results of phase III trials should be made public; it is argued that less innovative firms could benefit unfairly, while others believe that greater transparency would enhance competition, by permitting more widespread examination of claims made for new products.

The overview paragraph from Dr. Cookson's report is worth reproducing in full:

> Industry representatives argue that limitations in the evaluation of comparative effectiveness are due to unavoidable ethical, methodological or commercial difficulties in trial design – for instance, the need to protect patents, to achieve statistical validity, and to meet marketing time frames. While most academic specialists accept that genuine difficulties of this kind exist, they argue that nevertheless there is considerable scope for improving the evidence base. Both industry specialists and academics agree that the additional limitations in the evaluation of cost effectiveness are primarily due to lack of demand from large purchasers, and that there is substantial scope for improvement.

Challenges

Greater open-ness?

The report advocates greater open-ness unequivocally, and implicitly criticises governments and health departments for its lack. *Criticisms of national purchasers are directly related to the concern about public spending which is an important underlying theme of health economics. It is claimed that evidence is used mostly to inform health sector management decisions, rather than to inform health policy concerns about (for example) equity and general health standards, or to take into account societal costs, rather than health service costs. This is a reflection of a wider political failure on the part of EU societies, in which the effects of one department's decisions on other departments' responsibilities are simply ignored. This is inevitable, given the way that national political systems have adopted the objective of minimising public sector spending. Greater open-ness is only one aspect of a solution to the problems of making technological choices in democratic societies.*

Also, open-ness about health decisions is desireable only if the prioritisers are able to make the right decision; this depends on having the right evidence. It is by no means clear that such decisions are possible even in principle, given the constantly changing technologies in the health sector, the time taken to collect evidence, and the scarcity of the specialised personnel able to analyse it. The unavoidable necessity that prioritisation decisions must ultimately stand on value judgements is a further factor against open-ness on the part of senior civil servants and politicians.

EU Initiatives?

Cost-effectiveness comparisons, that is, health valuations, are expensive; once established, they should be communicated. However, it is widely appreciated that the volume of medical evidence is such that it is not possible for general practititioners to keep up to date with the literature. It appears to follow that any health service should regard knowledge management systems as basic infrastructure. In Europe, many practitioners do not have access to the Cochrane systematic reviews, and it may be appropriate to create multi-disciplinary and multi-national networks to reach a wider audience, even by simply translating material into languages other than English. The Canadian Institutes of Health Research might be worth imitating; they aim to "foster multidisciplinary approaches to health questions, and (to) provide talented investigators with the resources needed to address the health challenges faced by Canadians." (Government of Canada (1999)).

In general, there appears to be considerable scope for the generation of electronic and internet-based information exchange. The UK has the National Electronic Library For Health, which provides access to the recommendations of the National Institute for Clinical Excellence, as well as the NHS Centre for Reviews and Dissemination, and in France, there is the Social Health Network, which provides clinical practice guidelines, databases, and on-line textbooks.

Presumably, a common EU-wide methodology for EHI would increase the evaluation of drugs, through better standards of evaluation, and the exchange of evidence which can be interpreted and applied between countries, so that the health impact per unit of cost of the drug budget will increase. However, health care financing and provision seem likely to remain firmly under the control of national governments, while harmonisation in any respect will depend on a common approach to evaluation by governments. Previous EU attempts to harmonise methodological standards (the HARMET project) have met with differences which could not be resolved.

One means of increasing health valuation in the EU might be to require cost-effectiveness as part of the licensing decisions of the European Medicines Evaluation Agency. This is less simple than it sounds. Efficiency, effectiveness, and cost-effectiveness may vary between countries, for many different reasons, and there is also the danger that approval by the Agency could be used, inappropriately, to lobby for drug funding in countries other than the one for which the drug was found to be cost-effective.

Some of the possible gains might be achieved by a European clearing house for EHI information; it would be a means of adding value to the current work of existing agencies, it would enable greater critical analysis of results and practices throughout the EU, and it could lead to the development of a body of work for each country which would guide the interpretation and application of international results to that particular context. However, this kind of communication work tends not appeal to academics, who are focused on original research, and the publications which result.

Conclusion

The ASTEC project's findings suggest that, in practice, valuing health is not simply another dimension of scientific enquiry; valuation methods and approaches, the dissemination of valuation results, and the use of health technology guidelines, vary across the world. There also appears to be no reliable mechanism for disseminating scientific evidence, for the improvement of practice, in terms of either overall health impact, or the cost-effectiveness of health budgets. The ASTEC enquiry also indicated the importance of inter-country differences for the relevance and interpretation of health valuation results, and some of the problems in the way of their resolution.

Chapter 9

Review

Introduction

Must health sector choices be allowed to occur, or should we describe them, and make them explicit? The economist in the health sector rests his case on the unquestionable ground that more health is preferable to less; all health sector resource allocations involve choice, and there is an imperative to make sure that health impacts from the available resources are as large as possible.

But this depends on a proposition that physicians and others have questioned: valuing health in practice, on which the definition of such choices depends, requires assumptions and procedures which are not value free, and which can therefore be challenged from a number of standpoints. Evidently, value judgements and health priorities are inextricable, so that some value judgements are unavoidable; it then becomes a question of which value judgements are acceptable, and which are not. The aim here has been to make clear the reasonable character of the procedures which have been adopted to value health, so that the QALY approach, and at least one of its resulting measures, may be acceptable to the reader. The QALY work by no means resolves the problems in the way of an acceptable system of health sector resource allocation, but it makes an essential beginning.

We now review the ground covered, summarising and considering again some of the important points.

Review

We started with the example of a candidate for a bypass procedure, who seemed to move up the priority list after communicating his interest in suicide to a researcher. In terms of choice formats, such a case could fit into either of the three alternatives outlined, Programmed Budgeting and Marginal Analysis, Cost-Effectiveness Analysis, and Cost Benefit Analysis. In a PBMA, this patient would have been compared with other candidates in terms of a number of criteria, and a judgement made about who should get the procedure, without a summary quantitative measure being used. A CEA could have used a survival impact assessment, to compare patients in terms of cost per year of survival, or candidates' potential gains could have been measured using a QALY, that is, valuations of the patients' health states, identified using a questionniare, which had been established in previous research. Either way, priority would have been given in terms of the measured impact on health per unit of cost. In a CBA, we have to compare benefits and costs in money terms; this usually requires a "willingness to pay" analysis, which values benefits in terms of individuals' willingness to pay for them. An assessment of the different individuals' priority for a CABG would therefore need a comparison of the benefit/cost ratio for each.

The question is often raised, how meaningful are such exercises? This is the wrong question; rather, do we prefer current levels of ignorance about our priorities, to the greater knowledge about what the health sector is doing, that such techniques would introduce? When the assumptions of QALY measures are examined, and their development reasonably considered, it is hard to resist the conclusion that, at the least, QALY measures do make evident the important choices that are happening in health services, and that such information could improve decision-making and resource allocation.

Moving on to QALY measurement, the problems of health state valuation had to be considered. Once the need for choice is accepted, valuation is inescapable; the problems of making one set of valuations have to be compared with the problems of making another set, because the status quo means allowing choices to happen which have no justification whatever. Reliability in hrqol measures is different from the reliability of scientific instruments, given the ability and right of human beings to change their views, but workable health state values have resulted from QALY research, particularly the work relating to the EuroQol. On the other hand, validity cannot be determined, in the sense of comparison with a "gold standard" measure, though "criterion" validity can be established, by comparing the measure with another which is expected to have a particular relationship with it. Since valuation is inescapable, we are looking for what is relatively the best method of determining values; all valuation methods face similar problems, which may be solved more or less well.

The review of health profiles in chapter 4 raises the question of the distinctive contribution of the QALY approach. It seems important to ensure that health states are compared with death, as happens in QALY research, whatever the measure. This means that respondents place all states on a continuum from zero to unity, to provide an empirical basis for the zero. When profile scores are used to calculate percentage improvements, the assumption is being made that the zero, the value of the state of full health in the minds of the respondents, was the same. This may or may not be an acceptable assumption, but when such percentages are used, the assumption should at least be made explicit.

The testing of the Rosser QALY in chapter 4 demonstrated the use of convergent validity for QALY validation; comparing the rank ordering of patient health states between profiles and a QALY measure is a useful test, though it could be that the comparsion of value judgements, when consensus is important, may require a different approach than the Spearman test, which compares rankings with what could have occurred by chance. Departures from agreement, plus an allowance for error, might be a better measure of agreement, and hence of validity for QALY measures.

Chapter 5 laid on one side all the difficulties presented by the use of QALY for prioritisation, and used the project data to show how QALY values could be used for this purpose. The graphical approach also developed is a means for carrying out and explaining sensitivity analysis, which is an essential part of choice clarification.

In chapter 6, we encountered some of the realities of the empirical measurement of QALYs, in a context where the unrestrained use of outcome measures could affect the career prospects of surgeons, and/or the funding of cardiac surgery in a particular region. This is not intended as a criticism of the surgeons involved in the research project, who appeared to be as helpful as anyone could reasonably have expected, given the uncertainties surrounding the diagnosis of cardiac disease, and the prospect of litigation from patients who could be led to expect more than the surgeon could deliver. To the extent that such uncertainties occur elsewhere, these problems will be general.

We also described the use and relevance of randomised controlled trial evidence; there are serious reservations about the use of survival estimates by physicians to determine the QALY value of their procedures. To say the least, a reliance on judgement, not analysis, is at variance with the careful development and testing of the health state values used in QALY measures. Hence the proposal for the "Mean Expected QALY Indicator", or MEQI, which establishes a figure for assessing the performance of a cardiac (or other) sector over time, in terms of both health impacts and costs. The MEQI relies on a "database analysis" approach [Knaus (1995)], which has been applied in a number of fields [for example, Eggleston et al (1998), Canto et al (1999)]; its key feature is the use of scientific analysis to determine the performance of the sector as a whole, taking into account the costs of diagnosis, as well as the health, of all the patients who have been included as suffering from heart disease.

An important caveat is the necessity of defining which patients are to become "members" of a particular sector, such as the cardiac or arthritis sectors; "symptom inflation" could occur, as patients who were less and less ill became included, to make sure that the resources allocated to the sector were maintained. However, given strict definitions of membership, the Expected QALY Deficit, which took into account the difference between population health averages and the sector average, would be a measure of sector "need", and might permit the comparison of sectors, possibly to influence the allocation of resources between sectors.

These measures seem straightforward, though expensive in terms of the resources necessary to collect the data; currently, we simply do not know whether we are achieving anything like a maximum possible impact on health from the resources available, even within a particular sector, let alone generally. Would we rather know, or not? Currently, we are mostly choosing not to know.

In turning to the problems presented by Alzheimer's Disease, a distinction was maintained which might not always be easy to maintain, between AD, and other forms of dementia. This is acceptable when considering the first two sections, the drug companies' evidence, and the extended post-marketing surveillance trial, which was a direct response to the problems identified in that evidence. A focus on the drugs intended to treat AD requires a focus on AD patients; the use of the MEQI with AD patients considers the removal of the distinction, and points up some of the more uncomfortable implications of a measure of "need", though the logic of an approach is different from a requirement to follow through on its implications. By contrast, the lattice analysis is included as an example of choice-making which avoids measurement; it is of limited application because the number of patients who could reasonably be included can number no more than about 20 or 25.

The attempt by the ASTEC project to assess the extent of health evaluation in Europe could be described as ambitious, though the use of pharmacoeconomic guidelines might have been expected to produce systematic evidence and inter-country comparisons, so that definite conclusions about the cost-effectiveness of different drugs could be reached. In fact, the picture is varied and confusing, and is affected by inter-country variations in the finance and organisation of health care. The economic evaluation of health production remains a relatively small-scale activity, despite the availability of QALY and health profile measures, and despite the introduction in several countries of guidelines for the evaluation of new health technologies, which the drug companies have adopted as marketing "hurdles" for their products.

It is perhaps not widely appreciated that a drug could be cost-effective for one group (for example, the members of a Health Maintenance Organisation) and not cost-effective for another (such as the population served by a national health service). Even if the QALY impact was found to be the same for two groups, the impact on the costs of one group's members could be more favourable. The finding of whether or not a drug is cost-effective is a value judgement, which will depend on the assumptions made, and on the context. Lastly, the cost of determining whether or not a technology is cost-effective is more easily borne by large firms; if getting into the market place depends on achieving some definition of cost-effectiveness, government regulations which require this procedure discriminate in favour of large firms. In practice, this seems likely to reduce the scope of innovation, because the large firms will effectively control access to markets.

Conclusion

We cannot choose not to make health care choices; do we want to know what choices we are making? Valuing health in practice is possible, and can be done reasonably and convincingly. It seems obvious that QALY measures (such as the EuroQol) offer possible means of determining what the alternatives are, in the 21st century's approaching crises of ageing, medical manpower, and healthcare finance.

Appendix 1

The Health Measurement Questionnaire

QUALITY OF LIFE ASSESSMENT (SIMPLIFIED) SELF-COMPLETED QUESTIONNAIRE

GENERAL MOBILITY

Which one of these statements best describes your situation?

1.	I can move around indoors and outdoors on my own easily with no aids or help	
2.	I can move around indoors and outdoors on my own with a little difficulty but with no aids of help	
3.	I can get about indoors and outdoors on my own *but* I have to use a walking aid	
4.	I can move around the house without anyone's help but I need someone's help to get outdoors	
5.	I spend nearly all my time confined to a chair (other than a wheelchair)	
6.	I have to spend nearly all my time in bed	

USUAL ACTIVITY

During the past week has your health affected any of the things you usually do (e.g., at work or study or at home)?

1.	Not at all	
2.	Slightly affected	
3.	Severely affected	
4.	Unable to do usual activities at all	

SELF-CARE

Do you need help with

Washing yourself?	YES		NO	
Dressing?	YES		NO	
Eating or drinking?	YES		NO	
Using the toilet?	YES		NO	

SOCIAL AND PERSONAL RELATIONSHIPS

Does your state of health seriously affect any of the following?

Your social life?	YES		NO	
Seeing friends or relatives?	YES		NO	
Your hobbies or leasure activities?	YES		NO	
Your sex life?	YES		NO	

DISTRESS

How much does your state of health distress you overall? Mark a cross on the line.

NO DISTRESS   EXTREME
AT ALL   DISTRESS
_____

CALCULATING ROSSER-KIND VALUES FROM HMQ RESPONSES

This worked example shows the calculation of 1) the Disability Level, and 2) the Distress Level, from HMQ responses by two patients, X and Y.

1) The Disability Level: Respondents indicate which statement applies to them by marking a box opposite the appropriate statement.

General Mobility (GM)

	Patient	
	X	Y
Which one of these statements best describes your situation?		
1. I can move around indoors and outdoors on my own easily without help		
2. I can move around indoors and outdoors on my own with a little difficulty but with no aids or help	✔	
3. I can get about indoors and outdoors on my own *but* I have to use a walking aid e.g.stick, frame, wheelchair, etc		✔
4. I can move around the house without anyone's help but I need someone's help to get outdoors		
5. I spend nearly all my time confined to a chair (other than a wheelchair)		
6. I have to spend nearly all my time in bed		
Patient GM Score	2	3

Usual Activity (UA)

	Patient	
	X	Y
During the past week has your health affected any of the things you usually do (e.g. at work or study or at home) ?		
1. Not at all		
2. Slightly affected	✔	
3. Severely affected		✔
4. Unable to do usual activities at all		
Patient UA Score	2	3

Self-Care (SC)

			Patient	
			X	Y
Do you need help with:				
washing yourself?			N	Y
dressing?			N	Y
eating or drinking?			N	N
using the toilet?			N	N
Patient SC Score:			0	2

Social and Personal Relationships (SP)

	Patient	
	X	Y
Does your state of health seriously affect any of the following?		
Your social life ?	Y	Y
Seeing friends and relatives?	N	Y
Your hobbies or leisure activities?	Y	Y
Your sex life?	N	Y
Patient SP Score:	2	4

Translating HMQ responses into R-K disability levels

Scoring responses

As our examples indicate, "General Mobility" responses are already coded 1 to 6; "Self-Care" responses score 1 for each "YES", giving a total range of scores from 0 to 4; "Usual Activities" are already coded 1 to 4; and "Social Relationships" score 1 for each "YES", giving a total range of scores from 0 to 4.

Patient Scores on each Dimension:

	Patient	
Dimension	X	Y
General Mobility	2	3
Usual Activity	2	3
Self-Care	0	2
Social and Personal Relationships	2	4

The process of determining the disability level is explained with reference to the table on the next page.

Determining Disability Level from the scores

In the following table, first select the appropriate column, using the "General Mobility" response; as inspection of the table shows, for GM4 to GM6 no further action is needed, because all the combinations result in disability level 5, 6, or 7, respectively. For GM1 to GM3, determine the disability level by inspecting the response combinations, to find the one which applies.

General Mobility	1	2	3	4	5	6
Other Responses						
UA=1, SC=0, SP=0	1	2	3	5	6	7
UA=1, and SC=1or2, OR SP=1or2	2	2	3	5	6	7
UA=1, and SC=3or4, OR SP=3or4	3	3	4	5	6	7
UA=2, and SC<3 AND SP<3	3	3	3	5	6	7
UA=2, and SC>=3, OR SP>=3	3	3	4	5	6	7
UA=3	4	4	4	5	6	7
UA=4	5	5	5	5	6	7

For patient X, looking down the column for GM=2, we find that the other scores give a disability level of 3; for patient Y, looking down GM=3, we find that UA=3, and this means that whatever the value of SC or SP, the disability level is 4.

2) The Distress Level: The Analogue Scale

Referring to the example above, in the original questionnaire, the line was 100 mm long; suppose the patient crosses on the line were:

Patient X: 20 mm from the left; Patient Y: 60 mm from the left.

Measuring the position of the cross on the visual analogue scale in millimetres, with 0 at the left end and 100 at the right end, patients are allocated to Distress Categories A, B, C, or D as follows:

Distance from left	Distress Category
< or = 10 mm	A
>10 but < or = 50 mm	B
>50 but < or = 90 mm	C
>90 mm	D

This means that Patient X would be classified as Distress Category B, and Patient Y as Distress Category C.

Overall

It follows that Patient X is in health state 3B, and Patient Y is in health state 4C; in the R-K Matrix (Table 3.5), these are valued at 0.972 and 0.942 respectively.

Appendix 2

The Dataset

Table A.1 Waiting Patient Data
(These patients did not have a procedure during the project.)

Patient Code	Rosser Value	Disability Level	Distress Level	FLP Score	Age	Sex
W01	0.870	4	4	2423	65	F
W06	0.942	4	3	5749	62	M
W13	0.956	3	3	1104	63	M
W03	0.956	3	3	2722	67	M
W04	0.956	3	3	1197	52	M
W05	0.956	3	3	659	64	F
W10	0.972	3	2	1596	66	F
W11	0.972	3	2	1821	48	M
W14	0.972	3	2	2872	69	M
W02	0.980	3	1	452	61	M
W08	0.986	2	2	1125	51	M
W07	0.995	1	2	480	44	M
W09	0.995	1	2	361	59	M
W12	1.000	1	1	361	64	M

Table A.2 Pre-Routine CABG Patient Data

Patient Code	Rosser Value	Disability Level	Distress Level	FLP Score	Age	Sex
C09	0.000	6.0	4.0	6495	56	M
C11	0.870	4.0	4.0	1393	70	F
C06	0.900	5.0	3.0	3141	48	M
C03	0.912	3.0	4.0	1274	62	F
C01	0.942	4.0	3.0	1378	60	M
C02	0.942	4.0	3.0	3651	68	M
C10	0.942	4.0	3.0	1594	63	M
C08	0.956	3.0	3.0	2677	53	M
C12	0.956	4.0	2.0	2144	65	M
C04	0.972	3.0	2.0	3896	54	M
C05	0.972	3.0	2.0	1591	58	M
C07	0.972	3.0	2.0	1884	59	M

Table A.3 Post-Routine CABG Patient Data

Patient Code	Rosser Value	Disability Level	Distress Level	FLP Score	Age	Sex
C02	0.972	3.0	2.0	1783	68	M
C05	0.972	3.0	2.0	1503	58	M
C06	0.972	3.0	2.0	266	48	M
C09	0.972	3.0	2.0	2431	56	M
C10	0.972	3.0	2.0	477	63	M
C07	0.990	1.0	3.0	802	59	M
C08	0.990	1.0	3.0	845	53	M
C01	0.995	1.0	2.0	447	60	M
C03	0.995	1.0	2.0	115	62	F
C04	1.000	1.0	1.0	516	54	M
C11	1.000	1.0	1.0	287	70	F
C12	1.000	1.0	1.0	0	65	M

Table A.4 Pre-PTCA Patient Data

Patient Code	Rosser Value	Disability Level	Distress Level	FLP Score	Age	Sex
P27	0.700	5.0	4.0	4408	44	F
P30	0.900	5.0	3.0	3166	41	M
P04	0.932	2.0	4.0	1918	70	F
P01	0.935	5.0	2.0	2799	59	M
P31	0.935	5.0	2.0	839	41	M
P17	0.942	4.0	3.0	1466	56	M
P20	0.942	4.0	3.0	1205	54	F
P23	0.942	4.0	3.0	1829	53	M
P19	0.942	5.0	1.0	1770	50	M
P09	0.956	4.0	2.0	1495	70	F
P13	0.956	3.0	3.0	1640	52	F
P14	0.956	3.0	3.0	682	59	M
P16	0.956	3.0	3.0	746	68	M
P26	0.956	4.0	2.0	1419	71	M
P28	0.956	3.0	3.0	90	45	M
P06	0.972	3.0	2.0	2081	71	M
P07	0.972	3.0	2.0	687	39	M
P15	0.972	3.0	2.0	1697	63	M
P18	0.972	3.0	2.0	137	38	M
P22	0.972	3.0	2.0	2361	59	F
P24	0.972	3.0	2.0	546	55	M
P29	0.972	3.0	2.0	307	56	M
P08	0.986	2.0	2.0	972	48	M
P21	0.990	1.0	3.0	739	53	M
P05	0.995	1.0	2.0	201	54	F
P12	0.995	1.0	2.0	496	62	M
P25	0.995	1.0	2.0	1742	62	M
P02	1.000	1.0	1.0	0	62	M
P03	1.000	1.0	1.0	0	67	M
P10	1.000	1.0	1.0	178	68	M
P11	1.000	1.0	1.0	420	58	M

Table A.5 Post-PTCA Patient Data

Patient Code	Rosser Value	Disability Level	Distress Level	FLP Score	Age	Sex
P16	0.956	3.0	3.0	1222	68	M
P01	0.972	3.0	2.0	2268	59	M
P04	0.972	3.0	2.0	1544	70	F
P07	0.972	3.0	2.0	229	39	M
P08	0.972	3.0	2.0	1163	48	M
P17	0.972	3.0	2.0	1684	56	M
P21	0.972	3.0	2.0	244	53	M
P22	0.972	3.0	2.0	654	59	F
P23	0.972	3.0	2.0	178	53	M
P24	0.972	3.0	2.0	0	55	M
P10	0.980	3.0	1.0	98	68	M
P26	0.980	3.0	1.0	598	71	M
P06	0.986	2.0	2.0	1505	71	M
P14	0.990	1.0	3.0	1075	59	M
P25	0.990	1.0	3.0	812	62	M
P12	0.995	1.0	2.0	39	62	M
P19	0.995	1.0	2.0	361	50	M
P20	0.995	1.0	2.0	774	54	F
P27	0.995	1.0	1.0	854	44	F
P28	0.995	1.0	2.0	318	45	M
P02	1.000	1.0	1.0	0	62	M
P03	1.000	1.0	1.0	0	67	M
P05	1.000	1.0	1.0	129	54	F
P09	1.000	1.0	1.0	0	70	F
P11	1.000	1.0	1.0	420	58	M
P13	1.000	1.0	1.0	454	52	F
P15	1.000	1.0	1.0	361	63	M
P18	1.000	1.0	1.0	0	38	M
P29	1.000	1.0	1.0	0	56	M
P30	1.000	1.0	1.0	1272	41	M
P31	1.000	1.0	1.0	0	41	M

Table A.6.1 Post-Emergency CABG Patient Data (1)

Patient Code	Rosser Value	Disability Level	Distress Level	FLP Score	Age	Sex
EM42	0.700	5.0	4.0	4114	63	M
EM24	0.870	4.0	4.0	2044	54	M
EM40	0.870	4.0	4.0	2746	62	F
EM47	0.900	5.0	3.0	3018	29	M
EM28	0.956	4.0	2.0	2002	62	M
EM30	0.956	3.0	3.0	1330	42	F
EM08	0.972	3.0	2.0	1161	65	M
EM19	0.972	3.0	2.0	656	64	F
EM35	0.972	3.0	2.0	2069	64	M
EM23	0.980	3.0	1.0	300	62	M
EM27	0.980	3.0	1.0	0	60	M
EM33	0.980	3.0	1.0	967	51	M
EM25	0.986	2.0	2.0	960	59	M
EM36	0.986	2.0	2.0	1058	70	F
EM45	0.986	2.0	2.0	184	74	M
EM46	0.986	2.0	2.0	1248	51	M
EM04	0.990	1.0	3.0	1770	74	M
EM18	0.990	1.0	3.0	506	54	M
EM31	0.990	1.0	3.0	137	54	F
EM48	0.990	1.0	3.0	412	69	M
EM10	0.995	1.0	2.0	511	54	M
EM16	0.995	1.0	2.0	0	55	M
EM17	0.995	1.0	2.0	361	66	M
EM22	0.995	1.0	2.0	741	57	M

Table A.6.2 Post-Emergency CABG Patient Data (2)

Patient Code	Rosser Value	Disability Level	Distress Level	FLP Score	Age	Sex
EM32	0.995	1.0	2.0	383	56	M
EM38	0.995	1.0	2.0	86	64	M
EM01	1.000	1.0	1.0	98	72	M
EM02	1.000	1.0	1.0	0	62	M
EM03	1.000	1.0	1.0	849	68	F
EM05	1.000	1.0	1.0	190	52	M
EM06	1.000	1.0	1.0	59	73	M
EM07	1.000	1.0	1.0	0	69	M
EM09	1.000	1.0	1.0	52	48	M
EM11	1.000	1.0	1.0	64	67	M
EM12	1.000	1.0	1.0	0	57	F
EM13	1.000	1.0	1.0	145	62	M
EM14	1.000	1.0	1.0	361	47	M
EM15	1.000	1.0	1.0	0	58	M
EM20	1.000	1.0	1.0	267	57	M
EM21	1.000	1.0	1.0	52	71	M
EM26	1.000	1.0	1.0	471	62	M
EM29	1.000	1.0	1.0	34	70	M
EM34	1.000	1.0	1.0	52	48	M
EM37	1.000	1.0	1.0	446	52	M
EM39	1.000	1.0	1.0	447	61	M
EM41	1.000	1.0	1.0	52	56	M
EM43	1.000	1.0	1.0	0	79	M
EM44	1.000	1.0	1.0	86	54	M

Bibliography

Adami, H.-O., Baron, J.A., and Rothman, K.J. (1994), "Ethics of a prostate cancer screening trial", *The Lancet*, Vol. 343, pp. 958-960.

Agt van, H.M.E., Essink-Bot, M.L., Krabbe, P.F.M., and Bonsel, G.J. (1994), "Test-retest reliability of health state valuations collected with the EuroQol questionnaire", *Social Science and Medicine*, Vol. 39(11).

Alban, A., Gyldmark, M., Pedersen, A.V., and Sogaard, J. (1997), "The Danish Approach to Standards for Economic Evaluation Methodologies", *Pharmacoeconomics*, Vol. 12(6), pp. 626-636.

Alonso, J., Anto, J.M., and Moreno, C. (1990), "Spanish version of the Nottingham Health Profile: Translation and Preliminary Validity", *American Journal of Public Health*, Vol. 80(6), pp. 704-708.

Almqvist, O. (1998), "Assessment of Cognitive Functioning", in: A. Wimo, B. Jonsson, G. Karlsson and B. Winblad (eds), *Health Economics of Dementia*, Wiley, New York.

Andersen, T.F. and Mooney, G. (1990), *The Challenges of Medical Practice Variations*, Macmillan, London.

Arrow, K.J. (1951), *Social Choice and Individual Values*, Wiley, New York.

Arrow, K.J. (1963), "The Welfare Economics of Medical Care", in: M.H. Cooper and A.J. Culyer (eds), *Health Economics*, Pengin Books, Harmondsworth.

Bailey, K.R., (1994), "Generalising the results of randomised clinical trials", *Controlled Clinical Trials*, Vol. 15, pp. 15-23.

Baldwin, S., Godfrey, C. and Propper, C. (1990), *Quality of Life*, Routledge, London.

Banta, D. and Oortwijn, W. (1999), "Health technology assessment in the European Union", *Eurohealth*, Vol. 5(1), pp. 37-39.

Beck, J.R. and Pauker, S.G. (1983), "The Markov process in medical prognosis", *Medical Decision Making*, Vol. 3, pp. 419-458.

Bergmark, A. (2000), "Priorities in care and services for elderly people: a path without guidelines?", *Journal of Medical Ethics*, Vol. 26, pp. 312.

Bergner, L., Hallstrom, A.P. and Eisenberg, M. (1984), "Health status of survivors of out-of-hospital cardiac arrest six months later", *American Journal of Public Health*, Vol. 74(5), pp. 508-510.

Bergner, L., Hallstrom, A.P., Bergner, M., Eisenberg, M. and Cobb, L.A. (1985), "Health status of survivors of cardiac arrest and of myocardial infarction controls", *American Journal of Public Health*, Vol. 75, pp.1321-1323.

Bertrand, M.E., Lablanche, J.M., Bauters, C., Leroy, F., MacFadden, E. (1993), "Discordant results of visual and quantitative estimates of stenosis severity before and after coronary angioplasty", *Catheterisation and Cardiovascular Diagnosis*, Vol. 28, pp. 1-6.

Birch, S. and Gafni, A. (1993), Changing the problem to fit the solution: Johannesson and Weinstein's (mis)app.lication of economics to real world problems *Journal of Health Economics*, 12 pp. 471-476 1993.

Birch, S. and Gafni, A. (1994), "Cost-Effectiveness Ratios: in a League of their Own", *Health Policy*, Vol. 28, pp. 133-141.

Boehmer, P., Pain, C., Watt, A., Abernethy, P. and Sceats, J. (2001), "Maximising health gain within available resources in the New Zealand public health system", *Health Policy*, Vol. 55, pp. 37-50.

Bombardier, C., Ware, J., Russell, I.J., Larson, M., Chalmers, A., and Read, J.L. (1986), "Auranofin therapy and quality of life in patients with rheumatoid arthritis: results of a multicentre trial", *American Journal of Medicine*, Vol 81. (4), pp. 565-578.

Bombardier, C. and Maetzel, A. (1999), "Pharmacoeconomic evaluation of new treatments: efficacy versus effectiveness studies?", *Annals of the Rheumatic Diseases*, Vol. 58(1).

Bootman, L., Townsend, R. and McGrath, W. (1996), *Principles of Pharmacoeconomics*, Harvey Whitney Books, Cincinnati, Ohio.

Bosch, J.L., Graaf, Y. van der, Hunink, M.G.M, for the Dutch Iliac Stent Study Group (1999), "Health-Related Quality of Life After Angioplasty and Stent Replacement in Patients with Iliac Artery Occlusive Disease", *Circulation*, Vol. 99, pp. 3155-3160.

Bowling, A. (1991), *Measuring Health*, Open University Press, Buckingham.

Boyce, N. (1996), "Using Outcome data to Measure Quality in Health Care", *International Journal for Quality in Health Care*, Vol. 8(2), pp. 101-104.

Boyle, M.H., Torrance, G.W., Sinclair, J.C., and Horwood, S.P. (1983), "Economic Evaluation of Neonatal Intensive Care of very Low birthweight infants", *New England Journal of Medicine*, Vol. 308 (2), pp. 1330-1337.

Brazier, J. and Dixon, S. (1995), "The Use of Condition-Specific Outcome Measures in Economic Appraisal", *Health Economics*, Vol. 4(4), pp. 255-264.

Brazier, J., Jones, N. and Kind, P. (1996), "Testing the validity of the Euroqol and comparing it with the SF-36 health survey questionnaire", *Quality of Life Research*, Vol. 2, pp.169-180.

Brazier, J., Deverill, M., Green, C., Harper, R. and Booth, A. (1999), "A review of the use of health status measures in economic evaluation", *Health Technologyl Assessment*, Vol. 3(9).

Brooks, R.G. (1995), *Health Status Measurement: A Perspective on Change*, Macmillan, London.

Brooks, R. with the EuroQol Group (1996), "EuroQol: the current state of play", *Health Policy*, Vol. 18, pp. 870-877.

Broome, J. (1978), "Choice and Value in Economics", *Oxford Economic Papers*, Vol. 30, pp. 313-333.

Broome, J. (1993), "QALYs", *Journal of Public Economics*, Vol. 50.2.

de Bruin, A.F., de Witte, L.P., Stevens, F. and Diedericks, J.P.M. (1992), "Sickness Impact Profile: The State of the Art of a Generic Functional Status Measure", *Social Science and Medicine*, Vol. 35(8), pp.1003-1014.

Bucquet, D., Condon, S. and Ritchie, K. (1990), "The French version of the Nottingham Health Profile: A comparison of items weights with those of the source version", *Social Science and Medicine*, Vol. 30(7), pp. 829-835.

Bush, J.W., Anderson, J.P., Kaplan, R.M. and Blischke, W.R. (1982), "Counter-Intuitive Preferences in Health-Related Quality of Life Measurement", *Medical Care*, Vol. XX, no.5.

Busschbach, J., Brouwer, W.B.F., van der Donk, A., Passchier, J., Rutten, F.F.H. (1998), "An Outline for a Cost-Effectiveness Analysis of a Drug for Patients With Al.zheimer's Disease", *Pharmacoeconomics*, Vol.13, pp 21-34.

Buxton, M.J., Drummond, M.F., van Hout, B.A., Prince, R.L., Sheldon, T.A., Szucs, T., and Vray, M. (1997), "Modelling in Economic Evaluation: An Unavoidable Fact of Life", *Health Economics*, Vol 6(3), pp. 217-228.

CABG Panel Consensus Development Conference: Coronary Artery Bypass Grafting (1984), *British Medical Journal*, Vol. 289, pp. 1527-1529.

Cairns, J., Johnston, K. and McKenzie, L. (1991), *Developing QALYs from condition-specific outcome measures,* Health Economics Research Unit, Discussion Paper 14/91, University of Aberdeen.

Canadian Co-ordinating Office for Health Technology Assessment (CCOHTA) (1996), *A Guidance Document for the Costing Process,* CCOHTA, Ottawa, Canada.

Canadian Co-ordinating Office for Health Technology Assessment (CCOHTA) (1997), *Guidelines for Economic Evaluation of Pharmaceuticals: Canada 2nd edition,* CCOHTA, Ottawa, Canada.

Canto, J.G., Keife, K.I., Williams, O.D., Barron, H.V. and Rogers, W.J. (1999), "Comparison of outcomes research with clinical trials using pre-existing data", *The American Journal of Cardiology,* Vol. 84, no.8.

Carlin, P.S. and Sandy, R. (1991), "Estimating the implicit value of a young child's life", *Southern Economic Journal,* Vol. 58, pp. 186-202.

Carr-Hill, R.A. (1989), "Assumptions of the QALY procedure", *Social Science and Medicine,* Vol. 29, pp. 469-477.

Carr-Hill, R.A. (1991), "Allocating Resources to Health Care: Is the QALY a technical solution to a political problem?", *International Journal of Health Services,* Vol. 21(2), pp. 351-363.

Carter, W.B., Bobbitt, R., Bergner, M. and Gilson, B.S. (1976), "Validation of an Interval Scaling: the Sickness Impact Profile", *Health Services Research,* Vol. 11(4), pp.516-528.

Charlton, B.G. (1995), "Mega-Trials: methodological issues and clinical implications", *Journal of the Royal College of Physicians,* Vol. 29, pp. 96-100.

Charlton, B.G., Taylor, P.R.A. and Proctor, S.J. (1997), "The PACE (Population-adjusted clinical epidemiology) Strategy: a new approach to multi-centred clinical trials", *Quarterly Journal of Medicine,* Vol. 90, pp. 147-151.

Charlton, J.R.H., Patrick, D.L and Peach, H. (1983), "Use of multivariate measures of disability in health surveys", *Journal of Epidemiology and Community Health,* Vol. 37, pp. 296-304.

Chisholm, D. (1996), "Characterising mental health: implications for health economic research", *Mental Health Research Review,* Number 3, PSSRU/CEMH (University of Kent at Canterbury).

Chisholm, D. (2000), " "Mind how you go": issues in the analysis of cost-effectiveness in mental health care", *Mental Health Research Review,* Vol. 7.

Churchill, D.L., Torrance, G.W., Taylor D.W., Barnes C.C., Ludwin, D., Shimizu, A., and Smith E.K.M. (1987), "Measurement of quality of life in end-stage renal disease: the time trade-off approach", *Clinical Investigative Medicine,* Vol. 10, pp. 14-20.

Clarke, P., Gray, A., and Holman, R. (2002), "Estimating utility values for health states of type 2 diabetic patients using the EQ-5D (UKPDS 62)", *Medical Decision Making,* Vol. 22(4), pp. 340-349.

Claxton, K. and Posnett, J. (1996), "An Economic Approach to Clinical Trial Design and Research Priority Setting", *Health Economics,* Vol. 5(6), pp. 513-524.

Coast, J. (1993), "Developing the QALY concept", *Pharmacoeconomics,* Vol. 4, pp. 240-246.

Coast, J., Donovan, J. and Frankel, S. (1996), *Priority Setting: The Health Care Debate,* Wiley, Chichester.

Commonwealth Department of Human Services and Health (CDHSH) (1993), *Background Document (on the use of economic analysis as a basis for inclusion of pharmaceutical products on the Pharmaceutical Benefits Scheme),* Australian Government Publishing Service, Canberra.

Commonwealth Department of Human Services and Health (CDHSH) (1995), *Guidelines for the Pharmaceutical Industry on the Preparation of Submissions to the Pharmaceutical Benefits Advisory Committee*, Australian Government Publishing Service, Canberra.

Connolly, S. and Munro, A. (1999), *Economics of the Public Sector*, Prentice Hall, New York.

Cook, D.J., Mulrow, C.D. and Haynes, R.B. (1997), "Systematic reviews: synthesis of best evidence for clinical decisions", *Annals of Internal Medicine*, Vol. 126(5), pp. 376-380.

Cookson, R., Maynard, A., McDaid, D., Sassi, F. and Sheldon, T. (eds) (2000) *Analysis of the Scientific and Technical Evaluation of Health Care Interventions in the European Union* LSE Health, London School of Economics and Political Science, London.

Cookson, R. and Dolan, P. (2000), "Priority setting in healthcare; of course we should ask the taxpayer", *British Medical Journal,*, Vol. 321, pp. 323-329.

Cranshaw, J. and Evans, T.W. (2001), "Lung Volume Reduction Surgery: a quality operation?", *The Lancet*, Vol. 357.

Crombie, I.K. (1996), *Research in Health Care: Design, Conduct, and Interpretation of Health Services Research*, Wiley, Chichester.

Culyer, A.J. (1971), "The nature of the commodity "health care", and its efficient allocation", *Oxford Economic Papers*, Vol. 23, pp.189-211.

Culyer, A.J. (1989), "The normative economics of health care finance and provision", *Oxford Review of Economic Policy*, Vol. 5, pp. 34-58.

Culyer, A.J. (1990), "Commodities, characteristics of commodities, characteristics of people, utilities, and the quality of life", in S. Baldwin C. Godfrey, and C. Propper. (eds), *The Quality of Life: Perspectives and Policies,* Routledge, London.

Culyer, A.J. (1995), "Need: the idea won't do, but we still need it" (Editorial), *Social Science and Medicine,* Vol. 40(6) pp. 727-730.

Culyer, A.J., Maynard, A.K. and Posnett, J.W. (1990), *Competition in Health Care; Reforming the NHS*, Macmillan, Basingstoke.

D'Agostino, R.B. and Kwan, H (1995), Measuring Effectiveness *Medical Care*, Vol. 33(4), pp. AS5-AS105.

Daniels, N. (2000), "Accountability for reasonableness", *British Medical Journal*, Vol. 321, pp. 1300-1301.

Davis, C.E. (1994), "Generalising from clinical trials", *Controlled Clinical Trials*, Vol. 15, pp. 11-14.

Department of Health (UK) (1989), *Working for Patients, Command Paper 555,* Her Majesty's Stationery Office, London.

Department of Health (UK) (1995), *Policy Appraisal and Health*, Department of Health, London.

Detsky, A.S. (1995), "Evidence of effectiveness: evaluating its quality", in: F.A. Sloan (ed.), *Valuing Health Care*, Cambridge University Press, Cambridge.

Department of Health and Social Services (DHSS) (1983), *Performance Indicators: National Summary for 1981,* London.

Department of Health and Social Services (Northern Ireland) (DHSS(NI)) (1992), *Review of Cardiac Surgery in Northern Ireland: Report by the Chief Medical Officer (Dr. McKenna),* (mimeo) DHSS (NI), Belfast.

Department of Health and Social Services (Northern Ireland) (DHSS (NI)) (1995), *Regional Strategy for Health and Social Well-being,* (mimeo) DHSS (NI), Belfast.

Deyo, R.A. and Inui, T.S. (1984), "Towards clinical applications of health status measures: sensitivity of scales to clinically important changes", *Health Services Research*, Vol. 19, pp. 275-289.

Doessel, D.P. (1992), *The Economics of Medical Diagnosis: Technological Change and Health Expenditure,* Avebury Press, Aldershot.

Dolan, P. (1997), "The Nature of Individual Preferences: A Prologue to Johanesson, Jonsson, and Karlsson", *Health Economics,* Vol. 6(1) pp. 91-94.

Dolan, P. (on behalf of the Euroqol Group) (1994), "Search for a critical appraisal of the Euroqol: a response by the Euroqol Group to Gafni and Birch", *Health Policy,* Vol. 28, pp. 67-69.

Dolan, P., Gudex, C., Kind, P. and Williams, A. (1995), *A social tariff for the Euroqol: Results from a UK General Population Survey,* Centre for Health Economics Discussion Paper 138, York.

Donaldson, C., Atkinson, A. and Bond, J. (1988), "Should QALYs be programme-specific?", *Journal of Health Economics,* Vol. 7, pp. 239-257.

Donaldson, C., Handley, V. and McIntosh, E. (1996), "Using Economics alongside clinical trials; why we cannot choose the evaluation technique in advance" (Letter), *Health Economics,* Vol. 5(3), pp. 267-269.

Donaldson, C., Walker, A. and Craig, N. (1995), *Programme Budgeting and Marginal Analaysis: A Handbook for Applying Economics in Health Care Purchasing,* Scottish Forum for Public Health, Glasgow.

Dorman, P.J., Waddell, F., Slattery, J., Dennis, M. and Sandercock, P. (1997a), "Is the EuroQol a valid measure of health-related quality of life after stroke?", *Stroke,* Vol. 28(10).

Dorman, P.J., Waddell, F., Slattery, J., Dennis, M. and Sandercock, P. (1997b), "Are proxy assessments of health status after stroke with the EuroQol questionnaire feasible, accurate, and unbiased?", *Stroke,* 28(10).

Dowie, J. (1996), The Research-Practice Gap and the Role of Decision Analysis in Closing It, *Health Care Analysis,* Vol. 4, pp. 5-18.

Dowie, J. (1996), "'Evidence-based", "cost-effective", and "preference-driven" medicine: decision analysis based medical decision making is the pre-requisite', *Journal of Health Services Research and Policy,* Vol. 1(2).

Droitcour, J., Silberman, G. and Chelimsky, E. (1993), "Cross-Design Synthesis", *International Journal of Technology Assessment in Health Care,* Vol. 9(3), pp. 440-449.

Drummond, M. (1995), "Economic analysis al.ongside clinical trials: problems and potential", *Journal of Rheumatology,* Vol. 22, pp. 1403-7.

Drummond, M. and McGuire, A. (2001), *Economic Evaluation in Health Care,* Oxford University Press, Oxford.

Drummond, M.F., Stoddart, L.G. and Torrance, G.W. (1987), *Methods for the Economic Evaluation of Health Care Programmes,* Oxford University Press, Oxford.

Drummond, M.F., Mohide, E.A., Tew, M., Streiner, D.L., Pringle, D.M. and Gilbert, J.R. (1991), "Economic evaluation of a support program for caregivers of demented elderly", *International Journal of Technology Assessment in Health Care,* Vol. 7(2), pp. 209-219.

Drummond, M., Torrance, G. and Mason, J. (1993), "Cost-effectiveness league tables: more good than harm?", *Social Science and Medicine,* Vol. 37, pp. 33-40.

Editor (1995), "Evidence-Based Medicine in its place", *Lancet,* Vol. 346, no. 8978, pp. 785.

Eggleston, A., Wigerinck, A., Huijghebaert, S., Dubois, D. and Haycox, A. (1998), "Cost-effectiveness of treatment for gastro-oesophageal reflux disease in clinical practice: A clinical database analysis", *Gut,* Vol. 42, no. 1, pp. 13-19.

Enthoven, A.C. (1985), *Reflections on the Management of the National Health Service,* Nuffield Provincial Hospitals Trust, London.

Euroqol Group (1990), "Euroqol - a new facility for the measurement of health-related quality of life", *Health Policy,* Vol. 16(3), pp. 199-208.

Fanshel, S. and Bush, J.W. (1970), "A health status index and its application to health services outcomes", *Operational Research,* Vol. 18(6), pp. 1021-66.

Fayers, P.M. and Hand, D.J. (1997), "Generalising from phase III clinical trials: survival, quality of life, and health economics", *The Lancet,* Vol. 350, pp. 1025-1027.

Fayers, P. and Bjordal, K. (2001), "Should quality-of-life needs influence resource allocation?", *The Lancet,* Vol. 357.

Fenn, P. and Gray, A. (1999), "Estimating Long Term Cost Savings from Treatment of Alzheimer's Disease: A Modelling Approach", *Pharmacoeconomics,* Vol. 16(2), pp. 165-174.

Fletcher, A., Hunt, B. and Bulpitt, C.J., (1987), "Evaluation of Quality of Life in Clinical Trials of Cardiovascular Disease", *Journal of Chronic Disease,* Vol. 40(6).

Fletcher, A., McLoone, P., and Bulpitt, C. (1988), "Quality of Life on Angina Therapy: a randomised controlled trial of transdermal blyceryl trinitrate against placebo", *The Lancet,* Vol 341, pp. 216-230.

Folland, S., Goodman, A.C. and Stano, M. (1993), *The Economics of Health and Health Care,* Macmillan, London.

Frankel, S. (1991), "The epidemiology of indications" (Editorial*) Journal of Epidemiology and Community Health,* Vol. 45, pp. 257-259.

Frankel, S. and West, R. (1993), *Rationing and Rationality in the National Health Service,* Macmillan, London.

Frater, A. and Sheldon, T.A. (1993), "The outcomes movement in the USA and the UK", in M.F. Drummond and A. Maynard (eds), *Purchasing and Providing Cost-Effective Health Care,* Churchill Livingstone, Edinburgh.

Freemantle, N. and Maynard, A. (1994), "Something Rotten in the State of Clinical and Economic Valuations?", *Health Economics,* Vol. 3(2), pp. 63-67.

Fuchs, V.R. (1974), *Who Shall Live? Health, economics, and social choice,* Basic Books, New York.

Garattini, L., Grilli, R., Scopelliti, D. and Mantovani, L. (1995), "A Proposal for Italian Guidelines in Pharmacoeconomics", *Pharmacoeconomics,* Vol . 7(1), pp. 1-6.

Garber, A.M. and Phelps, C.E. (1997), "Economic foundations of cost-effectiveness analysis", *Journal of Health Economics,* Vol 16, pp. 1-31.

Garellick, G., Malchau, H. and Herberts, P. (1998), "Specific or general health outcome measures in the evaluation of total hip replacement: a comparison between the Harriss hip score and the Nottingham Health Profile", *Journal of Bone and Joint Surgery,* Vol. 80(4).

Gemmert, W.G. van, Adang, E.M., Greve, J. and Soeters, P.B. (1998), "Quality of life assessment of morbidly obese patients; effects of weight-reducing surgery", *American Journal of Clinical Nutrition,* 67(2), 197-201.

George, B., Harris, A. and Mitchell, A. (2001), "Cost-Effectiveness Analysis and the Consistency of Decision Making", *Pharmacoeconomics,* Vol. 19(11), pp. 1103-1109.

Gerard, K. and Mooney, G. (1993), "QALY League Tables: handle with care", *Health Economics,* Vol. 2, pp. 59-64.

Gerard, K., Dobson, M. and Hall, J. "Framing and Labelling Effects in Health Descriptions: quality of life years for treatment of breast cancer", *Journal of Clinical Epidemiology,* Vol. 46, pp.77-84.

Ginsberg, G.M. and Lev, B. (1997), "Cost-Benefit Analysis of Riluzole for the Treatment of Amyotrophic Lateral Sclerosis", *Pharmacoeconomics,* Vol. 12(5), pp. 578-584.

Glick, H., Kinosian, B., Schulman, K. (1994), "Decision-Analytic Modelling: Some Uses in the Evaluation of New Pharmaceuticals", *Drug Information Journal,* Vol. 28, pp. 691-707.

Gorham, P. (1995), "Cost-Effectiveness Guidelines - the Experience of Australian Manufacturers", *Pharmacoeconomics,* Vol. 8(5), pp. 369-373.

Gold, M.R., Siegel, J.R., Russell, L.B. and Weinstein, M.C. (eds) (1996), *Cost-effectiveness in Health and Medicine,* Oxford University Press, New York.

Gomm, R., Needham, G. and Bullman, A. (2000), *Evaluating Research in Health and Social Care,* Open University/Sage Publications, London.

Griffiths, R. (1983), *NHS Management Enquiry,* DHSS, London.

Gudex, C. (1986), *QALYs and their use in the health service,* Centre for Health Economics, York University, Discussion Paper no 20.

Gudex, C. (1990), "The QALY: How can it be used?", in S. Baldwin, C. Godfrey, and C. Propper (eds), *Quality of Life: Persepectives and Policies,* Routledge, London.

Gunnell, D. and Smith, L. (1994), *The Invasive Management of Ischaemic Heart Disease,* Health Care Evaluation Unit, University of Bristol, Bristol.

Gyrd-Hansen, D., Sogaard, J. and Kronberg, O. (1998), "Colorectal Cancer Screening: Efficiency and Effectiveness", *Health Economics,* Vol. 7(1), pp. 9-20.

Hannan, E.L., Kumar, D., and the Ischaemic Heart Disease Patient Outcomes Research Team [PORT] (1997), "Geographic variation in the utilization and choice of procedures for treating coronary artery disease in New York State", *Journal of Health Services Research and Policy,* Vol. 2(3), pp. 137-143.

Hannan, E.L., Siu, T. and Chassin, M.R. (1997), "Assessment of CABG surgery performance in New York: Is there a bias against taking high risk patients?", *Medical Care,* Vol. 35(1).

Harris, J. (1985), *The Value of Life,* Routledge and Kegan Paul, London.

Harris, J. (1991), "Unprincipled QALYs: A Response to Cubbon", *Journal of Medical Ethics,* Vol. 17 pp.185-188.

Henry, D. (1992), "Economic Analysis as an Aid to Subsidisation Decisions: the Development of Australian Guidelines for Pharmaceuticals", *Pharmacoeconomics,* Vol. 1, pp. 54-67.

Herman, J. (1995), "The Demise of the Randomized Controlled Trial", *Journal of Clinical Epidemiology,* Vol. 48(7), pp. 985-988.

Higgs, J. and Jones, M. (1995), *Clinical Reasoning in the health professions,* Butterworth-Heinemann, London.

Hilden, J. and Habbema, J.D. (1990), "The Marriage of Clinical Trials and Clinical Decision Science", *Statistics in Medicine,* Vol. 9, pp. 1243-1257.

Hillner, B., Hollenberg, J.P. and Pauker, S.P. (1986), "Postmenopausal estrogens in prevention of osteoporosis", *American Journal of Medicine,* Vol. 80, pp. 1115-1127.

Hinton, P.R. (1995), *Statistics Explained,* Routledge, London.

Hirst, M. (1990), "Multidimensional Representation of Disablement", in S. Baldwin, C. Godfrey and C. Propper (eds), *Quality of Life - Perspectives and Policies,* Routledge, London, pp. 72-83.

Hurst, N.P., Jobanputra, P., Hunter, M., Lambert, M., Lochhead, A. and Brown, H. (1994), "Validity of EuroQol – a generic health status instrument – in patients with rheumatoid arthritis", *British Journal of Rheumatology,* Vol. 33, pp. 655-662.

Holliday, I. (1992), *The NHS Transformed,* Baseline Books, Manchester.

Hughes, D.A., Bagust, A., Haycox, A. and Walley, T. (2001), "Accounting for Noncompliance in Pharmacoeconomic evaluations", *Pharmacoeconomics,* Vol. 19(12), pp. 1185-1197.

Hunt, S.M., McEwen, J. and McKenna, S.P. (1986), *Measuring Health Status*, Croom Helm, London.

Hunt, S.M., McKenna, S.P. and McEwen, J.A. (1980), "A quantitative app.roach to perceived health status: a validation study", *Journal of Epidemiology and Community Health*, Vol. 34, pp. 281-285.

Hunt, S.M. and McKenna, S.P. (1991), *The Nottingham Health Profile User's Manual*, Galen Research and Consultancy, Manchester.

Hunter, D.J. (1995), "Rationing health care: the political perspective", in R.J. Maxwell (ed.), *Rationing Health Care*, Churchill Livingstone, Edinburgh.

Hurst, J.W. and Mooney, G.H. (1983), "Implicit values in administrative decisions", in A.J. Culyer (ed), *Health Indicators: an international study for the European Science Foundation*, New York.

Indredavik, B., Bakke, F., Slordahl, S., Rokseth, R. and Hehim, L. (1998), "Stroke unit treatment improves long-term quality of life: a randomized controlled trial", *Stroke*, Vol. 29(5).

Jabobs, L. and Marmor, T. (1999), "The Oregon Health Plan and the Political Paradox of Rationing: What Advocates and Critics have claimed and what Oregon did", *Journal of Health Politics, Policy, and Law*, Vol. 24(1).

Jacobs, P., Bachynsky, J. and Baladi, J.-F. (1995), "A Comprehensive Review of Pharmacoeconomic Guidelines", *Pharmacoeconomics*, Vol. 8(3), pp. 182-189.

Jankovski, R.F. (2001), "Implementing national guidelines at local level", *British Medical Journal*, Vol. 322, pp. 1258-1259.

Jefferson, T., Demicheli, V. and Mugford, M. (1996), *Elementary Economic Evaluation in Health Care*, British Medical Journal, BMJ Publications, London.

Jenicek, M. (1989), "Meta-Analysis in Medicine: Where are we, and where do we want to go?", *Journal of Clinical Epidemiology*, Vol. 42(1), pp. 35-44.

Jenkinson, C., Fitzpatrick, R. and Argyle, M. (1988), "The Nottingham Health Profile: an analysis of its sensitivity in differentiating illness groups", *Social Science and Medicine*, Vol. 27(12), pp. 1411-1414.

Johannesson, M. and Meltzer, D. (1998), "Some Reflections on Cost-Effectiveness Analysis", *Health Economics*, Vol. 7(1), pp. 1-7.

Johannesson, M., Jonsson, B. and Karlsson, G. (1996), "Outcome Measurement in Economic Evaluation", *Health Economics*, Vol. 5(4), pp. 279-296.

Johannesson, M. and Weinstein, M.C. (1993), "On the decision rules of cost-effectiveness analysis", *Journal of Health Economics*, Vol. 12, pp. 459-467.

Joint Cardiology Committee of the Royal College of Physicians and the Royal College of Surgeons of England, Fourth Report (1992), "Provision of service for the diagnosis and treatment of heart disease", *British Heart Journal*, Vol. 67, pp.106-116.

Kahneman, D. and Tversky, A. (1979), "Prospect theory: an analysis of decision under risk", *Econometrica*, Vol. 47(2), pp. 263-291.

Karlsen, H.K., Larsen, J.P., Tandberg, E. and Maeland, J.G. (1999), "Influence of clinical and demographic variables on quality of life in patients with Parkinson's Disease", *Journal of Neurology, Neurosurgery, and Psychiatry*, Vol. 66(4).

Kassirer, J.P., Kuipers, B.J. and Gorry, G.A. (1982), "Towards a theory of clinical expertise", *American Journal of Medicine*, Vol. 73(2).

Kee, F., McDonald, P., Unwin, J.R., Patterson, C.C. and Love, G. (1997), "The stated and tacit impact of demographic and lifestyle factors on prioritisation decisions for cardiac surgery", *Quarterly Journal of Medicine*, Vol. 90(2), pp. 117-123.

Kee, F., Gaffney, B. and O'Reilly, D. (1993), "Access to coronary catheterisation: fair shares for all?", *British Medical Journal*, Vol. 307, pp. 1305-1307.

Kerrison, S. (1993), "Contracting and the quality of medical care", in I. Tilley (ed.), *Managing the Internal Market*, Paul Chapman, London.

Kind, P., Dolan, P., Gudex, C. and Williams, A. (1998), "Variations in population health status: Results from a United Kingdom national questionnaire survey", *British Medical Journal*, Vol. 316, pp. 736-741.

Kind, P., Rosser, R. and Williams, A. (1978), "Valuation of the quality of life: some psychometric evidence", in M.W. Jones-Lee (ed.), *The Value of Life and Safety*, North Holland, Amsterdam.

Kind, P. and Rosser, R. (1988), "The quantification of health", *European Journal of Social Psychology*, Vol. 18, pp. 63-77.

Kind, P. (1990), "Issues in the Design and Construction of a Quality of Life Measure", in S. Baldwin, C. Godfrey, and C. Propper (eds), *Quality of Life: Prospects and Policies*, Routledge, London.

Kind, P. and Gudex, C. (1991), *The HMQ: Measuring Health Status in the Community*, Centre for Health Economics, Discussion Paper 93, York University, York.

Kind, P. (1994), "Practical and methodological issues in the development of the EuroQol: the York experience", in G. Albrecht and R. Fitzpatrick (eds), *Advances in Medical Sociology Vol. 5: Quality of Life in Health Care*, JAI Press, London.

Kind, P. [no date], *The Design and Construction of Quality of Life Measures*, Centre for Health Economics, Discussion Paper 43, York University, York.

Kleiman, N.S., Rodriguez, A.R. and Raizner, A.E. (1992), "Interobserver variability in grading of coronary arterial narrowings using the American College of Cardiology/American Heart Association grading criteria", *American Journal of Cardiology*, Vol. 69, pp. 413-415.

Klein, R. (1983), *The Politics of the National Health Service*, Longman.

Knaus, W.A., Wagner, D.P., Harrell, F.E. and Draper, E.A. (1994), "What determines prognosis in sepsis? Evidence for a comprehensive individual patient risk assessment approach to the design and analysis of clinical trials", *Theoretical Surgery*, Vol. 9, pp. 20-27.

Krabbe, P., Essink-Bot, M.L. and Bonsel, G.J. (1997), "The comparability and reliabilty of five health-state valuation methods", *Social Science and Medicine*, Vol. 45(11), pp. 1641-1652.

Kula, E. I. (1997), *Time Discounting and Future Generations*, Quorum Books, Westport, Connecticut.

Launois, R., Henry, B., Marty, J.R., Gersberg, m., Lassale, C., Benoist, M., and Goehrs, J-M. (1994), "Chemonucleolysis versus Surgical Discotomy for Sciatica Secondary to Lumbar Disc Herniation", *Pharmacoeconomics*, Vol. 6(5), pp. 453-463.

Le Grand, J., Winter, D. and Wooley, F. (1990), "The National Health Service: Safe in Whose Hands?", in J. Hills (ed.), *The State of Welfare: The Welfare State in Britain since 1974*, Clarendon Press, Oxford.

Leakey, R. (1995), *The Sixth Extinction*, Routledge, London.

Leu, R.E. (1978), "Comment on Kind, Rosser and Williams", in M.W. Jones-Lee (ed.), *The Value of Life and Safety*, North Holland, Amsterdam.

Little, I.M.D. (1965), *A Critique of Welfare Economics*, Oxford University Press, Oxford.

Llewellyn-Thomas, H., Sutherland, H.J., Tibshirani, R., Ciampi, A., Till, J.E., and Boyd, N.F. (1984), "Describing Health States: Methodologic issues in obtaining values for health states", *Medical Care*, Vol. 22(6), pp. 543-552.

Loomes, G. and Mackenzie, L. (1989), "The Use of QALYs in Health Care Decision-Making", *Social Science and Medicine*, Vol. 28(4), pp. 299-308.

Lunt, N. and Coyle D (1996), *Welfare and Policy: Research Agendas and Issues,* Taylor and Francis, London.

McCloskey, B. (2001), "Prioritisation: The new growth of the NHS", *British Medical Journal,* Vol. 322, p. 499.

McCulloch, D.W. (1989), *Who Needs QALYs?* Occasional Paper No. 19, Policy Planning and Research Unit, Department of Finance and Personnel, Stormont.

McCulloch, D.W. (1991), "Can we measure "output"? Quality-Adjusted Life Years, Health Indices, and Occupational Therapy", *British Journal of Occupational Therapy,* Vol. 54(6), pp. 219-221.McCulloch, D.W., Barry, M., Ryan, M. and Heerey, A. (2000), "The economic evaluation of a drug for patients with Alzheimer's Disease", *European Hospital Pharmacy,* Vol. 6(2), pp. 64-68.

McCulloch, D.W. (1998), *The Quality-Adjusted Life Year (QALY) Approach as a Basis for Health Care Resource allocation: the Validity of a QALY measure, and the Application of QALYs to Clinical Practice,* University of Ulster PhD thesis, Belfast.

McDonald. R., Haycox, A. and Walley, T. (2001), "The Impact of Health Economics on Healthcare Delivery", *Pharmacoeconomics,* Vol. 19(8), pp. 803-809.

McGuire, A., Henderson, J. and Mooney, G. (1988), *The Economics of Health Care,* Routledge, London.

McKenna, S. (1993), "Commonly used measures of health status in European clinical trials", *British Journal of Medical Economics,* Vol. 6C, pp. 3-15.

McKenna, S. (1995), "Quality of Life Assessment in the Conduct of Economic Evaluations of Medicines", *British Journal of Medical Economics,* Vol. 8, pp. 33-38.

McNeil, B.J., Pauker, S.G., Sox, H.C., and Tversky, A. (1982), "On the elicitation of preferences for alternative therapies", *New England Journal of Medicine,* Vol. 305, pp. 982-987.

MacTavish, C.F. and Sundeen, J. (1968), *Assessment of the Quality of Medical Care: An Annotated Bibliography,* American Rehabilitation Foundation, Minneapolis.

Malcomson, J.M. and Chalkey, M. (1995), *Contracts and Competition in the NHS,* Discussion Paper in Economics and Econometrics No 9513, University of Southampton, Southampton.

Malek, M. (ed.) (1994), *Setting Priorities in Health Care,* Wiley, Chichester.

Margolis, H. (1982), *Selfishness, Altruism, and Rationality,* Cambridge University Press, Cambridge.

Marmor, T.R. and Boyum, D. (1999), "Medical care and public policy: the benefits and burdens of asking fundamental questions", *Health Policy,* Vol. 49, pp. 27-43.

Mason, J., Drummond, M. and Torrance, G. (1993), "Some guidelines on the use of cost-effectiveness league tables", *British Medical Journal,* Vol. 306, pp. 570-572.

Maynard, A. (1993), "Creating competition in the NHS: Is it possible? Will it work?", in I. Tilley (ed), *Managing the Internal Market,* Paul Chapman, London.

Maynard, A. (1997), "Economic Evaluation Techniques in Health Care", *Pharmacoeconomics,* Vol. 11(2), pp. 115-118.

Maynard, A. and Cookson, R.F. (1998), "Computer Modelling: The Need for Careful Evaluation and Public Audit", *Pharmacoeconomics,* Vol. 14 Suppl.2, pp. 67-72.

Mehrez, A. and Gafni, A. (1987), "An empirical evaluation of two assessment methods for utility measurement for life-years", *Socio-Economic Planning Sciences,* Vol. 21(6), pp. 371-375.

Mehrez, A. and Gafni, A. (1991), "The healthy-years equivalents: how to measure them using the standard gamble approach", *Medical Decision-Making,* Vol. 11, pp. 140-146.

Miller, D.M., Rudick, R.A., Cutter, G., Baier, M. and Fischer, J.S. (2000), "Clinical significance of the multiple sclerosis functional composite: Relationship to patient-reported quality of life", *Archives of Neurology*, Vol. 57(9).

Miller, P. and Vale, L. (2001), "Programme approach to managing informed commissioning", *Health Services Management Research*, Vol. 14(3).

Mitton, C., Donaldson, C., Dean, S. and West, B. (2000), "Program budgeting and marginal analysis: a priority setting framework for Canadian Regional Health Authorities", *Health Care Management Forum*, Vol. 13(4), pp. 24-31.

Monks, J. (1988), "Interpretation of subjective measures in a clinical trial of hyperbaric oxygen therapy for multiple sclerosis", *Journal of Psychosomatic Research*, Vol. 32 (4-5), pp. 365-372.

Mooney, G. and Olsen, J.A. (1994), "QALYs: Where Next?", in A. McGuire (ed.), *Providing Health Care*, Oxford University Press, Oxford.

Moses, L.E. (1995), "Measuring Effects Without Randomized Trials?", *Medical Care*, Vol. 33(4), pp. AS8-AS14.

Mulkay, M., Ashmore, M. and Pinch, T. (1987), "Measuring the Quality of Life: a sociological invention concerning the application of economics to health care", *Sociology*, Vol. 21(4), pp. 541-564.

Musgrove, P. (2000), "Cost-effectiveness as a criterion for public spending on health: a reply to William Jack's "second opinion" ", *Health Policy*, Vol. 54, pp. 229-233.

NHS Executive (1994), *The Operation of the Internal Market*, HMSO, London.

NHS Executive (1995), *1996/7 Purchaser Efficiency Index and HA Resources FDL(95)60*, HMSO, London.

Nord, E. A. (1990), "Comment on the meaning of numerical valuations of health states", *Social Science and Medicine*, Vol. 30 pp. 943-944.

Nord, E. (1991), "EuroQol: health-related quality of life measurement: Valuations of health states by the general public in Norway", *Health Policy*, Vol. 18, pp. 25-36.

Nord, E. (1992), "An alternative to QALYs: the saved young life equivalent", *British Medical Journal*, Vol. 305, pp. 875-877.

Nord, E. (1992), "Methods for the quality-adjustment of life years", *Social Science and Medicine*, Vol. 34(5), pp. 559-569.

Nord, E. (1993a), "Social Evaluation of Health Care versus Personal Evaluation of Health States", *International Journal of Technology Assessment in Health Care*, Vol. 9(4), pp. 463-478.

Nord, E. (1993b), "Unjustified use of the Quality of Well-Being scale in priority setting in Oregon", *Health Policy*, Vol. 24, pp.45-53.

Nord, E. (1993c), "The relevance of health state after treatment in prioritising between different patients", *Journal of Medical Ethics*, Vol. 19, pp. 37-42.

Nord, E. (1994), "The QALY - A measure of social value rather than individual utility?", *Health Economics*, Vol. 3(2), pp. 89-94.

Nord, E. (1999), *Cost-Value Analysis in Health Care; Making Sense Out Of QALYs*, Cambridge University Press, Cambridge.

Nuitjen, M., Hadjadjeba, L., Evans, C. and van der Berg, J. (1998), "Cost Effectiveness of Fluvoxamine in the Treatment of Recurrent Depression in France", *Pharmacoeconomics*, Vol. 14(4), pp. 433-445.

Nunally, J.C. (1970), *Introduction to Psychological Measurement*, McGraw-Hill, Basingstoke.

O'Brien, B.J. (1988), "Assessment of Treatment in Heart Disease", in G. Teeling-Smith (ed), *Measuring Health: A Practical Approach*, Wiley, London.

O'Brien, B.J., Buxton, M.J. and Ferguson, B.A. (1987), "Measuring the effectiveness of heart transplant programmes: quality of life data and their relationship to survival analysis", *Journal of Chronic Disease* Vol. 40, Supp.l, pp. 137S-153S.

O'Brien, B.J., Banner, N.R., Gibson, S. and Yacoub, M.H. (1998), "The Nottingham Health Profile as a measure of quality of life following combined heart and lung transplantation", *Journal of Epidemiology and Community Health,* Vol. 42(3), pp. 232-234.

O'Brien, B.J., Anderson, D.R. and Goeree, R. (1994), "Cost-effectiveness of enoxaparin versus warfarin prophylaxis against deep-vein thrombosis after total hip replacement", *Canadian Medical Association Journal,* Vol. 150(7), pp. 1083-1094.

O'Brien, B., Goeree, R., Hux, M., Iskedjian, M., Blackhouse, G., Gauthier, S. and Gagnon, M. (1999), "Economic Evaluation of Donepezil for the Treatment of Alzheimer's Disease in Canada", *Journal of the American Geriatric Society,* Vol. 47, pp. 570-578.

O'Connor, G.T., Plume, S.K., Olmstead, E.M., and Morton, J.R. (1996), "A Regional Intervention to Improve the Hospital Mortality Associated with Coronary Artery Bypass Graft Surgery", *Journal of the American Medical Association,* Vol. 275(11).

Oliver, A. (2002), *At the End of the Beginning: Eliciting Cardinal Values for Health States,* LSE Health and Social Care Discussion Paper No. 2, London School of Economics and Political Science, London.

O'Neill, C., Normand, C., Cupples, M. and McKnight, A. (1996), "A comparison of three measures of perceived distress: results from a study of angina patients in general practice in Northern Ireland", *Journal of Epidemiology and Community Health,* Vol. 50(2), pp. 202-206.

Ormel, J., Lindenberg, S., Steverink, N. and Vonkorff, M. (1997), "Quality of Life and Social Production Functions: A Framework for Understanding Health Effects", *Social Science and Medicine,* Vol. 45(7), pp. 1051-1063.

Ott, C.R., Sivarajan, E.S., Newton, K.M., Almes, M.J., Bruce, R.A., Bergner, M., and Gilson, B.S. (1983), "A controlled randomised study of early cardiac rehabilitation: the Sickness Impact Profile as an assessment tool", *Heart and Lung,* Vol. 12(2) pp. 162-170.

Patrick, D.L. (1976), "Constructing social metrics for health status indexes", *International Journal of Health Services,* Vol. 6(3), pp. 443-453.

Patrick, D.L. (1981), "Standardisation of comparative health status measures: using scales developed in America in an English-speaking country" *Health Survey Research Methods 3rd Biennial conference*, Hyattsville, Maryland, US Dept of Health and Human Services, pp. 216-219, Publication no. PHS 81-236, Washington DC.

Patrick, D.L., Bush, J.W. and Chen, M.M. (1973), "Towards an Operational Definition of Health", *Journal of Health and Social Behaviour,* Vol. 14, pp. 6-23.

Patrick, D.L., Bush, J.W. and Chen, M.M. (1973), "Methods for Measuring Levels of Well-Being for a Health Status Index", *Health Services Research,* Fall, pp. 228-245.

Patrick, D.L. and Erickson, P. (1993), *Health Status and Health Policy,* Oxford University Press, New York.

Patrick, D.L. and Peach, H. (eds) (1989), *Disablement in the Community,* Oxford University Press, Oxford.

Patrick, D.L., Sittampalam, Y., Somerville, S.M., Carter, W.B., and Bergner, M. (1985), "A cross-cultural comparison of health status values", *American Journal of Public Health,* Vol. 75(12), pp. 1402-1407.

Patrick, D.L., Peach, H. and Gregg, I. (1982), "Disablement and Care: a comparison of patient views and general practitioner knowledge", *Journal of the Royal College of General Practitioners,* Vol. 32, pp. 429-434.

Pauker, S.G. and McNeil, B.J. (1981), "Impact of patient preferences on the selection of therapy", *Journal of Chronic Diseases*, Vol. 34, pp. 77-86.

Petitti, D.B. (2000), *Meta-analysis, decision analysis, and cost-effectiveness analysis*, Oxford University Press, New York.

Petrou, S., Malek, M. and Davey, P.G. (1993), "The Reliability of Cost-Utility Estimates in Cost-per-QALY League Tables", *Pharmacoeconomics*, Vol. 3(5), pp. 345-353.

Pollard, B. and Johnston, M. (2001), "Problems with the Sickness Impact Profile: A theoretically based analysis and a proposal for a new method of implementation and scoring", *Social Science and Medicine*, Vol. 52(6), pp. 921-934.

Pollard, W.E., Bobbitt, R.A., Bergner, M., Martin, D.P., and Gilson, B.S. (1976), "The Sickness Impact Profile: Reliability of a Health Status Measure", *Medical Care*, Vol. XIV(2), pp. 146-155.

Pollard, W.E., Bobbitt, R.A. and Bergner, R.M. (1978), "Examination of variable errors of measurement in a survey-based social indicator", *Social Indicators Research*, Vol. 5, pp. 279-301.

Post, P.N., Stigglebout, A.M., and Wakker, P.P. (2001), "The utility of health states after stroke: a systematic review of the literature", *Stroke*, Vol. 32(6), pp. 1425-1429.

Raftery, J. (1994), "Limitations on the use of cost-effectiveness information: ways forward", in T. Delamonthe (ed.), *Outcomes into Clinical Practice*, BMJ Publishing, London.

Ratcliffe, J., Donaldson, C. and Macphee, S. (1996), "Programme budgeting and marginal analysis: a case study of maternity services", *Journal of Public Health Medicine*, Vol. 18(2), pp. 175-182.

Rawls, J. (1971), *A Theory of Justice*, Harvard University Press, Cambridge, Massachusetts.

Rayner, M. (1994), *Coronary Heart Disease Statistics*, British Heart Foundation, London.

Reinhardt, U. (1997), "Making Economic Evaluations Respectable", *Social Science and Medicine*, Vol. 45(4), pp. 555-562.

Reinhardt, U. (1998), "Abstracting from Distributional Effects, the Policy is Efficient", in M.L. Barer, T.E. Getzen, and G.L. Stoddart (eds), *Health, Health Care, and Health Economics*, Wiley, New York.

Reves, R., Johnson, P., and Ericsson, C. (1988), "A cost-effectiveness comparison of the use of antimicrobial agents for the treatment or prophylaxis of traveller's diarrhoea", *Archives of Internal Medicine*, Vol. 148, pp. 2421-2427.

Richards, D.M. and Irving, M.H. (1997), "Assessing the quality of life of patients with intestinal failure", *Gut*, Vol. 40(2).

Richardson, J. (1994), "Cost-Utility Analysis: What should be measured?", *Social Science and Medicine*, Vol. 39(1), pp. 7-21.

Rittenhouse, B.E. (1995), "The Relevance of Searching for Effects under a Clinical-trial Lamp-post", *Medical Decision-Making*, Vol. 15(4), pp. 348-357.

Rittenhouse, B.E. (1996), "Another Deficit Problem: The Deficit of Relevant Information When Clinical Trials are the Basis of Pharmacoeconomics", *Journal of Research in Pharmaceutical Economics*, Vol. 7(3), pp. 3-15.

Rittenhouse, B.E. and O'Brien, B.J. (1996), "Threats to the Validity of Pharmacoeconomic Analyses Based on Clinical Trials", in B. Spilker (ed.), *Quality of Life and Pharmacoeconomics in Clinical Trials*, Lippincott-Raven, Philadelphia.

Robinson, A. (1997), "Valuing Health States Using VAS and TTO: What Lies Behind the Numbers?", *Social Science and Medicine*, Vol. 45(8), pp.1289-1297.

Robinson, R. (1993), "Cost-Utility Analysis", *British Medical Journal*, Vol. 307, pp. 859-862.

Rovira, J. and Antonanzas, F. (1995), "Economic Analysis of Health Technologies and Programmes: A Spanish Proposal for Methodological Standardisation", *Pharmacoeconomics*, Vol. 8(3), pp. 245-252.

Rosser, R.M. and Watts V.C. (1972), "The Measurement of Hospital Output", *International Journal of Epidemiology*, Vol. 1(4), pp. 361-368.

Rosser, R.M. and Kind, P. A. (1978), "Scale of Valuations of States of Illness: Is there a social consensus?", *International Journal of Epidemiology*, Vol. 7(4), pp. 347-358.

Rothwell, P.M. (1994), "Can overall results of clinical trials be applied to all patients?", *The Lancet*, Vol. 345, pp. 1616-1619.

Rubins, H.B. (1994), "From clinical trials to clinical practice: generalising from participant to patient", *Controlled Clinical Trials*, Vol. 15, pp. 7-10.

Ruta, D.A., Donaldson, C. and Gilray, I. (1996), "Economics, public health and health care purchasing: the Tayside experience of programme budgeting and marginal analysis", *Journal of Health Services Research and Policy*, Vol. 1(4), pp. 185-193.

Sackett, D.L. and Rosenberg, W.M.C. (1995), "On the need for Evidence-Based Medicine", *Health Economics*, Vol. 4, pp. 249-254.

Sackett, D.L. and Torrance, G.W. (1978), "The Utility of Different Health States as perceived by the general public", *Journal of Chronic Diseases*, Vol. 31, pp. 697-704.

Sackman, H. (1975), *Delphi critique: expert opinion, forecasting, and group process*, Lexington Books, Lexington, Massachusetts.

Salek, S.S., Walker, M.D. and Bayer, A.J. (1999), "A review of quality of life in Alzheimer's Disease, Part 2: issues in assessing drug effects", *Pharmacoeconomics*, Vol. 14(6), pp. 613-627.

Sanders, B.S. (1964), "Measuring Community Health Levels", *American Journal of Public Health*, Vol. 54, pp. 1063-1070.

Santerre, R.E., and Neun S.P. (1996), *Health Economics: Theories, Insights, and Industry Studies*, Irwin, Chicago.

Schneider, E.C. and Epstein, A.M. "Influence of Cardiac-Surgery Performance Reports on Referral Practice and Access to Care", *New England Journal of Medicine*, Vol. 335(4), pp. 251-256.

Sen, A.K. (1979), "Personal Utilities and Public Judgements; or, What's Wrong with Welfare Economics", *Economic Journal*, Vol. 89, pp. 537-58.

Sheldon, T.A. (1996), "Problems of Using Modelling in the Economic Evaluation of Health Care", *Health Economics*, Vol. 5(1), pp. 1-11.

Siegel, J.E., Torrance, G.W., Russell, L.B., Luce, B.R., Weinstein, M.B. and Gold, M.R. (1997), "Guidelines for Pharmacoeconomic studies", *Pharmacoeconomics*, Vol. 11(2), pp. 159-168.

Singer, P.A., Martin, D.K., Giacommi, M. and Purdy, L. (2000), "Priority setting for new technologies in medicine; Qualitative case study", *British Medical Journal*, Vol. 321, pp. 1316-1319.

Sloan, F.A. (ed.) (1995), *Valuing Health Care*, Cambridge University Press, New York.

Smith, A. (1987), "Qualms about QALYs", *The Lancet*, Vol. 987, pp. 1134-1136.

Smith, P. (ed.) (1996), *Measuring Outcomes in the Public Sector*, Taylor and Smith, London.

Smith, R. (1992), "The ethics of ignorance", *Journal of Medical Ethics*, Vol. 18, pp.117-118.

Somerville, S., Silver, R. and Patrick, D. (1983), "Services for disabled people: what criteria should we use to assess disability?", *Community Medicine*, Vol. 5(4), pp. 304-310.

Stewart, A., Phillips, R. and Dempsey, G. (1998), "Pharmacotherapy for People with Alzheimer's Disease: A Markov-Style Evaluation of Five Years" Therapy Using Donepezil", *International Journal of Geriatric Psychiatry,* Vol. 13, pp. 445 - 453.

Stinnett, A.A. and Paltiel, A.D. (1996), Mathematical Programming for the efficient allocation of health care resources, *Journal of Health Economics,* Vol. 15(6), pp. 641-653.

Sugden, R. and Williams, A. (1978), *The Principles of Practical Cost-Benefit Analysis,* Oxford University Press, Oxford.

Sullivan, D.F. (1966), *Conceptual Problems in Developing an Index of Health,* United States Office of Health Statistical Analysis, National Centre for Health Statistics Series no. 2, no.17.

Tate, R., Hodgkinson, A., Veerabangsa, A. and Maggiotto, S. (1999), "Measuring psychosocial recovery after traumatic brain inury: psychometric properties of a new scale", *Journal of Head Trauma Rehabilitation,* Vol. 14(6), pp. 543-557.

Teeling-Smith, G. (ed.) (1988), *Measuring Health: a Practical Approach,* Wiley, Chichester.

Thomas, M.G. and Feinstein, A.R. "A Critical Appraisal of the Quality of Quality of Life Measurements", *Journal of the American Medical Association,* Vol. 272 (8), pp. 619-626.

Thurstone, L. (1959), *The Measurement of Value,* University of Chicago Press, Chicago.

Tilley, I. (ed.) (1993), *Managing the Internal Market,* Paul Chapman, London.

Tombaugh, T.N. and McIntyre, N.J. (1992), The Mini-Mental State Examination: A Comprehensive Review, *Journal of the American Geriatric Society,* Vol. 39, pp. 876-880.

Torgerson, D.J. and Gosden, T. (2000), "Priority setting in health care: Should we ask the tax payer?", *British Medical Journal,* Vol. 320, p. 1679.

Torgerson, W.S. (1958), *Theory and Methods of Scaling,* Wiley, New York.

Torrance, G.W. (1976a), "Toward a utility theory foundation for health status index models", *Health Services Research,* Vol. 11(4), pp. 364-369.

Torrance, G.W. (1976b), Social Preferences for Health States: an empirical evaluation of three measurement techniques, *Socio-Economic Planning Sciences,* Vol. 10, pp. 128-136.

Torrance, G.W., Thomas, W.H. and Sackett, D.L. (1972), "A utility maximisation model for the evaluation of health care programs", *Health Services Research,* Vol. 7(2), pp. 118-133.

Torrens, M., San, L., Martinez, A., Castillo, C., Domingo-Salvany, A. and Alonso, J. (1997) "Use of the Nottingham Health Profile for measuring health status of patients in methadone maintenance treatment", *Addiction,* Vol. 92(6), pp. 707-716.

Vandenburg, M.J. (1988), "Measuring the quality of life of patients with angina", in S.R. Walker and R. Rosser (eds), *Quality of life: assessment and application,* MTP Press, Lancaster.

Walker, M.D., Salek, S.S. and Bayer, A.J. (1998), "A review of quality of life in Alzheimer's Disease. Part I: issues in assessing disease impact", *Pharmacoeconomics,* Vol. 14(5), pp. 499-530.

Weinstein, M.C. (1980), "Estrogen use in postmenopausal women - costs, risks, benefits", *New England Journal of Medicine,* Vol. 303, pp. 308-316.

Weinstein, M.C. (1986), "Risky choices in medical decision-making: a survey", *The Geneva Papers on Risk and Insurance,* Vol. 11(40), pp.197-216.

Weinstein, M.C. (1995), "From cost-effectiveness ratios to resource allocation: where to draw the line?" in F. Sloan (ed.), *Valuing Health Care,* Cambridge University Press, New York.

Weisbrod, B.A. (1997), "Economics of mental illness: costs, benefits, and incentives", in B. Ronsson and J. Rosenbaum (eds.), *Health Economics of Depression,* Wiley, Chichester.

Whynes, D.K. (1996), "Towards an Evidence-Based National Health Service?", *Economic Journal,* Vol. 106, pp. 1702-1713.

Whynes, D.K. and Neilson, A.R. (1993), "Convergent validity of two measures of the quality of life", *Health Economics,* Vol. 2, pp. 229-235.

Whynes, D.K., Neilson, A.R., Walker, A.R., Hardcastle, J.D. (1998), "Faecal Occult Blood Screening for Colorectal Cancer: Is It Cost-Effective?", *Health Economics,* Vol. 7(1), pp. 21-30.

Wiklund, I., Romanus, B, and Hunt, S.M. (1988), "Self-assessed disability in patients with arthrosis of the hip joint; reliability of the Swedish version of the Nottingham Health Profile", *International Disability Studies,* Vol. 10(4), pp. 159-163.

Williams, A. (1976), *Cost benefit analysis in public health and medical care: Comments on a thesis written by Bengt Jonsson,* Report 1976:28, Department of Economics, University of Lund, Sweden.

Williams, A. (1985), "Economics of Coronary Artery Bypass Grafting", *British Medical Journal,* Vol. 291, pp. 326-329.

Williams, A. (1987), "Measuring Quality of Life", in G. Teeling-Smith (ed.), *Health Economics,* Croom Helm, London.

Williams, A. (1988a), "Applications in management", in G. Teeling-Smith (ed.), *Measuring Health: a Practical Approach,* Wiley, Chichester.

Williams, A. (1988b), "Economics and the rational use of medical technology", in F.F.H. Rutten and S.J. Reiser (eds), *The Economics of Medical Technology,* Springer, Berlin.

Williams, A. (1991), "Is the QALY a technical solution to a political problem? Of course not!", *International Journal of Health Services,* Vol. 21(2), pp. 365-369.

Williams, A. (1992), "Health and Health Care", in P. Smith (ed.), *Measuring Outcome in the Public Sector,* Taylor and Francis, London.

Wilson, A., Parker, H., Wynn, A., Jagger, C., Spiers, N. (1999), "Randomised controlled trial of effectiveness of Leicester hospital at home scheme compared with hospital care", *British Medical Journal,* Vol. 319, pp. 1524-1546.

Wit, A.G. de, Ramsteijn, P.G. and Charro, F.T.H. (1998), "Economic evaluation of end-stage renal disease treatment", *Health Policy,* Vol. 44, pp. 215-232.

Wolfe, F. and Hawley, D.J. (1997), "Measurement of the quality of life in rheumatic disorders using the EuroQol", *British Journal of Rheumatology,* Vol. 36(7), pp.786-793.

World Health Organisation (1957), *Measurement of Levels of Health; Report of a study group,* WHO, Geneva.

Zethraeus, N. (1998), "Willingness to pay for hormone replacement therapy", *Health Economics,* Vol. 7(1), pp. 31-38.

Index